Jacy

CSLI Studies in Computational Linguistics

This series covers all areas of computational linguistics and language technology, with a special emphasis on work which has direct relevance to practical applications, makes formal advances, and incorporates insights into natural language processing from other fields, especially linguistics and psychology. Books in this series describe groundbreaking research or provide an accessible and up-to-date overview of an area for nonspecialists. Also included are works documenting freely available resources for language processing, such as software, grammars, dictionaries, and corpora.

Series edited by Ann Copestake

CSLI Studies in
Computational Linguistics

Jacy
An Implemented
Grammar of Japanese

Melanie Siegel, Emily M. Bender, and Francis Bond

Center for the Study of
Language and Information
Stanford, California

Copyright © 2016
CSLI Publications
Center for the Study of Language and Information
Leland Stanford Junior University
Printed in the United States
20 19 18 17 16   1 2 3 4 5

Library of Congress Cataloging-in-Publication Data

Names: Siegel, Melanie, author. | Bender, Emily M., 1973- author. | Bond, Francis, 1967- author.

Title: Jacy : an implemented grammar of Japanese / Melanie Siegel, Emily M. Bender, and Francis Bond.

Description: Stanford : CSLI Publications, [2016] | Series: CSLI Studies in computational linguistics | Includes bibliographical references and index.

Identifiers: LCCN 2016029800 (print) | LCCN 2016047895 (ebook) |
ISBN 9781684000180 (pbk. : alk. paper) |
ISBN 1684000181 (pbk. : alk. paper) |
ISBN 9781684000197 (electronic) |
ISBN 168400019X (electronic)

Subjects: LCSH: Japanese language–Grammar, Generative. | Japanese language–Syntax. | Head-driven phrase structure grammar. | Computational linguistics.

Classification: LCC PL534 .S64 2016 (print) |
LCC PL534 (ebook) |
DCC 495.6501/823–dc23

LC record available at https://lccn.loc.gov/2016029800

CIP

∞ The acid-free paper used in this book meets the minimum requirements of the American National Standard for Information Sciences—Permanence of Paper for Printed Library Materials, ANSI Z39.48-1984.

CSLI was founded in 1983 by researchers from Stanford University, SRI International, and Xerox PARC to further the research and development of integrated theories of language, information, and computation. CSLI headquarters and CSLI Publications are located on the campus of Stanford University.

Visit our web site at
http://cslipublications.stanford.edu/
for comments on this and other titles, as well as for changes and corrections by the author and publisher.

言　　行　　一致
gen　kou　itchi
word　deed　unify
"Deeds match words."

Preface

This book aims to outline a linguistically motivated, precise head-driven phrase structure grammar of Japanese along with its computational implementation. We also sketch the multiple NLP applications the grammar has been developed and used in.

The research that is described in this book was done over a period of twenty years in various research contexts. The developers were during these years employed at different sites, including DFKI Saarbrücken, Universität des Saarlandes, YY Technologies, Stanford University, the University of Washington, Nippon Telephone and Telegraph Corporation (NTT), Nanyang Technological University, Acrolinx GmbH, and Darmstadt University of Applied Sciences. The different research projects were funded by the German Federal Ministry of Education and Research, by YY Technologies, by the European Commission (through the Erasmus Mundus Multi), by NTT, by the Japanese Society for the Promotion of Science and the Singapore Ministry of Education.

In 2006, the first in-depth description of the work in **Jacy** was presented as Melanie's habilitation thesis (Siegel, 2006), submitted to the University of Bielefeld. This thesis was the start of the current book and we would like to thank the thesis reviewers Dieter Metzing, Dan Flickinger and Takao Gunji.

Throughout this time, we have been members of the DELPH-IN consortium, whose members we would like to thank for fruitful discussions and motivation both as we developed the grammar and as we restructured and revised the document from Melanie's habilitation thesis to this book. Other researchers have helped in the development of this grammar, especially Sanae Fujita, Michael Goodman, Chikara Hashimoto, Petter Haugereid, Akira Kusamoto, Takayuki Kuribayashi, Takaaki Tanaka, Eric Nichols and Akira Ohtani. 感謝しております。

We would also like to thank Edith Aldridge, Timothy Baldwin,

Ulrich Callmeier, Dan Flickinger, Shigeko Nariyama, Stephan Oepen, Toshiyuki Ogihara, Sanghoun Song and Matsumoto Yuji for their input and for helpful discussions. All remaining infelicities are our own.

Contents

Preface   vii

Notational Conventions and Symbols   xv

1   Introduction   1
1.1   History of the Grammar   4
1.2   Theoretical Framework and Development Tools   5
1.3   **Jacy** among other HPSG Grammars of Japanese   6
1.4   **Jacy** and Multilingual Grammar Engineering   6
1.5   How this Book is Structured   7
1.6   Further Reading   7

2   Jacy in Different Application Domains   9
2.1   Appointment Scheduling in Machine Translation   10
2.2   Email in the Banking Domain   15
2.3   Hybrid Language Processing   17
2.4   Dictionary Definition Sentences   20
2.5   Open Source Machine Translation   23
2.6   The Full **Jacy** System   27
2.7   Summary and Further Reading   28

3   Basic Japanese Phrase Structure   29
3.1   Overview of HPSG   29
3.2   Core Phrase Structure Rules   30
3.2.1   Head-Subject Phrase   32
3.2.2   Head-Complement Phrases   33

3.2.3 Head-Adjunct Phrases   35
3.2.4 Coordinated Structures   37
3.2.5 Head-Specifier Constructions   41
3.2.6 Head-Marker Constructions   42
3.2.7 Utterance Rules   44
3.3 Head-Initial Constructions   45
3.3.1 The Position of Syntactic Heads in Japanese   45
3.3.2 Head-Initial Modification   49
3.3.3 Head-Initial Complementation   56
3.3.4 Corpus Study   60
3.4 Semantic Representations   61
3.5 Summary and Further Reading   65

4 Word Order and Subcategorization   67
4.1 Properties of Japanese Arguments   67
4.2 Previous Analyses   70
4.3 **Jacy**'s Approach   71
4.3.1 The Feature OPT   71
4.3.2 Required Adjacency   72
4.3.3 Zero Pronominalization and Obligatory Overt Realization   73
4.4 Summary and Further Reading   75

5 Verbs and Adjectives   77
5.1 Verbal Subcategorization Types   77
5.1.1 Intransitive Verbs   78
5.1.2 Transitive Verbs   80
5.1.3 Ditransitive Verbs   83
5.1.4 Copula Verbs   85
5.1.5 Adjective Subcategorization Types   89
5.2 Inflectional and Derivational Rules   89
5.2.1 Stem Classes   91
5.2.2 Ending Types   93
5.2.3 Inflectional Rules   93
5.2.4 Sample Derivation   95
5.2.5 Stand-Alone Stems   98
5.2.6 Derivational Rules   98
5.2.7 Adjective Inflectional Types   99
5.3 Auxiliary Constructions   100
5.3.1 Aspect Auxiliaries   100

5.3.2	Content Auxiliaries 102
5.3.3	Perspective Auxiliaries 103
5.3.4	Auxiliaries and Honorification 104
5.3.5	Contracted Auxiliaries 105
5.3.6	Summary 106
5.4	Passive Constructions 106
5.4.1	Simple Passives 106
5.4.2	Adversative Passive 109
5.4.3	Honorification with Passive Morphology 111
5.4.4	Potential with Passive Morphology 112
5.5	Causative 112
5.6	Summary and Further Reading 116

6 Nominal Structures: Linking Syntax, Semantics and Pragmatics 119

6.1	Ordinary Nouns and Noun Phrases 120
6.2	Names and Named Entities 123
6.3	Pronouns 125
6.3.1	Demonstrative Pronouns 125
6.3.2	Locative Pronouns 126
6.3.3	Personal Pronouns 127
6.3.4	The Reflexive *jibun* 128
6.4	Nominalizers 134
6.5	Temporal Nouns 136
6.6	Noun Modification 138
6.6.1	Noun Modification by Post-Positional Phrases 138
6.6.2	Relative Clause Constructions 139
6.6.3	Pre-Nominal Adjectives 142
6.7	Numeral Classifiers 143
6.7.1	Semantic Representations 147
6.7.2	The Analysis 149
6.8	Summary and Further Reading 159

7 Particles 163

7.1	Cooccurrence of Particles 164
7.2	The Type Hierarchy of Japanese Particles 168
7.3	Case Particles *case-p-lex* 169
7.3.1	General Properties of Case Particles 170

xii / JACY

7.3.2 The Case Particle *ga*   175
7.3.3 The Case Particle *wo*   177
7.3.4 The Case Particle *ni*   180
7.3.5 Other Case Particles   181
7.4 Other Semantically Empty Particles   182
7.4.1 Complementizers   182
7.4.2 Coordination Particles   183
7.5 Particles with Semantic Content *cont-p-lex*   184
7.5.1 Adnominal-Specifying *no*   184
7.5.2 Modifying Particles *mod-p-lex*   185
7.5.3 Topic Particles   189
7.5.4 Noun Phrase Conjunctions *conj-p-lex*   196
7.6 Sentence Particles and Sentence Force *sa-p-lex*   198
7.7 Omitted Particles   199
7.8 Evaluation of Case and Modifying Particles   200
7.9 Summary and Further Reading   201

8 Other Word Classes   203
8.1 Adverbs   203
8.1.1 Adverb Morphology and Derived Adverbs   203
8.1.2 Types of Adverbial Modification   204
8.2 Interrogatives   205
8.3 Demonstratives   206
8.4 Summary and Further Reading   208

9 Honorifics   209
9.1 Honorific Forms in Japanese   210
9.1.1 Three Types of Honorifics   210
9.1.2 Interaction of Different Kinds of Honorification   212
9.2 Previous Approaches   214
9.3 Japanese Honorification in **Jacy**   217
9.4 Evaluation   223
9.5 Honorification and Machine Translation   223
9.6 Honorification in Other Languages   224
9.7 Summary   225

10 Grammar Engineering   227
10.1   The Development Environment   227
10.2   The Grammar Development Cycle   228
10.3   Integrating Treebanking   230
10.4   Embedded Documentation: The Lexical Type Database   234
10.4.1   Linguistic Discussion   235
10.4.2   Exemplification   236
10.4.3   Implementation   236
10.4.4   Building the Lexical Type Database   238
10.5   Automatic Error Detection and Correction   239
10.6   Summary and Further Reading   239

11 The Current State of the Grammar   243
11.1   What is the Size of the Grammar?   244
11.2   What is the General Coverage on Different Kinds of Data?   245
11.2.1   Test Suites and Coverage   246
11.2.2   The Hinoki Treebank   247
11.3   How Can We Select the Best Interpretation?   250
11.4   How Domain-Adaptable is the Grammar?   252
11.5   How Far Can the Grammar Be Used in Multilingual Applications?   254
11.6   Summary and Further Reading   254

12 Conclusion   255

References   261

Index   279

Notational Conventions and Symbols

- *Italic font* is used for citing sentences, words and other forms. Japanese forms are given in the Hepburn transliteration (see Lunde 1999, 30–35); long vowels are shown as they are written in hiragana: e.g., *oo* or *ou*, long vowels from words written in katakana with ― are shown as double vowels. ん is transliterated as *n* except when it is followed by a vowel; in such cases it is transliterated as *N*.
- "Glosses" are given in double quotes immediately after the words or phrase.
- 'lit:' is used to mark literal glosses or translations
  e.g., *watashi no kono hon* "I ADN this book (lit: my this book)"
- SMALL CAPS are used for names of features and also for grammatical glosses.
- *Italic sans serif* is used for names of types.
- Sans serif is used for the names of predicates.
- Underlining is used to highlight areas of interest in examples.
- * (asterisk) indicates that the following example is ungrammatical.
- # (hash) indicates that the following example is pragmatically odd — it cannot have the desired interpretation, although it is grammatical under some other interpretation.
- ? indicates that the following example is of questionable grammaticality.
- Square brackets [like this] are used to show relevant context.
- Dropped arguments in Japanese are represented by suitable overt pronouns in the English translation and marked as such with parentheses only when argument drop is directly relevant to the discussion.

The following abbreviations are used for Japanese adpositions, affixes and other grammatical elements. Note that we generally do not gloss non-past (NONPST), negative addressee honorification, or neutral subject honorification explicitly, except where these features are directly relevant to the discussion around the example. When citing examples from other sources, we normalize the transliteration and glossing to our own conventions. Most sources do not give examples with standard Japanese orthography, which we have also added throughout. In this table, we give examples of each grammatical category. When the grammatical category is a particular inflected form of a verb, we illustrate with the verb 食べる *taberu* "eat".

Abbr.	Name	Example
\multicolumn{3}{c}{Honorification}		
HON	nominal affix	御 *go*, さん *san*
AHON:+	addressee, positive	[食べ *tabe*]-ます *masu*
AHON:−	addressee, negative	[食べ *tabe*]-る *ru*
SHON:+	subject, positive	召し上がる *meshiagaru* "eat"
SHON:±	subject, neutral	食べる *taberu*
SHON:−	subject, negative	いただく *itadaku* "eat"
\multicolumn{3}{c}{Tense/aspect}		
NONPST	non-past	[食べ *tabe*]-る *ru*
PST	past	[食べ *tabe*]-た *ta*
PFV	perfective	[食べて *tabete*] ある *aru*
PROG	progressive	[食べて *tabete*] いる *iru*
TERM	terminative	[食べて *tabete*] しまう *shimau*
\multicolumn{3}{c}{Other verbal elements}		
HOR	hortative	[食べ *tabe*]-よう *you* "let's eat"
INF	infinitival	[食べ *tabe*]-て *te*
CAUS	causative	[食べ *tabe*]-させる *saseru* "cause to eat"
COND	conditional	[食べ *tabe*]-たら *tara* "if X eats"
NEG	negative	[食べ *tabe*]-ない *nai* "don't eat"
PASS	passive	[食べ *tabe*]-られる *rareru* "be eaten"
POT	potential	[食べ *tabe*]-られる *rareru* "able to eat"
COP	copula	です *desu*
\multicolumn{3}{c}{Particles: Case markers}		
ACC	accusative	を *wo*
ADN	adnominal	の *no*
COM	comitative	と *to*
DAT	dative	に *ni*
DIR	directional	へ *e*
INS	instrumental	で *de*

continue on next page

Abbr.	Name	Example
Particles: Case markers (cont.)		
LOC	locative[1]	に *ni*, で *de*
NOM	nominative	が *ga*
Particles: Other		
COMP	complementizer	という *toiu*
QUOT	quotative	と *to*
TOP	topic	は *wa*, も *mo*
Particles: Sentence final		
Q	interrogative	か *ka*
SFP	other sentence final particles	けれども *keredomo*
TAG	tag	ね *ne*
Pronouns		
1	first person	私 *watashi* "I/me"
2	second person	あなた *anata* "you"
3	third person	彼女 *kanojo* "she/her"
F	feminine	彼女 *kanojo* "she/her"
M	masculine	かれ *kare* "he/him"
PL	plural	君達 *kimitachi* "you"
SG	singular	かれ *kare* "he/him"
Other		
COL	collectivizing suffix	達 *tachi*
CONJ	conjunction	し *shi*
INTERJ	interjection	で *de*
NMLZ	nominalizer/ nominalization	の *no*
NUMCL	numeral classifier	匹 *hiki*
REFL	reflexive	自分 *jibun*

---

[1] We use the gram LOC to gloss all occurrences of semantically-contentful に *ni*, and many uses of semantically-contentful で *de*, though their meanings are very broad and include uses, such as in the phrase ため に *tame ni* "for the purpose of", which wouldn't ordinarily be considered locative.

When describing feature structures, following the conventions of TDL, we will use . to separate feature names in paths.

The following paths are often shortened.

Abbr.	Full Path	Comment
VAL	(SYNSEM.)LOCAL.CAT.VAL	Valence (SPR, COMPS, SUBJ, SPEC)
HEAD	(SYNSEM.)LOCAL.CAT.HEAD	Head properties
CASE	(SYNSEM.)LOCAL.CAT.HEAD.CASE	Case
MOD	(SYNSEM.)LOCAL.CAT.HEAD.MOD	Mod list
INDEX	(SYNSEM.LOCAL.CONT.)HOOK.INDEX	Semantic index
LTOP	(LOCAL.CONT.)HOOK.LTOP	Local top handle
XARG	(LOCAL.CONT.)HOOK.XARG	External argument
CONT	(SYNSEM.)LOCAL.CONT	Semantic constraints
CTXT	(SYNSEM.)LOCAL.CTXT	Pragmatic constraints
LKEYS	SYNSEM.LKEYS	Pointer to main sem. contribution

1

Introduction

In this book, we present **Jacy**, a grammar of Japanese implemented within the Head-Driven Phrase Structure Grammar framework (HPSG; Pollard and Sag 1994). As HPSG provides both a rich formalism that allows for a clear description of a variety of linguistic phenomena and the possibility of efficient processing, the grammar is useful for both theoretical linguistic research and practical applications, and thus we address this book to linguists, HPSG researchers, and language technology researchers. We begin by exploring the motivation behind the grammar development effort.

From the point of view of linguistics, **Jacy** and other similar grammars are of interest as an approach to testing linguistic hypotheses in the context of interacting phenomena. As Bender (2008) argues, if we are to model natural languages in their full complexity and attempt to understand the constraints that analyses of one phenomenon put on the analyses of others, we in fact require the assistance of a computer.[1] Implementing our HPSG grammar allows us to explore not only the interaction among various syntactic phenomena, but also interactions that cross linguistic levels, including syntax, semantics, morphology, and even pragmatics. We will show how constraints from all of these levels combine to produce the meaning associated with a given string and the possible strings associated with a given meaning.

The primary power of an implemented grammar comes not from parsing individual sentences, but from applying the grammar to large bodies of data (Oepen and Flickinger, 1998). On the one hand, this allows us to validate theoretical claims against large amounts of data (both naturally occurring and hand-constructed) and show the relevance of such theoretical claims to language as spoken (or written) by native speakers. In this view, the implemented grammar can be seen as

---

[1] See also Bierwisch 1963, 163 and Müller 1999, Ch. 22.

a (detailed and ever-more-complete) model of linguistic competence. In addition, by processing large amounts of data with the grammar, we can provide the community with rich annotations over the data, such as in the Redwoods treebank for English (Oepen et al., 2004b) or the Hinoki treebank for Japanese (Bond et al., 2004a). Resources such as these enable further research, including both linguistic investigations of rare phenomena and automatic learning of linguistic structure.

With a large implemented HPSG grammar we provide a linguistically sound high-level grammatical description of Japanese. Such a treatment of any language is of great scientific interest, and Japanese is no exception: The language (and accordingly our model of it) contains interesting interactions between syntactic, semantic and pragmatic information, including elliptical phenomena, as we will show in this book. In addition, the strong tradition of linguistic research on Japanese provides both a solid foundation and a wide variety of hypotheses to test to our implementation efforts.

Historically, grammar engineering has often required compromising the linguistic soundness and precision of a grammar in order to achieve efficient processing. However, recent advancements in HPSG processing (Oepen et al., 2002b; Dridan, 2013; Zhang et al., 2007b) mean that HPSG developers do not need to make this compromise any more. Therefore, we can concentrate on building linguistically motivated grammars, allowing us to validate the HPSG approach with a language that has a very different structure from English. While there is a wealth of theoretical work applying HPSG to a wide variety of typologically diverse languages, our approach allows us to complement that research with a working proof that HPSG analyses scale up to broad coverage for a language typologically and genealogically far from English.

As noted above, the motivation for developing **Jacy** extends beyond its scientific (linguistic) interest. Natural language processing technology is used in a wide range of applications and we have reached a point where applications need more linguistic information than just part-of-speech tags or tree structures. Applications such as information extraction, machine translation, email categorization, dialogue understanding or question answering require natural language understanding, or at least an approximation thereof, and the annotation of large amounts of linguistic data, if they are to be used in a realistic way. Modeling the required linguistic information is expensive, and in fact too expensive to be recreated for each new application. The resource grammar approach leverages the fact that most of the linguistic competence required is largely the same across application domains and focuses on the development of a single consistent grammar (per language) across different applications always with an eye towards linguistic soundness and generality (see also Flickinger 2011). With **Jacy**, we have built a general, reusable competence system that can be the basis for different applications. A stringent test of this generality is generation. Even more than in applications requiring natural language understanding, applications involving natural language generation require precision and a sharp notion of grammaticality. **Jacy**, like other HPSG grammars, is designed to be usable in generation as well as parsing.

However, if the technology is to meet the demands of real-world applications, this precision must not come at the cost of robustness. Robustness requires not only wide coverage by the grammar (in both syntax and semantics), but also a large and extensible lexicon and interfaces to preprocessing systems for named-entity recognition, non-linguistic structures such as addresses, etc. Depending on the task, there are quite different constraints on robustness, accuracy, and processing speed. Therefore, the high-level precision grammar that forms the core of **Jacy** has rules for unknown word handling and can be combined with named-entity recognition systems if necessary.

Ideally, applications built on deep NLP technology should be extensible to multiple languages. This can be achieved relatively straightforwardly if the grammars involve flexible yet well-defined semantic representations that can be adapted to grammars of many different languages. **Jacy** produces semantic representations in Minimal Recursion Semantics (MRS; Copestake et al. 2005), a framework developed to be linguistically sound and computationally tractable and honed in the context of multilingual grammar development to ensure crosslinguistic applicability.

This book does two things. Firstly, it describes a grammar of Japanese, focusing on the morphology, syntax and semantics. We hope it will be of interest to people interested in the Japanese language. It differs from other Japanese grammars in that the grammar has been implemented as a computational grammar which both parses and generates Japanese text. This book must of course omit some of the detail of the implemented grammar, but the entire grammar is freely available to be examined and used. It can be downloaded from `http://www.delph-in.net/jacy/` which also links to an online demonstration. The grammar and tools needed to parse and generate with it are all open source. Secondly, the book describes the best practices in grammar engineering used to make this grammar. It should therefore be useful to people who wish to develop their own computational grammar.

1.1 History of the Grammar

Jacy was first implemented for the Verbmobil Machine Translation project (Siegel, 2000). The focus point of that first version of the grammar was the processing of spontaneous Japanese dialogues. Therefore, a description of spoken Japanese phenomena was essential. A strong emphasis was set on robustness in coverage. Parsing spoken language means that we had to deal with full sentences as well as sentence fragments. The Verbmobil project provided a large amount of test and development data, such that the grammar was based on empirical material from the start.

The next application area was interpreting email for automated response. This phase of the grammar development is described in Oepen et al. 2002a. Analyzing email also required robust analysis and handling styles similar to spoken language. In addition, it was necessary to work with the Japanese writing system. This required the introduction of an external tokenization module to separate words.

Project DeepThought embedded the Japanese grammar in a multilingual grammar development framework for hybrid natural language processing (Uszkoreit et al., 2004; Callmeier et al., 2004). **Jacy** was used for the task of understanding material about mobile phones available on the internet. In order to enhance the robustness of the grammars involved, the theoretical focus was the integration of shallow and deep modules for language analysis. In the case of Japanese, the results of tokenization, morphology interpretation, POS tagging and named-entity recognition were integrated into the analysis results of **Jacy**. This enabled the grammar to deal with unknown words and named entities.

Parallel to this, **Jacy** was being used for ontology extraction in the Hinoki project at Nippon Telegraph and Telephone Corporation (Bond et al., 2008a). For this purpose the vocabulary was expanded to cover the entire fundamental vocabulary of Lexeed (Kanasugi et al., 2002), some 30,000 commonly used words. Extensive treebanking was carried out, using the Redwoods treebanking approach (Oepen et al., 2004b) to produce the Hinoki treebank (Bond et al., 2008a). The treebank was built from dictionary definitions, native speaker examples, and news text.

The treebank was used to test the grammar and build statistical models for parse selection and generation ranking. It was also used to make a large-scale and detailed database of Japanese lexical types (Hashimoto et al., 2007). The lexical database includes detailed linguistic information and helps treebank annotators and grammar developers share precise knowledge about the grammatical status of words, allowing for consistent large-scale treebanking and grammar development.

In addition, **Jacy** was used in a machine translation project in cooperation with the LOGON initiative (Bond et al. 2005, Nichols et al. 2007). The LOGON initiative provided the infrastructure to produce open-source semantic transfer-based machine translation systems (Lønning et al., 2004). **Jacy** was used for setting up a Japanese-English machine translation system, as well as proof-of-concept systems for English-Japanese, Japanese-Norwegian and Korean-Japanese.

These development contexts share the following characteristics:

- The grammar was deployed in practical applications and developed to handle large and realistic corpora. Such development contexts require the treatment of peripheral as well as core phenomena of the language.
- The domain focus was spoken or near-spoken language.
- The focus of the grammar was to treat phenomena occurring in real data, rather than theoretically interesting but rarely occurring phenomena.

1.2 Theoretical Framework and Development Tools

The grammar is couched in the theoretical framework of Head-Driven Phrase Structure Grammar (HPSG; Pollard and Sag 1994; Sag et al. 2003), with semantic representations in Minimal Recursion Semantics (MRS; Copestake et al. 2005). We give an overview of these frameworks in Chapter 3. HPSG is well-suited to the task of multilingual development of broad-coverage grammars: It is flexible enough (analyses can be shared across languages but also tailored as necessary) and has a rich theoretical literature from which to draw analyses and inspiration. The characteristic type hierarchy of HPSG also facilitates the development of grammars that are easy to extend. MRS is a flat semantic formalism that is designed to work well with typed feature structures and is flexible in that it provides structures that are under-specified for scopal information. These structures give compact representations of ambiguities that are often irrelevant to the task at hand. HPSG and MRS have the further advantage that there are practical and useful open-source tools for writing, testing, and efficiently processing grammars written in these formalisms.

The tools we are using include the LKB system (Copestake, 2002b) for grammar development, [incr tsdb()] (Oepen and Carroll, 2000) for testing the grammar, tracking changes and annotating treebanks, and PET (Callmeier, 2000), a very efficient HPSG parser, for processing. We also use the **ChaSen** tokenizer and POS tagger (Asahara and Matsumoto, 2000).

1.3 Jacy among other HPSG Grammars of Japanese

Gunji 1987 was the first HPSG grammar of Japanese. While the book gave a description of several major aspects of the language and approaches in HPSG grammar descriptions, there was no implementation of the theoretical work.

While couched within the same general framework (HPSG), our approach differs from that of Kanayama et al. (2000). The work described there achieves impressive coverage (83.7% on the EDR corpus of newspaper text) with an underspecified grammar consisting of a small number of lexical entries, lexical types associated with parts of speech, and six underspecified grammar rules. In contrast, our grammar is much larger in terms of the number of lexical entries, the number of grammar rules, and the constraints on both, and takes correspondingly more effort to bring up to that level of coverage. The higher level of detail allows us to output precise semantic representations as well as to use syntactic, semantic and lexical information to reduce ambiguity and rank parses.

Other existing descriptions of implemented HPSG grammars of Japanese, such as Yoshimoto 1998, Miyata et al. 2001 and Hashimoto and Bond 2005 give very detailed descriptions and implementations of certain aspects of the Japanese syntax and semantics. Insights from these gave important inspirations for the implementation of our broad-coverage grammar, covering the main aspects of the Japanese language.

1.4 Jacy and Multilingual Grammar Engineering

Multilingual grammar engineering involves the parallel or otherwise coordinated development of grammars for different languages within the same framework and formalism (see, e.g., Butt et al. 1999, Butt et al. 2002 and Bender et al. 2005). Within the DELPH-IN consortium, the **Jacy** grammar has been developed alongside the English Resource Grammar (ERG: Flickinger 2000, 2011) and the German HPSG Grammar (Müller and Kasper 2000; Crysmann 2005) and more recently grammars for other languages including Norwegian (Hellan and Haugereid 2003; Haugereid 2009), Spanish (Marimon, 2010), Modern Greek (Kordoni and Neu, 2005), Portuguese (Branco and Costa, 2010) and Korean (Song et al., 2010). Among other advantages, multilingual grammar engineering facilitates cross-linguistic hypothesis testing, as well as the development of cross-linguistically applicable representations and technologies, as mentioned above.

The Grammar Matrix (Bender et al., 2002, 2010) aims to facilitate the development of further grammars in this framework. Indeed, the

Norwegian, Spanish, Modern Greek, Portuguese and Korean grammars mentioned above were based on early versions of the Grammar Matrix, which significantly sped up their initial development time while also promoting consistency in their semantic representations. This initial version of the Grammar Matrix grew out of the ERG, with reference to the German HPSG grammar and especially to **Jacy**. **Jacy** was later adapted to be consistent with the core grammar files provided by the Grammar Matrix.

1.5 How this Book is Structured

In the next chapter (Chapter 2), we show how **Jacy** was developed and used in different application domains and how the applications influenced the grammar. The data that has to be covered is of different nature in different applications and similarly the applications have different demands for precision and robustness of the grammatical analysis.

Chapter 3 provides background on HPSG and then gives a detailed description of our treatment of phrase structure in **Jacy**. This immediately leads to the problem of subcategorization in Japanese and the methods for the treatment of optionality and scrambling, presented in Chapter 4. We elaborate further on verbal constructions, verbal valence, morphology, auxiliary constructions, passive and causative and the organization of the verbal type hierarchy, as well as the treatment of adjectives, in Chapter 5.

The description of nominal constructions and the nominal type hierarchy in Chapter 6 shows the interrelation between the information on different linguistic levels. Chapter 7 presents our analysis of particles, which play a central role in Japanese syntax and semantics. We complete the discussion of lexical types in Chapter 8, with a description of adverbs and other minor categories. Our analysis of honorification (Chapter 9) links the information of syntax, semantics and pragmatics.

In Chapter 10, we describe aspects of our grammar engineering methodology, including the development environment, treebanking and regression testing, embedded documentation, and automatic error detection and correction. Chapter 11 looks at the current state of the grammar and briefly describes it quantitatively.

1.6 Further Reading

The basic general introduction to HPSG is the book by Pollard and Sag (1994). For a textbook presentation, see Sag et al. 2003. Copestake (2002b) provides an introduction to the LKB and LKB-based grammar engineering. The first comprehensive HPSG grammar of Japanese

(Japanese Phrase Structure Grammar: JPSG) is described in Gunji 1987. Copestake et al. (2005) give an introduction to Minimal Recursion Semantics (MRS).

2
Jacy in Different Application Domains

Before we discuss the **Jacy** as a grammar, we will introduce some of the applications that have used it, and describe its place in a larger system. **Jacy** itself is a grammar, a declarative description of the syntax and semantics of Japanese. When we use **Jacy**, it is embedded in a system that includes pre-processors (for segmentation and identification of unknown words), a parsing or generation engine, and post-processors to integrate other knowledge sources.

During the development history of the grammar, different applications with different application domains were modeled:

- Appointment scheduling in machine translation of spoken language
- Emails in the banking domain for an automatic email correspondence system
- Parallel multilingual grammar development embedded in hybrid natural language processing for domain-independent information extraction
- Extracting relations from dictionary definition sentences to build ontologies
- Semantic-transfer-based Japanese-to-English machine translation

Each of these required analysis of specialized vocabulary and grammatical constructions, had different processing needs and got quite different input. In order to address these needs, the grammar had to be highly modular, easy to extend and flexible to configure in usage. Finally, the grammar has been used as a test-bed for research on parsing efficiency, allowing the research community to show results for languages beyond just English.

2.1 Appointment Scheduling in Machine Translation

The grammar was first developed for the purpose of machine translation of spoken dialogs as part of the Verbmobil project (Wahlster, 2000). Therefore, it had to deal with spontaneous spoken dialogue language, erroneous speech recognition input and unclear sentence boundaries. In this genre, utterances are relatively short and often fragmentary. Speakers make heavy use of sentence end particles and honorification to express their empathy and thoughts and to reflect the social situation. There are three main features that are characteristic for turns in spoken dialogue language, as opposed to sentences in written language:

- They can be sequences of sentences.
- They can be fragments.
- They can obey syntactic rules that are not valid for written language.

The syntax distinguishes between core sentences that contain the main syntactic components (mainly PP and VP) and utterances that have some reference to the addressee. This can be a honorific form or inflection or a sentence-final particle like けれども *keredomo* or ね *ne*. A turn — on the other hand — can consist of not only one utterance but also of a sequence of utterances:[1]

(1) 今日　は　　です　　　　　ね　ちょっと 夕方　　　まで　授業
　　kyou　wa　desu　　　　　ne　chotto　　yuugata made　jugyou
　　today TOP COP.AHON:+ TAG a.bit　　evening until　lesson
　　も　入っ　て ます　　　　し　で　　　午前 中　　　　　も
　　mo　hait　te-masu　　　shi　de　　　gozen-chuu　　　mo
　　also insert PROG-AHON:+ and INTERJ morning-during also
　　鈴木　さん と　　打ち合わせ が　　　入って
　　Suzuki san　to　　uchiawase　　ga　　hait-te
　　Suzuki HON COM meeting　　　　NOM insert-INF
　　おり ます　　　　　　　　　ので　　ちょっと 今日　　という の
　　ori-masu　　　　　　　　　node　　chotto　　kyou　　toiu　　no
　　PROG.SHON:--AHON:+ because a.bit　　today COMP　NMLZ
　　は　むり なん です　　　　けれども
　　wa　muri nandesu　　　　keredomo
　　TOP bad COP.AHON:+ SFP

"Because today there are lessons until evening and in the morning well there is a meeting with Mr/Ms Suzuki, today is a bit difficult."

---

[1] In Verbmobil, the input to the grammar was in *romaji* (the romanized Japanese encoding), coming from the speech recognizer. Here we give the sentence in Japanese characters for ease of understanding as well.

There are two ways of sequencing: One is to combine a finite sentence and a conjunction with other sentences. The whole coordinated structure must be an utterance in reference to the dialogue situation. In the above example the finite sentence (*kyoo wa desu ne chotto yuugata made jugyoo mo haittemasu*) is conjoined with the rest via the conjunction *shi*. The other way is to combine an utterance with others without a conjunction. As 'utterance' is defined for spoken language, it refers to the dialogue situation, where it is often unclear where the sentence boundaries are. Consider the following example:

(2) 十七　日　の　火曜日　です　　　ね　そう
    juu nana nichi no kayoubi desu   ne sou
    ten seven day ADN Tuesday COP.AHON:+ TAG so
    です　　　ね　一時　まで　会議　そのた
    desu   ne ichi-ji made kaigi sonota
    COP.AHON:+ TAG one-hour until meeting and.so.on
    あります　　ので　一時　　すぎ　から
    ari-masu   node ichi-ji sugi kara
    exist-AHON:+ because one-hour after from
    でしたら　　　　　　なんとか　予定　が　取れる
    deshi-tara   nantoka yotei ga to-reru
    COP.AHON:+-COND   somehow plan NOM take-POT
    んです　　　が　そちら　の　ご都合　　　　は　いかが
    ndesu   ga sochira no go-tsugou   wa ikaga
    COP.AHON:+ but you ADN HON-convenience TOP how
    でしょう　　か
    deshou   ka
    COP.AHON:+ Q

"That's Tuesday the 17th, isn't it? Well, until one o'clock there are meetings and so on, if it would be after one o'clock, I could somehow take some time, how is that for you?"

The first segment (*juu nana nichi no kayoobi desu ne*) has the honorific form *desu* of the copula and the tag-particle *ne*, as does the second segment (*soo desu ne*). The third one has the honorific form *ndesu* and the sentence-final particle *ga*. These three (complete) utterances are strung together without any marking of the combination.

In addition to handling such run-on sentences, the grammar also accepts incomplete inputs (fragments) and produces semantics for them. An example of a fragmentary utterance from the Verbmobil corpus is (3):

(3) イナーシティホテル
    inaa-shiti-hoteru
    inner-city-hotel

    "inner city hotel"

This is just a noun. We build a structure for it where is an underspecified argument of a default event. This makes it easy to integrate with post-processing. The processing module is modeled as described in Schlangen and Skantze 2009 and allows the combination of fragments with existing representations. The parser is therefore enabled to compute analyses for utterances as consisting of only phrases, if full-sentence analyses are not available.

If an utterance is corrupted by not being fully recognized, the parser delivers analyses for those parts that could be understood. The speech recognition system[2] often gives several possibilities for what word sequence the speech signal could correspond to. These possibilities are combined for a sentence in a directed graph structure, called a word lattice. Using probability methods, the speech recognition system gives the most probable path through the word lattice, the so-called best hypothesis. This hypothesis is a sentence that is then sent to the syntax analysis system, the parser. The parser also takes the word lattice into account.

An example is the following best hypothesis from the speech recognizer in a system test:

(4) そうです　　　ね　私　　の　ほうは　大丈夫
    sou desu   ne watakushi no hou wa daijoubu
    so COP.AHON:+ TAG 1SG   ADN side TOP okay
    です　　　　　だがこの日　は　火曜日　です　　　　ね
    desu   daga kono hi wa kayoubi desu   ne
    COP.AHON:+   but this day TOP Tuesday COP.AHON:+ TAG

    "Well, it is okay for my side, but this day is Tuesday, isn't it?"

Here, analyses for the following fragments are delivered (where the parser found *opera wa* in the word lattice, but not in the hypothesis):

(5) そうです　　　ね　私　　の　ほうは　大丈夫
    sou desu   ne watakushi no hou wa daijoubu
    so COP.AHON:+ TAG I   ADN side TOP okay
    です　　　　　ね
    desu   ne
    COP.AHON:+   TAG

    "Well, it is okay for my side."

---

[2]For a description of the speech recognition system see Waibel et al. 2000

(6) オペラ は
    opera wa
    opera TOP

   "The opera"

(7) この 日 は 火曜日 です   ね
    kono hi wa kayoubi desu   ne
    this day TOP Tuesday COP.AHON:+ TAG

   "This day is Tuesday, isn't it?"

Another motivation for partial analysis comes from real-time restrictions imposed by the Verbmobil system. If the parser is—due to time restrictions—not allowed to produce a spanning analysis, it delivers best partial fragments (see Kiefer et al. 2000 for further details).

In addition to processing effects, spoken language also provides a range of linguistic phenomena not typical of text. The grammar covers many of these. Typical features are the extensive use of topicalization and the omission of particles. Serialization of particles also occurs more often than in written language (Siegel, 1999). A well-defined type hierarchy of Japanese particles is necessary here to describe their functions in the dialogues, as described in Chapter 7. Extensive use of honorification is also characteristic of spoken Japanese.

Compare the following sentences:

(8) a. 十 一 日 の 日 は セミナー が 一日中
       juu ichi nichi no hi wa seminaa ga ichinichijuu
       ten one day ADN day TOP seminar NOM whole.day
       入って いる
       hait-te   iru
       insert-INF PROG

      "There's a whole-day seminar on the 11th."

   b. 十 一 日 の 日 は セミナー が 一日中
       juu ichi nichi no hi wa seminaa ga ichinichijuu
       ten one day ADN day TOP seminar NOM whole.day
       入って おり ます
       hait-te   ori-masu
       insert-INF SHON:--AHON:+

      "There is a whole-day seminar on the 11th."

The first one is a syntactically correct sentence. In a dialogue though, it can only be uttered in an informal situation, in a dialogue between friends. The second one refers to the dialogue situation via honorifics: The speaker as the agent of the utterance refers to himself with the 'humble' auxiliary *oru* and such defines the social interaction between the dialogue participants as a distant one. The ending *masu* is a verbal inflection that also expresses social distance to the addressee.

A detailed description of honorification is necessary for multiple purposes in an MT system: honorification is a syntactic restrictor in subject-verb agreement and certain subordinate sentences. Furthermore, it is a very useful source of information for the resolution of zero pronouns, as described in Metzing and Siegel 1994. Finally, it is necessary for Japanese generation in order to find the appropriate honorific forms (Mima et al., 1997). The sign-based information structure of HPSG makes it simple to describe honorification across the different levels of linguistic structure: In our analysis of honorification, we include constraints on the syntactic level for agreement phenomena, on the contextual level for anaphora resolution and connection to speaker and addressee reference, and with co-indexing to the semantic level. Our solutions to the generation and representation of honorific knowledge are described in Chapter 9. Connected to honorification is the extensive use of auxiliary and light verb constructions that require solutions in the linked areas of morpho-syntax, semantics, and context.

Finally, a severe problem of the Japanese grammar in the MT dialogue translation task is the high potential of ambiguity arising from the syntax of Japanese itself, and especially from the syntax of Japanese spoken language. For example, the Japanese particle が *ga* marks verbal arguments in most cases. There are, however, occurrences of *ga* that are assigned to verbal adjuncts (topics), especially in spoken language. Allowing *ga* in any case to mark arguments or adjuncts would lead to a high potential of (spurious) ambiguity. Thus, a restriction was set on the adjunctive *ga*, requiring the modified verb not to have any unsaturated *ga* arguments.

The Japanese language allows many verbal arguments to be optional; where a pronoun might be used in English, for example, Japanese opts for zero anaphora instead. This phenomenon is fundamental to spoken Japanese, and as a result the syntax urgently needs a clear distinction between optional and obligatory arguments. We therefore used a description of subcategorization that differs from the HPSG description of other languages in that it explicitly states the optionality of arguments, as described in Chapter 4.

After Verbmobil, the grammar contained about 3,000 lexical entries (full forms) in Latin writing (*romaji*), rules for the basic Japanese constructions (such as utterances and phrases, nouns, particles, verbs, adjectives, copula, adverbs, honorification, empathy, zero pronouns, topicalization and light verb constructions) and facilities adapted to the special needs of Japanese spoken language processing.

2.2 Email in the Banking Domain

The next context for **Jacy** grammar development was at YY Technologies USA (in collaboration with DFKI Germany), where it was part of an automated customer service product, specifically in the domain of online banking. Language in email, like speech, typically contains many short sentences and fragments. Additionally, email language contains special abbreviations, greetings, tabular-like formatting and some punctuation. To extend **Jacy** to this domain, the lexicon required expansion. Many idiomatic expressions and abbreviations had to be included, including many multiword expressions. At this time we further developed inflectional and derivational rules instead of using a fullform lexicon.

The switch from spoken language (represented in Latin characters from the output of the speech recognizer) to written language (in standard orthography) entailed the addition of multiple forms for each word to the lexicon. A more significant change to the processing set-up involved tokenization: As Japanese orthography does not use whitespace to indicate word boundaries, a preprocessing system is required in order to handle written Japanese. We integrated **ChaSen** (Asahara and Matsumoto, 2000), a tool that provides word segmentation as well as part-of-speech tags and morphological information such as verbal inflection.[3] As the lexical coverage of **ChaSen** is higher than that of the HPSG lexicon, default part-of-speech entries are inserted into the lexicon. These are triggered by the part-of-speech information given by **ChaSen**, if there is no existing entry in the lexicon. These specific default entries assign a type to the word that contains features typical to its part-of-speech. For example, if a word is recognized as a noun by **ChaSen** but has no entry in the **Jacy** lexicon, we can still analyze the sentence by assuming that this noun behaves just like the majority of Japanese nouns. This default mechanism is often used for different kinds of names and 'ordinary' nouns, but also for adverbs, interjections and verbal nouns (where we assume a default transitive valence pattern). Within this project the **ChaSen** lexicon was extended with a domain-specific lexicon, containing, among others, names in the domain of banking.

For verbs and adjectives, **ChaSen** gives information about stems and inflection that is used in a similar way. The inflection type is translated to an HPSG type. These types interact with the inflectional rules in the

---

[3]We would like to thank Stephan Oepen and Ulrich Callmeier for their help with integrating **ChaSen**.

grammar such that the default entries for unknown words are inflected just as known words would be.

Grammar extensions were done in collaborative work with Stephan Oepen, Ulrich Callmeier and Daniel Flickinger (Oepen et al., 2002a). The grammarians were working on different sides of the world, contributing to the grammar. There was a continuous demand for improving coverage and quality of analyses, as the grammar was used in a commercial product of automatic email correspondence. Thus, the grammar was put into a version control system in order to make submission and tracking of changes possible. A strong focus was set on collaboration with the grammar developers of the English and Spanish grammars, requiring a careful design and discussion of MRS output structures. The goal was to make them as compatible as possible to simplify downstream processing, such that the same components could be easily adapted for English, Japanese or Spanish. The grammar was already fairly complex, such that one had to be careful about side effects of changes. The adding of an auxiliary verb to the lexicon could have the effect of a massive increase of overall parsing ambiguity, for example. Thus, phenomena-oriented test sets were set up and an integrated competence and performance profiling was extensively used: the [incr tsdb()] system (Oepen and Carroll, 2000).

The banking domain contains a variety of numeral expressions; accordingly it was necessary to extend and refine the analysis of numeral classifiers (see § 6.7). Another phrase type that occurred quite regularly was two noun phrases with a colon, such as:

(9)   ID : 1 0
        ID : 10
        ID : 10
        "ID: 10"

This is semantically similar to an expression with a topic marker:

(10)   ID は 1 0
        ID wa 10
        ID TOP 10
        "The ID is 10"

Thus we analyze the expression in (9) analogously to that in (10), handling both as fragments. The fragment rule introduces an underspecified event into the semantics, with ID as the first argument and 10 as the second. Symbols like dash, arrow or brackets also occurred in this data, such that we had to give an account for these. For example, we inserted "∼" and ":" as *case-p-lex-np* and *adv-p-lex-np* into the grammar, carefully observing their syntactic behavior and semantic functions in the corpus.

As the grammatical coverage grew, the ambiguity rate did as well. Accordingly, a good deal of effort was spent on reduction of spurious ambiguity, which especially arose in compounds, conjuncts and zero pronoun processing.

2.3 Hybrid Language Processing

Jacy was next used to parse Japanese in the DeepThought project (Crysmann et al., 2002; Uszkoreit et al., 2004). This project combined deep and shallow processing for a wide selection of languages. The following two principles strongly influenced the grammar development:

1. The development of grammars in a multilingual environment, with an emphasis on collaboration with developers of other grammars, in order to provide compatible and comparable grammar output from multiple languages
2. The embedding of these grammars in a hybrid architecture (the Heart-of-Gold; Callmeier et al. 2004) that allowed the connection of various NLP modules of different preciseness and robustness in different modes, but with a common and compatible output format: Robust Minimal Recursion Semantics (RMRS) (Copestake, 2003)

A new approach to parallel multilingual grammar development was developed in the context of the DeepThought project. First, a shared core (the Grammar Matrix) was extracted from the Japanese and English grammars (Bender et al., 2002). The aim of the Grammar Matrix is to provide a common set of lexical and rule types to provide the basis for new grammars. Sharing the core both speeds up initial development and facilitates interoperability across languages.

In the project (and connected to the project), new grammars of Norwegian (Hellan and Haugereid, 2003), Italian and Greek (Kordoni and Neu, 2005) were set up. The existing grammars of Japanese, English and German were adapted to Matrix principles by inserting and connecting the Matrix types to the grammars. This process was bidirectional: in some cases, a grammar writer came up with a phenomenon that could not be described when using the Matrix types, such that the Matrix had to be revised. Some changes to **Jacy** that were necessary when including Matrix types were:

- **Naming Conventions for MRS Feature Names.** The feature naming conventions were made consistent with standard reference

on MRS. Therefore, feature name replacements were necessary, as well as some reorganization of features.
- **Introduction of the** HOOK **Attribute.** To ensure that composition happens cleanly, the externally visible attributes of an MRS were grouped within a single attribute called HOOK, which exposes pointers into the semantic structure of a constituent that are required for further composition.[4]
- **Naming of Argument Roles**: (ARG1, ARG2, ARG3, ARG4). Each relation now assigns its first (least oblique) argument to ARG1, its next argument to ARG2, and so on. The major change from previous grammar versions was to assign objects of transitive verbs to ARG2 rather than ARG3, and similarly for objects of prepositions.
- **Basic Relation Types**. The inventory of basic relation types has been simplified. New relation types had to be introduced to the grammars, such as a relation type for quantifiers (quant-rel). The basic relation type named-rel has also been incorporated into the grammars, and its inherent constant is now the C-ARG.
- **Subcategorization**. A new multilingual approach to subcategorization was introduced into the Japanese and English grammars and tested. In order to give a direct encoding to the division of optional and obligatory arguments, as well as scrambling and adjacent arguments, the argument status is explicitly stated in an attribute OPT. This contains information about the saturation status of subcategorized arguments. It is an advantage of this approach that it provides a straightforward and easy-to-process way of dealing with scrambling and optionality of arguments. There are no lexical rules necessary that move arguments from valence to adjacency or slash lists, there is no need for traces and slashs. We tested on the Japanese grammar that the treatment is still adequate for the phenomena associated with Japanese subcategorization. This is discussed in more detail in Chapter 4.

As a result of these efforts, grammars of various languages provide compatible output for similar semantics (Figure 1). Comparing the output of the different languages shows the compatibility of the different language's grammars. Although the actual semantic relations are different for each language, there are similar relation names for propositions and determiner relations, as well as arguments, labels and scoping restrictions.

---

[4]See Copestake et al. 2005 for more detail.

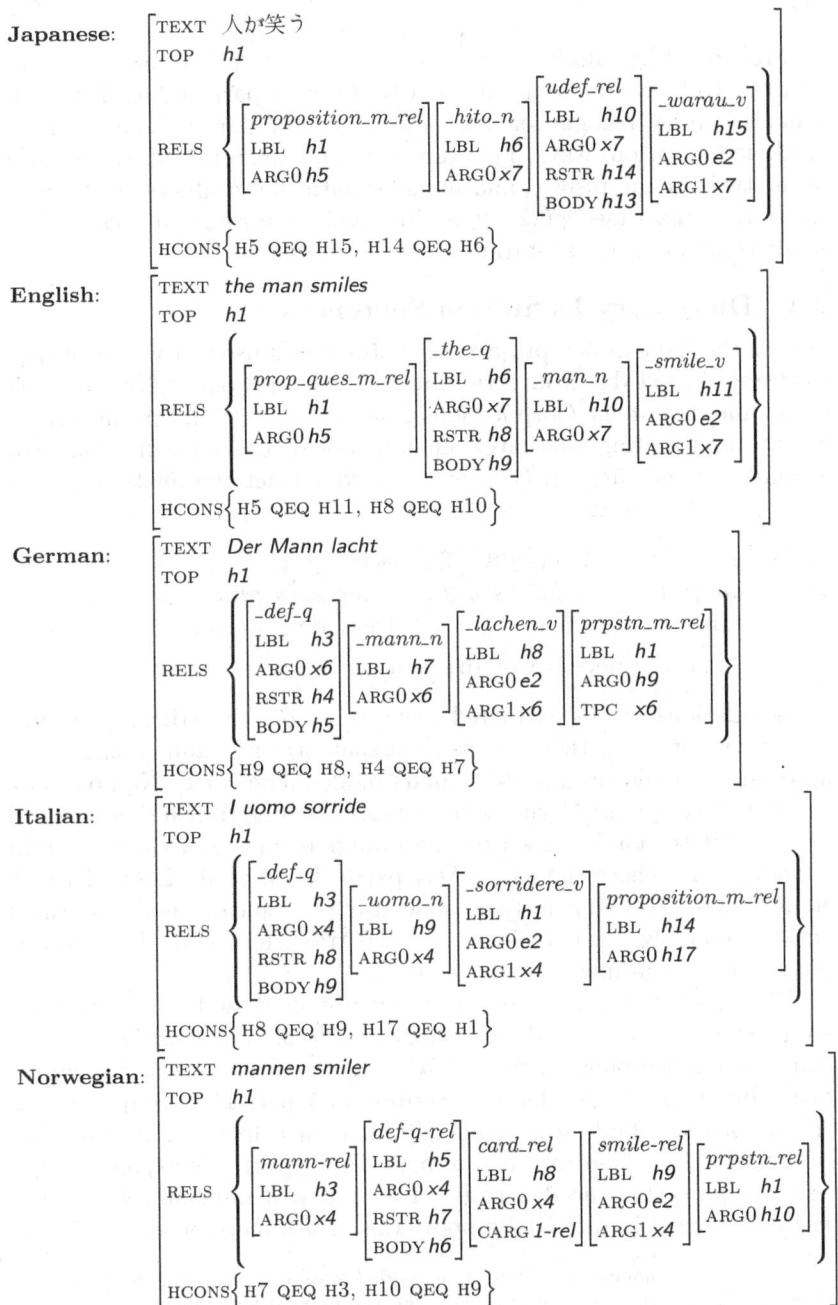

FIGURE 1 Parses of "the man smiles" in five languages.

Multiple NLP modules can also be integrated. For Japanese, the Heart-of-Gold contains, in addition to **Jacy**, a part of speech tagger, a named-entity recognition tool and a shallow parser. These can be combined in various ways. The standard approach is to take the deepest of the two parsing results, and merge it with the results of the named-entity recognizer (see § 6.2). It is also possible to return all results in a single combined representation.

2.4 Dictionary Definition Sentences

One of the next major projects that **Jacy** was used in was a project to extract knowledge from structured text, carried out at Nippon Telegraph and Telephone Corporation (Bond et al., 2004c). Specifically we looked at extracting relations from Japanese dictionary definitions. For example, in the entry in (11), we want to extract the relation ドライバー ⊂ 人 "driver is-a person".

(11) ドライバー ： 自動車 を 運転 する 人
     doraibaa : *jidousha wo unten suru hito*
     driver : car ACC drive do person

"driver: a person who drives a car"

These relations can be extracted accurately from the MRS representation of the sentence. However, as most sentences are ambiguous, it was necessary to build up a parse-ranking model. The NTT (Nippon Telegraph and Telephone Corporation Japan) machine translation research group built treebanks based on the grammar and used these to train a model which chose the most likely parse (Bond et al., 2004e; Nichols et al., 2006). Ranking is then done using stochastic models trained on the manually evaluated and selected trees, following the methods proposed by Toutanova et al. (2005).[5]

Dictionary definitions contain relatively short and well-structured sentences covering a broad vocabulary and domain. Definitions contain many nominalizations, such that a precise analysis of these is necessary. Our approach to this is described in § 6.4. The group working on dictionary definition sentences brought in a huge number of lexical items to be added to the grammar. To support this expansion, the lexical type system needed to be clear and well understandable; and was reorganized in order to support this (Hashimoto et al., 2007). As

---

[5] At YY Technologies, such stochastic models were not yet available, and so we attempted to handle parse selection through the manual assignment of weights to rules. This was extremely difficult to maintain and not at all scalable. Treebank-trained stochastic parse selection models are clearly a far superior solution.

part of this we moved more of the documentation online to facilitate collaboration (http://www.delph-in.net/jacy).

We give an example of the extraction process, for the Japanese word ドライバー *doraibaa* "driver". (12) is a simplified entry (missing two senses) from the Lexeed semantic database of Japanese (Kasahara et al., 2004). Lexeed is a machine-readable dictionary consisting of headwords and their definitions for the 28,000 most familiar open class words of Japanese, with all the definitions using only those 28,000 words (and some function words).

(12) $\begin{bmatrix} \text{INDEX} & \text{ドライバー} & \textit{doraibaa} \\ \text{POS} & \textit{noun} \\ \text{SENSE 1} & \begin{bmatrix} \text{DEFINITION} & \begin{bmatrix} S_1 & \text{自動車を運転する}\underline{\text{人}}\text{。} \\ & \text{\underline{Someone} who drives a car} \end{bmatrix} \\ \text{HYPERNYM} & \text{人}_1 \textit{ hito} \text{ "person"} \end{bmatrix} \\ \text{SENSE 2} & \begin{bmatrix} \text{DEFINITION} & \begin{bmatrix} S_1 & \text{ゴルフで、遠距離用の}\underline{\text{クラブ}}\text{。} \\ & \text{In golf, a long-distance \underline{club}.} \\ S_2 & \text{一番/ウッド。/} \\ & \text{A number one wood .} \end{bmatrix} \\ \text{HYPERNYM} & \text{クラブ}_2 \textit{ kurabu} \text{ "club"} \\ \text{DOMAIN} & \text{ゴルフ}_1 \textit{ gorufu} \text{ "golf"} \end{bmatrix} \end{bmatrix}$

In most cases, the first sentence of a dictionary definition consists of a fragment headed by the same part of speech as the headword. Thus the noun *driver* is defined by a noun phrase. The noun phrase consists of a genus term (*person*) and differentia (*who drives a car*).[6] The genus term is generally the most semantically salient word in the definition sentence. For example, for sense 1 of the word ドライバー *doraibaa*, the hypernym is 人 *hito* "person" (Figure 2). Although the actual hypernym is in very different positions in the Japanese and English definition sentences, it is the head of the NP in both cases, meaning that its INDEX value is available as the underspecified argument ARG of the unknown_rel in both the semantic representations.

We parse the definition sentences and then extract the relations from the semantic output, shown in Figure 2. Using the parse results is attractive for various reasons. The first is that it makes our knowledge acquisition more language independent. If we have a parser that can produce MRS, and a machine readable dictionary for that language, the knowledge acquisition system can easily be ported. As we can see here,

---

[6]Also know as superordinate and discriminator or restriction.

the MRS for two sentences that are very different syntactically are close to identical. Another common approach, to use regular expressions, needs them to be rewritten for each language.

The second reason is that we can go on to use the parser and acquisition system to acquire knowledge from non-dictionary sources. Fujii and Ishikawa (2004) have shown how it is possible to identify definitions semi-automatically, however these sources are not as standard as dictionaries and thus harder to parse using only regular expressions. The third reason is that we can more easily acquire knowledge beyond simple hypernyms, for example, identifying synonyms through common definition patterns as proposed by Tsuchiya et al. (2001).

$$\left\langle h_1, \left\{ \begin{array}{l} h_3\text{:unknown}(e_2, x_4 \{\text{PERS } 3\}), \\ h_5\text{:udef\_q}(x_6 \{\text{PERS } 3\}, h_7, h_8), \\ h_9\text{:\_jidousha\_n}(x_6), \\ h_{10}\text{:\_unten\_s\_2}(e_{11} \{\text{TENSE } pres\}, x_4, x_6) \\ h_{12}\text{:udef\_q}(x_4, h_{13}, h_{14}), \\ h_{10}\text{:\_hito\_n}(x_4), \end{array} \right\} \right\rangle,$$
$$\{h_7 =_q h_9, h_{13} =_q h_{10}\}$$

「自動車 を 運転 する 人」 "car-ACC drive do person"

$$\left\langle h_1, \left\{ \begin{array}{l} h_3\text{:unknown}(e_2, x_4 \{\text{PERS } 3\}), \\ h_5\text{:\_a\_q}(x_6 \{\text{PERS } 3\}, h_7, h_8), \\ h_9\text{:\_car\_n}(x_6), \\ h_{10}\text{:\_drive\_v\_1}(e_{11} \{\text{TENSE } pres\}, x_4, x_6) \\ h_{12}\text{:\_some\_q}(x_4, h_{13}, h_{14}), \\ h_{10}\text{:person\_n}(x_4), \end{array} \right\} \right\rangle,$$
$$\{h_7 =_q h_9, h_{13} =_q h_{10}\}$$

somebody who drives a car

FIGURE 2 Simplified MRS representations for the definition of *doraibaa$_2$* "driver" and the English definition of *driver*

We also extract information not explicitly labeled, such as the domain of the word (in sense 2). Here the actual entry is an NP fragment modified by a PP expressing the domain in which the interpretation applies. Thus we interpret "In golf, a club for playing long strokes" as if it were the sentence "In golf, [a driver$_3$ is] a club for playing long strokes", where the PP modifies the (actually unexpressed) head verb of the whole clause. To parse this, we added a construction to the grammar that allows an NP fragment heading an utterance to have an adpositional modifier. We then extract these modifiers and take the head of the noun phrase to be the domain. This is hard to distinguish reliably with regular expressions. An initial NP followed by で *de* could be a copula phrase or a PP that attaches anywhere within the definition — not all such initial phrases restrict the domain. The grammar produces all the possibilities and ranks them with a statistical model, where as a regular expression will match them all. Most of the domains extracted fall under a few superordinate terms, mainly sport, games and religion. For example, as a result of this processing we identified Japanese equivalents of the following words having a sense marked as being in the domain golf: *approach, edge, down, tee, driver, handicap, pin, long shot*.

Nichols et al. (2005) compared relation extraction using just a part-of-speech tagger (**ChaSen**) to using **Jacy** or a combination (**Deepest: Jacy** if it parsed the definition, **ChaSen** otherwise). The results for all parts of speech are shown in Table 1. The results were automatically evaluated by comparing against existing ontologies (they thus under-estimate the precision as we found new entries not in the existing ontologies).

Using **Jacy**, we achieved a confirmation rate of **55.74%** from 46,000 relations. Parsing also allows us to extract multiple relations from a single sentence by processing coordinate clauses. This allowed us to extract an extra 3,300 relations. Just using **ChaSen** gave **49.32%** confirmed out of 53,000 relations. Using the deepest parse available, we confirmed **50.49%** overall for over 60,000 relations. This is comparable in precision to the results reported in Bond et al. 2004e using only **Jacy**, but extracts over 10,000 more confirmed ontological relations using the combination of deep and shallow techniques. The extraction process was also successfully applied to English (Nichols et al., 2006) using the English Resource Grammar. Because the MRS abstracts away from language particular structure it is easy to port semantic post-processing to new languages.

2.5 Open Source Machine Translation

Jacy is also being used in an open source machine translation system: **Jaen**. **Jaen** is a rule-based machine translation system employing semantic transfer rules built using the LOGON infrastructure (Lønning et al., 2004; Oepen et al., 2007). The medium for the semantic transfer is Minimal Recursion Semantics, (MRS; Copestake et al. 2005). The system consists of the two HPSG grammars: **Jacy** used to parse the Japanese input and the ERG, used for the generation of the English

ChaSen

Relation	Confirmed Precision	Extracted	%
hypernym	18,609	42,756	43.52
synonym	7,898	10,992	71.85
total	26,507	53,748	49.32

Jacy

Relation	Confirmed Precision	Extracted	%
hypernym	17,050	33,545	50.83
synonym	8,436	11,900	70.89
abbreviation	64	156	41.03
domain	75	372	20.16
other	125	225	55.56
total	25,750	46,198	55.74

Deepest

Relation	Confirmed Precision	Extracted	%
hypernym	21,680	47,149	45.98
synonym	8,730	12,489	69.90
abbreviation	64	156	41.03
domain	75	372	20.16
other	125	225	55.56
total	30,674	60,391	50.79

TABLE 1 Results confirmed for Lexeed (for 46,000 senses)

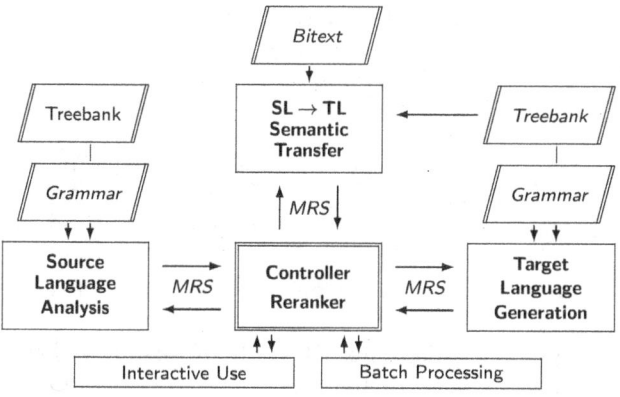

FIGURE 3 Architecture of the **Jaen** MT system.

output (Flickinger, 2000). The third component of the system is the transfer grammar, which transfers the MRS representation produced by the Japanese grammar into an MRS representation that the English grammar can generate from. For more details see Bond et al. 2011 and Haugereid and Bond 2011.

At each step of the translation process, the output is ranked by stochastic models. In the default configuration, only the 5 top ranked outputs at each step are kept, so the maximum number of translations is 125 ($5 \times 5 \times 5$). There is also a final reranking using a combined model (Oepen et al., 2007).

A small core of transfer rules is constructed by hand, and the rest learned from 20 million words of parallel Japanese-English text aligned at the sub-sentence level with the help of statistical machine translation phrase aligners. The architecture of the MT system is illustrated in Figure 3 (taken from Bond et al. 2011), where the contribution of the transfer rule extraction from parallel corpora is depicted by the arrow going from Bitext to Semantic Transfer.

We compared **Jaen** to the statistical machine translation system Moses (Koehn et al., 2007). The results are given in Table 2, taken from Bond et al. 2011. Accuracy is measured using two standard automatic scores based on comparison to a reference translation BLEU (Papineni et al., 2002) and METEOR (Lavie and Agarwa, 2007) and a human score. In the human scoring, the evaluator was given the Japanese source, a reference translation and the output from the two systems, randomly presented as A or B. They then indicated which they preferred, or if the quality was the same (in which case each system gets

0.5). All the translations, including the reference translations, were tokenized and lower-cased. Moses gets better BLEU and METEOR scores, while the **Jaen** translation is preferred by the human evaluator in 58 out of 100 cases.

	BLEU	METEOR	HUMAN
JaEn First	16.77	28.02	**58**
Moses	**30.19**	**31.98**	42

TABLE 2 BLEU Comparison of **Jaen** and Moses (1194 items)

The two systems make different kinds of mistakes. The output of **Jaen** is mostly grammatical, but it may not always make sense. An example of a nonsense translation from **Jaen** is given in (13).[7]

(13) S: 我々は魚を生で食べる。
      R: We eat fish raw.
      M: We eat fish raw.
      J: We eat fish in the camcorder.

Jaen sometimes gets the arguments wrong:

(14) S: 彼は大統領に選ばれた。
      R: He was elected president.
      M: He was elected president.
      J: The president chose him.

The output of Moses on the other hand is more likely to lack words in the translation, and it is also more likely to be ungrammatical. Translations with missing words are shown in (15)–(16).

(15) S: カーテンがゆっくり引かれた。
      R: The curtains were drawn slowly.
      M: The curtain was slowly.
      J: The curtain was drawn slowly.

Missing words are especially problematic when a negation is not transferred, which happens for almost two thirds of negative sentences translated by Moses (Wetzel and Bond, 2012).

(16) S: 偏見は持つべきではない。
      R: We shouldn't have any prejudice.
      M: You should have a bias.
      J: I shouldn't have prejudice.

---

[7] The examples below are taken from the development data of the Tanaka Corpus. 'S' stands for 'Source', 'R' stands for 'Reference translation', 'M' stands for 'Moses translation', and 'J' stands for '**Jaen** translation'.

Sometimes the Moses output is lacking so many words that it is impossible to follow the meaning:

(17) S: 脳 が 私 達 の 活動 を 支配 し て いる 。
      R: Our brains control our activities.
      M: The brain to us.
      J: The brain is controlling our activities.

Also the output of Moses is more likely to be ungrammatical, as illustrated in (18) and (19)

(18) S: 私 は 日本 を 深く 愛 し て いる 。
      R: I have a deep love for Japan.
      M: I is devoted to Japan.
      J: I am deeply loving Japan.

(19) S: 彼女 は タオル を 固く 絞った 。
      R: She wrung the towel dry.
      M: She squeezed pressed the towel.
      J: She wrung the towel hard.

Using the semantic output of the grammars allows to ensure that the translation preserves meaning. The current weaknesses in the **Jaen** system stem from the lack of robustness: neither **Jacy** nor the transfer grammar have anything near full coverage.

2.6 The Full Jacy System

Currently **Jacy** is open source, facilitating its use in future applications of varying types. It is distributed in a package that contains:

- The grammar/lexicon itself
    - Includes in-line documentation that can be compiled out into the lexical type database (see § 10.4)
- Scripts to load it for the LKB grammar development system/parser/generator
- Scripts to load it in the PET efficient parser
- Scripts to load it in the ACE efficient parser/generator
- Some test suites and treebanks (see § 11.2.1)
- A stochastic model for parse ranking
- Scripts for integrating the **ChaSen** pre-processor for on-the-fly tokenization and unknown word handling

Because details of how to use the grammar change as systems evolve, we keep this documentation in a wiki (http://moin.delph-in.net/

JacyTop), which includes information on downloading and installing, other online documentation and links to relevant papers. We describe the current state of the grammar in more detail in Chapter 11.

2.7 Summary and Further Reading

The chapter gave an overview on the different applications **Jacy** has been embedded in in the course of its development. It shows that a grammar with precise semantic descriptions of the language can be used in various language technology applications: Machine translation, automatic email response, information extraction, and ontology induction, as well as providing information on the different contexts in which the grammar was developed.

More information about the machine translation project Verbmobil is given in Wahlster 2000. The procedure of developing parallel grammars in different locations of the world and in different time zones is described in Oepen et al. 2002a. Siegel and Bender (2002) give an overview of the state of the grammar in 2002. The architecture for linguistic processing of the project DeepThought is described in Callmeier et al. 2004. Robust Minimal Recursion Semantics (RMRS) was developed to facilitate the hybrid processing pursued in DeepThought. For more information on RMRS read Copestake 2007. Bender et al. (2002) give an overview of the Grammar Matrix, which was partially derived from the English and Japanese grammars. It has since been used in various projects to develop new HPSG grammars.

Jacy has also been used to provide data for a range of experiments including: parse ranking (Blunsom and Baldwin, 2006; Dridan and Baldwin, 2010); acquisition of deep lexical types using supertagging (Zhang et al., 2007a); calculation of sentence similarity using lexical and structural semantics (Dridan and Bond, 2006); semantic role labelling (Zhang et al., 2009); question classification for question answering (Dridan and Baldwin, 2007) and paraphrasing to produce statistical machine translation training data (Nichols et al., 2010; Wetzel and Bond, 2012).

For a different approach to the same problems, there is another grammar with similar design goals, also developed within a multilingual context, using the Lexical-Functional Grammar framework (Masuichi and Ohkuma, 2003; Butt et al., 2002). For more information on interesting problems in Japanese Natural Language Processing and their solutions, we recommend Bond et al. (2016).

3
Basic Japanese Phrase Structure

As noted in Chapter 1, the **Jacy** grammar is couched within the framework of Head-driven Phrase Structure Grammar (HPSG; Pollard and Sag 1994). HPSG is a strongly lexicalist framework, in which relatively streamlined phrase structure rules combine words and phrases into larger structures according to constraints carried by lexical entries. In this chapter, we give a brief overview of HPSG (§ 3.1) and then present the core phrase structure rules posited in the **Jacy** grammar (§ 3.2). In § 3.3, we take up the issue of direction of headedness in Japanese: while most phrases in Japanese are head-final, in applying the **Jacy** grammar to a broad range of data, we found a handful of constructions that went against this trend. Finally, in § 3.4 we describe the semantic representations produced by **Jacy** and how they will be depicted in this book.

3.1 Overview of HPSG

The fundamental unit in HPSG is the *sign*. A sign, as in the Saussurean sense (Saussure, 1949), is a pairing of form and meaning, where for our purposes, form includes both orthographic form and syntactic information. In HPSG, signs are modeled through a system of typed feature structures.[1] A feature structure is an object with zero or more features, each of whose values is another feature structure. Features are declared as appropriate for particular types. The typed feature structures are arranged into a hierarchy: when a type is defined, it is given one or more supertypes. The new type inherits the constraints associated with its supertypes, i.e., the features which are declared as appropriate and the constraints on their values, and can also add further constraints and/or further appropriate features.

---

[1] There are multiple formalisms for typed feature structures. **Jacy** uses the DELPH-IN joint reference formalism (Copestake, 2002a).

The use of a type hierarchy is one prominent difference between HPSG and other unification-based approaches to syntax. The type hierarchy has both theoretical and practical benefits. First and foremost, it allows us to capture generalizations: types of phrases (constructions), lexical entries, or lexical rules that share properties in common inherit from common supertypes. The shared properties are expressed only one time each as constraints on the supertypes. Using this system, we can capture generalizations at varying levels of granularity: Broad generalizations are located high in the hierarchy, while more fine-grained ones, applying to smaller sets of types, are located lower down. Capturing generalizations is not only of theoretical interest: It also helps with grammar maintenance. If a constraint is found to be incorrect, it needs only be changed in one place. Secondly, types can be used to create more efficient grammars. For example, Flickinger (2000) exploits the type hierarchy in order to move away from disjunctive constraints which were expensive to process.

The type hierarchy comprises types for phrase structure rules, lexical entries and lexical rules, as well as ancillary types that are called on in those definitions. The grammar also includes a series of instantiations of rules and lexical entries that the parser will use to construct analyses. Thus lexical entries, lexical rules and phrase structure rules are all feature structures. The rules have a distinguished feature ARGS whose value is a list. The elements of this list are the daughters of the rule. Feature structures representing smaller constituents are combined via the operation of unification with the elements of the ARGS list of a rule. If this unification succeeds, then the larger constituent is licensed. The information on the mother of this constituent (including both syntactic and semantic information) is calculated on the basis of the constraints on the rule and the information provided by the daughters.

3.2 Core Phrase Structure Rules

Pollard and Sag (1994) posit six basic schemata used in HPSG grammars:

1. Head-Subject Schema
2. Head-Complement Schema
3. Head-Subject-Complement Schema
4. Head-Marker Schema
5. Head-Adjunct Schema
6. Head-Filler Schema

In **Jacy** we have direct analogues of four of these (Head-Subject Schema, Head-Complement Schema, Head-Adjunct Schema, and the

Head-Marker Schema), as well as for the Head-Specifier Schema, not included in the Appendix to Pollard and Sag 1994 but discussed in their Chapter 9. The Head-Filler Schema concerns long-distance dependencies, for which we found different solutions.[2] The Head-Subject-Complement Schema is replaced by a mechanism for scrambling, which is significant for parsing a language like Japanese. These are both described in Chapter 4. This section illustrates how the schemata are used and modified for parsing Japanese, including the instances of these general rule schemata, and necessary additions. Further, it will introduce a schema for coordinated structures and head-specifier constructions.

The phrase structure rules are relatively schematized, with information coming from the lexical entries serving both to control the applicability of the rules and to provide information defining the characteristics of the mother of the rule. One key kind of information is that provided by the *valence features*. The valence features of a word provide information about the other words/phrases it needs to combine with. For example, the lexical entry for the simple transitive verb 食べる *taberu* "eat" includes the constraints shown in Figure 4, which it inherits from its supertypes.[3] The SUBJ and COMPS values indicate that this word is looking for a *ga*-marked subject and a single *wo*-marked complement, respectively. The empty lists for SPR and SPEC indicate that it is neither seeking a specifier nor can serve as a specifier (for more on head-specifier constructions, see § 3.2.5 below).[4]

The types used to define the phrase structure rules are arranged into a hierarchy. This allows us to state constraints shared across the phrase structure rules in just one place. The part of the type hierarchy relevant for the rules discussed in this section (and somewhat simplified for clarity of exposition) is shown in Figure 5. The type *head-nexus-phrase*, which serves as the root of this small hierarchy, inherits from *headed-phrase*. *headed-phrase*, in turn, is the locus of the Head Feature Principle: According to the Head Feature Principle, the HEAD value of

---

[2] The three canonical uses of the Head-Filler Schema are *wh*-questions, relative clauses and topicalization. Japanese has *wh* in situ and thus in our surface-oriented framework, Japanese *wh*-questions do not involve long-distance dependencies. For our analysis of relative clauses, see Section 6.6.2. For topicalization, see Section 7.5.3.

[3] This feature structure is abbreviated for clarity, shortening feature paths and using (e.g.,) 'PP[ga]' to stand in for a feature structure describing a PP headed by *ga*.

[4] In this organization of the valence information, we are following the English Resource Grammar (Flickinger, 2000), the Grammar Matrix (Bender et al., 2002), as well as Chapter 9 of Pollard and Sag 1994 in using multiple lists rather than just one, and in distinguishing specifiers from subjects. **Jacy** departs from the Matrix and other work in HPSG in treating SPEC as a head feature, rather than a valence feature.

$$\begin{bmatrix} \text{VAL} & \begin{bmatrix} \text{SUBJ} & \langle \text{PP[ga]} \rangle \\ \text{COMPS} & \langle \text{PP[wo]} \rangle \\ \text{SPR} & \langle \rangle \end{bmatrix} \\ \text{HEAD} & \begin{bmatrix} \text{SPEC} & \langle \rangle \end{bmatrix} \end{bmatrix}$$

FIGURE 4 Valence constraints on *taberu* "eat"

the mother is identified with the HEAD value of the head daughter. This constraint is shown in Figure 6, where identities are shown with boxed numbers.[5] The head feature includes information on the part of speech (CAT), what can be modified (MOD) and the case of the phrase (CASE).

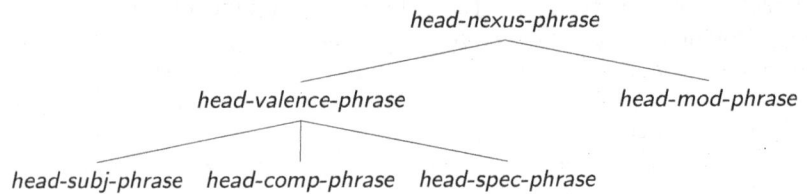

FIGURE 5 Type hierarchy excerpt: Phrase structure types

$$\begin{bmatrix} \text{SYNSEM.LOCAL.CAT.HEAD} & \boxed{1} \\ \text{HEAD-DTR.SYNSEM.LOCAL.CAT.HEAD} & \boxed{1} \end{bmatrix}$$

FIGURE 6 A Constraint on *headed-phrase*: The Head Feature Principle

3.2.1 Head-Subject Phrase

Figure 7 shows the basic head-subject-phrase in **Jacy**, with the mother on the right and its daughters on the left. The left-hand daughter is the subject (non-head daughter) and the right-hand daughter is the head (shown preceded by **H**). Note that the SYNSEM value of the non-head daughter must match the subject requirement (SUBJ value) of the head daughter. This is how the phrase structure rule enforces the constraints that the head daughter (and ultimately the lexical entry

---

[5]Note that this constraint makes reference to the attribute HEAD-DTR rather than ARGS. The linking between the features HEAD-DTR and NON-HEAD-DTR and the elements of the ARGS list is done by other types which define the order of daughters in the rules (see § 3.3 below).

$$\left[\text{VAL} \begin{bmatrix} \text{SUBJ} & \langle \, \rangle \\ \text{COMPS} & \boxed{2} \\ \text{SPR} & \boxed{3} \end{bmatrix} \right] \rightarrow \boxed{5}\bigl[\text{VAL.COMPS} \quad \textit{olist}\bigr] \quad \mathbf{H} \left| \text{VAL} \begin{bmatrix} \text{SUBJ} & \langle \, \boxed{5} \, \rangle \\ \text{COMPS} & \boxed{2}\textit{olist} \\ \text{SPR} & \boxed{3}\textit{olist} \end{bmatrix} \right.$$

FIGURE 7 Head-subject type in **Jacy**

for the lexical head of the sentence) places on its subject. In addition to requiring this identity, the rule also "copies up" the other valence properties of the head, and checks to make sure that any complements which must be adjacent to the head are already saturated (with the constraint [COMPS *olist*]).[6]

The **Jacy** head subject type given in Figure 7 differs from the Head-Subject Schema of Pollard and Sag (1994) in several ways:

- The subcategorization value (VAL in **Jacy**) is not a single list, but a complex structure containing multiple lists.
- The complement list is not necessarily empty when binding the subject.
- SLASH is not used in the Japanese structure.

These differences illustrate the fact that the basic treatment of subcategorization in **Jacy** differs from the treatment of subcategorization in Pollard and Sag 1994. We explain and motivate these differences in Chapter 4.

3.2.2 Head-Complement Phrases

Head-complement phrases are licensed by rules that combine a head daughter with something on its COMPS list. **Jacy** has three different head-complement rules. Their relationship within the type hierarchy is shown in Figure 8. They all inherit from the type *basic-head-complement-type*. *head-complement-type* realizes the first element of the COMPS list, and it is further specialized by *head-complement-hf-type* for the ordinary head complement phrases where the head appears on the right and *head-complement-hi-type* for the rare head-initial cases (see § 3.3). These are instantiated by *head-complement-hf-rule* and *head-complement-hi-rule* respectively. Finally, there is *head-complement2-type* (instantiated by the *head-complement2-rule*), which realizes the second element on the COMPS list, allowing for scrambling among the complements of ditransitive verbs.

---

[6]This constraint is related to the analysis of argument optionality and scrambling, as discussed in the following chapter.

34 / Jacy

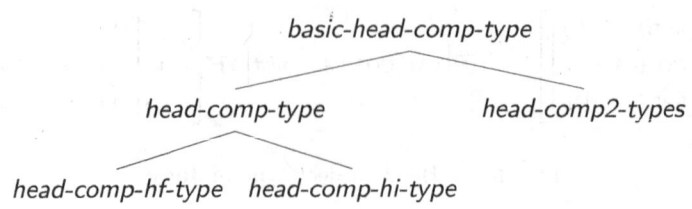

FIGURE 8 Types and instances of the basic head complement type

Jacy's basic head-complement rule type does not constrain its Head-Daughter value to be a word, as the notion of word is in principle problematic in Japanese language processing.

The type *head-complement-rule-type*, which all rules realizing the first thing on the COMPS list ultimately inherit from, is subject to the constraints shown in Figure 9. These constraints are displayed in avm notation (rather than as a rule as in Figure 7), because at the level of this type, the order of the daughters is not yet determined.

$$\begin{bmatrix} \text{SYNSEM.LOCAL.CAT.VAL} & \begin{bmatrix} \text{SUBJ} & \boxed{1} \\ \text{SPR} & \boxed{2} \\ \text{COMPS} & \boxed{3}\textit{0-1-list} \end{bmatrix} \\ \text{NON-HEAD-DTR.SYNSEM} & \boxed{4} \\ \text{HEAD-DTR.SYNSEM.LOCAL.CAT.VAL} & \begin{bmatrix} \text{SUBJ} & \boxed{1}\textit{olist} \\ \text{SPR} & \boxed{2}\textit{olist} \\ \text{COMPS} & \langle \boxed{4} \rangle \oplus \boxed{3} \end{bmatrix} \end{bmatrix}$$

FIGURE 9 Head-complement type in **Jacy**

As noted above, *head-complement2-rule* realizes the second element of the COMPS list, skipping over the first. This is implemented through the constraints on *head-complement2-type*, shown in Figure 10 (here we do use the rule notation, because all *head-complement2-type* rules in **Jacy** are head-final).

$$\begin{bmatrix} \text{SYNSEM.LOCAL.CAT.VAL} \begin{bmatrix} \text{SUBJ} & \boxed{1} \\ \text{SPR} & \boxed{2} \\ \text{COMPS} & \langle \boxed{3} \rangle \end{bmatrix} \end{bmatrix} \rightarrow$$

$$\begin{bmatrix} \text{SYNSEM} & \boxed{4} \end{bmatrix} \text{H} \begin{bmatrix} \text{SYNSEM.LOCAL.CAT.VAL} \begin{bmatrix} \text{SUBJ} & \boxed{1}\textit{olist} \\ \text{SPR} & \boxed{2}\textit{olist} \\ \text{COMPS} & \langle \boxed{3}[\text{OPT} \; +], \boxed{4} \rangle \end{bmatrix} \end{bmatrix}$$

FIGURE 10   Head-complement2 type

3.2.3   Head-Adjunct Phrases

As in Pollard and Sag (1994), head-adjunct phrases in **Jacy** combine modifiers with the heads they modify, with reference to the feature MOD (inside HEAD), which allows modifiers to constrain the type of head they can combine with. In addition, the head-adjunct phrase requires that the modified head have picked up any of its complements that are required to be adjacent before it gets modified. For example, modifiers that attach to verbal projections (e.g., きっと *kitto* "surely") cannot attach between the copula and its complement NP (20).

(20) きっと 彼 だ
   kitto   kare   da
   surely 3SG.M COP

   "Surely it's him."

(21) *彼 きっと だ
   **kare kitto   da*
   3SG.M surely COP

   Intended: "Surely it's him."

This is implemented by constraining the COMPS value of the head daughter to be *olist*, a list of optional complements. These constraints on *head-adjunct-rule-type* are shown in Figure 11. The order of the daughters is determined by more specific subtypes (see below), so Figure 11 uses avm notation, rather than the rule notation.

As there were for *head-complement-type*, there are subtypes and instances to the *head-adjunct-rule-type*. These subtypes are cross-classified along two dimensions. The first, familiar from *head-complement-type* is the order of the daughters, as head-final or head-initial. The second is a semantic dimension. Following Flickinger (2000) (see also Flickinger and Bender 2003), we have separate rules for intersective and scopal

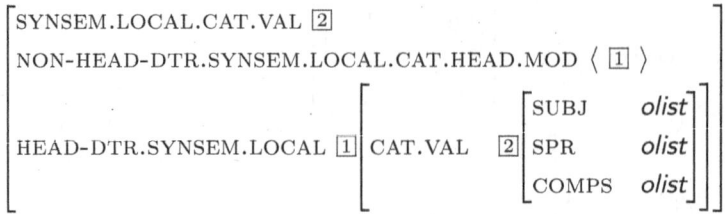

FIGURE 11 Head-adjunct-rule-type

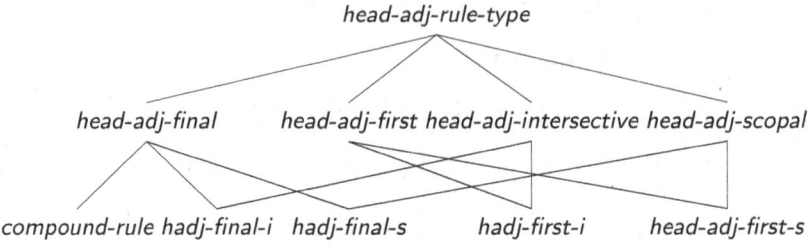

FIGURE 12 The head-adjunct rule type

modification, as they differ in the constraints required to build the correct semantic representations. The semantic dimension also includes a special type for compound constructions, which must introduce the compound relation and a quantifier for the head noun, so cannot be directly assimilated to either intersective or scopal modification. This shows up in the hierarchy as an extra subtype of *head-adjunct-rule-final*. The cross-classification is shown in Figure 12.[7]

Two features are used to ensure that particular modifiers only combine via the correct head-adjunct rules. First, we need to distinguish between scopal and intersective modifiers. We follow the ERG (Flickinger, 2000) in taking advantage of the feature LOCAL for this purpose. We posit two subtypes of *local* (*intersective_mod* and *scopal_mod*), and the scopal and intersective modifiers constrain the LOCAL value of the element of their MOD lists accordingly. Secondly, we need to distinguish between modifiers that appear before their heads, those that appear after, and those that can appear in either position. This is done with the HEAD feature POSTHEAD. In addition to controlling the distribution in the various head-adjunct phrases discussed here, the POSTHEAD feature is also used to distinguish predicates in the appropriate form to head conjuncts (*coord*), and predicates which can head relative clauses

---

[7]The type names have been shortened slightly so that they could fit.

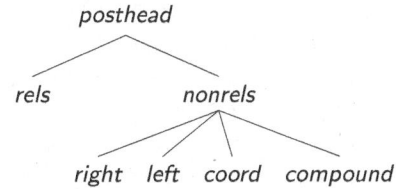

FIGURE 13 Posthead type hierarchy

(*rels*; see 6.6.2). Accordingly, the type *posthead* has the subtypes shown in Figure 13, where *left* is the value for pre-head modifiers required by *head-adjunct-rule-final* and *right* is the value for post-head modifiers required by *head-adjunct-rule-first*.

An *i*-adjective has the POSTHEAD value *rels*, such that it can participate in relative sentence constructions. Pre-nominal modifiers like プラス *purasu* "plus" have the POSTHEAD value *left*, such that they can be the modifier in head-final modification, while posthead noun modifiers like など *nado* "and so on" have the POSTHEAD value *right*. The verbal *te*-form adds POSTHEAD *coord* to the verb's HEAD, such that it can undergo sentence coordination rules.

3.2.4 Coordinated Structures

Kurohashi and Nagao (1994) identify three types of coordination structures in Japanese:[8]

Conjunctive noun phrases: Noun phrases can be conjoined, with each conjunct phrase including its own modifiers (see (22) and (23)).

Conjunctive predicative clauses: Predicative clauses can be conjoined (see (24) and (25)).

Incomplete conjunctive predicative clauses: Verbal arguments can be conjoined (see (26)).

(22) 原　　言語　　の　解析　　と　　相手　言語　　の
gen　gengo　no　kaiseki　to　aite　gengo　no
source language ADN analysis CONJ target language ADN
生成　　　を
seisei　　wo
generation ACC

"The analysis of the source language text and the generation of the target language text"

---

[8](22)–(26) are from Kurohashi and Nagao (1994, 510).

(23) 原　　言語　　を　　解析　　する 処理　　　と　　　相手
　　　gen　gengo　wo　kaiseki　suru　shori　　to　　aite
　　　source language ACC analyze do　processing CONJ target
　　　言語　　を　　生成　　する 処理　　　を
　　　gengo　wo　seisei　suru shori　　wo
　　　language ACC generate do　processing ACC

　　　"The processing of analyzing the source language text and generating the target language text"

(24) 原　　言語　　を　　解析　　し、相手 言語　　を
　　　gen　gengo　wo　kaiseki　shi,　aite　gengo　wo
　　　source language ACC analyze do　target language ACC
　　　生成　　する
　　　seisei　suru
　　　generate do

　　　"Analyzing the source language text, generating the target language text"

(25) 解析　　で　　は　　利用　　する が、生成　　　で　　は　　利用
　　　kaiseki　de　wa　riyou　suru ga,　seisei　de　wa　riyou
　　　analysis LOC TOP use　do　but　generation LOC TOP use
　　　し ない
　　　shi-nai
　　　do-NEG

　　　"Use for analysis, but do not use for generation."

(26) 前者　　を　　解析　　に、後者　　を　　生成　　　に
　　　zensha wo　kaiseki　ni,　kousha wo　seisei　　ni
　　　former ACC analysis LOC latter ACC generation LOC

　　　"The former for analysis, the latter for generation"

We give analyses for the first and the second type of conjoined structures, but not for the third one, which needs further investigation.[9]

In keeping with our general use of binary tree structures, we provide a binary-branching analysis of coordination constructions. An example is shown in Figure 14. *conj-rule* instantiates the type *conj-rule-type* which in turn inherits from *binary-type-conj* and ultimately *binary-modification-type*.

Such structures are licensed by lexical entries for the conjunctions (here と *to* "and") in combination with the rule *conj-rule*. The conjunc-

---

[9]For an analysis of constructions like (26) in terms of ellipsis, see Ito and Chaves 2008, which builds on Beavers and Sag 2004. Mouret (2006) argues against an ellipsis-based account for similar French data.

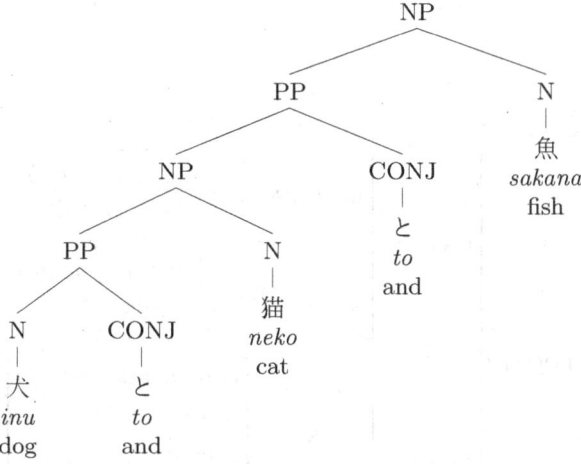

FIGURE 14 Binary-branching coordination structure

tion combines with the conjunct to its left via the *head-complement-hf-rule*, and then with the conjunct to its right via the *conj-rule*. The *conj-rule* uses a new feature C-MOD, which like the MOD feature, allows conjunction to specify what it can attach to. The constraints on the lexical entry for the conjunction と *to* "and" are illustrated in Figure 15 and the *conj-rule* in Figure 16.[10] The same structure is used for coordinated predicative phrases that contain a predicative conjunction like *ga* "and, but" が, *keredomo* "however" けれども or *node* "because" ので.

The constraints shown in Figure 15 include both syntactic and semantic information, to illustrate how the conjunction relates the semantic representations of the conjuncts to the semantic representation of the conjoined NP. These representations will be described further in § 3.4 below. For now, note that the index of the coordinated noun phrase comes from the *conjunction-relation*, which in turn takes the indices of each of the conjuncts as arguments.

The *conj-rule* combines a left-hand daughter marked for coordination with another conjunct as the right-hand daughter. It insists that both conjuncts be valence saturated, and takes the HEAD value from the right-hand daughter. Since the conjunctions all require the same type of HEAD value of their complements and their C-MODs, the HEAD values of the conjuncts will all be of the same type, ensuring NPs coor-

---

[10]This approach differs from that of Drellishak and Bender (2005), who locate more of the information about coordination in the coordination constructions and less in the conjunctions themselves.

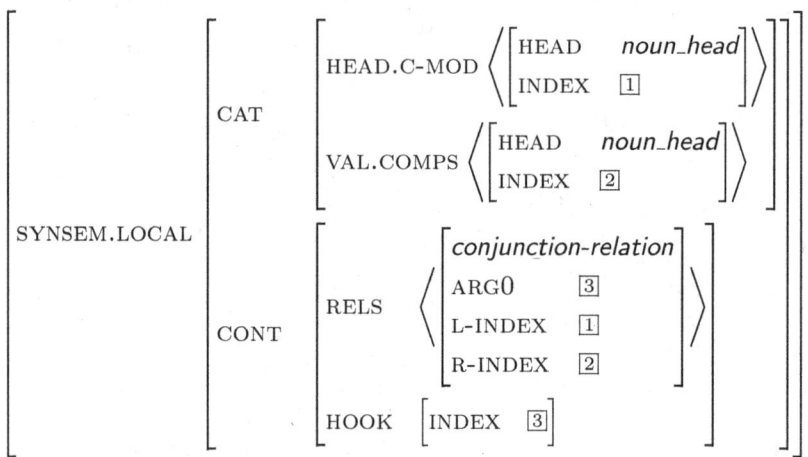

FIGURE 15 Lexical entry for *to* "and"

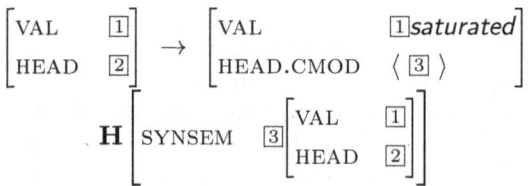

FIGURE 16 *conj-rule*

dinated with NPs, etc. Note, too, that this analysis requires all non-final conjuncts to be marked by some coordination marker.

Sentential coordination in Japanese can also be achieved through inflection, where the non-final conjuncts are marked by the form of the predicate, rather than a separate conjunction. An example is given in (27).

(27) 花子　　が　　ご飯　を　食べて、　早く　　寝た
　　　Hanako ga　gohan wo　tabe-te,　hayaku ne-ta
　　　Hanako NOM rice　ACC eat-INF,　quickly sleep-PST

"Hanako ate rice and went to bed quickly."

This kind of coordinated structure is licensed by *sentence-te-coordination-rule*, which shares many constraints with *conj-rule*, introduced above. In particular, it uses the C-MOD feature in the same way to allow the coordination marker to constrain the type of the right hand conjunct. Here, the coordination marker is the verbal ending て *te*. The *sentence-te-coord-rule* differs from the *conj-rule* primarily in that in sentential coordination, it is the rule that introduces the coordination relation. This allows us to use the same verb form in non-coordinated contexts as well.

In the case of more than two conjuncts, we keep the general binary construction policy and semantically let the second conjunction refer to the C-ARG of the first conjunct in its L-INDEX.

3.2.5 Head-Specifier Constructions

In HPSG, head-specifier constructions allow for mutual selection between the head and specifier daughters, through the SPR and SPEC features, respectively. As shown in Figure 17, the rule matches the requirements from each daughter to the information about the other. In addition to determiner-noun combinations (the original use of head-specifier constructions in HPSG; cf. Pollard and Sag 1994), we have found a handful of other constructions requiring mutual selection.

Figure 17 shows the basics of the *head-specifier-rule*. The head daughter subcategorizes for a specifier, a *synsem* which is identified with the non-head daughter's SYNSEM value, and the VAL.SPR on the mother is saturated, i.e., null. The HEAD information, as well as the SUBJ and COMPS lists on the mother come from the head daughter. The COMPS list on the non-head daughter must be either empty or a list of optional arguments, to ensure that all required adjacent arguments within that constituent have been picked up. The non-head daughter selects for syntactic (HEAD) and semantic (CONT) properties of the head daughter via its SPEC feature.

$$\begin{bmatrix} \text{HEAD} & \boxed{1} \\ \text{VAL} & \begin{bmatrix} \text{SUBJ} & \boxed{2} \\ \text{SPR} & \mathit{null} \\ \text{COMPS} & \boxed{3} \end{bmatrix} \end{bmatrix} \rightarrow$$

$$\begin{bmatrix} \text{SYNSEM } \boxed{4} \begin{bmatrix} \text{HEAD.SPEC} & \left\langle \begin{bmatrix} \text{HEAD} & \boxed{1} \\ \text{CONT} & \boxed{5} \end{bmatrix} \right\rangle \\ \text{VAL.COMPS } \mathit{olist} \end{bmatrix} \end{bmatrix} \mathbf{H}, \begin{bmatrix} \text{HEAD} & \boxed{1} \\ \text{VAL} & \begin{bmatrix} \text{SUBJ} & \boxed{2} \\ \text{SPR} & \langle \boxed{4} \rangle \\ \text{COMPS} & \boxed{3} \end{bmatrix} \\ \text{CONT} & \boxed{5} \end{bmatrix}$$

FIGURE 17 Head-specifier rule type

In a determiner-noun construction like (28), the determiner specifies a *noun_head* in HEAD.SPEC and the noun subcategorizes for an optional determiner.

(28) その 人
sono hito
that person

Other constructions built via the *head-specifier-rule* or a specialized subtype thereof include the combination of verbal stems with verbal endings (*vstem-vend*, see § 5.2), the combination of verbs and auxiliaries (see § 5.3), and both number names (§ 3.3.3) and numeral classifier constructions (§ 6.7).

3.2.6 Head-Marker Constructions

A special treatment is needed for Japanese verbal noun + light verb constructions. In these cases, a word that combines the qualities of a noun with those of a verb occurs in a construction with a verb that has only marginal semantic information. The syntactic, semantic and pragmatic information on the complex is a combination of the information of the two. Most inflectional morphology appears on the light verb, while the verbal noun has a constant form, modulo honorifics. However, the verbal noun does specify the valence frame (intransitive, transitive or ditransitive) and gives sortal restrictions for its arguments. When the light verb appears, the verbal noun is obligatory and must be adjacent to it. The verbal noun + light verb complex forms the predicate.[11]

---

[11] Dubinsky (1997) explains the atypical behavior of verbal nouns.

$$\begin{bmatrix} \text{HEAD} & \boxed{1} \text{ \textit{light-verb\_head}} \\ \text{VAL} & \boxed{2} \end{bmatrix} \rightarrow$$

$$\begin{bmatrix} \text{HEAD} & \boxed{3} \begin{bmatrix} \textit{vn\_head} \\ \text{MARK} & \langle [\text{HEAD } \boxed{1}] \rangle \end{bmatrix} \\ \text{BAR} & - \end{bmatrix} \quad \text{H,} \quad \begin{bmatrix} \text{HEAD} & \boxed{1} \\ \text{VAL.SPR} & \langle \begin{bmatrix} \text{HEAD} & \boxed{3} \\ \text{VAL} & \boxed{2} \end{bmatrix} \rangle \end{bmatrix}$$

FIGURE 18 *vn-light-rule*

Consider (29):

(29) 花子　が　勉強　した
Hanako ga benkyou shi-ta
Hanako NOM study do-PST
"Hanako studied."

The verbal noun 勉強 *benkyou* "study" contains subcategorization information (transitive), as well as semantic information (the _benkyou_s relation and its semantic arguments). The light verb *shita* supplies tense information (**past**). Pragmatic information can be supplied by both parts of the construction, as in the formal form *o-benkyou shi-mashi-ta*.

One approach (e.g., Grimshaw and Mester 1988) analyzes this construction in terms of "argument-transfer", where the light verb is the head of the complex and adopts the arguments of the verbal noun. Our analysis is based on the viewpoint that the verbal noun + light verb complex is sub-syntactic, i.e., at the boarder of morphology and syntax. It needs a special rule that allows the combination of the information from both components. The rule that licenses this type of combination is the *vn-light-rule* (see Figure 18), an instance of the *head-marker-rule-type*. The *vn-light-rule* combines the HEAD information from the light verb with the valence and semantic information from the verbal noun. At the same time, the daughters mutually select for each other, using the SPR feature on the light verb and the MARK feature on the verbal noun. Though this treats the light verb formally as the head daughter, the sub-syntactic nature of this construction is seen in the way that the properties usually passed from the head daughter to the mother (HEAD, VAL) are shared across the two daughters. Formally, we use the constraint [BAR −] to mark the verbal noun as sub-syntactic.

The *head-marker-rule-type* is used for the combination of verbal endings as well. In ChaSen's segmentation, (30) is broken into three morphemes:

(30) 面白く なかった
    omoshiroku-nakat-ta
    interesting-NEG-PST
    "It was not interesting."

The rule which combines *na* and *katta* (*vend-vend-rule*) combines information from both in a way that is similarly typical of sub-syntactic constructions.

3.2.7 Utterance Rules

Jacy makes use of a series of **utterance rules**, non-branching rules which apply at the root of the tree. These rules enforce saturation constraints while also making semantic contributions, specifically related to sentential force (the distinction between propositions, questions and commands) and honorifics. These semantic contributions in turn are keyed to morphosyntactic properties of the daughter of the utterance rule. All of the utterance rules constrain their daughter to be [VAL *saturated*]. The type *saturated* (a subtype of *valence*) is constrained as in Figure 19. The type *zlist* and its role in the analysis of dropped arguments is described in § 4.3.3.

$$\begin{bmatrix} \text{SUBJ} & \textit{zlist} \\ \text{COMPS} & \textit{zlist} \\ \text{SPR} & \langle\,\rangle \end{bmatrix}$$

FIGURE 19 Constraints on the type *saturated*

As an example, the utterance rule type for *wh*-questions without a question particle is shown in Figure 20. The non-empty QUE value on the daughter reflects the presence of a *wh*-word, and the constraint [SF *ques*] on the mother's C-CONT.HOOK.INDEX is the correlated semantic information that this utterance is a question.

$$\begin{bmatrix} \text{C-CONT.HOOK.INDEX.SF } \textit{ques} \end{bmatrix} \rightarrow \begin{bmatrix} \text{SYNSEM} \begin{bmatrix} \text{VAL} & \textit{saturated} \\ \text{NON-LOCAL.QUE} & \langle!\,[\,]\,!\rangle \end{bmatrix} \end{bmatrix}$$

FIGURE 20 *utterance-rule_wh_without_ka*

In addition, utterance rules are critical to our analysis of sentence fragments. The grammar contains four utterance rules each specialized to a different type of constituent which can appear as a stand-alone utterance despite not meeting the criterion of being a full sentence (NPs,

PPs, scopal and non-scopal adverbs) as well as four rules to handle sequences of two constituents that similarly can function as a stand-alone utterance despite not forming a constituent in the analogous complete sentences. These include what look like copula clauses missing their copula, as well as clausal modifiers appearing together with an NP or PP fragment. We illustrate the latter case with the example in (31).

(31) ゴルフ で、 遠距離 用 の クラブ
 gorufu de, enkyori you no kurabu
 golf LOC, long.distance use ADN club

"In golf, a long-distance club."

The grammar assigns the example in (31) the phrase structure and MRS shown in Figure 21. Here, the intended interpretation has the PP *gorufu de* "in golf" attaching not inside the NP but rather higher than it. That is, the PP restricts the domain of use of the definition, not the use of the club. Accordingly, our fragment rule (*frag-pp-np-rule*, shown in Figure 22) combines the two constituents, and adds through its C-CONT an underspecified predication (unknown) which takes the index of the NP as its argument and is in turn modified by the PP.

3.3 Head-Initial Constructions

Japanese is generally taken to be strictly head-final in its syntax (Gunji, 1987), and so far in this chapter we have focused on head-final constructions (though we have mentioned in passing the possibility of head-initial ones). This is exactly the sort of broad claim that is particularly interesting to test by implementing grammars that can be used to process naturally occurring text. Indeed, in our work on **Jacy**, we have found a few minor exceptions to the broad trend towards head-final order in Japanese.[12]

3.3.1 The Position of Syntactic Heads in Japanese

Zwicky (1993) identifies several characteristics which have been taken to differentiate heads and dependents, and points out that they do not correlate all that well.[13]

HPSG theory only recognizes some of these characteristics in the identification of syntactic heads,[14] namely required v. accessory, category determinant v. non-determinant, and external representative v. externally transparent. The central intuition is that the syntactic head

---

[12]This section is adapted from Siegel and Bender (2004).

[13]In modifier constructions, the semantic functor is not the head, but the modifier, cf. Zwicky 1993.

[14]Note that the syntactic head need not to be the semantic head.

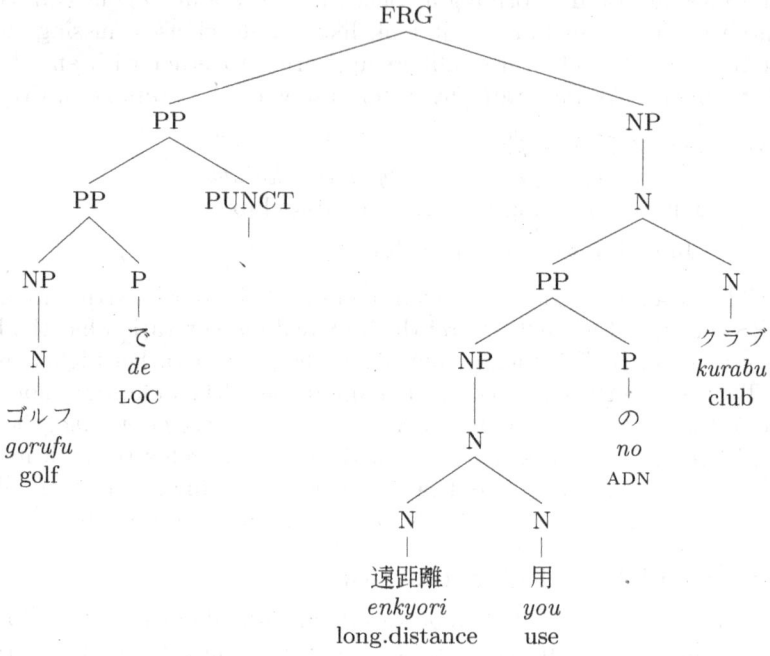

$\left\langle h_1, \left\{ \begin{array}{l} h_3\text{:udef\_q}(x_4 \{\text{PERS } 3\}, h_5, h_6), \\ h_7\text{:\_gorufu\_n\_1}(x_4), \\ h_8\text{:\_de\_p}(e_9 \{\text{TENSE } untensed\}, e_2 \{\text{TENSE } tense\}, x_4) \\ h_{10}\text{:udef\_q}(x_{11} \{\text{PERS } 3\}, h_{12}, h_{13}), \\ h_{14}\text{:\_enkyori\_n\_1}(x_{15} \{\text{PERS } 3\}), \\ h_{16}\text{:\_you\_n\_task}(x_{11}), \\ h_{16}\text{:compound}(e_{17} \{\text{TENSE } untensed\}, x_{11}, x_{15}) \\ h_{18}\text{:udef\_q}(x_{15}, h_{19}, h_{20}), \\ h_{21}\text{:\_no\_p}(e_{23} \{\text{TENSE } untensed\}, x_{22} \{\text{PERS } 3\}, x_{11}) \\ h_{24}\text{:udef\_q}(x_{22}, h_{25}, h_{26}), \\ h_{21}\text{:\_kurabu\_n}(x_{22}), \\ h_8\text{:unknown}(e_2, x_{22}), \end{array} \right\}, \right\rangle$
$\{h_5 =_q h_7, h_{12} =_q h_{16}, h_{19} =_q h_{14}, h_{25} =_q h_{21}\}$

FIGURE 21 PP-NP fragment: Phrase structure tree and MRS

$$\begin{bmatrix} \text{HEAD} & \textit{fragment\_head} \\ \text{C-CONT.RELS} & \left\langle !\begin{bmatrix} \text{PRED} & \textit{unknown} \\ \text{LBL} & \boxed{1} \\ \text{ARG0} & \boxed{2} \\ \text{ARG} & \boxed{3} \end{bmatrix}! \right\rangle \end{bmatrix} \rightarrow$$

$$\begin{bmatrix} \text{HEAD} & \begin{bmatrix} \textit{vmod-p\_head} \\ \text{MOD} & \left\langle \begin{bmatrix} \text{LTOP} & \boxed{1} \\ \text{INDEX} & \boxed{2} \end{bmatrix} \right\rangle \end{bmatrix} \\ \text{VAL} & \textit{saturated} \end{bmatrix} \begin{bmatrix} \text{HEAD} & \textit{noun\_head} \\ \text{VAL} & \textit{saturated} \\ \text{INDEX} & \boxed{3} \end{bmatrix}$$

FIGURE 22 Constraints on binary fragment rule: *frag-pp-np-rule*

	Head	Dependent
Semantics	characterizing	contributory
Syntax	required	accessory
	word rank	phrase rank
	category determinant	non-determinant
	externally representative	externally transparent
Morphology	morpho-syntactic locus	morpho-syntactically irrelevant

TABLE 3 Characteristics of head and dependents, from Zwicky 1993

of a construction is that subconstituent which determines the syntactic distribution of the whole. This notion of head is, of course, fundamental to HPSG and is encoded in the Head Feature (Pollard and Sag, 1994) and Subcategorization (Borsley, 1993) Principles. Given an HPSG grammar, the head of any constituent parsed as a headed phrase by the grammar is well-defined. The HEAD values encode precisely the kind of part of speech information which determines the syntactic distribution of an element (such as case, preposition form, and modification possibilities) and the Head Feature Principle propagates this information to the mother of the phrase. Likewise, the Subcategorization Principle distinguishes heads from arguments, in general making the valence requirements of a phrase some function of the valence requirements of its head.[15] Determining which element is the head for

---

[15]In some cases these 'functions' get fairly elaborate and also refer to the valence requirements of the non-head daughter, as in argument transfer and composition in constructions like that combining verbal nouns and light verbs in Japanese.

the purposes of writing the grammar, on the other hand, can be trickier. Deciding on the head constituent in a phrase requires observing which constituent contributes the head information and the subcategorization information. By this definition, it is true that most heads in Japanese follow both arguments and adjuncts: Verbs appear at the end of clauses, as can be seen in (32).

(32) 田中　が　本　を　読んだ
Tanaka ga　hon　wo　yon-da
Tanaka NOM book ACC read-PST

"Tanaka read a book."

Adjectives, adnominals, and relative clauses precede nouns:

(33) 田中　の　やさしい 友達　が　来た
Tanaka no　yasashii tomodachi ga　ki-ta
Tanaka ADN nice　friend　NOM come-PST

"Tanaka's nice friend came."

The language has post-positions, including both contentful elements such as *kara* "from" (34), and the case marking post-positions *ga, wo, ni* (35), which both follow nouns.

(34) 東京　から 来た
Toukyou kara ki-ta
Tokyo　from come-PST

"They came from Tokyo."

(35) 何時　から が　よろしい です　か
nan-ji　kara ga　yoroshii desu　ka
what-hour from NOM good　COP.AHON:+ Q

"From what time would be good?"

That contentful post-positions should head their phrases is relatively uncontroversial. Applying the same treatment to the case markers might be more surprising, especially as they are sometimes considered to be nominal inflection (e.g., Sag et al. 2003). However, we will argue in Chapter 7 that Japanese case particles should best be treated as syntactic heads. We illustrate the argument here with the examples in (34)–(35) above and (36)–(37), which together show that *ga* is crucial in determining the combinatoric potential of its phrase.

(36) 何時　から 集まります　か
nan-ji　kara atsumari-masu ka
what-hour from gather-AHON:+ Q

"From what time are people gathering?"

(37) *何時   から が   集まります   か
      *nan-ji kara ga atsumari-masu ka
      what-hour from NOM gather-AHON:+ Q

   Intended: "From what time are people gathering?"

In (35), there is a single constituent (何時から が *nanji kara ga*) containing both a contentful post-position (から *kara* "from") and a case-marking post-position *ga*. Constituents ending in *kara* are verbal adjuncts ((34) and (36)). When *ga* attaches, the result is eligible to appear in an argument (here, subject) position (35), and no longer can appear as a verbal adjunct (37). If *ga* were merely a marker that otherwise preserved the category information of the constituent it attaches to, this behavior would be hard to explain. Note that on this analysis, the Japanese case particles look fairly similar to English 'case-marking prepositions', such as *to* in *Kim gave the book to Sandy*. For our purposes here, the main point is that PPs, with both contentful and case marking post-positions, are also head-final. We now turn to the exceptions we have found to the general head-final trend, which can be classified into two groups: head-initial modification and head-initial complementation.[16]

3.3.2 Head-Initial Modification

Using the definition above of the syntactic head in a construction, we can find some elements that behave as non-heads, although they occur final in a construction. In this class, we find the modifiers だけ *dake*, のみ *nomi*, ばかり *bakari* (in two distinct uses), ごろ *goro*, くらい *kurai*, ほど *hodo*, and certain instances of numeral classifiers.

だけ **Dake** "only" The modifier だけ *dake* "only" modifies at least NPs, predicative PPs, and adverbs. The noun-modification use is illustrated in (38):

(38) a. 野村   さん だけ が   来た
         Nomura san dake ga   ki-ta
         Nomura HON only NOM come-PST

   "Only Mr/Ms Nomura came."

---

[16]In general, distinguishing morphology and syntax is not very clear-cut in this agglutinating language Shibatani and Kageyama (1988); Kageyama (2001). For better or for worse, the orthography does not provide any clues, lacking inter-word spaces. For practical (engineering) purposes, we tend towards regarding syntax over morphology, as ChaSen Matsumoto et al. (1999) provides near-morpheme-level segmentation. Along the way, we will point out evidence that the cases presented here involve syntactically separate words (clitics or otherwise).

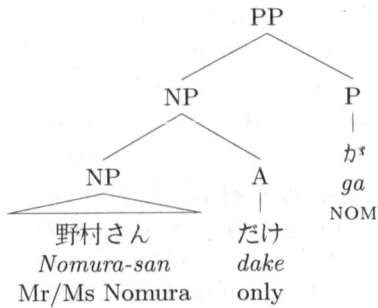

FIGURE 23 Structure of PP with *dake*

b. 野村　さんがﾞ　来た
   Nomura san   ga   ki-ta
   Nomura HON NOM come-PST

   "Mr/Ms Nomura came."

c. *だけがﾞ　来た
   **dake ga   ki-ta*
   only   NOM come-PST

   Intended: "Only came."

The head of the construction *Nomura-san dake ga* is the case particle *ga* (see above). The head of *Nomura-san dake* must be *Nomura-san*, because *ga* selects for a noun. Leaving *dake* out in this construction leads to a grammatical sentence *Nomura-san ga kita*, while leaving *Nomura-san* out gives an ungrammatical sentence. *Dake* is optional in all registers, the noun is obligatory in all, and the case particle is obligatory in some.[17] Therefore we conclude that *dake* in this construction is a modifier to *Nomura-san*, even though it follows the head.

The use of *dake* as a modifier of predicative PPs is illustrated in (39):

(39) 利用者 は　東京　から (だけ) で は ない
      riyousha wa   toukyou kara (dake) dewa-nai
      user   TOP Tokyo from (only) COP-NEG

      "The users were not only from Tokyo."

The fact that *dake* is optional in this example lends support to the conclusion that *toukyou kara dake* is a head-initial construction. Further support comes from the fact that the order of the particles is flexible, as illustrated in (40) (from Makino and Tsutsui 1986, 95).

---

[17]For our analysis of the optionality of case particles, which is consistent with treating them as heads, see 7.3.1.

(40) a. この 車　　は　アルコール で だけ
　　　　 kono kuruma wa arukooru de dake
　　　　 this car　　 TOP alcohol INS only
　　　　 動け ます
　　　　 ugoke-masu
　　　　 move.POT-AHON:+

　　　　 "This car runs only on alcohol."

　　 b. この 車　　は　アルコール だけ で
　　　　 kono kuruma wa arukooru dake de
　　　　 this car　　 TOP alcohol only INS
　　　　 動け ます
　　　　 ugoke-masu
　　　　 move.POT-AHON:+

　　　　 "This car runs on alcohol alone."

As indicated in the glosses, *dake* can modify (semantically as well as syntactically) either the NP or the PP. It can appear in either position without affecting combinatoric potential. Thus, *arukouru de dake* and *arukouru dake* are head-initial.

Finally, adverbs can also be modified (head-initially) by *dake*, as illustrated in Example 41 (from Makino and Tsutsui 1986, 94).

(41) 私　　は　日本　へ 一度　(だけ) 行った
　　　 watashi wa nihon e ichido (dake) it-ta
　　　 1SG　 TOP Japan to once (only) go-PST

　　　 "I went to Japan (only) once."

To summarize the observations for *dake*, we can say that it combines with (at least) NP, PP, and ADV to form a category of the same type. The relative non-specificity of the host suggests a syntactic rather than a morphological combination. The distributional facts support treating *dake* as a non-head, even though it is final in its constituent.[18] A second element, *nomi* 'only', is very similar to *dake*, except that it cannot follow adjectives and quantifiers. It is used in formal speech and written Japanese, but seldom in the registers found in our corpora.

ばかり Bakari "only" Our second example is ばかり *bakari* "only". It can also modify PPs, VPs (or possibly Vs) and NPS. Consider first the example in (42), from the newspaper *Mainichi Shinbun*. Here, *bakari* is a PP modifier:

---

[18]Makino and Tsutsui (1986) also note a use of *dake* where it attaches to verbs and adjectives to make nominal constituents. In this case, *dake* appears to be a nominalizing head and the examples are not relevant to the point at hand.

(42) a. 衝突　　に　　ばかり　関心　　が　　集まった
　　　　shoutotsu ni　bakari　kanshin ga　atsumat-ta
　　　　collision　LOC　only　　concern　NOM collect-PST

"It is only on the collision that concern is concentrated."

b. 衝突　　に　　関心　　が　　集まった
　　shoutotsu ni　kanshin ga　atsumat-ta
　　collision　LOC concern　NOM collect-PST

"It is on the collision that concern is concentrated."

c. 衝突　　ばかり　関心　　が　　集まった
　　shoutotsu bakari　kanshin ga　atsumat-ta
　　collision　only　　concern　NOM collect-PST

Intended: "It is only on the collision that concern is concentrated."

In the first example, the particle に *ni* "to" determines the combinatoric potential of the whole phrase, leaving *bakari* the role of a modifier. There are also examples of head-initial verb modification, including the following attested in *Mainichi Shinbun* in 2002:

(43) 学校　の　先生　　を　　怒らせて　　　ばかり　いた
　　　Gakkou no　sensei　wo　okora-se-te　bakari　i-ta
　　　school ADN teacher ACC upset-CAUS-INF only　PROG-PST

"The only thing he was doing was upsetting the school's teacher."

This is one exception to the general rule that nothing should intervene between a verb in the *-te* form and an auxiliary. The exception can be handled if *bakari* modifies *okorasete*. We therefore introduce one instance of *bakari* that can be a post-head modifier of verbs with *-te* inflection.

But in the third example (42c), *bakari* acts both to restrict the focus and as a post-position that takes a NP as complement and then modifies a VP.

Bakari and other forms meaning 'about' There is another post-head modifier *bakari* meaning 'about', which modifies temporal expressions. We illustrate it here with another *Mainichi Shinbun* example:

(44) 東京　　から　車　　　で　二　時間　ばかり　の　近郊　　の
　　　Toukyou kara kuruma de　ni　jikan bakari　no　kinkou no
　　　Tokyo　from car　INS two hour only　ADN suburb ADN
　　　温泉　　に　朝　　七時　　　ごろ　出発　　　する
　　　onsen　ni　asa　shichi-ji　goro　shuppatsu suru
　　　hotspring LOC morning seven-hour around depart　do

"We depart at about 7 a.m. for a hotspring in the suburbs which is about two hours from Tokyo by car."

The relevant construction here is *nijikan bakari no*. The head of the construction is の *no*, because it carries the information that the construction can modify an NP. *no*, in turn, selects for the temporal noun *nijikan* and *nijikan* is modified by *bakari*. The sentence would be perfectly grammatical without *bakari*. Similarly, for ごろ *goro*, くらい *kurai* and ほど *hodo*, one finds several examples for head-initial modification of temporal expressions, such as (45):

(45) 今日 何時 ごろ まで 寝て いました か
kyou nan-ji goro made ne-te i-mashi-ta ka
today what-hour about until sleep-INF PROG-AHON:+-PST Q

"Until about what time did you sleep today?"

Leaving out *goro* in (46a) simply removes the 'approximate' meaning from the sentence, while leaving out *nanji* (46b) changes the meaning drastically: *Goro* becomes a modifier of *kyou*. Leaving out *made* (46c) gives the sentence another meaning, 'At about what time did you fall asleep today?'. Leaving out both *goro* and *made* gives 'At what time did you fall asleep today?'

(46) a. 今日 何時 まで 寝て いました か
kyou nan-ji made ne-te i-mashi-ta ka
today what-hour until sleep-INF PROG-AHON:+-PST Q

"Until what time did you sleep today?"

b. 今日 ごろ まで 寝て いました か
kyou goro made ne-te i-mashi-ta ka
today about until sleep-INF PROG-AHON:+-PST Q

"Were you sleeping until about today?"

c. 今日 何時 ごろ 寝て いました か
kyou nan-ji goro ne-te i-mashi-ta ka
today what-hour about sleep-INF PROG-AHON:+-PST Q

"At about what time were you sleeping today?"

d. 今日 何時 寝て いました か
kyou nan-ji ne-te i-mashi-ta ka
today what-hour sleep-INF PROG-AHON:+-PST Q

"At what time were you sleeping today?"

Once again, we see a modifier (*goro*) which can attach to multiple different constituents. Unlike *made*, *goro* does not affect the way the constituent it is attached to interacts with the rest of the sentence. Therefore, we propose the structure in Figure 24 for *nanji goro made*.

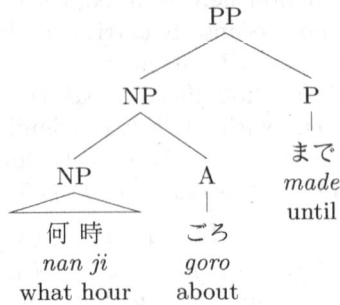

FIGURE 24 Structure of *nanji goro made* 'until about what time'

Numeral classifiers Finally, on our analysis, numeral classifier phrases appearing between a noun and its case particle or immediately after a case particle are post-head modifiers. Some examples are given in (47). See Bender and Siegel 2004, as well as § 6.7 for further details.

(47) a. 猫 二 匹 を 飼う
neko ni hiki wo kau
cat two NUMCL ACC raise

"I am raising two cats."

b. 猫 を 二 匹 家 で 飼う
neko wo ni hiki ie de kau
cat ACC two NUMCL house LOC raise

"I am raising two cats in my house."

In this section, we have seen post-head modification of nominal, post-positional, adverbial and verbal constituents. Many of the modifiers can modify multiple different parts of speech. Others (numeral classifier phrases) are internally complex (potentially containing arbitrarily large number names) and further more can appear before or after the phrases they modify, or 'floated' away from them (Bender and Siegel, 2004). These properties suggest that we are dealing with a syntactic rather than morphological phenomenon.

Our analysis for head-initial modification consists of:

1. A lexical type hierarchy containing types that allow for head-initial constructions.

2. Grammar rules for head-initial modification and head-initial complementation.
3. A head feature POSTHEAD that is referenced by head-adjunct rules.

Figure 25 shows part of the type hierarchy of lexical signs, containing lexical items that modify nouns, post-positions and verbs, and which are divided into left-modifying and right-modifying items.

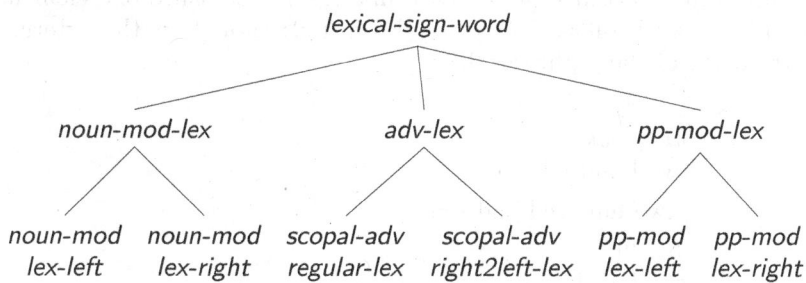

FIGURE 25 Partial hierarchy of lexical types for modifiers

The inventory of grammar rules contains rules for both head-initial and head-final modification, which differ in the order of the daughters. The rules reference the HEAD.POSTHEAD value of the modifier daughter in order to constrain the distribution of lexical items across the constructions. POSTHEAD can be *left* or *right*, or can be left unspecified for those items that can modify in both directions. Head-initial modifier rules (scopal or intersective) bear the constraints shown in Figure 26, where the feature ARGS encodes the daughters of the rule and the order in which they appear.

$$\begin{bmatrix} \text{HEAD-DTR} & \boxed{1} \\ \text{NON-HEAD-DTR} & \boxed{2}[\text{HEAD.POSTHEAD} \quad \textit{right}] \\ \text{ARGS} & \langle \boxed{1}, \boxed{2} \rangle \end{bmatrix}$$

FIGURE 26 Constraints on head-initial modifier rules

Modifiers of type *pp-mod-lex-right*, etc., are constrained to be [POSTHEAD *right*] and are compatible with head-initial modifier rules. In contrast, *pp-mod-lex-left*, etc., are [POSTHEAD *left*] and are thus incompatible with head-initial modifier rules. In principle, modifiers could be underspecified for POSTHEAD, thus appearing on either side. Our lexicon does not currently contain any such modifiers.[19]

3.3.3 Head-Initial Complementation

We have found two clear cases of head-initial complementation, the first in number names and the second in numeral classifiers. In both cases, one optional argument follows the head. We argue that number names like 二百十 *ni hyaku juu* "210" are head-medial on the basis of examples like (48) and (49). (48b) and (48c) each share one element in common with (48a). The examples in (49) show that the external distribution of these phrases differs.

(48) a. 二 百 十
 ni hyaku juu
 two hundred ten
 "two hundred and ten"

 b. 五 百 三
 go hyaku san
 five hundred three
 "five hundred and three"

 c. 二 千 三
 ni sen san
 two thousand three
 "two thousand and three"

(49) a. 六 千 二 百 十
 roku sen ni hyaku juu
 six thousand two hundred ten
 "six thousand two hundred and ten"

 b. 六 千 五 百 三
 roku sen go hyaku san
 six thousand five hundred three
 "six thousand five hundred and three"

 c. *六 千 二 千 三
 **roku sen ni sen san*
 six thousand two thousand three

---

[19]It might appear that numeral classifiers would constitute a case of modifiers attaching either to the left or to the right of their heads. However, in pre-head uses of numeral classifiers there is always an intervening の *no* (adnominal) particle. We treat this particle as a head which selects for a numeral classifier phrase and mediates the modification of the noun by the numeral classifier. For details, see Bender and Siegel 2004.

BASIC JAPANESE PHRASE STRUCTURE / 57

Intended: "six thousand two thousand and three"

d. *六　千　　　五　千　　　十
　*roku sen　　go sen　　juu
　six　thousand　five thousand　ten

Intended: "six thousand five thousand and ten"

Expressions with 百 *hyaku* (48a,b) have the same combinatoric potential. Expressions without *hyaku* differ. The other elements of (48) 二 *ni* "two" and 十 *juu* "ten" are not relevant. Thus, we take *hyaku* to be the head of (48). If we forget for the moment that Japanese is supposed to be head-final, this isn't very surprising: English number names work the same way (see Smith 1999). So do number names in another SVO language: Chinese, the source from which Japanese borrowed this system.[20] One might argue that this is actually a morphological process, in which case the head-medial structure is less surprising. However, Martin (1988) finds that while some local combinations within number names (e.g., the names for 11 through 19, 20, 30, 200, 300, etc.) form single phonological words, longer combinations made up of these pieces (such as 三百十一 *sanbyaku juuichi* "311") show phrasal phonology.

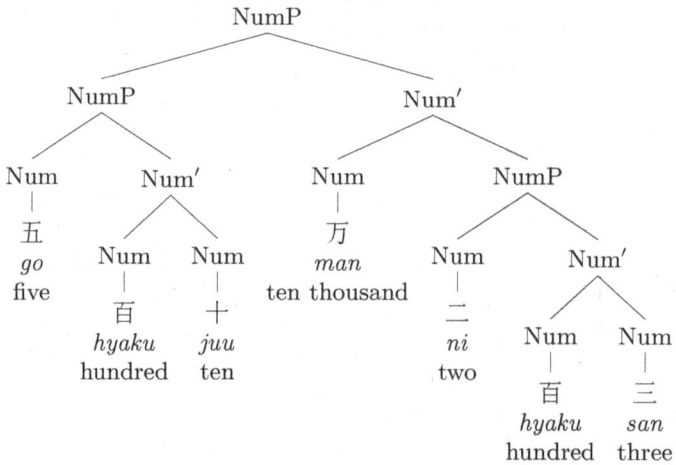

FIGURE 27 Recursive structure in number name expressions

Moreover, number names show a recursive constituent structure (where full number names can show up as subcomponents of larger

---

[20]According to Frellesvig (2010), Sino-Japanese numerals are thought to have been borrowed into Japanese in the Early Middle Japanese period (800–1200 C.E.) (p. 289).

number names) that is well-modeled with phrase structure grammar but not with finite-state techniques (see Figure 27). This kind of recursion is (to our knowledge) unattested elsewhere in morphology. The analysis presented here was developed within the context of an application that takes text-based input. As such, it was most convenient to apply the phrasal analysis uniformly. A similar analysis could be developed that provides lexical entries for every combination that forms a phonological word. It would still involve head-initial structures: In a phrase like 三百十一 *sanbyaku juiuichi*, the phonological words are 三百 *sanbyaku* "three hundred" and 十一 *juuichi* "eleven". Following the same argumentation as above, *sanbyaku* (and within it, *hyaku* "hundred") determines the distribution of the phrase within larger number names.

(50) a. 一 千 [三 百 十 一]
    is sen [san byaku juu ichi]
    one thousand [three hundred ten one]

    "one thousand three hundred eleven"

b. *五 百 [三 百 十 一]
    **go hyaku [san byaku juu ichi]*
    five hundred [three hundred ten one]

    Intended: "five hundred three hundred eleven"

c. 五 百 十 一
    go hyaku juu ichi
    five hundred ten one"

    "five hundred eleven"

The second type of head-initial complementation involves numeral classifiers. All numeral classifiers combine with a number name to their left, but certain mensural numeral classifiers such as 年 *nen* "year" can also take the word 半 *han* "half" to their right (51). Syntactically, the numeral classifier determines the combinatorics of the phrase (being able to modify nouns, not being able to show up as the specifier of a larger number name). The presence or absence of *han* has no effect on the distribution. The numeral classifier is also in a better position to integrate the semantics of *han* than vice versa (Bender and Siegel, 2004).

(51) a. 二 年 半
    ni nen han
    two year half

    "two and a half years"

b. 二　年
   ni　*nen*
   two year
   "two years"

Our analysis of both of these instances of head-initial complementation consists of:

1. Two head-complement rules, differing in the order of the daughters, and sensitive to the HEAD type of the head.
2. A high-level distinction in the subtypes of *head* into *init_head* and *final_head*.

In the case of head-initial complementation, we do not posit an additional feature, but instead take advantage of the type hierarchy and posit a split between initial heads and final heads. Most head types inherit from *final_head*, including *noun-or-case-p_head* (subsuming nouns and the case particles), *verb_head*, and *p_head*, for the contentful post-positions. The two subtypes of *init_head* are *int_head* (for number names) and *num-cl_head* (for numeral classifiers). The latter point is a bit subtle: The only numeral classifiers that take complements at all are those that can appear with *han* (as a complement).[21] As the classification into *final_head* and *init_head* is only referenced by the head-complement rules, it is simplest to make numeral classifiers all *init_head*.

$$\begin{bmatrix} \text{HEAD-DTR} & \boxed{1}\begin{bmatrix}\text{HEAD} & \textit{final\_head}\end{bmatrix} \\ \text{NON-HEAD-DTR} & \boxed{2} \\ \text{ARGS} & \langle\,\boxed{2},\,\boxed{1}\,\rangle \end{bmatrix}$$

FIGURE 28 Head-complement-head-final-rule

The constraints on the two head-complement rules shown in Figure 28 capture the necessary contrast. The ordering constraints relating HEAD-DTR, NON-HEAD-DTR, and ARGS are inherited from a supertype that is also applicable to the head-modifier cases. In our current implementation, there are no head types which are indeterminate between

---

[21] We have actually found it convenient to posit one more kind of numeral classifier which takes a complement: namely currency symbols such as '$' and '¥', which appear to the left of a numerical expression but otherwise function syntactically and semantically like currency words such as ドル *doru* "dollars" and 円 *en* "yen", which appear to the right of a number name. Most numeral classifiers select their dependent number name.

$$\begin{bmatrix} \text{HEAD-DTR} & \boxed{1}\begin{bmatrix} \text{HEAD} & \textit{init\_head} \end{bmatrix} \\ \text{NON-HEAD-DTR} & \boxed{2} \\ \text{ARGS} & \langle \boxed{1}, \boxed{2} \rangle \end{bmatrix}$$

FIGURE 29 Head-complement-head-initial-rule

Arity	Head	Frequency	%	Example
1	H	20,944	19.18	quantify-n-rule
1	—	10,049	9.20	utterance_rule-decl-finite, adv_np_rule
2	R	77,170	70.66	hf-complement-rule, head_subj_rule
2	L	1,021	0.93	hi-adj-s-rule, hi-complement-rule
2	—	22	0.02	frg-cop

TABLE 4 **Jacy** (1301) Headedness from the Tanaka Corpus (6–15), 8,797 sentences

init_head and *final_head*. All head types inherit from exactly one of these. It would of course be possible to cross-classify the ordering dimension with the part of speech dimension, should this be necessary, if some elements of a certain head type preceded their complements and others followed or if all elements of some head type could appear in either order with respect to their complements. Our investigations so far suggest that this is not the case for Japanese. It might be relevant for another language with relatively free order in general, but with some heads showing a more fixed order.

3.3.4 Corpus Study

We use the Tanaka-Corpus treebank (see Section 11.2.2.2) to investigate the distribution of headedness. We count all rules and determine whether they are unary or binary (Arity of 1 or 2) and whether they are **H**eaded (and for binary rules whether the head is **L**eft or **R**ight). The results, with some example rules, are given in Table 4 for Japanese and, for comparison, Table 5 for English.

For Japanese, 28.4% of rule tokens are unary, of which 67.6% are headed. Of the binary rule tokens, 98.7% are right-headed 1.2% are left-headed and almost none are non-headed. For English, there are more unary rule tokens (32.8%) and the binary rules are much more evenly split: 39.5% are right-headed, 55.0% are left-headed and the rest are non-headed. Thus we see that while broad-coverage, precision analysis of Japanese requires head-initial rules, their token frequency in a corpus is quite low. For this reason, it is not surprising that linguists generally take the language to be strictly head-final.

Arity	Head	Frequency	%
1	H	230,855	28.27
1	—	37,087	4.50
2	R	216,808	26.55
2	L	301,542	36.92
2	—	30,265	3.71

TABLE 5 ERG (1212) Headedness from the Redwoods Corpus, 47,926 sentences

3.4 Semantic Representations

The **Jacy** grammar produces semantic representations in the format of Minimal Recursion Semantics (MRS; Copestake et al. 2005). These representations are central to the grammar: When extending the grammar to cover a new phenomenon, the first step is to design the target semantic representations. Significant effort has been put into 'harmonizing' the representations of **Jacy** with the English Resource Grammar (ERG; Flickinger 2000), though in some cases, differences between the two languages necessitate differences in the output semantic representations and in others there was no model available in the ERG. In this section, we briefly overview the structure of the MRS representations and present the format we will use to depict them throughout the book.

The heart of an MRS representation (or "MRS") is a bag of elementary predications. Each elementary predication has a predicate name (encoded as the value of the feature PRED) and a label (encoded as the value of the feature LBL), and one or more arguments (encoded as the value of the features ARG0–ARG3). In the simplest case, the arguments to predications can be variables standing for events (e) or individuals (x). For example, Figure 30 shows the MRS for (52).

(52) 猫　が　ケーキ を　食べ た
neko ga　keeki　wo　tabe-ta
cat　NOM cake　ACC eat-PST

"The cat ate the cake."

In this MRS, the variable e_2 stands for the eating event, x_4 for the cat, and x_9 for the cake. Accordingly, x_4 and x_9 are the values of ARG1 and ARG2 of the _taberu_v_1 predication, as well as the ARG0 of the _neko_n and _keeki_n predications, respectively. The variables are associated with "variable properties", such as person or number for nominal indices and tense, aspect or sentential force for event variables. These appear as feature-value pairs on the indices themselves.

The more elaborate case comes in with scope-taking predicates.

$$\begin{bmatrix} \text{TOP} & h1 \\ \text{INDEX} & e2 \\ \text{RELS} & \left\{ \begin{bmatrix} \text{PRED} & \_neko\_n \\ \text{LBL} & h3 \\ \text{ARG0} & x4[\text{PERS } 3] \end{bmatrix}, \begin{bmatrix} \text{PRED} & udef \\ \text{LBL} & h5 \\ \text{ARG0} & x4 \\ \text{RSTR} & h7 \\ \text{BODY} & h6 \end{bmatrix}, \begin{bmatrix} \text{PRED} & \_keeki\_n \\ \text{LBL} & h8 \\ \text{ARG0} & x9[\text{PERS } 3] \end{bmatrix}, \begin{bmatrix} \text{PRED} & udef \\ \text{LBL} & h10 \\ \text{ARG0} & x9 \\ \text{RSTR} & h12 \\ \text{BODY} & h11 \end{bmatrix}, \begin{bmatrix} \text{PRED} & \_taberu\_v\_1 \\ \text{ARG0} & e2[\text{TENSE } past] \\ \text{ARG1} & x4 \\ \text{ARG2} & x9 \end{bmatrix} \right\} \\ \text{HCONS} & \left\{ \text{H}12 =_Q \text{H}8, \text{H}7 =_Q \text{H}3 \right\} \end{bmatrix}$$

FIGURE 30 MRS representation of 猫がケーキを食べた "The cat ate the cake"

These include quantifiers as well as clause-embedding verbs, scopal modifiers and scopal operators (such as negation). With scope-taking predicates, one or more argument positions point to the label of the predicate they scope over. However, this is done indirectly through handle constraints (the value of the feature HCONS). This indirection allows for the underspecification of quantifier scope.[22] The udef predicates in Figure 30 are the underspecified quantifier predications provided for the NPs in that example. Another example, with negation, is provided in Figure 31, the MRS for (53).

(53) 猫   が   ケーキ を   食べ なかった
     neko ga keeki wo tabe-nakat-ta
     cat NOM cake   ACC eat-NEG-PST

"The cat did not eat the cake."

Here, the negation is represented by the scopal predicate _neg_v. The ARG1 of this predicate is the handle h_{15}, which is linked through the handle constraint "$h_{15} =_q h_{13}$" to the label (LBL) of the _taberu_v predication. This means that unless a quantifer scopes in between, the argument of negation will be the 'eating' predication.

---

[22]For the details, we refer the reader to Copestake et al. 2005.

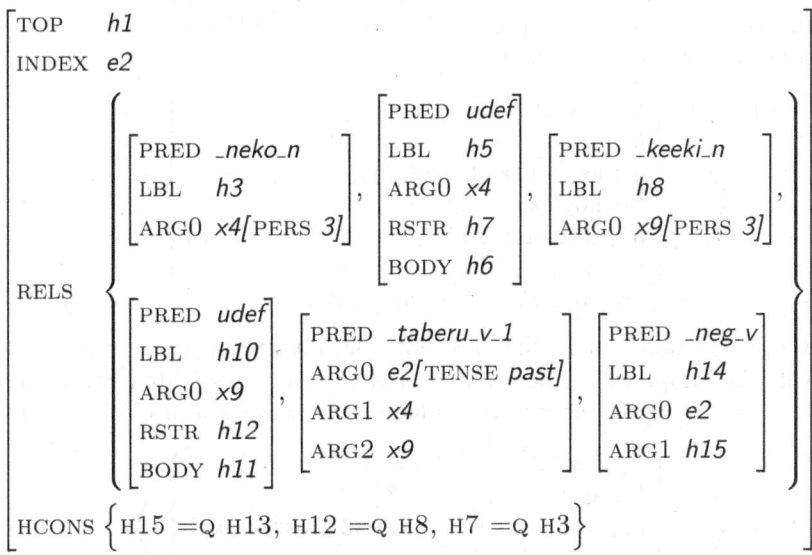

FIGURE 31 MRS representation of 猫がケーキを食べなかった "The cat did not eat the cake"

Finally, note that in addition to the bags of predications (RELS) and handle constraints (HCONS), each MRS is associated with a top handle (TOP) and an index (INDEX). These serve as pointers into the RELS list, both for post-processing of MRSs and for composition of MRSs for larger constituents. Composition of MRSs in **Jacy** proceeds broadly as specified in the MRS algebra (Copestake et al., 2001): The RELS and HCONS lists of a constituent is built up of the lists of its daughters and those of its C-CONT (CONSTRUCTIONAL-CONTENT; the semantic contribution of a rule). The TOP and INDEX come from those of the C-CONT, which, depending on the rule, may identify them with the TOP and INDEX of either daughter or with values from within the C-CONT.RELS.[23]

This brief introduction has used the avm notation for MRSs in order to make it easier to talk about the relationships between the elementary predications. In the remainder of the book, we will use the format shown

---

[23]Note, however, that **Jacy** is not necessarily fully algebra-compliant. There are certainly rules that specify linkages between semantic representations that go beyond the operators anticipated by the algebra as published, see for example footnote 19 on page 156. We leave to future work the questions of identifying these rules and determining which motivate extensions to the algebra and which could be revised into compliance.

in (54). This format is more concise, suppressing the feature names, but otherwise presents the same information.

(54) $\left\langle h_1, \left\{\begin{array}{l} h_3\text{:\_neko\_n}(x_4 \{\text{PERS } 3\}), \\ h_5\text{:udef}(x_4, h_7, h_6), \\ h_8\text{:\_keeki\_n}(x_9 \{\text{PERS } 3\}), \\ h_{10}\text{:udef}(x_9, h_{12}, h_{11}), \\ h_{13}\text{:\_taberu\_v\_1}\left(e_2 \{\text{TENSE } past\} x_4, x_9\right), \\ h_{14}\text{:\_neg\_v}(e_2, h_{15}) \end{array}\right\} \right\rangle$,
$\{h_{15} =_q h_{13}, h_{12} =_q h_8, h_7 =_q h_3\}$

In addition, where they are not relevant to the point at hand, we will also suppress any udef quantifiers and their associated handle constraints, giving the even more concise representation in (55) for (53).

(55) $\left\langle h_1, \left\{\begin{array}{l} h_3\text{:\_neko\_n}(x_4 \{\text{PERS } 3\}), \\ h_8\text{:\_keeki\_n}(x_9 \{\text{PERS } 3\}), \\ h_{13}\text{:\_taberu\_v\_1}\left(e_2 \{\text{TENSE } pres\} x_4, x_9\right), \\ h_{14}\text{:\_neg\_v}(e_2, h_{15}) \end{array}\right\} \right\rangle$,
$\{h_{15} =_q h_{13}\}$

Predicate names for real predicates (those introduced directly by lexical items) take the form of lemma_pos_sense, following the conventions introduced by Robust Minimal Recursion Semantics in the Deep Thought project (Copestake, 2007; Callmeier et al., 2004). The lemma portion of a predicate name is typically the romanization of the base form of the word. Part-of-speech (pos) is the rough part of speech, summarized in Table 6.

pos	Definition	Example
n := u	Noun	_inu_n_1 "dog"
v := u	Verb	_hoeru_v_1 "bark"
a := u	Adjective or Adverb	_furui_a_1 "old"
r := a	Adverb	_tabun_r_rel "probably"
s := n; s := v	Verbal noun	_benkyou_s_1 "study"
c := u	Conjunction	_ya_c_1 "and"
p := u	Adposition (pre-/post-position)	_kara_p_1 "from"
q := u	Quantifier	_kaku_q_1 "each"
x := u	Other closed class	_chikushou_x_1_rel "beast"

TABLE 6 MRS Part-of-Speech labels

Two words may have the same predicate if we consider them to have identical meaning. The most common case of this is kanji and non-kanji spellings, such as 欲しい and ほしい for *hoshii* "want". In any case, two words with the same predicate must have the same number of arguments and their roles should be the same.

3.5 Summary and Further Reading

This chapter has presented the basic phrase structure rules used in **Jacy**. Along the way, we have given a brief overview of HPSG and MRS. For a comprehensive introduction to HPSG, see Pollard and Sag 1994. MRS is introduced in Copestake et al. 2005. While most of the phrase types needed for Japanese are head-final (see Gunji 1987 for the argumentation), in our work on extending the grammar to cover naturally occurring text, including both core and non-core phenomena, we did find a handful of instances of head-initial phrases. The phrase structure rules, both head-initial and head-final, fall into the classes generally assumed in HPSG: phrases for combining heads with complements, subjects, specifiers and modifiers, along with special schemata for coordination and sub-syntactic head-marker constructions. Zwicky (1993) explains the theoretical difference between heads and dependents. A general introduction to Japanese grammar is given by Tsujimura (2006). As is typical for strongly lexicalist HPSG grammars, most of the information is in the lexicon, and the phrase structure rules serve largely to project and mediate this lexical information. A grammar based on the same principles is the English ERG, described in Flickinger et al. 2000. Flickinger (2000) illuminates the usage of type hierarchies in HPSG grammars.

The following chapters describe various kinds of lexical constraints and assume the phrase structure rules presented here as background.

4

Word Order and Subcategorization

This chapter describes our approach to subcategorization in Japanese. At a sufficiently abstract level, we treat Japanese subcategorization like that of any other language: heads select for arguments while modifiers are not selected by heads. However, there are several phenomena specific to the realization of Japanese arguments that differentiate it from English and that must be modeled in a robust, precise grammar. To wit:

1. The great majority of Japanese arguments are optional, i.e., can be (and often are) realized as zero pronouns.
2. Japanese allows scrambling of most arguments.
3. Non-optionality correlates with strict word order in Japanese, such that non-optional arguments also must be directly adjacent to their selecting head.

In addition, we note that subjects are distinguished from other arguments (as they are in English). In Japanese, the distinguishing properties include the fact that subjects are never obligatory, the interaction with honorification, and a privileged position with respect to the binding of reflexives. In this chapter we illustrate the properties of Japanese arguments mentioned above (§ 4.1), briefly review previous analyses (§ 4.2) and present the analyses of these phenomena that are implemented in **Jacy** (§ 4.3).

4.1 Properties of Japanese Arguments

The examples in (56) illustrate the pervasive optionality of arguments in Japanese. These examples are all felicitous, given an appropriate context. Furthermore, subjects and objects that refer to the speaker are typically omitted (rather than overt) in Japanese, but zero anaphora do not have to be interpreted as referring to the speaker.

(56) a. 花子 が ご飯 を 食べた
Hanako ga   gohan wo   tabe-ta
Hanako NOM rice   ACC eat-PST

"Hanako ate rice."

b. ご飯 を 食べた
gohan wo   tabe-ta
rice   ACC eat-PST

"ate rice"

c. 食べた
tabe-ta
eat-PST

"ate"

A second characteristic of Japanese argument realization is that arguments of a predicate can appear in any order as can be seen in (57):

(57) ご飯 を 花子 が 食べた
gohan wo   Hanako ga   tabe-ta
rice   ACC Hanako NOM eat-PST

"Hanako ate rice."

On the other hand, there are arguments, which are both obligatory (cannot be dropped) and must appear adjacent to their selecting head. The complement of the copula is one such example, as illustrated in (58). (58a) is drawn from the Verbmobil corpus; (58b,c) show that the complement of です *desu* "be" is obligatory and (58d) that it must appear directly before the copula.

(58) a. 会議 は 二 時間 ぐらい です
kaigi   wa   ni   jikan gurai   desu
meeting TOP two hour about COP.AHON:+

"The meeting is about two hours."

b. *会議 は です
**kaigi   wa   desu*
meeting TOP COP.AHON:+

Intended: "The meeting is"

c. *です
**desu*
COP.AHON:+

Intended: "is"

d. *二 時間 ぐらい 会議 は です
   *ni jikan gurai kaigi wa desu
   two hour about meeting TOP COP.AHON:+

   Intended: "The meeting is about two hours."

Subjects in Japanese can be differentiated from other arguments in several ways. First, subjects are always optional: we have encountered no example of a predicate that selects for an obligatory subject. Second, subjects are referenced by subject honorifics, as illustrated in (59) and discussed further in Chapter 9. Finally, as illustrated in (60) (from McCawley 1976) and discussed further in § 6.3.4, the reflexive pronoun 自分 *jibun*, if bound by an argument in the sentence, takes a subject as its antecedent.

(59) 先生 を お待ち します
   sensei wo o-machi shi-masu
   teacher ACC SHON:−-wait SHON:−-AHON:+

   "I wait for the teacher."

(60) 佐藤 は 田中 が 原田 に 自分 が 好き
   Satou$_i$ wa Tanaka$_k$ ga Harada ni jibun$_{i/k}$ ga suki
   Satou TOP Tanaka NOM Harada DAT REFL NOM like
   な 娘 を 紹介 した こと に 驚いた
   na musume wo shoukai shi-ta koto ni odoroi-ta
   COP girl ACC introduce do-PST NMLZ DAT surprise-PST

   "Satou$_i$ was surprised that Tanaka$_k$ introduced to Harada the girl he$_{i/k}$ loves."

It is far from trivial to distinguish arguments from adjuncts in Japanese, where the distinction is made murkier by the properties of pervasive optionality and scrambling. Our working hypotheses are as follows:

1. Subjects are arguments.
2. Obligatory dependents are arguments.
3. Dependents marked by を *wo* (accusative) are arguments.
4. Dependents that can be promoted via passivation are arguments.
5. Dependents that get a selectional restriction from the head are arguments.

In the following section, we review previous HPSG analyses of Japanese subcategorization in light of these observations.

4.2 Previous Analyses

The standard HPSG approach to the realization of selected arguments in HPSG, as outlined in Pollard and Sag 1994 and also in Sag et al. 2003 encodes the argument requirements on one or two lists (possibly distinguishing the subject) and then realizes those arguments via phrase structure schemata (or rules) which attach the arguments in the order specified by the lists.

It has long been noted that this approach needs to be extended to handle the argument optionality and scrambling characteristic of Japanese. An analysis based on the SLASH mechanism provided by HPSG to handle long-distance dependencies won't suffice, as scrambling is clause-bounded (i.e., not long-distance).[1] Finally, the standard HPSG approach needs augmentation to handle the phenomenon of necessarily adjacent arguments and the correlation between obligatoriness and required adjacency. Here we quickly review previous approaches to the realization of Japanese arguments from the HPSG literature.

Gunji (1987) (and similarly the NAIST JPSG grammar (Ohtani et al., 2000)) models the value of SUBCAT as a set rather than as a list to account for argument scrambling, but this approach does not distinguish between optional and obligatory arguments, nor between subjects and non-subject arguments. Gunji (1991) adds the list-valued feature ADJACENT to distinguish adjacent arguments from others.[2] Similarly, Sirai (1996) posits two attributes to account for subcategorization in the Japanese Phrase Structure Grammar: SUBCAT, which takes a set of arguments that are optional and can be scrambled, and ADJACENT, which takes one obligatory argument which cannot be scrambled. This approach treats adjacency and obligatoriness as just one property that arguments can have, which is correct for Japanese, as Gunji notes.

There are several other strategies that have been or could be tried for handling Japanese subcategorization: An earlier version of this grammar had separate grammatical functions for each verbal argument (not unlike LFG (Bresnan and Kaplan, 1982) or the approach of Haugereid (2009)). This approach was abandoned with the move to developing **Jacy** in a multilingual context, because it is not followed by the Grammar Matrix. Another alternative is providing several different lexical entries for each lexeme, one for each possible ordering of the arguments. This was a strategy adopted in an earlier version of the

---

[1] Furthermore, a SLASH-based analysis has nothing to say about argument optionality.

[2] Though this feature is list-valued, the order of the list is not important to the grammar rules.

German HPSG in Verbmobil (Müller and Kasper, 2000). This approach has the disadvantage that the lexicon becomes very large. A third possibility is to produce the lexical structures with the various required orderings of the subcategorization list by lexical rule. While this would allow us to capture underlying generalizations about the arguments for each lexeme, it would run the risk of significantly slowing down processing time, and we have not explored it. Finally, there is the popular approach from the HPSG literature of using linearization (Reape, 1993; Yatabe, 2007), which effectively disassociates phenogrammatical from tectogrammatical structure. This is not applicable in our case as the relevant operators do not form part of the DELPH-IN formalism in which **Jacy** is implemented, due to the difficulty of implementing them efficiently.

4.3 Jacy's Approach

This section describes in more detail **Jacy**'s analyses of scrambling, zero pronominalization and obligatorily adjacent arguments, which can be summarized as follows: **Jacy** follows Pollard and Sag 1994, Chapter 9, the ERG, and the Grammar Matrix (inter alia) in positing separate lists for SUBJ, COMPS and SPR. This supports analyses of phenomena for which we need to distinguish the subject. **Jacy** handles scrambling by (a) not requiring complements to be saturated before subjects and (b) including both an ordinary *head-complement* rule (which realizes the first element of the COMPS list) as well as a *head-complement2* rule, which skips over the first element and realizes the second (leaving a COMPS list with just the first thing on it, to be realized later). **Jacy** handles argument optionality by defining the notion of a saturated constituent not as one with empty valence lists, but as one whose valence lists (if non-empty) include only arguments that are optional. The possibility of both scrambling and zero pronominalization are controlled by the feature OPT, described immediately below.

4.3.1 The Feature OPT

The boolean-valued feature OPT (adopted from the ERG) is a feature of objects of type *synsem*. No constituent ever constrains its own OPT value. Instead, selecting heads use it to specify whether a given argument must be overtly realized adjacent to the head. In this case, the head marks the corresponding element of its valence list as [OPT −], as in the definition of the type *suru_noun_ditransitive* (Figure 32) which in turn is used in the definition of する *suru* as used in (61).

$$\begin{bmatrix} \textit{suru\_noun\_ditransitive} \\ \text{SUBJ} \left\langle \begin{bmatrix} \text{HEAD} \begin{bmatrix} \textit{ga-or-wo-case-p\_head} \\ \text{CASE } \textit{ga} \end{bmatrix} \end{bmatrix} \right\rangle \\ \text{COMPS} \left\langle \begin{bmatrix} \text{OPT} & - \\ \text{HEAD} \begin{bmatrix} \textit{case-p\_head} \\ \text{CASE } \textit{ni-or-to} \end{bmatrix} \end{bmatrix}, \begin{bmatrix} \text{HEAD} \begin{bmatrix} \textit{ga-or-wo-case-p\_head} \\ \text{CASE } \textit{wo} \end{bmatrix} \end{bmatrix} \right\rangle \end{bmatrix}$$

FIGURE 32 Type illustrating use of OPT: *suru_noun_ditransitive*

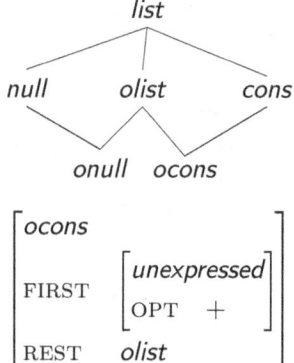

$$\begin{bmatrix} \textit{ocons} \\ \text{FIRST} \begin{bmatrix} \textit{unexpressed} \\ \text{OPT} & + \end{bmatrix} \\ \text{REST} & \textit{olist} \end{bmatrix}$$

FIGURE 33 Type hierarchy and type constraint for *olist*

(61) 彼   が   鉛   を   銀   に   した
　　　kare *ga* *namari* *wo* *gin* *ni* *si-ta*
　　　3SG.M NOM lead   ACC silver DAT do-PST

"He made lead into silver."

Again following the ERG, we define parameterized list types to implement the notion 'list of optional arguments', as shown in Figure 33. The type *olist* is consistent with either the empty list (*null*) or a list in which every single element is a *synsem* whose OPT value is compatible with + (i.e., left underspecified or constrained as +).

4.3.2 Required Adjacency

As described in § 3.2.2, **Jacy**'s phrase structure rules provide the flexibility to realize the arguments of a head in any order. However, certain arguments in Japanese must be realized directly adjacent to their selecting heads. The selecting heads enforce this by constraining the obligatorily adjacent arguments to be [OPT −]. In order for this to have the desired effect, the phrase structure rules must also be sensitive to this feature. This is achieved by making sure that any (head-final) rule combining a head with anything other than the first element of its COMPS list requires the (other) elements of the COMPS list to be [OPT +]

Taking the example in (61) above, we wish the rules to block the variants in (62):

(62) a. *鉛 を 銀 に 彼 が した
         *namari wo gin ni kare ga si-ta
         lead   ACC silver DAT 3SG.M NOM do-PST

   Intended: "He made lead into silver."

   b. *彼 が 銀 に 鉛 を した
      *kare ga gin ni namari wo si-ta
      3SG.M NOM silver DAT lead   ACC do-PST

   Intended: "He made lead into silver."

   c. *彼 が 鉛 を 銀 に はやくした
      *kare ga namari wo gin ni hayaku si-ta
      3SG.M NOM lead   ACC silver DAT quickly do-PST

   Intended: "He quickly made lead into silver."

In order for the grammar to license (62a), the *head-subject* rule would have to combine 彼 *kare* "3SG.M" with した *sita*. But the *head-subject* rule's head daughter is constrained to be [COMPS *olist*]. The COMPS list of the relevant lexical entry for する *suru* has one element that is [OPT −], and so this unification fails. Similarly, in order to license (62b), the *head-complement2* rule (see Figure 10 on page 35) would have to combine 鉛 を *namari wo* "lead ACC" with した *sita*. This rule checks whether the complement it is skipping over is compatible with [OPT +]. Finally, the *head-adjunct* rule that would attach はやく *hayaku* "quickly" to した *sita* also requires the head daughter's COMPS list to be an *olist*.[3]

4.3.3 Zero Pronominalization and Obligatory Overt Realization

Previous versions of **Jacy** handled zero pronominalization via a unary-branching phrase structure rule which discharged an element of a valence list without any overt element corresponding to it. This rule could

---

[3]This same mechanism is also applied to the SUBJ and SPR lists, to allow heads to select obligatorily adjacent subjects or specifiers. Any given head may have, of course, at most one obligatorily adjacent argument.

$$\begin{bmatrix} \textit{saturated} \\ \text{SUBJ} & \textit{zlist} \\ \text{COMPS} & \textit{zlist} \\ \text{SPR} & \textit{null} \end{bmatrix}$$

FIGURE 34 Saturated Valence allowing Zero Pronouns

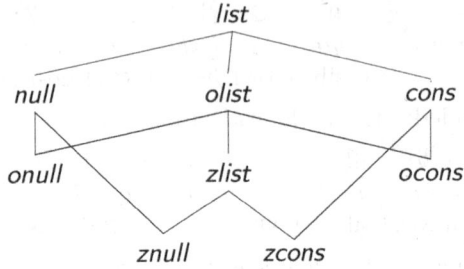

$$\begin{bmatrix} \textit{zcons} \\ \text{FIRST.LOCAL.CONT.HOOK.INDEX} & \textit{zpro\_ref-ind} \\ \text{REST} & \textit{zlist} \end{bmatrix}$$

FIGURE 35 Type hierarchy and type constraint for *zlist*

then insert a semantic relation (and associated quantifier) corresponding to the dropped argument. In the current version of **Jacy**, we forgo introducing a pronoun relation for a dropped argument, which obviates the need for these rules as well. We still require a semantic reflex of the argument drop, but rather than putting in elementary predications, we simply constrain the type of the INDEX of the argument to be of a distinguished type (*zpro_ref-ind*). This information is added in not by the application of any additional grammar rules, but rather through the definition of a type, *saturated*, which is used everywhere in the grammar that a saturated category is selected. This type in turn makes use of another parameterized list type, closely related to *olist*, called *zlist*. The definitions of these types are shown in Figure 34 and Figure 35.[4]

We illustrate how this works with the simple example in (63).

(63) 吠え　　た
　　　hoe-ta
　　　bark-PST

　　　"(It) barked."

---

[4]Thanks to Dan Flickinger for suggesting the analysis and helping to implement it.

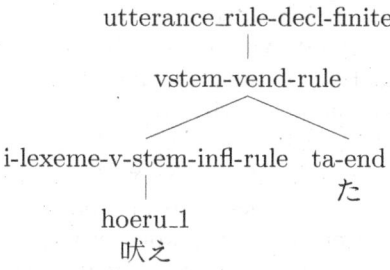

FIGURE 36 Derivation tree for (63)

As can be seen in derivation tree for this item in Figure 36, the analysis involves the rule combining the verbal stem with its ending (*vstem-vend*; see Chapter 5) and the utterance rule for declarative sentences.[5] The utterance rule constrains its daughter to be [VAL *saturated*], meaning that its daughter may or may not contain overt realizations of all of the arguments required by its head, but any arguments that are not overtly realized are resolved to [INDEX *zpro_ref-ind*] per the constraints on *saturated* and *zcons* described above. In this case, the constituent licensed by the *vstem-vend* rule has a non-empty SUBJ list; this argument is optional (i.e., not [OPT −]), so the constituent can serve directly as a sentence. In addition to the daughter positions of the utterance rules, the type *saturated* is also invoked by the rules licensing fragments, the subcategorization features of heads selecting saturated constituents as arguments, the MOD values of modifiers attaching to saturated constituents, etc.

This analysis is far more efficient than an earlier analysis which used pumping rules to discharge the arguments and mark them as zero pronouns: the *zlist*-based analysis requires fewer edges in the chart and is faster.

4.4 Summary and Further Reading

This chapter reviewed key properties of the realization of subcategorized arguments in Japanese, namely that they can typically be omitted (zero pronouns) and realized in any order (scrambling). Importantly, however, some arguments are obligatorily overt and must be realized adjacent to the head. Furthermore, as in many languages, subjects are distinguished from other arguments in Japanese. We present the **Jacy** analyses of these phenomena, in which the feature OPT and the notions of parameterized lists play a central role.

---

[5]On utterance rules, see § 3.2.7.

For a detailed discussion of scrambling (and much more) we recommend Miyagawa (1989). Vermeulen (2012) gives and overview of the information structure of Japanese and the research discussion on this topic. The classic unification-based account is Gunji (1987). Gunji (1991) introduced the ADJACENT feature. The other main theoretical approach is linearization (Reape, 1993), with it applied to Japanese by Yatabe (1996). To see the type-based approach used here applied to a language with an even more free word order, we recommend Bender (2008). Finally, for an introductory movement-based account see Tsujimura (1996, § 5.3).

5

Verbs and Adjectives

The previous chapter laid out our general approach to subcategorization. In this chapter, we look more closely at **Jacy**'s treatment of verbs and adjectives, including subcategorization frames, morphology (inflectional and derivational), and auxiliary constructions. The presentation of the subcategorization types and inflectional morphology is intended to give the reader a general picture of the verbal type classification. The exploration of auxiliary constructions, passivation and causativization sheds light on how our analysis treats valence-changing phenomena.

This chapter is structured as follows. First, we describe the various subcategorization frames available for verbs, verbal nouns, and adjectives (§ 5.1), before moving on to how inflection is handled (§ 5.2). Then we discuss auxiliaries and passive and causative constructions (§ 5.3, 5.4, 5.5).

5.1 Verbal Subcategorization Types

Verb lexical entries encode information about subcategorization, linking, inflection, and honorifics. In this section, we focus on subcategorization, including the number of arguments and their syntactic properties (part of speech, post-position selection). Any analysis of subcategorization must be situated with respect to the larger theoretical discussion of this aspect of linguistic structure. On the one hand, there is the debate about the status of notions such as subject and object. Some authors (e.g., Chomsky 1981) treat phrase structure as fundamental, and the grammatical functions as derivative notions, which can be stated in terms of phrase-structural configurations. Others (e.g., Bresnan and Kaplan 1982) have argued that grammatical functions should be primitives of syntactic theory. In keeping with the typical HPSG approach, we take *subject* and *complement* to be grammatical primitives, but rely on the order of arguments within the COMPS list to distinguish non-subject arguments. Nonetheless, grammatical function is not defined in terms of phrase structural configurations.

Another important theoretical issue which connects with subcategorization is linking, or the relationship between semantic and syntactic arguments. Some authors (e.g., Bresnan and Zaenen 1990; Butt et al. 1997) attempt to derive (to the extent possible) the syntactic functions on the basis of systematic patterns of semantics to syntax linking. Nonetheless, a certain degree of lexical idiosyncrasy remains Koenig and Davis (2006). In the present work, our focus is on capturing the range of possible syntactic subcategorization patterns and associating lexical items wih the correct ones in a broad-coverage lexicon. Each syntactic argument is linked to a semantic argument, but following general practice in MRS (see Copestake 2009) we do not distinguish thematic roles. Instead, semantic arguments are only differentiated by obliqueness, which in turn is closely connected to syntactic obliqueness. This aspect of **Jacy** could be used in combination with a lexical semantic resource specifying more detailed semantic representations to study, in a data-driven fashion, the predictability of syntactic patterns from semantic patterns.

Table 7 outlines the subcategorization types in **Jacy**, including one, two and three argument verbs. All subjects are optional in Japanese. Complements, on the other hand, can be either optional or obligatory. This is indicated in Table 7 after each COMPS element. In the implementation, subjects and other optional arguments are [OPT +] while obligatory (non-optional) complements are marked as [OPT −].[1] Japanese verbal nouns basically follow the same subcategorization principles. As discussed in § 3.2.6, verbal nouns combine with a light verb through a sub-syntactic construction. The verbal noun + light verb constituent inherits the subcategorization information from the verbal noun. Table 8 shows the subcategorization patterns of verbal nouns in **Jacy**. The following subsections describe and illustrate the major subcategorization types.

5.1.1 Intransitive Verbs

5.1.1.1 Simple Intransitive

Most intransitive verbs in **Jacy** are of the type *v_-_lt*, which specifies that they take a subject (always optional, for all verbs) and no complements. The subject is headed by a particle whose case is *ga*. An example of an intransitive verb is the verb 太る *futoru* "to become fat", as in

---

[1] In fact, it would be sufficient to put [OPT −] on the non-optional arguments and leave the optional ones underspecified. We use [OPT +] for clarity.

Verbal type	Subcategorization pattern SBJ	COMPS	Example
v_-_lt	P-ga		太る
v_pp_wo_lt	P-ga	P-wo (opt)	見守る
v_pp_ni_lt	P-ga	P-ni (opt)	乗る
v_adv*_lt	P-ga	ADV (obl)	なる
v_pp*_ni+to_lt	P-ga	P-ni-or-to (obl)	なる
v_to*cp_lt	P-ga	P-to (obl)	言う
v_pp-pp_wo-ni_lt	P-ga	P-wo (opt), P-ni (opt)	置く
v_to_lt	P-ga	P-to (opt)	付き合う
v_pp_ni+to_lt[†]	P-ga	P-ni-or-to (opt)	入れ替わる
v_np*_lt	P-ga	N (obl)	書き送る
v_np*_coparg-subj_lt	P-ga-or-coparg[‡]	N (obl)	です
cop-light-lt		Adj (obl)	です

* is used to mark obligatory arguments.
[†] v_pp_ni+to_lt also differs from v_pp*_ni+to_lt semantically: v_pp*_ni+to_lt inserts a cop-id_rel.
[‡] cop-arg is the case given to colons, when these are used in the same way as case particles and to the topic particle *wa* in copula constructions.

TABLE 7 Verb Subcategorization Types

Verbal noun type	Subcategorization pattern SBJ	COMPS	Example
vn-intrans-lt	P-ga		発生
vn-trans1-lt	P-ga	P-wo (opt)	アレンジ
vn-trans2-lt	P-ga	P-ni	電話
vn-trans3-lt	P-ga	P-to (opt)	結婚
vn-trans8-lt	P-ga	N (obl)	お願い
vn-ditrans-lt	P-ga	P-wo (opt), P-ni (opt)	掲載
vn-ditrans-toni-lt	P-ga	P-wo (opt), P-ni-or-to (opt)	略

TABLE 8 Subcategorization Patterns of Verbal Nouns

(64a). In addition to specifying the part of speech and case of the subject, the type v_-_lt specifies that the subject's INDEX value is linked to the value of ARG1 in the elementary predication contributed by the verb to the semantics (shown as x_4 in (64b)).

(64) a. 猫　が　太った
　　　 neko ga futot-ta
　　　 cat NOM become.fat-PST

　　　 "The cat became fat."

b. $\langle h_1, \left\{ \begin{array}{l} h_3\text{:\_neko\_n}(x_4 \{\text{PERS } 3\}), \\ h_5\text{:udef}(x_4, h_7, h_6), \\ h_8\text{:\_futoru\_v}(e_2 \{\text{TENSE } past\}, x_4) \end{array} \right\} \rangle$,
$\{h_7 =_q h_3\}$

5.1.2 Transitive Verbs
5.1.2.1 Simple Transitive

Prototypical transitive verbs take two PP arguments, both of which are optional. There is a range of case-marking possibilities, which **Jacy** accommodates by providing three lexical types for this general kind of transitive verb. v_pp_wo_lt is the most typical case (4361 verbs in **Jacy**), providing for a *ga*-marked subject and an *wo*-marked object. An example is the verb 食べる *taberu* "eat", as in (65). v_pp_ni_lt handles the pattern where the object is marked instead by *ni*, as shown for 乗る *noru* "ride" in (66). We have 315 verbs of this type. Finally, there are two-argument verbs which allow either *ni* or *to* to mark the complement, 25 verbs in **Jacy**. These are modeled by v_pp_ni+to_lt, which underspecifies the case requirement on the complement appropriately. An example is 合う *au* "meet", illustrated in (67).

(65) 花子　　が　ご飯　　を　食べた
　　 Hanako ga gohan wo tabe-ta
　　 Hanako NOM rice ACC eat-PST

　　 "Hanako ate rice."

(66) 花子　　が　（バス　に）　乗る
　　 Hanako ga (basu ni) noru
　　 Hanako NOM (bus DAT) ride

　　 "Hanako rides the bus."

(67) 私　　　　が　花子　　に/と　会いました
　　 watashi ga Hanako ni/to ai-mashi-ta
　　 1SG　　 NOM Hanako DAT/COM meet-AHON:+-PST

　　 "I met Hanako."

The semantics for these verb types is straightforward. They all introduce semantic relations which take two indices as arguments (in addition to the ARG0 event variable corresponding to the verb itself). The subject of the verb is linked to the first argument (ARG1) and the complement to the second (ARG2), as shown in (68), which provides the MRS for (65).

(68) $\left\langle h_1, \begin{cases} h_3\text{:named}(x_4, \textit{hanako}), \\ h_5\text{:def}(x_4, h_6, h_7), \\ h_8\text{:\_gohan\_n}(x_9), \\ h_{10}\text{:udef}(x_9, h_{12}, h_{11}), \\ h_{13}\text{:\_taberu\_v\_1}\left(e_2\left\{\text{TENSE } \textit{past}\right\}, x_4, x_9\right) \end{cases} \right\rangle$,
$\{h_{12} =_q h_8, h_6 =_q h_3\}$

5.1.2.2 Clausal Complement Transitives

The next class of two-argument verbs, *v_cp*_to_lt*, takes nominal subjects and clausal complements. The subjects are marked with *ga* and the sentential complements, which are obligatory, are marked with *to*. To this class belong verbs like 存じる *zonjiru* "know", 語る *kataru* "relate" and 言う *iu* "say". An example is given in (69).

(69) a. 花子 が 良い と 言いました
Hanako ga yoi to ii-mashi-ta
Hanako NOM good QUOT say-AHON:+-PST

"Hanako said good."

b. $\left\langle h_1, \begin{cases} h_3\text{:def\_q}(x_4, h_5, h_6), \\ h_7\text{:named}(x_4, \textit{hanako}), \\ h_8\text{:\_ii\_a\_3}(e_{10}), \\ h_{11}\text{:\_iu\_v\_1}(e_2, x_4, h_{12}) \end{cases} \right\rangle$,
$\{h_5 =_q h_7, h_{12} =_q h_8\}$

As with the simple transitive verbs above, the elementary predication contributed by *iu* relates two arguments (in addition to the event variable). The referential index for the subject (x_4) fills the ARG1 role, while the ARG2 role is linked to the handle of the subordinate clause (h_8), via a qeq.

Note that most verbs of this type also occur as a transitive verb with an optional accusative NP (*v_pp_wo_lt*). Here ARG1 of the verbal semantics is linked to the subject and ARG2 is linked to the object.

(70) 花子 が (それ を) 言いました
Hanako ga (sore wo) ii-mashi-ta
Hanako NOM (that ACC) say-AHON:+-PST

"Hanako said (that)."

5.1.2.3 Subject Raising Transitives

Finally, we have two lexical types (v_adv*_lt and v_pp*_ni+to_lt) that together describe the uses of なる *naru* "become" as a subject raising verb. This verb can take an adjective argument (inflected to an adverb) (v_adv*_lt, illustrated in (71)) or a PP argument marked by *ni* or *to* (v_pp*_ni+to_lt, illustrated in (72)). In both cases the complement is obligatory. We require two types to describe this pattern because of differences in semantic construction required by the two types of complements. In addition, although we can underspecify the case on the PP argument, we cannot underspecify between PP and adverbial complements while still partially constraining the case on the PP.

(71) 辺り   が   明るく   なった
      atari   ga   akaruku   nat-ta
      neighborhood NOM bright   become-PST

  "The neighborhood became bright."

(72) 花子   が   大人   に/と   なった
      Hanako ga   otona ni/to   nat-ta
      Hanako NOM adult COP   become-PST

  "Hanako became an adult."

The hallmark of raising verbs is that they take a syntactic argument which is a semantic argument of their complement's. For subject raising verbs, the shared argument is realized overtly as the subject of the raising verb. v_adv*_lt is a canonical subject raising verb. Its subject (辺り *atari* "neighborhood" in (71)) plays no role in its semantic predication (_naru_v_5 in (73)), but rather appears in the semantics as the ARG1 of _akarui_a_1 "bright". The superficially similar *naru* in (72) is an instance of the type vp_pp*_ni+to_lt. In this case, since the complement (大人 に/と *otona ni/to* "adult COP") has no open semantic position, the verb itself contributes an extra predication that connects the two nouns. Thus in (74), cop_id relates x_4 (the ARG0 of the named relation, i.e., *Hanako*) and x_9 (the ARG0 of _otona_n_1, "adult").[2] The cop_id relation, in turn, is the argument of _naru_v_4 "become".[3]

---

[2] cop_id is the same predicate contributed by the identity copula; see § 5.1.4.1.

[3] Note that this means that verbs of the type vp_pp*_ni+to_lt are not strictly speaking raising verbs. We discuss them here together with the type v_adv*_lt because of their superficial similarity.

(73) $\left\langle h_1, \left\{ \begin{array}{l} h_3\text{:udef\_q}(x_4\,\{\text{PERS }3\}, h_5, h_6), \\ h_7\text{:\_atari\_n\_1}(x_4), \\ h_8\text{:\_akarui\_a\_1}\left(\begin{array}{l} e_9\,\{\text{TENSE }untensed\}, \\ e_2\,\{\text{TENSE }past\} \end{array}\right), \\ h_8\text{:\_naru\_v\_5}(e_2, x_4) \end{array} \right\} \right\rangle$

$\{h_5 =_q h_7\}$

(74) $\left\langle h_1, \left\{ \begin{array}{l} h_3\text{:udef\_q}(x_4, h_5, h_6), \\ h_7\text{:named}(x_4, hanako), \\ h_8\text{:udef\_q}(x_9\,\{\text{PERS }3\}, h_{10}, h_{11}), \\ h_{12}\text{:\_otona\_n\_1}(x_9), \\ h_{13}\text{:\_naru\_v\_4}(e_2\,\{\text{TENSE }past\}, h_{14}), \\ h_{15}\text{:cop\_id}(e_{16}, x_4, x_9) \end{array} \right\} \right\rangle$

$\{h_5 =_q h_7, h_{10} =_q h_{12}, h_{14} =_q h_{15}\}$

This semantic distinction, alongside the obligatoriness of the complement also differentiates *v_pp*_ni+to_lt* from the other type that allows *ni* or *to* marking of the complement (*v_pp_ni+to_lt*). An alternative analysis would forgo the lexical decomposition and posit only *_naru_v_4* as a two-place relation relating the two referential indices of the subject and the complement. This would make these verbs similar to those of type *v_pp_ni+to_lt*. Even in this case we would not be able to assimilate the two types into one, however, because the complement is optional in one case and obligatory in the other.

5.1.3 Ditransitive Verbs

Our grammar includes three types of ditransitive verbs, *v_pp-pp_wo-ni_lt* and two subject-object-complement verb types (similar to the verb complement types shown above).

5.1.3.1 Simple Ditransitive Verbs

Simple ditransitives take two optional complements, one marked with *wo* and the other with *ni*, in addition to a *ga*-marked subject, also optional. Semantically, these are three-place predicates. Note how the _oku_v relation in the MRS shown in (75b) takes the indices from the *ga*- (x_4; 花子 *Hanako*), *wo*- (x_9; 本 *hon* "book") and *ni*-marked (x_{14}; 本棚 *hondana* "bookshelf") arguments.

(75) a. 花子　が　本　を　本棚　に　置いた
　　　　Hanako ga   hon wo hondana ni   oi-ta
　　　　Hanako NOM book ACC bookshelf DAT put-PST

　　　"Hanako put the book on the bookshelf."

b. $h_1, \left\langle \left\{ \begin{array}{l} h_3\text{:def\_q}(x_4, h_5, h_6), \\ h_7\text{:named}(x_4, hanako), \\ h_8\text{:udef\_q}(x_9 \{\text{PERS } 3\}, h_{10}, h_{11}), \\ h_{12}\text{:\_hon\_n}(x_9), \\ h_{13}\text{:udef\_q}(x_{14} \{\text{PERS } 3\}, h_{15}, h_{16}), \\ h_{17}\text{:\_hondana\_n\_1}(x_{14}), \\ h_{18}\text{:\_oku\_v}(e_2 \{\text{TENSE } past\}, x_4, x_9, x_{14}) \end{array} \right\}, \right\rangle$
$\{h_5 =_q h_7, h_{10} =_q h_{12}, h_{15} =_q h_{17}\}$

5.1.3.2 Object Raising Verbs

Object raising verbs are similar to subject raising verbs (§ 5.1.2.3). In this case, it is the object of the raising verb that is semantically an argument of the embedded verb. The verb する *suru* can combine with *i*-adjectives or *na*-adjectives as in (76) and (77). Here the *wo*-marked element is the syntactic complement of *suru*, but functions semantically as the argument of the embedded predicate, as illustrated in the MRS for (77a), given in (77b).

(76) 花子　が　子供　を　賢く　　し　た
Hanako ga　kodomo wo　kashikoku　shi-ta
Hanako NOM child　ACC cleverly　do-PST

"Hanako made the child clever."

(77) a. 花子　が　子供　を　元気　に　し　た
Hanako ga　kodomo wo　genki　ni　shi-ta
Hanako NOM child　ACC healthy　COP do-PST

"Hanako made the child healthy."

b. $h_1, \left\langle \left\{ \begin{array}{l} h_3\text{:def\_q}(x_4, h_5, h_6), \\ h_7\text{:named}(x_4, hanako), \\ h_8\text{:udef\_q}(x_9 \{\text{PERS } 3\}, h_{10}, h_{11}), \\ h_{12}\text{:\_kodomo\_n}(x_9), \\ h_{13}\text{:\_genki\_a}(e_{14} \{\text{TENSE } tense\}, x_9), \\ h_{15}\text{:\_suru\_v\_soc}(e_2 \{\text{TENSE } past\}, x_4, h_{16}) \end{array} \right\}, \right\rangle$
$\{h_5 =_q h_7, h_{10} =_q h_{12}, h_{16} =_q h_{13}\}$

As with subject raising verbs, we also find a variant here which takes a PP complement and must contribute some extra semantics, as shown in (78b) which gives the MRS assigned by **Jacy** to the example in (78a). Note that the predicate introduced by *suru* (suru_v_soc) takes just two arguments (x_4, from its subject *Hanako*, the one doing the causing) and the embedded situation (h_{19}; the label of the cop_id relation). The surface complement of *suru* (子供 *kodomo* "child"; x_9) is semantically the first argument of cop_id. As with subject-raising *naru*, this *suru* contributes two relations (cop_id and _suru_v_soc).[4]

(78) a. 花子　が　子供　を　大人　に　した
　　　Hanako ga　kodomo wo　otona ni　shi-ta
　　　Hanako NOM child　　ACC adult COP do-PST

　　"Hanako made the child an adult."

b. $\left\langle h_1, \left\{ \begin{array}{l} h_3\text{:def\_q}(x_4, h_5, h_6), \\ h_7\text{:named}(x_4, hanako), \\ h_8\text{:udef\_q}(x_9 \{\text{PERS } 3\}, h_{10}, h_{11}), \\ h_{12}\text{:\_kodomo\_n}(x_9), \\ h_{13}\text{:udef\_q}(x_{14} \{\text{PERS } 3\}, h_{15}, h_{16}), \\ h_{17}\text{:\_otona\_n\_1}(x_{14}), \\ h_{18}\text{:\_suru\_v\_soc}\begin{pmatrix} e_2 \{\text{TENSE } past, \text{SF } prop\}, \\ x_4, h_{19} \end{pmatrix}, \\ h_{20}\text{:cop\_id}\begin{pmatrix} e_{21} \{\text{TENSE } tense, \text{SF } prop\}, \\ x_9, x_{14} \end{pmatrix} \end{array} \right\} \right\rangle$

$\{h_5 =_q h_7, h_{10} =_q h_{12}, h_{15} =_q h_{17}, h_{19} =_q h_{20}\}$

5.1.4 Copula Verbs

Having overviewed the subtypes of intransitive and transitive verbs, we now turn our attention to copula verbs. The class of copula verbs in **Jacy** includes です *desu*, だ *da*, and である *dearu*, negated forms such as ではない *dewanai*, and forms that are less obviously related, such as the question marking かしら *kashira*, pre-nominal な *na* Nightingale (1996), non-finite で *de* and conditional なら *nara*. Cutting across the morphosyntactic and semantic distinctions marked by these variations in form are variations in the syntax and semantics of the copula. In particular, we distinguish three general classes of use of the copula: (i) an identity copula, which takes a nominal complement as well as a nominal subject and introduces a semantic predication to relate the two, (ii) a semantically-empty copula, which attaches to saturated sentences headed by *i*-adjectives and other elements marked [COP-ARG +], and (iii) a semantically empty copula, which attaches to *na*-adjectives and raises the subject.[5]

---

[4]Again, this isn't a true raising predicate, since cop_id is contributed by *suru* itself, but we discuss it here because of the superficial similarity to the raising verbs in (76) and (77).

[5]The reason for this has to do with the analysis of pre-nominal adjective as relative clauses (see § 6.6.2 and § 6.6.3). We provide both gapped and non-gapped relative clauses, and analyze pre-nominal adjectives as actually heading relative clauses. For the gapped variant to be available, the relative clause (e.g., 元気 な *genki na* "healthy COP") needs to have a non-empty SUBJ value.

The types that model these subcategorization differences are explained (together with examples) in more detail below. We then take up the various syntactic and semantic contrasts that are morphologically marked on the copula.

5.1.4.1 Subcategorization Frames of the Copula

The type *v_np*_ga+coparg-subj_lt* models the type of copula verb which attaches to a nominal complement. This type selects for a *ga*-marked subject and an obligatory NP object (no case particle). This is illustrated in (79).

(79)   a.   花子   が   学者   です
             Hanako ga   gakusha desu
             Hanako NOM scholar COP.AHON:+

             "Hanako is a scholar."

   b. $\left\langle h_1, \left\{ \begin{array}{l} h_3\text{:def\_q}(x_4, h_5, h_6), \\ h_7\text{:named}(x_4, \textit{hanko}), \\ h_8\text{:udef\_q}(x_9 \{\text{PERS } 3\}, h_{10}, h_{11}), \\ h_{12}\text{:\_gakusha\_n\_1}(x_9), \\ h_{13}\text{:cop\_id}(e_2 \{\text{TENSE } \textit{pres}\}, x_4, x_9) \end{array} \right\} \right\rangle$,
       $\{h_5 =_q h_7, h_{10} =_q h_{12}\}$

The predicate cop_id is introduced by the copula. In its linking of its two arguments to this predication, this use of the copula is like an ordinary transitive verb. However, the copula is distinguished in the lack of case marking on the NP complement as well as in the morphological variations it exhibits, discussed below, and thus we do not assimilate this type to any of the other transitive verb lexical types.

The semantically empty copula that attaches to saturated sentences marked as [COP-ARG +] is modeled by *cop-light-lt*. This type takes only a single complement and no subject. Elements that are [COP-ARG +] include *i*-adjectives such as おもしろい *omoshiroi* "interesting", wh-adverbs such as なぜ *naze* "why", post-positions such as から *kara* "from", and verbal endings such as the desiderative (showing desire) -たい *-tai* "want to". An example is given in (80). Note that the MRS shows no predication corresponding to the copula.

(80)   a.   花子   が   賢い   です
             hanako ga   kashikoi desu
             Hanako NOM clever   COP.AHON:+

             "Hanako is clever."

b. $\left\langle h_1, \left\{ \begin{array}{l} h_3\text{:def\_q}(x_4, h_5, h_6), \\ h_7\text{:named}(x_4, \textit{hanako}), \\ h_8\text{:\_kashikoi\_a\_1}\left(e_2\left\{\text{TENSE } \textit{pres}\right\}, x_4\right) \end{array} \right\}, \right\rangle$
$\{h_5 =_q h_7\}$

Finally, the type *reg-cop-stem-lt* models copulas that attach to *na*-adjectives, illustrated in (81). As with *cop-light-lt*, this type does not contribute any semantic predications. Unlike those of *cop-light-lt* (which combine with saturated sentences), copula verbs of type *reg-cop-stem-lt* combine with projections of *na*-adjectives that are still subject-seeking.⁶ Accordingly, the type *reg-cop-stem-lt* identifies its own SUBJ value with that of its complement. In other words, we analyze copula verbs of this type as raising verbs.⁷

(81) a. 花子　が　元気　です
Hanako ga　genki　desu
Hanako NOM healthy COP.AHON:+

"Hanako is healthy."

b. $\left\langle h_1, \left\{ \begin{array}{l} h_3\text{:named}(x_4, \textit{hanako}), \\ h_5\text{:def}(x_4, h_6, h_7), \\ h_8\text{:\_genki\_a}\left(e_2\left\{\text{TENSE } \textit{pres}, \text{SF } \textit{prop}\right\}, x_4\right) \end{array} \right\}, \right\rangle$
$\{h_6 =_q h_3\}$

As *na*-adjectives, unlike *i*-adjectives, cannot inflect on their own, the copula will carry information such as tense, negation, or honorification.

5.1.4.2 Negative Copulas

All three of the primary copula types described above have negated counterparts. Rather than modeling this via a lexical rule which attaches a negative morpheme, we model these as lexically negated copulas, which each introduces a neg_v predication. This is the same predication that is introduced by the negative verbal ending ない *nai*. Thus the negated identity copula, *cop-id-neg-stem-lt*, introduces two elementary predications (neg_v and cop_id), while the other negated copulas, *cop-neg-lt* and *cop-neg-stem-lt*, each only introduce one. An example of the negated identity copula is shown in (82).

(82) a. 花子　が　花　じゃ　ない
Hanako ga　hana ja-nai
Hanako NOM flower COP-NEG

"Hanako isn't a flower."

---

⁶See note 5 on page 85.
⁷On raising verbs, see § 5.1.2.3 and Chapter 12 of Sag et al. 2003.

b. $\langle h_1, \left\{ \begin{array}{l} h_3\text{:def\_q}(x_4, h_5, h_6), \\ h_7\text{:named}(x_4, \textit{hanako}), \\ h_8\text{:udef\_q}(x_9 \{\text{PERS } 3\}, h_{10}, h_{11}), \\ h_{12}\text{:\_hana\_n}(x_9), \\ h_{13}\text{:neg\_v}(e_2 \{\text{TENSE } \textit{pres}, \text{SF } \textit{prop}\}, h_{14}) \\ h_{15}\text{:cop\_id}(e_{16} \{\text{SF } \textit{prop}\}, x_4, x_9) \end{array} \right\} \rangle$

$\{h_5 =_q h_7, h_{10} =_q h_{12}, h_{14} =_q h_{15}\}$

5.1.4.3 Question Marking Copulas

While forms of the copula can cooccur with the ordinary question particle か *ka*, there are also specialized forms of the copula which directly encode question marking. These include かい *kai*, かなあ *kanaa*, and かしら *kashira*, as well as だい *dai*, which has the special property that it requires its complement to contain an interrogative (See § 8.2). All of the different subcategorization types for the copula have subtypes which model the question forms and add the constraint that the sentential force of the utterance is *ques*. For the *dai* form we add the constraint that the non-local feature QUE value must be non-empty. Since interrogatives (and nothing else) introduce non-empty QUE values, this ensures that *dai* always has an interrogative in its complement.

5.1.4.4 Copulas as Modifiers

Another dimension of variation among forms of the copula is whether or not they can head clauses which modify nouns. Copula forms like だ *da*, です *desu*, なんです *nandesu* and なのです *nanodesu* cannot, as shown in (83). They are blocked from modifying with the constraint [SYNSEM.LOCAL.CAT.HEAD.MOD *null*].

(83) a. *元気 です 人
 *genki desu hito
 healthy COP.AHON:+ person

 Intended: "a healthy person"

 b. 元気 な 人
 genki na hito
 healthy COP person

 "a healthy person"

Other forms of the copula, such as である *dearu*, でござる *degozaru*, and the な *na* of *na*-adjectives (cf. Nightingale 1996), can be used as modifiers. Among these, な *na* is distinguished in that it can only serve as a modifier, and cannot head stand-alone clauses (modeled by [SYNSEM.LOCAL.CAT.HEAD.MAIN-PRD −]).

5.1.4.5 Honorific or Stylistically Marked Copulas

Many forms of the copula bear marking for pragmatic information. This includes addressee honorification (see Chapter 9) as well as forms that are considered stylistically masculine or feminine. As before, these distinctions cross-cut the subcategorization distinctions among copula types. Subtypes constrain the feature AHON to indicate honorification in polite forms (e.g., です *desu*, でしょう *deshou*) or negative honorification in forms such as だい *dai* or だろう *darou*. Stylistically marked forms bear constraints on the gender of the SPEAKER within the pragmatic C(ONTEXTUAL)-INDICES feature. For example, かしら *kashira* is marked as feminine.[8]

5.1.5 Adjective Subcategorization Types

As with verbs, adjectives vary in their subcategorization. Among the adjective lexical types in **Jacy**, we find the subcategorization frames shown in Table 9. Frequency is given for the lexicon and the corpus (Tanaka Corpus, § 11.2.2.2), for example, *eval-rashii* only has one entry in the lexicon, but is used 13 times in the corpus.

As with verbs, the subjects are always optional but the complements can vary in their optionality, as shown in the table. The vast majority of adjectives (of both morphological types) is intransitive. There are a few special cases listed in Table 9. Prominent among these are the desiderative adjective 欲しい *hoshii* and the evidential (or 'semblative' (Martin, 1988, 986)) adjective らしい *rashii*. These and the other adjectives which subcategorize for non-PP complements in fact function much like derivational suffixes. Note that some do not even select for a subject.[9]

This concludes our tour of the lexical types for verbs and adjectives. In the next section, we consider the lexical rules that combine with lexical items of these types.

5.2 Inflectional and Derivational Rules

Among Japanese lexical items, the major inflecting classes are verbs and adjectives. These lexical items combine with suffixes ("endings") expressing various grammatical and pragmatic information (tense, nega-

---

[8]Though **Jacy** models this with constraints on a feature named GEN, this does not literally mean that the sentence would be ungrammatical if uttered by a man. Rather, we understand gender-marked forms as resources for the construction of social identities through language (Eckert and McConnell-Ginet, 1992).

[9]The *ga-wo_transitive* pattern is quite rare for adjectives, and indeed some native speakers reject examples with the listed adjectives and this case pattern. However, Martin (1988, 198–199) notes that there are attested examples.

Subcat type	Subcategorization SBJ	COMPS	Examples & Freq *i*-adjective		*na*-adjective	
ga+	P-ga		明るい 807	1,417	丁寧 1,027	2,272
ga-ga	P-ga	P-ga	欲しい 7	14	好き 9	121
ga-wo	P-ga	P-wo	欲しい 2	7	好き 5	11
ni-ga	P-ni	P-ga	欲しい 2	2	必要 1	9
eval-rashii		V:past-or-pres	らしい 1	13		
eval-te+ii		V:te	欲しい 14	59		

TABLE 9 Adjective Subcategorization Types

tion, honorifics, etc.), as illustrated in (84).[10]

(84) a. 食べる
    taberu.NONPST.AHON:−
    eat
    "eat"

b. 食べた
    tabe-ta
    eat-PST.AHON:−
    "ate"

c. 食べました
    tabe-mashi-ta
    eat-AHON:+-PST
    "ate"

d. 食べられた
    tabe-rare-ta
    eat-PASS-PST.AHON:−
    "was eaten"

In **Jacy**, the combination of stems with endings is handled with subsyntactic phrase structure rules.[11] However, there is still a need for lexical (i.e., morphological) rules, as the stems can change form depending on the endings. Furthermore, there are subclasses of verbs

---

[10] Although we treat the non-past form as a single word, some scholars and NLP applications separate the plain non-past form into a stem and an ending: 食べる *taberu*. As noted in the front matter (p. xvi), in most of the text, we generally do not gloss NONPST and AHON:− forms as such. Here we make these glosses explicit to clarify the contrasts illustrated in (84).

[11] We adopted the segmentation guidelines of the Information-Technology Promotion Agency (IPA, 1987) as implemented in ChaSen (Matsumoto et al., 2000), which splits off all endings except simple non-past into separate tokens.

which express different morphological generalizations in the formation of the various stems. Thus, for each fully inflected word, there are zero or more suffixes, a stem type, and a particular inflected form of the stem. The grammar must ensure that the suffixes combine with the correct stem forms and that the stem inflectional rules only apply to the correct stem classes.

For both verbs and adjectives, there are two major groups: one consisting mainly of native Japanese words and one consisting mainly of borrowed words (mainly from Chinese). The first group (verbs and *i*-adjectives) inflects, for the second (verbal nouns and *na*-adjectives) the inflection is carried by a light verb. The native Japanese verbs and adjectives form a large but relatively closed class, it is rare for new members to be added. In contrast, almost any word that is semantically appropriate can be used as a verbal noun or *na*-adjective (Hasegawa, 2014, pp 64–66). The subcategorization patterns are basically the same for the two groups, as discussed above, but their morphology differs.

5.2.1 Stem Classes

The major stem forms across the primary stem classes are summarized in Table 10. The root is the form as it is stored in the lexicon. The various other forms (labeled in the left-most column) are those that are called for by the different endings, exemplified in the right-most column. The five middle columns represent the stem classes: While all *i*-adjectives form a single class (and generally take fewer endings), regular verbs fall into one of two regular classes which we call **c-stem**[12] and **v-stem**[13]. All verbs end in /u/. **v-stem** verbs must end in /iru/ or /eru/, but some verbs that end in *iru/eru* are **c-stem**. There are also a small number of irregular verbs, with the most common being 来る *kuru* "come" and する *suru* "do". Each cell in the body of Table 10 shows the form of an example stem for the relevant class and inflected form. The character Q represents the first half of a geminate consonant, which takes its phonetic properties from the initial consonant in the ending.

To ensure that the correct inflection rules apply to the correct stems, each verb lexical entry has a value for the feature STEMTYPE. The hierarchy of values for those features is shown in Figure 37. Japanese has very few irregular verbs. There are a few consonant verbs that differ only in one inflection (before *-te/-ta*), which we call **c2-stem** and then *kuru* and *suru* which have different endings and so can be combined into a single type. Finally, there are the non–main-verb inflections for copula verbs and adjectives.

---

[12] Also called consonant-stem, type 1 or 五段 *godan* verbs.
[13] Also called vowel-stem, type 2 or 一段 *ichidan* verbs.

Form	v-stem	c-stem	suru	kuru	adj-stem	example ending
root	食べる	打つ	する	来る	古い	
gloss	"eat"	"hit"	"come"	"do"	"old"	
(u-morph)	*taberu*	*utsu*	*suru*	*kuru*	*furui*	—
a-morph	*tabe*	*uta*	*shi*	*ko*	*furuku*	-*nai*
i-morph	*tabe*	*uchi*	*shi*	*ki*	—	-*masu*
e-morph	*tabe*	*ute*	*se*	*ku*	*furuke*	-*reba/ba*
o-morph	*tabe*	*uto*	*shiyo*	*kiyo*	—	-*you/-u*
t-morph	*tabe*	*uQ*	*shi*	*ki*	*furukaQ*	-*ta*

TABLE 10 Major Japanese Inflectional Forms

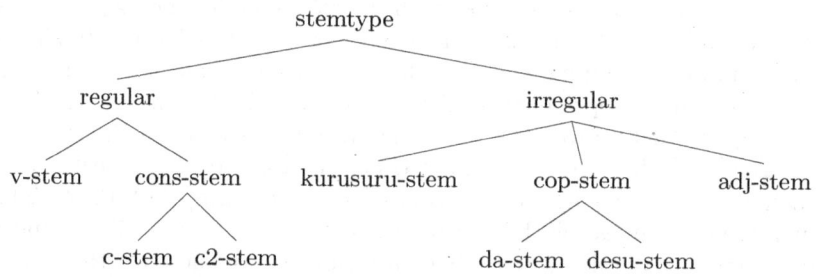

FIGURE 37 Type Hierarchy of Stemtypes

Stem	Inflection for *tmorph*: with -*ta*/*te*	Example	
v-stem	delete る	食べる → 食べ	*taberu* → *tabe*
c-stem	る→っ, う→っ, つ→っ	切る→切っ	*kiru* → *kiQ*
	く→い, ぐ→い, す→し,	聞く→聞い	*kiku* → *kii*
	む→ん, ぶ→ん,		
	ぬ→ん	呼ぶ→呼ん	*yobu* → *yon*
c2-stem	く→っ, る→っ、		
	う→う	行く→行っ	*iku* → *iQ*
	来る→来、くる→き、		
kurusuru-stem	する→し	来る→来	*kuru* → *ki*
cop-stem	だ→だっ、す→し	です→でし	*desu* → *deshi*
adj-stem	い→かっ	高い→高かっ	*takai* → *takakaQ*

TABLE 11 Inflection Types and Combination with Past Tense

Table 11 illustrates the differences in inflection by summarizing the morphological changes associated with creating the stem which comes with -*ta* or -*te* for each stem type (***tmorph***). Note that this table illustrates the use of one intermediate type: ***cop-stem***, the mother of ***desu-stem*** and ***da-stem*** in the type hierarchy of stemtype. The distinction between these two is not needed for past tense marking, but for other inflections.

5.2.2 Ending Types

In order to ensure that the suffixes combine with only the correct inflected stem forms, we use the features LMORPH-BIND-TYPE and RMORPH-BIND-TYPE. When an ending attaches to a stem, its LMORPH-BIND-TYPE must match the stem's RMORPH-BIND-TYPE. The combination will still have values for both features: LMORPH-BIND-TYPE is set to ***nomorphbind*** to show that the combination cannot itself be an ending, but RMORPH-BIND-TYPE will come from the ending, and reflect the possibilities for further suffixation. Table 12 lists the endings associated with various values of RMORPH-BIND-TYPE. Note that some of these values are supertypes in the ***morphbindtype*** hierarchy, meaning that they produce forms compatible with the union of the endings compatible with their subtypes.

5.2.3 Inflectional Rules

The lexical rules which create the inflected stem forms associate appropriate values for STEM-TYPE with their input and RMORPH-BIND-TYPE with their output. These are illustrated in Table 13, where the + symbol in the examples delimits the stem from the ending requiring that stem

morphbindtype	Endings	Example
vstem-morph	ます、ました、まして、ません、ませんでした、はじめる、ましたら、ましたらば、ながら、ましょう、よう、たい、たがる、たく、られる、なさい、た、たり、て、たら、たらば、てる、ちゃう、ありませんでした、ない、ありません、なさ、ぬ、ないで、ずに、なる、ざるをえません、なさ、う、させる、さす、られる	食べます *tabemasu*
i-morph	ます、ました、まして、ません、ませんでした、はじめる、ましたら、ましたらば、ながら、ましょう、よう、たい、たがる、たく、られる、なさい	読みます *yomimasu*
t-morph	た、たり、て、たら、たらば、てる、ちゃう	聞いた *kiita*
o-morph	う	読もう *yomou*
a-or-aa-morph	ず、ありませんでした、ない、ありません、なさ、ぬ、ないで、ずに、なる、ざるをえません	読まない *yomanai*
a-morph	ない、なさ、ぬ、ないで、ずに、なる、ざるをえません	来ない *konai*
aa-morph	ず	来ず *kozu*
pass-c-stem-moprh	せる、れる	読ませる *yomaseru*
cond-morph	ば、る	読めば *yomeba*
cond-exceptional-morph	ば、る	食べれば *tabereba*
nd-morph	だ、だり、で、だら、だらば、じゃう	読んだ *yonda*
mai-morph	まい、だけ	来まい *komai*

TABLE 12 *morphbindtype*s and Associated Endings

$$\begin{bmatrix} \text{RMORPH-BIND-TYPE} & \textit{i-morph} \\ \text{CAT.HEAD.MODUS} & \textit{indicative} \end{bmatrix} \rightarrow \begin{bmatrix} \text{STEMTYPE} & \textit{c-stem} \end{bmatrix}$$

FIGURE 38 Constraints on *i-lexeme-c-stem-infl-rule*

form. Note that multiple rules can map to the same output value for RMORPH-BIND-TYPE. These rules apply to words with different values of STEM-TYPE and apply different morphophonological changes to the stem. In one case (*pass-Iteme-stem*), a rule references an underspecified value of STEM-TYPE (*const-stem*) on the input, as it can apply to both subtypes. *cond-spoken-lexeme* is a rule that allows the so-called ranuki "ra-less" form, which is used in spoken language.

Figure 38 shows the morphosyntactic constraints on the rule *i-lexeme-c-stem-infl-rule*. Through the ARGS feature, it constrains the STEMTYPE of the lexical entries it can apply to. In addition to specifying a value of RMORPH-BIND-TYPE, the lexical rule also constrains the MODUS value to be *indicative*, as this constraint is common to all of the forms created of stems produced by this rule. The endings themselves add further constraints.

5.2.4 Sample Derivation

Figure 39 shows how the information on a verbal stem changes when going through an inflectional rule and then combining with an ending. Stem, ending and the stem-ending complex are lexical, i.e., [LEX +]. The lexical entry and the derived stem are both [J-NEEDS-AFFIX +], indicating that they must combine with an ending. The lexical item is marked as [STEMTYPE *v-stem*], restricting which inflectional rules can apply to it. The output (mother) of the inflectional rule has no value for this feature as STEMTYPE is not appropriate for lexical rules. The RMORPH-BIND-TYPE of the output of the lexical rule (食べ *tabe*) is *i-morph*.

The *vstem-vend* rule, a subtype of *head-specifier-rule-type* (see § 3.2.5), combines the inflected stem 食べ *tabe* with the ending ました *mashita* and matches the stem's RMORPH-BIND-TYPE value with the LMORPH-BIND-TYPE value of the ending. Since *vstem-morph* is a supertype of *i-morph*, the values unify and the combination is licensed. The ending is [BAR −], indicating that it is not a complete word, but the combination is [BAR +] and thus can serve as the daughter of non-lexical (i.e., syntactic) phrase structure rules.

The VAL (valence) information comes from the stem, while the HEAD information comes from the ending, which in this case contributes tense and formality information. The ending also constrains the TENSE and

Inflectional rule	Change of morphological type	Example
i-lexeme-c-stem	c-stem → i-morph	読み+ます *yomi+masu*
i-lexeme-c2-stem	c2-stem → i-morph	行き+ません *iki+masen*
i-lexeme-v-stem	v-stem → vstem-morph	食べ+ます *tabe+masu*
a-lexeme-negative-cons-stem	cons-stem → a-or-aa-morph	読ま+ない *yoma+nai*
pass-lexeme-stem	cons-stem → pass-c-stem-morph	読ま+せる *yoma+seru*
t-lexeme-c-stem	c-stem → t-morph	聞い+た *kii+ta*
tt-lexeme-c2-stem	c2-stem → t-morph	行っ+た *it+ta*
cond-lexeme	regular-stem → cond-morph	読め+ば *yome+ba*
cond-spoken-lexeme	v-stem → cond-exceptional-morph	食べ+れば *tabe+reba*
o-lexeme-c-stem	cons-stem → o-morph	読も+う *yomo+u*
o-lexeme-v-stem	v-stem → o-morph	食べよ+う *tabeyo+u*
nd-lexeme	c-stem → nd-morph	読ん+だ *yon+da*
tt-cop-lexeme	cop-stem → t-morph	だっ+た *dat+ta*
o-cop-lexeme	cop-stem → o-morph	でしょ+う *desho+u*
ki-lexeme	kurusuru-stem → i-morph	来+ません *ki+masen*
ka-lexeme	kurusuru-stem → a-morph	来+ない *ko+nai*
kaa-lexeme	kurusuru-stem → aa-morph	来+ず *koz+u*
kit-lexeme-c-stem	kurusuru-stem → t-morph	来+た *ki+ta*
ke-lexeme	kurusuru-stem → cond-morph	来れ+ば *kure+ba*
ko-lexeme	kurusuru-stem → o-morph	来+う *ko+u*
sa-lexeme	kurusuru-stem → pass-c-stem-morph	来さ+せる *kosa+seru*
mai-lexeme	kurusuru-stem → mai-morph	来+まい *ko+mai*
adj-te-t-lexeme-c-stem	adj-stem → t-morph	高なく+て *takanaku+te*
adj-past-t-lexeme-c-stem	adj-stem → t-morph	高なかっ+た *takanakat+ta*
adj-kere-lexeme	adj-stem → cond-morph	高なけれ+ば *takanakere+ba*

TABLE 13 Examples of Verb Inflectional Rules

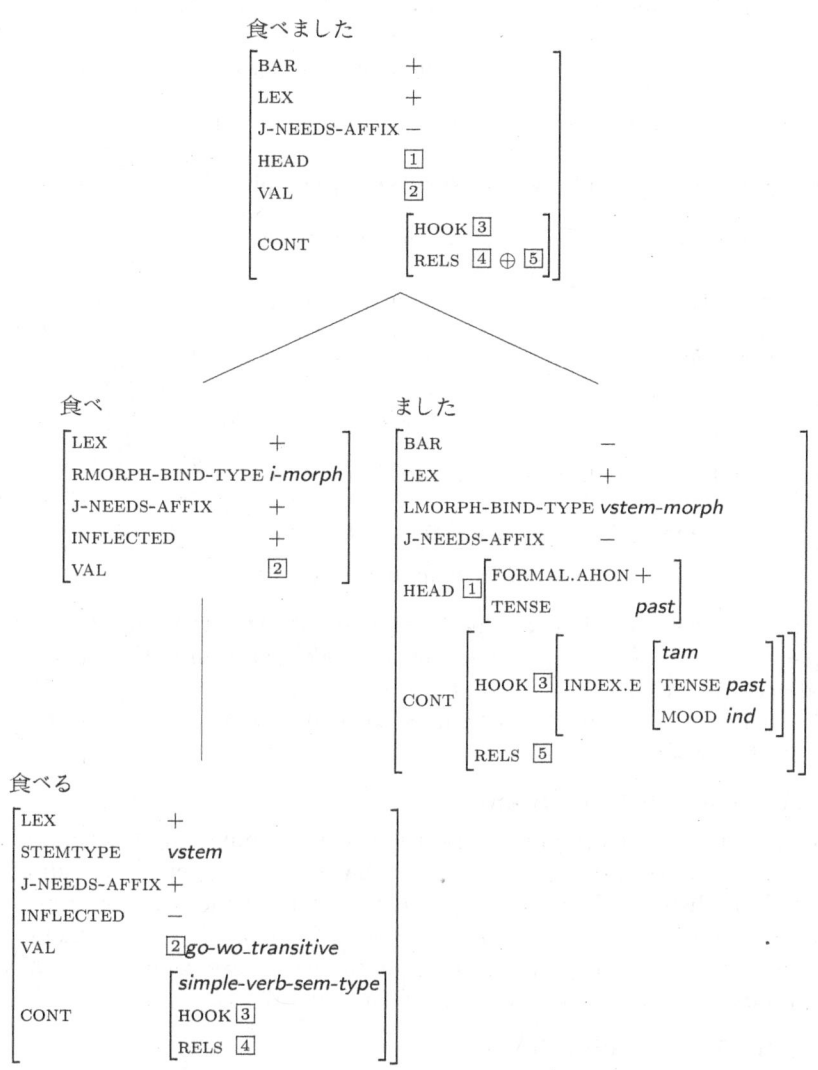

FIGURE 39 An Example of Verbal Inflection and Stem-End Combination

Inflection rule	Change of morphological type	Example
ru-lexeme-infl-rule	no change to the morphology	食べる *taberu*
eru-lexeme-infl-rule	regular-stem → u-morph	学べる *manaberu*
infinitive-lexeme-1-infl-rule	regular-stem → inf-morph	食べ *tabe*
imperative-c2-stem-infl-rule	c2-stem → imp-morph	下さい *kudasai*
desu-lexeme-infl-rule	cop-stem → u-morph	です *desu*
de-lexeme-infl-rule	desu-stem → u-morph	で *de*
ra-lexeme-infl-rule	da-stem → u-morph	なら *nara*
kuru-lexeme-infl-rule	kurusuru-stem → u-morph	来る *kuru*
infinitive-lexeme-2-infl-rule	kurusuru-stem → inf-morph	来 *ki*
adj-i-lexeme-infl-rule	adj-stem → u-morph	ではない *dewanai*

TABLE 14 Examples of Lexical Rules

MOOD values of the index, which is shared with the stem (and the complete word). The semantic relations are collected from both daughters, in accordance with our approach to semantic composition (see § 3.4). In this case, the ending contributes no relations, so mother's all come from the stem.

5.2.5 Stand-Alone Stems

In addition, there are inflectional rules which produce stem forms that can serve as stand-alone words, i.e., that do not require any endings. These are listed in Table 14. These rules contribute more morphosyntactic information as there are no separate endings involved. For example, Figure 40 shows some of the constraints on *eru-lexeme-infl-rule*, which produces the so-called "potential" form of verbs.

5.2.6 Derivational Rules

Jacy also has derivational rules which inflect stems while changing their syntactic category. These are in fact quite similar to inflectional rules in their operation, differing only in the feature values that are changed. There are two types of derivational rules that apply to verbs, with five subtypes between them, listed in Table 15: The various subtypes

$$\begin{bmatrix} \text{RMORPH-BIND-TYPE} & u\text{-}morph \\ \text{HEAD} & \begin{bmatrix} \text{MODUS} & potential \\ \text{MOD} & \langle [\text{HEAD} \quad noun\_head] \rangle \\ \text{FORMAL.AHON} & - \\ \text{FIN} & + \end{bmatrix} \\ \text{ARGS} & \langle [\text{STEMTYPE} \quad regular\text{-}stem] \rangle \end{bmatrix}$$

FIGURE 40 Constraints on *eru-lexeme-infl-rule*

Rule	Derivation	Example
v2vn-v-infl-rule	verb (v-stem) → vn	食べる → 食べ
v2vn-c-infl-rule	verb (c-stem) → vn	楽しむ → 楽しみ
v2vn-c2-stem-infl-rule	verb (c2-stem) → vn	なさる → なさい
v2n-vstem-kata-infl-rule	verb (v-stem) → n	食べる → 食べ方
v2n-cstem-kata-infl-rule	verb (cons-stem) → n	読む → 読み方

TABLE 15 Derivational Rules that Apply to Verbal Stems

of *v2vn-infl-rule* change the syntactic category to a verbal noun and produces a form akin to those produced by *i-lexeme-c-stem*, *i-lexeme-c2-stem*, and *i-lexeme-v-stem* lexical rules, while the subtypes of *v2n-kata-rule* changes the syntactic category to a noun by attaching 方 *kata*. The different subtypes of *v2vn-infl-rule* and *v2n-kata-rule* handle the different stem classes.

5.2.7 Adjective Inflectional Types

There are three major inflection types for adjectives in Japanese. The *i*-adjectives inflect, and their treatment has been covered along with the inflected forms of verbs above (see e.g., Tables 10, 11 and 13). The second kind is *na*-adjectives (and the small class of *no*-adjectives, not yet handled in **Jacy**, see Kuroda et al. 2011). The *na*-adjectives are also called adjectival nouns (e.g., by Tsujimura (1996, 136–138) and Martin (1988, 179–183)). However because they lack two of the defining properties of nouns (they cannot take case particles nor demonstratives), we consider them to be closer to adjectives. We follow Nightingale (1996) in treating な *na* as a copula (see § 5.1.4). Thus what might appear to be different inflected forms of *na*-adjectives actually involve different forms of the copula. The *no*-adjectives (what Martin (1988, 179–183) calls pre-copular nouns) do not inflect at all.

The final type of adjective is the non-inflecting adjective (*pred-adj-lex*, also known as rentaishi 連体詞). They attach to nouns directly as modifiers (rather than building relative clauses) and they cannot appear predicatively. There are only eight lexical entries of this type in **Jacy**: three spellings of 大きな *ookina* "big", two spellings each of 小さな *chiisana* "small" and 同じ *onaji* "same", and the entry for しかるべき *shikarubeki* "proper".

5.3 Auxiliary Constructions

Japanese has a rich set of auxiliaries which combine with verbs to express information about aspect or perspective. Here we call only the words that come after the *te-form* auxiliaries: formatives that attach to other verbal forms are called verbal endings (see § 5.2.2).

Many of the auxiliaries also carry information about honorification. Auxiliaries combine with main verbs via the *head-specifier-rule*, with the auxiliary as the head. In most cases, they combine with the saturated verbal projections, however, the perspective auxiliaries add an argument which must be able to interleave with the other verbal arguments. Similarly, certain aspect auxiliaries (like ある *aru* in (86) and the various alternatives with different politeness values such as ござる *gozaru*) suppress one valence element of the main verb and change the particle required for the other. These auxiliaries thus should combine with the lexical verb and raise its arguments.

We call the basic classes of auxiliaries aspect auxiliaries, content auxiliaries, and perspective auxiliaries. These are listed in Table 16.

5.3.1 Aspect Auxiliaries

Semantically, the aspect auxiliaries contribute only information about the feature ASPECT. This is illustrated in (85) and (86).[14]

(85) a. ケーキを 食べている
   keeki wo tabe-te iru
   cake ACC eat-INF PROG

"He is eating cake."

b. $\left\langle h_1, \left\{ \begin{array}{l} h_3\text{:udef\_q}(x_4 \{\text{PERS } 3\}, h_5, h_6), \\ h_7\text{:\_keeki\_n}(x_4), \\ h_8\text{:\_taberu\_v\_1}\left(e_2 \left\{ \begin{array}{l} \text{TENSE } pres, \\ \text{PROG } +, \\ \text{SF } prop \end{array} \right\}, i_9, x_4 \right) \end{array} \right\}, \right\rangle$

$\{h_5 =_q h_7\}$

---

[14] Actually, the progressive aspect can be further classified using the semantic context and is therefore a bit more complex than the English progressive. See Yoshimoto (1998) for a more detailed discussion and further classification of the progressive aspect of *iru*.

Verbs and Adjectives / 101

Auxiliary type	Example	Contracted
Aspect		
progressive	いる *iru*	てる *teru*
	おる *oru*	
	いらっしゃる *irassharu*	
prospective	おく *oku*	とく *toku*
inceptive	いく *iku*	
terminative	しまう *shimau*	ちゃう *chau*
perfective	ある *aru*	
	ござる *gozaru*	
perfect-progressive	くる *kuru*	
Content		
try	みる *miru*	
show I can	みせる *miseru*	
Perspective		
give	くれる *kureru*	
(ARG2 empathy)	くださる *kudasaru*	
give	あげる *ageru*	
(ARG1 empathy)	さしあげる *sashiageru*	
	やる *yaru*	
receive	もらう *morau*	
(ARG1 empathy)	いただく *itatadaku*	

TABLE 16 Auxiliary Types with Examples

Most aspect auxiliaries do not affect the valence of the main verb, although some auxiliaries make changes to the valence of the verbal complex, as can be seen in (86). These attach to a transitive verb, and constrain the verb's ARG1 (via its XARG) to be empty. The verb's ARG2 (accessed through its COMPS list) is marked with *ga*. These constraints are illustrated in Figure 41, which is instantiated by *aru* and its honorific equivalent *gozaru*.

(86) a. ケーキが　食べてある
    keeki   ga   tabe-te   aru
    cake   NOM   eat-INF   PFV

   "The cake has been eaten"

$$\begin{bmatrix} \textit{aspect-stem-lex} \\ \text{VAL} \begin{bmatrix} \text{SUBJ} & \left\langle \begin{bmatrix} \text{INDEX} & \boxed{1} \end{bmatrix} \right\rangle \\ \text{SPR} & \left\langle \begin{bmatrix} \text{VAL} \begin{bmatrix} \text{COMPS} & \left\langle \begin{bmatrix} \text{INDEX} & \boxed{1} \end{bmatrix}, \ldots \right\rangle \\ \text{XARG} & \textit{zpro_ref-ind} \end{bmatrix} \end{bmatrix} \right\rangle \end{bmatrix} \end{bmatrix}$$

FIGURE 41 Valence-related constraints on *aspect-stem-lex*

b. $$\left\langle h_1, \left\{ \begin{array}{l} h_3{:}\text{udef_q}(x_4 \{\text{PERS } \mathit{3}\}, h_5, h_6), \\ h_7{:}\text{_keeki_n}(x_4), \\ h_8{:}\text{_taberu_v_1}\left(e_2 \left\{ \begin{array}{l} \text{TENSE } \mathit{pres}, \\ \text{PERF } +, \\ \text{SF } \mathit{prop} \end{array} \right\}, i_9, x_4 \right) \end{array} \right\}, \{h_5 =_q h_7\} \right\rangle$$

5.3.2 Content Auxiliaries

The content auxiliaries add an elementary predication to the MRS, as illustrated in (87). There are only two みる *miru* "try" and みせる *miseru* "show I can".

(87) a. 花子 が ケーキ を 食べ て みる
Hanako ga keeki wo tabe-te miru
Hanako NOM cake ACC eat-INF try

"Hanako tries eating the cake."

b. $$\left\langle h_1, \left\{ \begin{array}{l} h_3{:}\text{def_q}(x_4, h_5, h_6), \\ h_7{:}\text{named}(x_4, \mathit{hanako}), \\ h_8{:}\text{udef_q}(x_9 \{\text{PERS } \mathit{3}\}, h_{10}, h_{11}), \\ h_{12}{:}\text{_keeki_n}(x_9), \\ h_{13}{:}\text{_taberu_v_1}\left(\begin{array}{l} e_{14} \{\text{TENSE } \mathit{tense}\}, \\ x_4, x_9 \end{array} \right), \\ h_{15}{:}\text{_miru_v_6}\left(e_2 \left\{ \begin{array}{l} \text{TENSE } \mathit{pres}, \\ \text{ASPECT } \mathit{modal} \end{array} \right\}, x_4, h_{16} \right) \end{array} \right\}, \{h_5 =_q h_7, h_{10} =_q h_{12}, h_{16} =_q h_{13}\} \right\rangle$$

(88) ケーキ を 全て 食べ て みせる
keeki wo subete tabe-te miseru
cake ACC all eat-INF show

"You will see, I will eat all the cake./I will show you I will eat all the cake."

Figure 42 shows the relevant constraints on the type *complex-aspect-stem-lex*, which is instantiated by the auxiliaries *miru* and *miseru*.

$$\begin{bmatrix} \text{VAL} & \begin{bmatrix} \text{SUBJ} & \langle \boxed{1}[\text{INDEX} \quad \boxed{2}] \rangle \\ \text{SPR} & \left\langle \begin{bmatrix} \text{SUBJ} & \langle \boxed{1} \rangle \\ \text{HOOK.LTOP} & \boxed{3} \end{bmatrix} \right\rangle \end{bmatrix} \\ \text{CONT} & \begin{bmatrix} \text{INDEX} & \boxed{4} \\ \text{RELS} & \left\langle ! \begin{bmatrix} \text{ARG0} & \boxed{4} \\ \text{ARG1} & \boxed{1} \\ \text{ARG2} & \boxed{5} \end{bmatrix} ! \right\rangle \\ \text{HCONS} & \langle ! \boxed{5} \; qeq \; \boxed{3} ! \rangle \end{bmatrix} \end{bmatrix}$$

FIGURE 42 Constraints on *complex-aspect-stem-lex*

The predication on the RELS list will have the PRED value _miru_v_6 or _miseru_v_2, accordingly.

5.3.3 Perspective Auxiliaries

The final class of auxiliaries also add a new predicate and also provide information about perspective or the point of view from which a situation is being described. These auxiliaries add a *ni*-marked argument to the argument structure of the whole predicate. There are two subclasses which differ in how they relate their arguments to the arguments of the verb. Verbs in one class (including くれる *kureru* "give"; see (89)) are treated as subject control verbs. The other class (including もらう *morau* "receive", see (90)) establishes a control relation between the *ni*-marked argument and the embedded subject. Figure 43 shows how these constraints are implemented for verbs in the *morau* class, which inherits from *aux-obj-id-stem-lex*.[15]

(89) a. 友達　　が　私　に　本　を　買って　くれた
 tomodachi ga watashi ni hon wo kat-te kure-ta
 friend　　NOM 1SG　DAT book ACC buy-INF give-PST

"My friend bought me a book." / "My friend bought a book for me."

---

[15] Some of these constraints are inherited from supertypes.

b. $\left\langle h_1, \left\{ \begin{array}{l} h_3:\text{udef\_q}(x_4 \{\text{PERS } 3\}, h_5, h_6), \\ h_7:\_\text{tomodachi\_n\_1}(x_4), \\ h_8:\text{pron}\left(x_9 \left\{ \begin{array}{l} \text{PERS } 1, \\ \text{NUM } sg, \\ \text{PRONTYPE } std\_pron \end{array} \right\} \right), \\ h_{10}:\text{def\_q}(x_9, h_{11}, h_{12}), \\ h_{13}:\text{udef\_q}(x_{14} \{\text{PERS } 3\}, h_{15}, h_{16}), \\ h_{17}:\_\text{hon\_n}(x_{14}), \\ h_{18}:\_\text{kau\_v\_1}(e_{19} \{\text{TENSE } tense\}, x_4, x_{14}), \\ h_{20}:\_\text{kureru\_v\_aux}(e_2 \{\text{TENSE } past\}, x_4, x_9, h_{21}) \end{array} \right\} \right\rangle$

$\{h_5 =_q h_7, h_{11} =_q h_8, h_{15} =_q h_{17}, h_{21} =_q h_{18}\}$

(90) a. 私　　が　　友達　　に　　本　　を　　買って
watashi ga　tomodachi ni　hon　wo　kat-te
1SG　　NOM　friend　　DAT　book ACC buy-INF

もらった
morat-ta
receive-PST

"My friend bought me a book." / "I got a book bought by my friend."

b. $\left\langle h_1, \left\{ \begin{array}{l} h_3:\text{pron}\left(x_4 \left\{ \begin{array}{l} \text{PERS } 1, \\ \text{NUM } sg, \\ \text{PRONTYPE } std\_pron \end{array} \right\} \right), \\ h_5:\text{def\_q}(x_4, h_6, h_7), \\ h_8:\text{udef\_q}(x_9 \{\text{PERS } 3\}, h_{10}, h_{11}), \\ h_{12}:\_\text{tomodachi\_n\_1}(x_9), \\ h_{13}:\text{udef\_q}(x_{14} \{\text{PERS } 3\}, h_{15}, h_{16}), \\ h_{17}:\_\text{hon\_n}(x_{14}), \\ h_{18}:\_\text{kau\_v\_1}(e_{19} \{\text{TENSE } tense\}, x_9, x_{14}), \\ h_{20}:\_\text{morau\_v\_2}(e_2 \{\text{TENSE } past\}, x_4, x_9, h_{21}) \end{array} \right\} \right\rangle$

$\{h_6 =_q h_3, h_{10} =_q h_{12}, h_{15} =_q h_{17}, h_{21} =_q h_{18}\}$

5.3.4 Auxiliaries and Honorification

There are different types of honorification information that can be added by aspect auxiliaries. For example, おる *oru* and おく *oku* add subject honorification with negative polarity, while いらっしゃる *irassharu* adds subject honorification with positive polarity. This information is added to the CONTEXT part of the sign. Perspective auxiliaries can also add honorification information. くださる *kudasaru* "give (ARG2 empathy)" adds subject honorification with positive polarity, while さしあげる *sashiageru* "give (ARG1 empathy)"

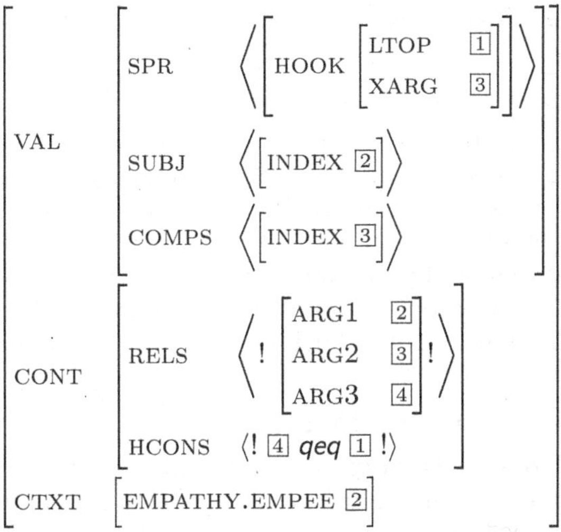

$$\begin{bmatrix} \text{VAL} & \begin{bmatrix} \text{SPR} & \left\langle \begin{bmatrix} \text{HOOK} & \begin{bmatrix} \text{LTOP} & \boxed{1} \\ \text{XARG} & \boxed{3} \end{bmatrix} \end{bmatrix} \right\rangle \\ \text{SUBJ} & \left\langle \begin{bmatrix} \text{INDEX} & \boxed{2} \end{bmatrix} \right\rangle \\ \text{COMPS} & \left\langle \begin{bmatrix} \text{INDEX} & \boxed{3} \end{bmatrix} \right\rangle \end{bmatrix} \\ \text{CONT} & \begin{bmatrix} \text{RELS} & \left\langle ! \begin{bmatrix} \text{ARG1} & \boxed{2} \\ \text{ARG2} & \boxed{3} \\ \text{ARG3} & \boxed{4} \end{bmatrix} ! \right\rangle \\ \text{HCONS} & \langle ! \boxed{4}\ \textit{qeq}\ \boxed{1}\ ! \rangle \end{bmatrix} \\ \text{CTXT} & \begin{bmatrix} \text{EMPATHY.EMPEE} & \boxed{2} \end{bmatrix} \end{bmatrix}$$

FIGURE 43 Constraints on *aux-obj-id-stem-lex*

adds subject honorification with negative polarity. They also add empathy information to the CONTEXT of the sentence (see § 6.3 for a discussion of empathy). The empathy is set to ARG1 in the cases of *ageru*, *sashiageru* and *yaru* and to ARG2 in the cases of *kureru* and *kudasaru*. The auxiliaries *morau* and *itadaku* are like *ageru*, *sashiageru* and *yaru* in setting the empathy to ARG1, but distinct in that they associate their ARG2 with the external argument (ARG1) of the other verb (the *ni*-marked argument).

5.3.5 Contracted Auxiliaries

Finally, we note that many of the auxiliaries also have contracted forms. These are shown in Table 16 and exemplified in (91).

(91) 吠え ている   → 吠え てる
     hoe-te iru   *hoe teru*
     bark-INF PROG   bark PROG

"The dog barks."

In the same way that て has two forms (て and で), most contracted auxiliaries also have two forms, e.g., (てる, でる). We treat these contracted auxiliaries as a single word. That is, while we segment a form such as 食べている *tabeteiru* "eat-PROG" as *tabete* and *iru*, the corresponding contracted form 食べてる *tabeteru* is segmented as *tabe* and *teru*. Because of this re-segmentation, the contracted auxiliaries are treated as verbal endings (combining with forms other than the *te-form*).

5.3.6 Summary

In this section, we have described the analysis of auxiliaries in **Jacy**. Our analysis distinguishes among aspect, content and perspective auxiliaries, and allows us to capture the semantic contributions of each, including aspectual information (modeled via features on events), predications introduced by the auxiliaries (e.g., _miru_v_6 in (87b)), and any honorification marked on the auxiliary. As **Jacy** has been developed with both spoken and written language, our analysis of auxiliaries also handles the contracted forms.

5.4 Passive Constructions

The Japanese passive is morphologically built by attaching *reru* to a c-stem verbal stem with a-inflection or *rareru* to a v-stem verbal stem (as in (92)–(93)).

(92) 話される
hanasa-reru
speak-PASS

(93) 食べられる
tabe-rareru
eat-PASS

There are two types of Japanese passives: The simple and the adversative passive (or, direct and indirect passive, as they are called by Uda (1996)). We describe our analysis of each of these in turn.

5.4.1 Simple Passives

The simple passive is (parallel to many other languages, including English) only available for transitive and ditransitive verbs and promotes an object to subject. An example of a simple transitive passive is (94).

(94) ご飯 が 井上 に 食べられた
gohan ga inoue ni tabe-rare-ta
rice NOM Inoue DAT eat-PASS-PST

"The rice was eaten by Inoue."

The verb that gets a passive ending changes its *ga*-marked subject into a complement that is marked by *ni* or *kara*. The *wo-* or *ni*-marked complement of the active form is marked in the passive by *ga*.

Oshima (2003) proposes to add a relation *lack-control-rel* to the MRS in all cases of passive. We rather leave the representation of the direct passive parallel to the analysis in other languages (as for example

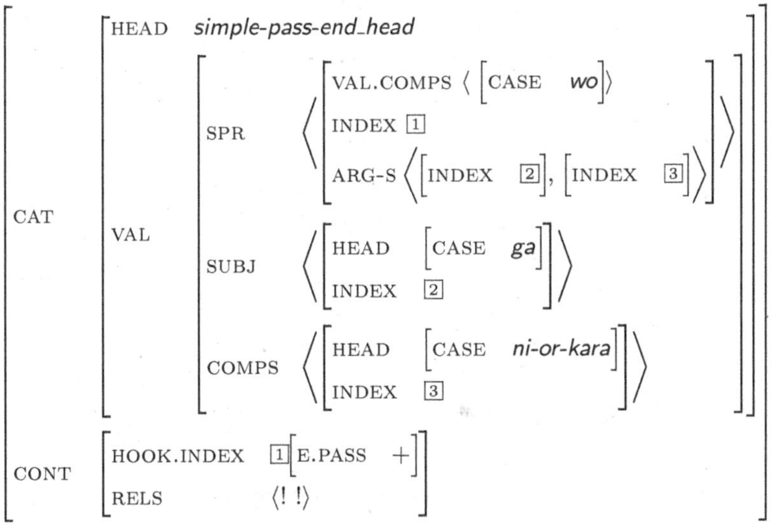

$$\begin{bmatrix} \text{CAT} & \begin{bmatrix} \text{HEAD} & \textit{simple-pass-end\_head} \\ \text{VAL} & \begin{bmatrix} \text{SPR} & \left\langle \begin{bmatrix} \text{VAL.COMPS} \left\langle \begin{bmatrix} \text{CASE} & \textit{wo} \end{bmatrix} \right\rangle \\ \text{INDEX} & \boxed{1} \\ \text{ARG-S} \left\langle \begin{bmatrix} \text{INDEX} & \boxed{2} \end{bmatrix}, \begin{bmatrix} \text{INDEX} & \boxed{3} \end{bmatrix} \right\rangle \end{bmatrix} \right\rangle \\ \text{SUBJ} & \left\langle \begin{bmatrix} \text{HEAD} & \begin{bmatrix} \text{CASE} & \textit{ga} \end{bmatrix} \\ \text{INDEX} & \boxed{2} \end{bmatrix} \right\rangle \\ \text{COMPS} & \left\langle \begin{bmatrix} \text{HEAD} & \begin{bmatrix} \text{CASE} & \textit{ni-or-kara} \end{bmatrix} \\ \text{INDEX} & \boxed{3} \end{bmatrix} \right\rangle \end{bmatrix} \end{bmatrix} \\ \text{CONT} & \begin{bmatrix} \text{HOOK.INDEX} & \boxed{1}\begin{bmatrix} \text{E.PASS} & + \end{bmatrix} \\ \text{RELS} & \langle ! \, ! \rangle \end{bmatrix} \end{bmatrix}$$

FIGURE 44 Feature Structure of a Passive Ending (*simple-pass-end-lex*)

Pollard and Sag (1994) do as well) and add a relation only in the case of the adversative passive. There is therefore no relation added to the MRS in the case of simple direct passive, such that the semantics of the passive sentence looks very much like the semantics of the active sentence. Passivation is reflected in the semantics with a feature PASS on the event variable of the verb as a placeholder until we have a fuller account of information structure, perhaps along the lines of Song 2014.

Figure 44 illustrates the constraints on the simple passive ending. This ending selects for the verbal stem via the SPR feature and identifies the indices of its SUBJ and COMPS elements with the ARG-S[16] elements of the verbal stem it combines with.[17] Since the *vstem-vend-rule* which combines this ending with the stem takes the valence information from the ending, these values will be the values of the combined lexical item. The ending stipulates the CASE values for each of the arguments, and contributes the value [PASS +], while adding no further relations ([RELS ⟨! !⟩]). The combination of this ending with a verbal stem is illustrated in Figure 45.

Ditransitive verbs can be passivated in two ways, such that both complements can be subjects of the compound, as can be seen in (96) and (97).[18]

---

[16]ARG-S is the argument structure list, whose elements are shared with the valence features.
[17]A separate passive ending is defined to handle passives of ditransitives.
[18]Thanks to T. Kuribayashi for the examples.

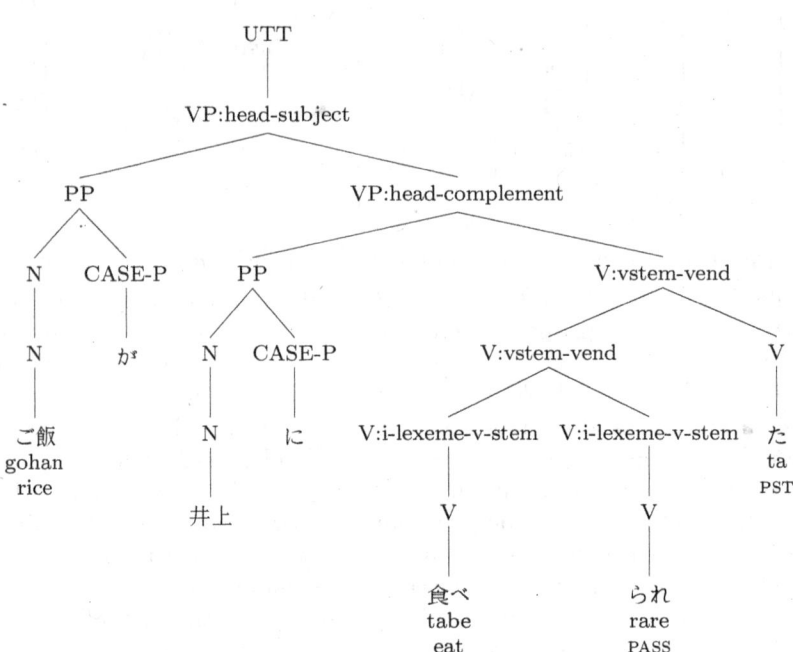

FIGURE 45 Example Passive Structure

(95) フランス が 田中 に ボール を 渡し た
Francis ga Tanaka ni booru wo watashi-ta
Francis NOM Tanaka DAT ball ACC hand-PST

"Francis handed Tanaka the ball."

(96) ボール が フランシス によって 田中 に
booru ga Francis niyotte Tanaka ni
ball NOM Francis DAT Tanaka DAT
渡さ れ た
watasa-re-ta
hand-PASS-PST

"The ball was handed to Tanaka, by Francis."

(97) 田中 が フランシス によって ボール を
Tanaka ga Francis niyotte booru wo
Tanaka NOM Francis DAT ball ACC
渡さ れ た
watasa-re-ta
hand-PASS-PST

"Tanaka was handed the ball by Francis"

5.4.2 Adversative Passive

Unlike English or German, the Japanese language has an adversative passive. This construction can be attached to intransitive as well as transitive verbs. It adds an argument (surface subject) and expresses the fact that this argument is adversely related by the action. An example of adversative passive with an intransitive verb is given in (98).

(98) a. 花子 が 弟 に 寝 られ た
Hanako ga otouto ni ne-rare-ta
Hanako NOM brother DAT sleep-PASS-PST

"Hanako was adversely affected by the fact that her brother slept."

b. $\left\langle h_1, \left\{ \begin{array}{l} h_3\text{:def\_q}(x_4, h_5, h_6), \\ h_7\text{:named}(x_4, \textit{hanako}), \\ h_8\text{:udef\_q}(x_9 \{\text{PERS } 3\}, h_{10}, h_{11}), \\ h_{12}\text{:\_otouto\_n}(x_9), \\ h_{13}\text{:\_neru\_v}(e_{14} \{\text{TENSE } \textit{pres}\}, x_9), \\ h_{15}\text{:adversative}(e_2 \{\text{TENSE } \textit{past}\}, x_9, h_{13}) \end{array} \right\} \right\rangle,$
$\{h_5 =_q h_7, h_{10} =_q h_{12}\}$

In this example, the *ga*-marked NP is affected by the event (linked in the MRS to the ARG1 of the **adversative** relation). The ARG1 of the

$$\begin{bmatrix} \text{VAL} & \begin{bmatrix} \text{SUBJ} & \left\langle \begin{bmatrix} \text{CASE} & ga \\ \text{INDEX} & \boxed{1} \end{bmatrix} \right\rangle \\ \text{SPR} & \left\langle \begin{bmatrix} \text{LTOP} & \boxed{2} \end{bmatrix} \right\rangle \end{bmatrix} \\ \text{CONT} & \begin{bmatrix} \text{RELS} & \left\langle ! \begin{bmatrix} \text{PRED} & \textit{adversative} \\ \text{ARG1} & \boxed{1} \\ \text{ARG2} & \boxed{2} \end{bmatrix} ! \right\rangle \end{bmatrix} \end{bmatrix}$$

FIGURE 46 Constraints on *adversative-pass-end-lt*

$$\begin{bmatrix} \text{VAL} & \begin{bmatrix} \text{COMPS} & \left\langle \begin{bmatrix} \text{CASE} & ni \\ \text{INDEX} & \boxed{1} \end{bmatrix} \right\rangle \\ \text{SPR} & \left\langle \begin{bmatrix} \text{XARG} & \boxed{1} \end{bmatrix} \right\rangle \end{bmatrix} \end{bmatrix}$$

FIGURE 47 Constraints on *adversative-intrans-pass-end-lt*

_neru_v ("sleep") relation is marked with *ni*. The adversative relation also takes the handle of _neru_v relation as an argument.

Jacy captures these adversative passives by putting constraints on the adversative passive ending that encode the additional semantic information and relates the compound verb's valence features to the valence of the verbal stem while adding the *ga*-marked argument. We posit a general type (*adversative-pass-end-lt*), shown in Figure 46, which has subtypes for endings that attach to intransitive and transitive verbs. As with simple passives, the adversative passive ending selects for the verbal stem through its SPR feature, so that it may combine with the stem via the *vstem-vend-rule*, a subtype of *head-specifier-rule*.

The intransitive subtype is shown in Figure 47. This type specifies that the verbal complex has exactly one complement, which is furthermore marked by *ni*. The ending identifies the index of this complement with the HOOK.XARG (i.e., the external argument) of the verbal stem. This ensures that the *ni*-marked argument is linked to the ARG1 of the stem.

The constraints on the adversative passive ending for transitive verbs are shown in Figure 48. In this case, the ending specifies two complements. The first is marked with *wo* and is identified with the first element of the COMPS list of the stem. The second is, as with the

$$\begin{bmatrix} \text{VAL} & \begin{bmatrix} \text{COMPS} & \left\langle \boxed{2}\begin{bmatrix} \text{CASE} & wo \end{bmatrix}, \begin{bmatrix} \text{CASE} & ni \\ \text{INDEX} & \boxed{1} \end{bmatrix} \right\rangle \\ \text{SPR} & \left\langle \begin{bmatrix} \text{VAL.COMPS} & \langle \boxed{2} \rangle \\ \text{XARG} & \boxed{1} \end{bmatrix} \right\rangle \end{bmatrix} \end{bmatrix}$$

FIGURE 48 Constraints on *adversative-trans-pass-end-lt*

intransitives, marked with *ni* and linked to the external argument of the stem.

An example of a transitive adversative is given in (99).

(99) a. 花子 が 弟 に ケーキ を 食べ られ た
Hanako ga otouto ni keeki wo tabe-rare-ta
Hanako NOM brother DAT cake ACC eat-PASS-PST

"Hanako was affected by the fact that her brother ate the cake."

b. $h_1, \left\langle \begin{Bmatrix} h_3\text{:def\_q}(x_4, h_5, h_6), \\ h_7\text{:named}(x_4, hanako), \\ h_8\text{:udef\_q}(x_9 \{\text{PERS } 3\}, h_{10}, h_{11}), \\ h_{12}\text{:\_otouto\_n}(x_9), \\ h_{13}\text{:udef\_q}(x_{14} \{\text{PERS } 3\}, h_{15}, h_{16}), \\ h_{17}\text{:\_keeki\_n}(x_{14}), \\ h_{18}\text{:\_taberu\_v\_1}(e_{19} \{\text{TENSE } tense\}, x_9, x_{14}), \\ h_{20}\text{:adversative}(e_2 \{\text{TENSE } past\}, x_4, h_{18}) \end{Bmatrix} \right\rangle,$
$\{h_5 =_q h_7, h_{10} =_q h_{12}, h_{15} =_q h_{17}\}$

5.4.3 Honorification with Passive Morphology

The same morphological process is also used for a different purpose: Honorification. Adding れる/られる *reru/rareru* to a verbal stem can have affect of honorification of the subject, as shown in (100).

(100) 先生 が ご飯 を 食べ られ た
sensei ga gohan wo tabe-rare-ta
teacher NOM rice ACC eat-SHON:+-PST

"The teacher ate rice."

This verbal ending adds BACKGROUND information (a *subj-honor_rel*)[19] to the feature structure, but does not affect the MRS. As it behaves morphologically just like the passive, there is systematic ambiguity between the honorific and the passive reading.

---

[19] For further discussion of our analysis of honorifics, see Chapter 9.

5.4.4 Potential with Passive Morphology

The same morphological process has yet another meaning: potential. Adding れる/られる *reru/rareru* to a verbal stem can have affect of expressing potential, as shown in (101).

(101) a. 先生　が　カレー　が/を　食べられる
　　　　 sensei ga   karee   ga/wo   tabe-rareru
　　　　 teacher NOM curry NOM/ACC eat-POT

"The teacher can eat curry."

b. $\left\langle h_1, \left\{ \begin{array}{l} h_3\text{:def\_q}(x_4, h_5, h_6), \\ h_7\text{:named}(x_4, \textit{hanako}), \\ h_8\text{:udef\_q}(x_9\,\{\text{PERS } 3\}, h_{10}, h_{11}), \\ h_{12}\text{:\_keeki\_n}(x_9), \\ h_{13}\text{:\_taberu\_v\_1}\,(e_{14}\,\{\text{TENSE } \textit{tense}\}, x_4, x_9) \\ h_{15}\text{:rareru\_v\_can}\,(e_2\,\{\text{TENSE } \textit{pres}\}, x_4, h_{16}) \end{array} \right\} \right\rangle,$

$\{h_5 =_q h_7, h_{10} =_q h_{12}, h_{16} =_q h_{13}\}$

This verbal ending adds another predicate to the feature structure *rare_v_can* which takes the subject as its ARG1 and the verb as its ARG2.

This use of the morphological form of the passive adds further ambiguity. Though case marking can sometimes restrict the range of analyses, in the worst case *rare* can be ambiguous with all four interpretations: simple, adversative, honorific and potential. In practice, adversative passives are rare, and honorific passives mainly used in conversation. In our corpus, we found 41 examples of sentences with simple passive, 4 examples of adversative passive, no examples of honorific passive and 52 examples of potential passives for *rare*.

5.5 Causative

The final verbal construction we address in this chapter is the causative. Japanese causatives are morphological (rather than periphrastic), and are indicated by the verbal endings せる/させる *seru/saseru*. These endings are differentiated by which type of stems they attach to (*c-stem* and *v-stem*, respectively) and constrain their LMORPH-BIND-TYPE to *pass-c-stem-lt* and *pass-v-stem-lt* accordingly.

Causatives can apply to intransitive or transitive verbs, as illustrated in (102) and (103), and even to ditransitive verbs (104).

(102) 花子　が　妹　に　ピアノ　を　習わせる
　　　 Hanako ga imooto ni piano wo narawa-seru
　　　 Hanako NOM sister DAT piano ACC learn-CAUS

"Hanako makes her sister learn piano."

(103) 花子 が 妹 に 寝させる
Hanako ga imooto ni ne-saseru
Hanako NOM sister DAT sleep-CAUS

"Hanako puts her sister to sleep."

(104) 祐美子 が 花子 に 太郎 に ケーキ を
Yumiko ga Hanako ni Tarou ni keeki wo
Yumiko NOM Hanako DAT Tarou DAT cake ACC
あげさせた
age-sase-ta
give-CAUS-PST

"Yumiko made Hanako give Tarou some cake."

There has been some debate in the research literature on the correct analysis of this construction. Gunji (1996) advocates a phrasal approach in light of the fact that modifiers can attach semantically to either verbal stem or the causative. Manning et al. (1998) argue that the morphological and phonological evidence requires a lexical approach where the stem plus ending form a single word and present an analysis which can handle the semantic facts while maintaining lexical construction of the causative.

The approach taken in **Jacy** to verbal morphology puts the combination of verbal stems with their endings right at the boundary of morphology and syntax. While the combination is achieved by means of a subtype of the *head-specifier-rule* (i.e., the *vstem-vend-rule*), this rule must apply low. That is, the left-hand daughter must be only the verbal stem, and not a projection thereof. Thus, our analysis is similar to that of Manning et al. (1998), though we achieve the semantic effects differently.

In order to account for the different possibilities to access the verb or the causative relation for semantic modification, we assume two types of causatives, which propagate the index of the causative relation or the verbal relation to the top. (105b,c) give the two MRSs assigned to (105a) the modification of the verbal and the cause event.[20]

(105) a. 紀子 が 勝 に 学校 で 走らせた
Noriko ga Masaru ni gakkou de hashira-se-ta
Noriko NOM Masaru DAT school LOC run-CAUS-PST

"Masaru made Noriko run at school."

---

[20]In fact, the current version of **Jacy** only finds the reading in (105b). This is considered a bug in the grammar, to be addressed as outlined here in future development.

b. $\left\langle h_1, \left\{ \begin{array}{l} h_3\text{:def\_q}(x_4, h_5, h_6), \\ h_7\text{:named}(x_4, \textit{noriko}), \\ h_8\text{:udef\_q}(x_9, h_{10}, h_{11}), \\ h_{12}\text{:named}(x_9, \textit{masaru}), \\ h_{13}\text{:udef\_q}(x_{14}\{\text{PERS } 3\}, h_{15}, h_{16}), \\ h_{17}\text{:\_gakkou\_n}(x_{14}), \\ h_{18}\text{:\_de\_p}(e_{19}\{\text{TENSE } \textit{untensed}\}, e_2, x_{14}), \\ h_{20}\text{:\_hashiru\_v}(e_{22}\{\text{TENSE } \textit{tense}\}, x_9, i_{21}), \\ h_{18}\text{:\_saseru\_v\_cause}(e_2\{\text{TENSE } \textit{past}\}, x_4, x_9, h_{23}) \end{array} \right\}, \right\rangle$
$\{h_5 =_q h_7, h_{10} =_q h_{12}, h_{15} =_q h_{17}, h_{23} =_q h_{20}\}$

c. $\left\langle h_1, \left\{ \begin{array}{l} h_3\text{:def\_q}(x_4, h_5, h_6), \\ h_7\text{:named}(x_4, \textit{noriko}), \\ h_8\text{:udef\_q}(x_9, h_{10}, h_{11}), \\ h_{12}\text{:named}(x_9, \textit{masaru}), \\ h_{13}\text{:udef\_q}(x_{14}\{\text{PERS } 3\}, h_{15}, h_{16}), \\ h_{17}\text{:\_gakkou\_n}(x_{14}), \\ h_{20}\text{:\_de\_p}(e_{19}\{\text{TENSE } \textit{untensed}\}, e_{22}, x_{14}), \\ h_{20}\text{:\_hashiru\_v}(e_{22}\{\text{TENSE } \textit{tense}\}, x_9, i_{21}), \\ h_{18}\text{:\_saseru\_v\_cause}(e_2\{\text{TENSE } \textit{past}\}, x_4, x_9, h_{23}) \end{array} \right\}, \right\rangle$
$\{h_5 =_q h_7, h_{10} =_q h_{12}, h_{15} =_q h_{17}, h_{23} =_q h_{20}\}$

The case marking facts require separate endings for transitive and intransitive causatives. In intransitive causatives, the causer (花子 *Hanako* in (103)) is marked by *ga* and the causee (妹 *imooto* "younger sister" in (103)) by *wo* or *ni*. In transitive causatives (e.g., (102)), the causer is marked by *ga* and the causee by *ni*. As with other **vstem-vend-rule** combinations, the valence information comes from the verbal ending. Thus, the verbal endings specify appropriate values for SUBJ and COMPS and link the indices of the elements on those lists to the XARG (and, in the case of transitives COMPS element) of the stem they combine with. This ensures the correct linking of the arguments in the MRS. The constraints that achieve this effect are illustrated for transitive causatives in Figure 49.

Finally, the causative endings also add the causative relation to the semantics and expose either the ARG0 of that relation or the ARG0 of the verbal stem as the HOOK.INDEX of the combined form. Figure 49 shows the case where the causative's ARG0 is exposed.[21]

---

[21] Some of the constraints shown in Figure 49 are inherited from the supertype *v-cause-op-end-lt*.

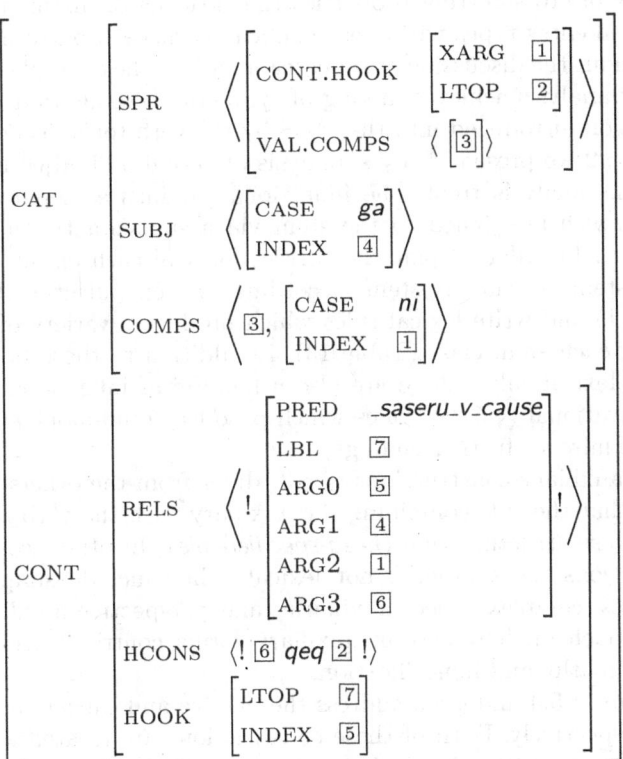

FIGURE 49 Constraints on *caus-trans-obj-end-lt*

5.6 Summary and Further Reading

This chapter details **Jacy**'s handling of verbs and adjectives, including subcategorization, inflection, derivation, auxiliary constructions, passive and causative. We outline the subcategorization types of verbs, verbal nouns and adjectives (§ 5.1). A special case of verb subcategorization is copula verbs. We present an overview of both the range of subcategorization properties of Japanese copula verbs as well as an overview of cross-cutting properties that lead us to distinguish different lexical entry types within each subcategorization pattern (§ 5.1.4). Throughout the discussion of subcategorization, the examples illustrate how our analysis achieves linking of syntactic to semantic roles in the predication introduced into the MRS by the verb (or adjective).

In § 5.2 we present **Jacy**'s analysis of verbal and adjectival inflection. This analysis treats the inflectional endings as separate lexical entries which are joined to the stem via a subsyntactic rule (*vstem-vend-rule*). In order to pair the correct form of each ending with the correct stem, we classify stems according to their inflectional patterns (Table 11) and write lexical rules which produce a variety of inflected forms of each stem class (Table 13). In addition to these bound stem forming lexical rules, there are also a handful of inflectional (§ 5.2.5) and derivational (§ 5.2.6) rules which produce stand-alone stem forms which require no further endings.

The auxiliary constructions (§ 5.3) differ from the others discussed here in that the rule combining the auxiliary with the verb is an ordinary phrase structure rule (*head-specifier-rule*). In other words, these constructions are syntactic, not lexical. They include simple aspect auxiliaries, complex aspect auxiliaries and perspective auxiliaries. We briefly touch on how certain auxiliary forms contribute information about empathy and honorification.

Finally, § 5.4 and § 5.5 address the passive and causative constructions, respectively. Both of these constructions are treated as subsyntactic, on a par with other verbal endings (cf. § 5.2). Our analysis of passives handles both simple passives and adversative passives. Our analysis of the causative construction takes a lexicalist approach, though not the same one as Manning et al. (1998). These analyses interact with our analyses of phrase structure (Chapter 3) and particles (Chapter 7) to license the structures we observe with the intended MRSs.

Kageyama (2001) presents a semantic classification of Japanese verbs making use of Lexical Conceptual Structure and gives a linking theory that accounts for the transitivity alternation, resultative constructions, tough constructions, among others, as well as illustrating corresponding English constructions. In Chapter 2 of Teramura 1984a, an extensive classification of Japanese verbs is presented that is based on the verbal meaning and the type of arguments they require. Teramura does not rely on any formal linguistic theory and gives an intuitive and comprehensive description of Japanese verbs.

The inflection of Japanese verbs is detailed in Chapter 4 of Teramura (1984b). Also, Masuoka and Takubo (1992) give a concise description of the Japanese verbal inflection in Chapter 2.

Voice constructions have been extensively studied in Japanese linguistics. Tsujimura (1999) summarizes issues of passive constructions in Chapter 7 and causative constructions in Chapter 8. Chapter 3 of Teramura (1984a) is also helpful to grasp the big picture of Japanese voice phenomena. For lexicalist analyzes of Japanese voice, Uda (1994) and Matsumoto (1996b) cover a broad range of phenomena. The former is based on HPSG and the latter is based on LFG.

Regarding auxiliaries, Teramura (1984b) classifies Japanese aspect and modality that are expressed by auxiliaries in Chapters 5 and 6. Masuoka and Takubo (1992) also present a catalog of Japanese aspect and modality. Chapter 11 of Tsujimura (1999) discusses issues pertaining to Japanese tense and aspect. Yoshimoto (1998) describes tense and aspect of Japanese in an HPSG framework. Finally, Matsumoto (1996a) embeds his analysis of the Japanese VP in an LFG framework.

6
Nominal Structures: Linking Syntax, Semantics and Pragmatics

This chapter describes our analysis of Japanese noun phrases. Semantically, noun phrases refer to entities, their characteristic variables (ARG0) typed as a referential index (x). Syntactically, noun phrases prototypically act as subject and object in sentences, marked with a case-marker (as described in Chapter 7). Japanese noun phrases are generally right-headed. Japanese nouns do not require the presence of a determiner and most have no complements. There is no morphological or syntactic distinction between singular and plural, or countable and uncountable. A collectivizing suffix such as -達 -*tachi* "and others") can attach to common nouns if their antecedent refers to a group, but this is normally done only if the antecedent is animate: 学生達 *gakusei-tachi* "the student and others (normally also students)".[1] It can even attach to proper nouns: 池原さん達 *Ikehara-san-tachi* "the group centered around Mr Ikehara". Collectivizing suffixes differ from English number in that they do not mark plurality (one or more discrete entities of the same kind), but rather denote a group of entities, with the one referred to by the noun being salient.

Noun phrase syntax and semantics have largely been neglected in earlier work on unification-based Japanese grammar. There is almost no discussion of NP internal structure in Gunji (1987) or Ohtani et al. (2000). This is a pity, as Japanese noun phrases show an interesting interaction of syntax, semantics and pragmatics and the HPSG grammar framework is well suited for building representations and restrictions for this interaction, as it makes use of complex signs. In this chapter, we describe some phenomena of Japanese noun phrases and how integrated analyses of their syntax, semantics and pragmatics can be used

---

[1] See Bond 2005, pp 84-86 for a fuller discussion.

for Japanese language processing.

We first describe the basic structures of Japanese ordinary nouns in our grammar in § 6.1, where it can already be seen how syntax, semantics and pragmatics interact. We then look at names in § 6.2. The analysis of named entities shows how information from external resources is included into the grammar. The analysis of Japanese pronouns is based on the analysis of ordinary nouns (which is reflected by the fact that the pronoun type hierarchy is part of the noun hierarchy). Their analysis, described in § 6.3, sets a stronger focus on the context. Although they are not commonly used, the characteristics of the Japanese reflexive pronouns reflect interesting interaction of linguistic levels. For this reason we describe reflexives in some detail in § 6.3.4.

We round out the discussion of nouns with explanations of our analyses of a few additional phenomena. § 6.4 addresses nominalizers and their restricted semantic content and subcategorization features. Next, we show how the analysis of temporal expressions fits well into the general account and does not need special grammar structures (§ 6.5). We then turn to noun modification in § 6.6, covering the adnominal particle and other noun modifiers, including the surprising similarities between relative clauses and pre-nominal adjectives. Finally, we present a detailed discussion of our analysis of numeral classifiers (§ 6.7).

6.1 Ordinary Nouns and Noun Phrases

An ordinary noun (belonging to the lexical type *ordinary-noun-lex*, the most common kind of noun) does not serve as the specifier for any other category. It can have different honorific forms and it can occur with or without a particle in spoken language. For example, 本 *hon* "book" is a non-honorific ordinary noun and 教授 *kyouju* "professor" is an honorific ordinary noun, which prefers pragmatic agreement with the verb when being in the subject position of the phrase headed by this verb (see Chapter 9 for discussion of honorific agreement). Semantically, ordinary nouns are one-place predicates with an ARG0 whose value is of the type *ref-ind* (referential index[2]) : $\text{hon\_n}(x_i)$.

Japanese noun phrases usually do not take determiners. However, determiners like この *kono* "this", その *sono* "that" or あの *ano* "that over there" are possible. Thus, the ordinary noun subcategorizes for an optional specifier, which is a determiner. The determiner, if expressed, adds quantificational information to the MRS of the noun phrase, as can be seen in (106).

---

[2]referential indices are represented by the letter x.

(106) a. この 時
 kono toki
 this time

b. $\left\langle h_1, \left\{ \begin{array}{l} h_5{:}\_kono\_q(x_4, h_6, h_7), \\ h_8{:}\_toki\_n(x_4) \end{array} \right\}, \right.$
 $\left. \{h_6 =_q h_8\} \right\rangle$

Most Japanese noun phrases have no overt determiner; however for compatibility with DELPH-IN-standard MRS well-formedness and interoperability with MRS representations produced by DELPH-IN grammars for other languages, such nouns must still be associated with a quantifier in the semantics. Therefore, we have a unary rule (*quantify-n-rule*) that takes a noun as its daughter, produces an NP mother, and adds an underspecified quantifier through its constructional context (C-CONT). The rule can be seen in Figure 50. This rule exemplifies how syntactic information, such as head type and valence information, is linked with semantic information when building relations in RELS. The C-CONT contains information that is added to the MRS by the rule. It contains the (underspecified) quantifier relation udef_q_rel, which takes as its bound variable the noun's index (ARG0 #i). The constraint on the RSTR feature reflects the (partial) information available about the quantifier's restriction, namely, that it includes the semantic contribution of the daughter of the rule (exclusive of any quantifiers embedded in it).

The resulting MRS for a noun phrase containing only the ordinary noun 本 *hon* "book" can be seen in (107). It is similar to the noun phrase containing a determiner and a noun, except for the underspecified quantifying relation udef_q_rel.

(107) a. 本
 hon
 book

b. $\left\langle h_1, \left\{ \begin{array}{l} h_5{:}udef\_q(x_4, h_6, h_7), \\ h_8{:}\_hon\_n(x_4) \end{array} \right\}, \right.$
 $\left. \{h_6 =_q h_8\} \right\rangle$

As noted, most Japanese noun phrases do not contain determiners (fewer than 17% of sentences in our data had any instance of the type *det-lex*). However, this claim is dependent on the analysis of the various nominal dependents. Our primary tests for determiners are that any given noun phrase can only have one, and it must be left-peripheral. According to this definition, demonstratives (この *kono* "this", その *sono* "that", *ano* "that over there" あの and どの *dono* "which", see § 8.3),

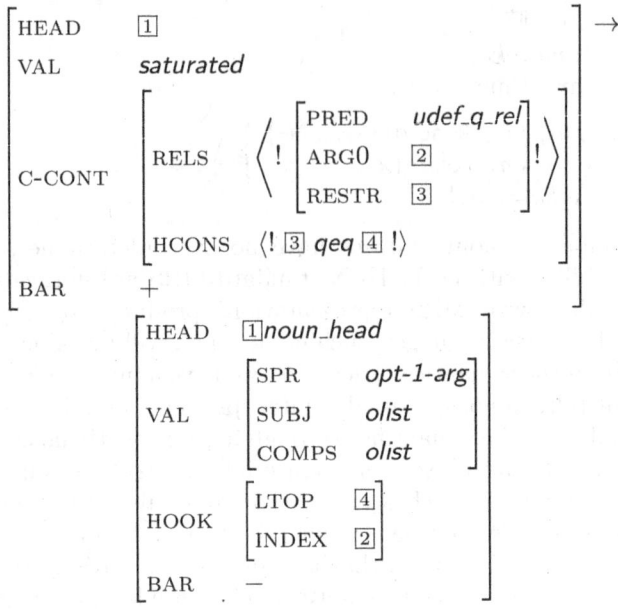

FIGURE 50 *quantify-n-rule*

and some words like 各 *kaku* "each", ある *aru* "a certain" qualify as determiners. Accordingly, these are the only words to contribute explicit quantifiers in our grammar.

Japanese has no articles, but the demonstratives, especially *sono* "that" are often used when referring to known entities, either identifiable from the situation (deictic) or previously mentioned (anaphoric), and translated in such cases as *the* rather than *that*. We give an example of this from the Tanaka Corpus (108).

(108) a. 最初、 私 は その テスト に 失敗 した
saisho, watashi wa <u>sono</u> tesuto ni shippai shi-ta
first, 1SG TOP that test DAT fail do-PST

"At first I failed <u>the</u> test."

The lack of determiners in Japanese is a problem when translating into languages like English or German. Siegel (1996b), Heine (1998) and Bond (2005) describe some of the problems this causes for machine translation and outline some solutions.

6.2 Names and Named Entities

Named entities are similar in structure to nouns, except that they all share the same predicate: named and are differentiated by the value of their constant argument (CARG) which is set to the name's string itself (or a transliteration). The interpretation is that we are introducing a referent whose name is the value of the constant argument. This follows the standard practice in DELPH-IN and is loosely based on Pollard and Sag (1994, 27).

Person names can occur with a determiner (as in (109), taken from the internet), but typically do not. Therefore, a person name undergoes a unary rule that inserts a quantifying relation, just as ordinary nouns. The difference, though, is that person names restrict their determiners to be definite in their lexical type. Thus they undergo the same rule as in Figure 50, but the quantifier is specialized from *udef_q* to *def_q*. We give an example of a noun phrase built from a person name and its semantics in (110).

(109) この 田中 先生 から
kono Tanaka sensei kara
this Tanaka Prof from

"From this Professor Tanaka [...]"

(110) a. 花子
Hanako
Hanako

b. $\langle h_1, \{ h_5\text{:named}(x_4, 鹿ノ台), h_6\text{:def\_q}(x_4, h_8, h_7) \}, \{h_8 =_q h_5\} \rangle$

Another strategy is to run **Jacy** in parallel with a named-entity recognizer and then merge the results, for example, using the Heart-of-Gold (see Callmeier et al. (2004) and § 2.3). This can be done using an extended semantic representation (RMRS: Robust MRS; Copestake 2007), which allows more underspecification than standard MRS. **Jacy** can return RMRS (by converting MRS) and this is combined with RMRS from the named-entity recognizer. In our implementation we used Sprout (Drozdzynski et al., 2004) as the named-entity recognition tool. As a result, names not available in the **Jacy** lexicon but recognized by the tool can be included into the parse results.

In many cases, the named-entity recognizer will simplify some internal structure. Consider (111), which **Jacy** analyses as a compound noun, headed by 大学 *daigaku* "university" (111a). This is a correct analysis, but not necessarily useful to post-processing. If the grammar is used in an application, such as machine translation, instead of getting the internal structure of the named entity, it is more useful to get the information that it is a named entity and should be translated as a unit. The named-entity recognizer treats the whole name as a single noun as in (111b), and gives more information about its type (*organization*), but no quantifier. The integrated architecture merges these, replacing the complicated NP with the simpler named entity (see Callmeier et al. (2004) for more details).

(111) 南洋　　理工　　　大学
      naNyou rikou   daigaku
      Nanyang Technological University

a. $\left\langle h_1, \left\{ \begin{array}{l} h_5\text{:named}(x_6, nanQyou\_2), \\ h_7\text{:\_rikou\_n\_3}(x_8\ \{\text{PERS } 3\}), \\ h_9\text{:\_daigaku\_n\_1}(x_4), \\ h_9\text{:compound}(e_{10}\ \{\text{TENSE } untensed\}, x_4, x_8), \\ h_{11}\text{:udef\_q}(x_8, h_{13}, h_{12}), \\ h_9\text{:compound}(e_{14}\ \{\text{TENSE } untensed\}, x_4, x_6), \\ h_{15}\text{:udef\_q}(x_6, h_{17}, h_{16}), \\ h_{18}\text{:udef\_q}(x_4, h_{20}, h_{19}) \end{array} \right\} \right\rangle,$

$\{h_{20} =_q h_9, h_{17} =_q h_5, h_{13} =_q h_7\}$

b. $\left\langle h_1, \left\{ \begin{array}{l} h_5\text{:named}(x_4, \text{南洋理工大学}), \\ h_6\text{:loctype}(x_5, x_4, organization) \end{array} \right\} \right\rangle,$

$\{\}$

Names are neutral concerning honorification. **Jacy** differentiates between first names, surnames, names of institutions, names of locations and product names.[3] They have different HEAD values (which are all subtypes of *noun_head*).

First names normally come after surnames in Japanese, but the other order is possible. The *compound-name-rule* takes a name and adds the possibility to modify another name. This rule inserts a relation named compound to the MRS, which combines the information on the names. The *compounds-rule*, an instance of head-final head-adjunct rules, combines the names. First names modify a surname; surnames and institutions do not modify, and location names modify institutions (e.g., 青山大学 *aoyama daigaku* "Aoyama University"). An example MRS for a personal name (栗林花子 *Kuribayashi Hanako*) is shown in (112):

---

[3] *ippan-name* is used for those cases where the named-entity recognition detects a name, but doesn't give the information about the name type.

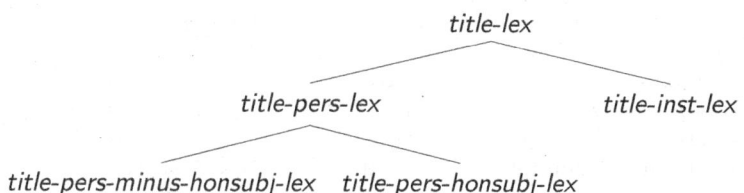

FIGURE 51 Type hierarchy of titles

(112) $\left\langle h_1, \left\{ \begin{array}{l} h_5\text{:def\_q}(x_4, h_6, h_7), \\ h_8\text{:named}(x_9, \textit{hanako}), \\ h_{10}\text{:named}(x_4, \textit{kuribayashi}), \\ h_{10}\text{:compound}\left(e_{11}\left\{\text{TENSE}\ \textit{untensed}\right\}, x_4, x_9\right) \\ h_{12}\text{:udef\_q}(x_9, h_{13}, h_{14}), \end{array} \right\} \right\rangle$
$\{h_6 =_q h_{10}, h_{13} =_q h_{18}\}$

All names can take an optional title as specifier. Titles are words like 教授 *kyouju* "professor", さん *san* "Mr/Ms", 君 *kun* "diminuitive", 様 *sama* "Mr/Ms (honorific)", and 先生 *sensei* "teacher" that subcategorize for a specifier that can be a human name, but also institutional titles like 研究室 *kenkyuushitsu* in 藤田研究室 *Fujita kenkyuushitsu* "Fujita research institute", or 大学 *daigaku* "university". Titles that attach to person names can add information on subject honorification with positive or negative polarity. They introduce two relations to the MRS: a title relation and a title-id_rel that combines the information on the title and the name. Institutional titles like *kenkyuushitsu* add their specific relation (such as _kenkyuushitsu_n_rel) and the title-id_rel.

6.3 Pronouns

Pronouns share many properties with nouns (they head noun phrases, and can be modified by similar things). We therefore treat them as a subtype of nouns and build their type hierarchy under *n-lex*. At the top level, we divide pronouns into two types: personal (*pers-pron-lex*), and locative/demonstrative (*pron-demon-lex*). Table 17 shows the pronoun types and examples.

6.3.1 Demonstrative Pronouns

Japanese has three demonstrative pronouns: これ *kore* "this", それ *sore* "that" and あれ *are* "over there" (also glossed as proximal, medial and distal). We decompose these into the equivalent of このもの *kono mono* "this thing", as shown in (113). See 8.3 for a fuller discussion. Unlike the personal pronouns, the demonstratives do not have any particular effects on empathy.

Type of Pronoun	Gloss	Example
pron-demon-lex	demonstrative	それ *sore* "that"
pron-loc-ref-lex	locative	そこ *soko* "there"
pron-firstpl-ref-lex	1PL	私達 *watashi-tachi* "we"
pron-firstahon-ref-lex	1.AHON:+	こちら *kochira* "I/we"
pron-firstsgminusahon-ref-lex	1SG.AHON:−	ぼく *boku* "I"
pron-firstsg-ahon-ref-lex	1SG.AHON:+	私 *watashi* "I"
pron-secondperson-ref-lex	2	そっち *socchi* "you"
pron-secondsg-ref-lex	2SG	あなた *anata* "you"
pron-secondpl-ref-lex	2PL	あなた達 *anatatachi* "you"
pron-secondminusahon-ref-lex	2.AHON:−	君 *kimi* "you"
pron-secondahon-ref-lex	2.AHON:+	そちら *sochira* "you"
pron-thirdsgmasc-ref-lex	3SG.M	かれ *kare* "he"
pron-thirdsgfem-ref-lex	3SG.F	彼女 *kanojo* "she"
pron-thirdpl-ref-lex	3PL.M	かれら *karera* "they"
reflexive-pronoun-lex	REFL	自分 *jibun* "self"
reflexive-pronoun-honsbj-lex	REFL.SHON:+	ご自分 *go-jibun* "self"

TABLE 17 Pronouns

(113) a. これ
           kore
           this

    "this (lit: this thing)"

  b. $\left\langle h_1, \left\{ \begin{array}{l} h_5\text{:generic-nom}(x_4), \\ h_6\text{:kono\_q}(x_4, h_7, h_8) \end{array} \right\}, \{h_7 =_q h_5\} \right\rangle$

6.3.2 Locative Pronouns

We decompose locative pronouns into a reference to a place, and a demonstrative pronoun. See 8.3 for a fuller discussion. Unlike English locative pronouns *here/there*, Japanese locatives cannot function as adverbs, they must have a post-position: *soko-ni ike* "go to there".

(114) a. ここ
           koko
           here

    "here (lit: this place)"

  b. $\left\langle h_5, \left\{ \begin{array}{l} h_5\text{:place\_n}(x_4), \\ h_6\text{:kono\_q}(x_4, h_7, h_8) \end{array} \right\}, \{h_7 =_q h_5\} \right\rangle$

6.3.3 Personal Pronouns

Pronouns that refer to persons encode person, number and gender — just as in English or German. In this sense, they are more specified than ordinary nouns in Japanese. Pronouns are always definite and thus get a definite quantifier in the semantic representation. Explicit pronouns are used far less in Japanese than in English. In most cases where English uses a pronoun, the Japanese equivalent will be to omit the element. For example, in a parallel text of 600 sentences, translated from English into Japanese, the English had 1,445 pronouns and the Japanese only 514 (Seah and Bond, 2014). The omitted pronouns are commonly referred to as zero pronouns; see § 4.3.3 for how these are handled in Jacy.

Japanese personal pronouns can contain further information about addressee honorification. This is reflected in the type hierarchy of personal pronouns, which links syntactic, semantic and pragmatic information in the types. Person, number and gender are added to the MRS (see (115) for a first person singular pronoun), while honorification is added as CTXT (CONTEXT) information. Additionally, they add and instance of *entity-honor_rel* with negative polarity to CTXT.BACKGROUND, in order to reflect the fact that reference to oneself usually happens in humble or neutral form with respect to honorification. The HEAD.FORMAL gets [SHON −] (subject honorification), such that agreement phenomena of honorification can be accounted for as well. The CTXT of a first person singular pronoun, as can be seen in Figure 52, thus co-indexes the speaker with the pronoun index, the empathy setting person as well as the person empathy is set to, and an *entity-honor_rel* in the BACKGROUND, which further identifies the honorer and the honored with a negative polarity.

Honorific second person pronouns on the other hand get [SHON +] in their HEAD information. They identify their INDEX with the ADDRESSEE and insert *entity-honor* with positive polarity into the CTXT.BACKGROUND.

(115) a. 私
    watashi
    1SG
    "me"

b. $\left\langle h_5, \left\{ \begin{array}{l} h_5\text{:pron}\,(x_4\,\{\text{PERS } 1, \text{NUM } sg\}), \\ h_6\text{:def\_q}(x_4, h_8, h_7) \\ \{h_8 =_q h_5\} \end{array} \right\} \right\rangle$

The usage of first person pronouns like 私 *watashi* is rare in

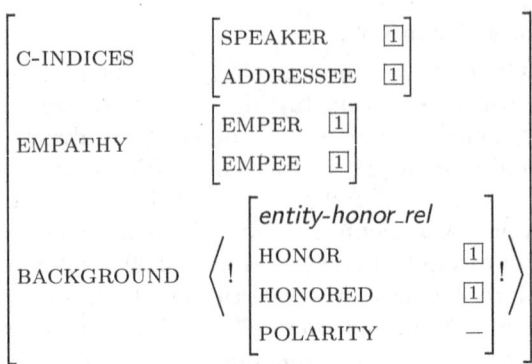

FIGURE 52 CTXT of a first person singular pronoun

Japanese spoken language. Japanese speakers leave out the first person pronoun, except when they want to put a special stress on the fact that they are referring to themselves. As honorification is based on the social distance between the speaker, the subject and the addressee, information about the pragmatic perspective of pronouns is essential to analyze Japanese sentences. First person pronouns set the pragmatic perspective (EMPATHY) to the speaker of the utterance and coindex the pronoun with the speaker. So, they identify their HOOK.INDEX in CONT with the EMPEE (empathisee) in CTXT.EMPATHY and the SPEAKER in C-INDS in CTXT.

6.3.4 The Reflexive *jibun*

The Japanese reflexive does not appear very frequently: we found no occurrences in the Verbmobil dialogue data and 自分 *jibun* accounts for only 0.009% of the word tokens in one year of Mainichi Shinbun newspaper data. It is slightly more common in essays (0.2%) and stories (0.07%) (Tan and Bond, 2012). Although this is the case, there is a considerable body of research on the binding properties of *jibun*. In light of the theoretical importance of this element, we have included it in the grammar, exploring its syntax, semantics and pragmatics and their interactions. We only model binding properties that should be expressed as restrictions (as opposed to preferences) and that are on the sentential level—we do not attempt to model interactions between sentences.

There is a fundamental difference between reflexive binding in Japanese and English, as discussed in e.g., Sag and Wasow (1999, 166f): The Japanese reflexive can be bound to a subject in a higher sentence or an external entity that is not contained in the ARG-ST of a verb. Furthermore, the Japanese reflexive typically lacks number and gender information.

At first sight, the Japanese reflexive syntactically looks like an ordinary noun. It is followed either by an adverbial particle or by a case particle (as in (116) from Makino and Tsutsui 1986, 159-162 and (117) from Sag and Wasow 1999, 168) and can therefore function as a verbal argument as well as an adjunct. It is different from a common noun in that it typically cannot take a determiner (see (118)). This qualifies the reflexive to be a personal pronoun, similar to 彼 *kare* "3SG.M" or 彼女 *kanojo* "3SG.F". The difference between the reflexive and the other pronouns is in the binding properties.

(116) a. メアリー$_i$ は 自分$_i$ で 何でも する
  Mearii$_i$ wa jibun$_i$ de nandemo suru
  Mary$_i$ TOP REFL$_i$ INS everything do

  "Mary$_i$ does everything by herself$_i$."

 b. 中川$_i$ は 自分$_i$ が 京大 に 入れる
  Nakagawa$_i$ wa jibun$_i$ ga Kyoudai ni haireru
  Nakagawa$_i$ TOP REFL$_i$ NOM Kyoto.Univ. LOC enter.POT
  と 思って いなかった
  to omot-te i-nakat-ta
  COMP think-INF PROG-NEG-PST

  "Nakagawa$_i$ didn't think that he$_i$ could enter Kyoto University."

 c. 和夫$_i$ は 自分$_i$ を 励ました
  Kazuo$_i$ wa jibun$_i$ wo hagemashi-ta
  Kazuo$_i$ TOP REFL$_i$ ACC brace-PST

  "Kazuo$_i$ braced himself$_i$."

(117) 花子$_i$ が 自分 を 敲いた
  Hanako$_i$ ga jibun$_i$ wo tatai-ta
  Hanako$_i$ NOM REFL$_i$ ACC hit-PST

  "Hanako$_i$ hit herself$_i$."

(118) *メアリー$_i$ は その 自分$_i$ で 何でも する
  **Mearii$_i$ wa sono jibun$_i$ de nandemo suru*
  Mary$_i$ TOP this REFL INS everything do

  Intended: "Mary$_i$ does everything by herself$_i$."

Motomura (2001) states that the reflexive is not a lexical element, but a grammatical formative introduced to save a derivation. This expresses the view that *jibun* has no semantics on its own: the reflexive inherits its semantics from its antecedent. Indeed, unlike the other personal pronouns, *jibun* carries no explicit information about gender or person; these are interpreted based on the antecedent. However, number information can be shown in the same way as with other pronouns by adding たち *-tachi* "and others": we treat *jibuntachi* as the lexicalized plural form of *jibun*, although *jibun* is underspecified for number. In addition, it is possible to encode honorification with the reflexive, in the form ご自分 *go-jibun*. The reflexive therefore has some semantic and pragmatic content: Though lacking person and gender information, it sometimes contains number and honorification. In discourse processing, this partial information will be combined with other partial information from the antecedent. We therefore view the reflexive as a personal pronoun with special implications to semantics and pragmatics. The semantics is fairly underspecified, but not empty, and can be enriched, when combined with the antecedent's content value.

The binding possibilities for the reflexive pronoun also show the mingled contributions of syntax, semantics and pragmatics. On the one hand, it is not obligatory for a reflexive to be bound in the clause (subjects of higher clauses are available as antecedents) or even in the sentence. Gunji 1983, 132 notes that some speakers allow *jibun* to be bound pragmatically (typically to the speaker of the sentence). On the other hand, there seem to be syntactic restrictions for reflexive binding. McCawley (1976) formulates the subject antecedent conditions as follows:

> "...the reflexive refers back to the subject in the same simplex sentence or the subject in any higher sentence." (page 53)
> "...the antecedent of the reflexive not only must be the subject but also must command the reflexive." (page 58)

Example (119), from McCawley (1976, 53), illustrates the subject antecedent condition. In this case, both subjects (*Satou*, subject of *odoroita* in the higher clause and *Tanaka*, subject of *shoukaishita* in the lower clause) are possible antecedents of *jibun*.

(119) 佐藤$_i$ は 田中$_j$ が 原 に 自分$_{i/j}$ が 好きな
Satou$_i$ wa Tanaka$_j$ ga Hara ni jibun$_{i/j}$ ga suki na
Satou$_i$ TOP Tanaka$_j$ NOM Hara DAT REFL$_{i/j}$ NOM like COP
娘 を 紹介 した こと に 驚いた
musume wo shoukai shi-ta koto ni odoroi-ta
girl ACC introduce do-PST NMLZ DAT surprise-PST

"Satou$_i$ was surprised that Tanaka$_j$ introduced to Hara the girl he$_{i/j}$ loves."

The command condition is illustrated by (120), from Gunji 1983, 133. Here there are two subjects that precede *jibun*, but only one is available as an antecedent, namely *Ken*, as the other (*Naomi*) is embedded in a lower (relative) clause.

(120) ケン$_i$ は 奈緒美$_j$ が 愛 し て いる 男 に
Ken$_i$ wa Naomi$_j$ ga ai shi-te iru otoko ni
Ken$_i$ TOP Naomi$_j$ NOM love do-INF PROG man DAT
自分$_{i/*j}$ の 話 を した
jibun$_{i/*j}$ no hanashi wo shi-ta
REFL$_{i/*j}$ ADN story ACC do-PST

"Ken$_i$ told the man who Naomi$_j$ loves his$_{i/*j}$ story."

A further way in which syntax constrains the binding of *jibun* is that multiple occurrences of *jibun* in one clause must be bound to the same antecedent, as in (121) from Gunji 1983, 141.

(121) ケン$_i$ は 奈緒美$_j$ が 自分$_{i/j/k}$ に 自分$_{i/j/k}$ の 本
Ken$_i$ wa Naomi$_j$ ga jibun$_{i/j/k}$ ni jibun$_{i/j/k}$ no hon
Ken$_i$ TOP Naomi$_j$ NOM REFL$_{i/j/k}$ DAT REFL$_{i/j/k}$ ADN book
を 送った と 思って いる
wo okut-ta to omot-te iru
ACC send-PST COMP think-INF PROG

"Ken$_i$ thinks that Naomi $_j$has sent herself$_j$ her$_j$ book." OR "Ken$_i$ thinks that Naomi$_j$ has sent himself$_i$ his$_i$ book." OR "Ken$_i$ thinks that Naomi$_j$ has sent Z$_k$ Z's$_k$ book."

Motomura (2001, 2) uses (122) to show that split antecedents are not allowed:

(122) 崇$_i$ が 真理子$_j$ に 健司$_k$ が 自分$_{i/k/*i+j/*i+k}$
Takashi$_i$ ga Mariko$_j$ ni Kenji$_k$ ga jibun$_{i/k/*i+j/*i+k}$
Takashi$_i$ NOM Mariko$_j$ DAT Kenji$_k$ NOM REFL$_{i/k/*i+j/*i+k}$
を 推薦 した と 告げた
wo suisen shi-ta to tsuge-ta
ACC recommend do-PST COMP report-PST

"Takashi$_i$ reported to Mariko$_j$ that Kenji$_k$ recommended self$_{i/k/*i+j/*i+k}$."

Looking further, however, we find exceptions to some of the proposed syntactic conditions on antecedents for *jibun*. In particular, causatives and adversative passives provide exceptions to the subject antecedent condition, as in the examples in (123) from Gunji 1983, 145:

(123) a. 健$_i$ が 奈緒美$_j$ に 自分$_{i/j}$ を 批判
Ken$_i$ ga Naomi$_j$ ni jibun$_{i/j}$ wo hihan
Ken$_i$ NOM Naomi$_j$ DAT REFL$_{i/j}$ ACC criticize
させた
sa-se-ta
do-CAUS-PST

"Ken$_i$ made Naomi$_j$ criticize him$_i$/herself$_j$."

b. 健$_i$ が 奈緒美$_j$ に 自分$_{i/j}$ を 批判 された
Ken$_i$ ga Naomi$_j$ ni jibun$_{i/j}$ wo hihan sa-re-ta
Ken$_i$ NOM Naomi$_j$ DAT REFL$_{i/j}$ ACC criticize do-PASS-PST

"Ken$_i$ was adversely affected by Naomi's criticizing him$_i$/herself$_j$."

In both of these examples, *Naomi* is available as a possible antecedent of *jibun*, even though it is not a surface subject. Thus the subject antecedent condition must be generalized to include as possible antecedents NPs which are not surface subjects but are prominent at some other level of representation. Manning and Sag (1998, 43), using examples from a couple of languages including Japanese, show that "theories of grammar that define binding on surface phrase structure configurations or surface valence lists are unable to satisfactorily account for binding patterns." They propose using the argument structure (ARG-ST, a list of all valence elements) as the locus of binding constraints.

While representing the syntactic constraints in terms of a level such as argument structure goes some way towards accounting for the data, we also find that there are significant semantic and pragmatic factors at play. Katagiri (1991, 439) gives a coreference rule for *jibun* that is based on world view and semantics:

"The use of '[j]ibun' is based on the identity of the referent of '[j]ibun' to the semantic agent of an action or to the semantic experiencer of a mental state described in the sentence."

This helps to account for the correlation between perspective auxiliaries and *jibun* binding. He gives the following examples (p.430):

(124) 花子$_i$ は 太郎$_j$ が 自分$_i$ に 本 を 読んで
Hanako$_i$ wa Tarou$_j$ ga jibun$_i$ ni hon wo yon-de
Hanako$_i$ TOP Tarou$_j$ NOM REFL$_i$ DAT book ACC read-INF

くれた こと を 覚えて　　いる
kure-ta koto wo oboe-te　　iru
give-PST NMLZ ACC remember-INF PROG

"Hanako$_i$ remembered that Tarou$_j$ read a book for her$_i$."

(125)　*花子$_i$ は 自分$_i$ が 太郎$_j$ に 本 を 読んで
　　　**Hanako$_i$ wa jibun$_i$ ga Tarou$_j$ ni hon wo yon-de*
　　　Hanako$_i$ TOP REFL$_i$ NOM Tarou$_j$ DAT book ACC read-INF
　　　くれた こと を 覚えて　　いる
　　　kure-ta koto wo oboe-te　　iru
　　　give-PST NMLZ ACC remember-INF PROG

Intended: "Hanako$_i$ remembered that she$_i$ read a book for Tarou$_j$."

As intra-sentential binding of reflexives is optional, we decided to leave its computation to a grammar-external module, just as with the resolution of other pronouns and coreference resolution more generally. Nonetheless, we give the necessary information that can be accessed from the linguistic input, such that it is available for such a module.

Information for reflexive binding restrictions in **Jacy** is stated on the semantic and pragmatic level, interconnecting the information available on these levels. The reflexive introduces REL to the NONLOCAL structure, reflecting the fact that antecedent and reflexive do not have to be bound locally. The value of REL is the semantic index of the reflexive pronoun. First of all, this locates the binding conditions to the semantic index and not to a syntactic function, following the arguments given above. NONLOCAL is passed up in the trees, as they are built. Thus, the reflexive index is available for binding at any place in the tree. On the other hand, it is not possible to parse a second reflexive that inserts a different semantic index (see (121)). Thus, the restriction that multiple occurrences of *jibun* must be bound to the same index is met. Furthermore, this representation correctly disallows split antecedents. By passing up the NONLOCAL.REL, the MRS of a sentence with two occurrences of *jibun* shows the same index for both pronoun relations.[4]

On the pragmatic level, the reflexive pronoun sets EMPATHY to its own index. This accounts for the fact that binding to entities outside and inside the sentence is possible, if the speaker's empathy is focused on the binding entity. If other entities in a sentence set empathy restrictions, for example, the adversative passive, the reflexive binding

---

[4]In future work, this analysis should be refined to state the restriction in terms of ICONS constraints Song (2014) rather than simple identity between the indices of the different occurrences of *jibun*.

will also be affected by these restrictions. This is due to the fact that empathy can be set maximally to one index in a sentence. This helps account for the possible antecedents in the perspective auxiliary examples.

An external component for anaphoric binding will make use of the information given by the grammar:

- Constraints on animacy on the index of the reflexive, which can be combined with external ontological information to make sure it only refers back to animate entities;
- Constraints on speaker empathy, which can be input to reasoning about empathy in the discourse context to constrain possible antecedents for the reflexive;
- Shared indices between multiple reflexives in the same sentence which require them all to be bound by the same antecedent; and
- Linking of speaker, addressee, perspective (empathy) and honorification, which together are the basic information required from the linguistic side for an account of the situatedness of binding in a physical and social environment, as described by Katagiri (1991).

6.4 Nominalizers

Japanese has a small class of nouns, including こと *koto*, ため *tame* and もの *mono*, which have little semantic content of their own and obligatorily combine with some dependent (determiner, adnominal, adjective or sentence). The external syntactic function of the phrase headed by these nouns is that of a noun. We call these nouns nominalizers.[5]

Nominalizers cannot occur by themselves and need an obligatory argument (see (126), (127), (128) and (129)). Typically, nominalizers take a verb phrase and nominalize it (as does *koto* in (126)). Examples for those nominalizing nouns are: ほう *hou* "side", こと *koto* "thing", ため *tame* "purpose", かたち *katachi* "form" and の *no*.[6] Some of the nominalizers, such as *hou, koto, tame* and *katachi,* can also take a determiner (*sono hou*) or noun with the particle *no* (*kochira no hou ni* (126)). The nominalizer *no* allows only a verb phrase. We analyze these arguments as obligatory specifiers.

(126) こちら の ほう で 四 時 に 終わる こと は
kochira no hou de yo-ji ni owaru koto wa
1 ADN side LOC four-hour LOC end NMLZ TOP

---

[5]They are also known as 形式名詞 *keishiki meishi* "formal nouns".

[6]*no* is so bleached of meaning there is no good English translation.

できます　　　けども
deki-masu　　　kedomo
do.POT-AHON:+ SFP

"We could end at 4 o'clock." [Verbmobil]

(127) *ことは　いい　です
koto wa　ii　desu
NMLZ TOP good COP.AHON:+

Intended: "[some]thing is good"

(128) そのため　に　ちょっと スケジュール の　ほうを　調整
sono tame　ni　chotto　sukejuuru　no hou wo　chousei
that purpose LOC somehow schedule ADN side ACC order
させて　　いただきたい　　と　思いまして
sa-se-te　itadaki-tai　　to　omoi-mashi-te
do-CAUS-INF receive.SHON:—-want COMP think-AHON:+-INF

"For that purpose, I think I want to order my schedule somehow."
[Verbmobil]

(129) *ため　です
tame desu
purpose COP.AHON:+

Intended: "It was the purpose."

The structures these nominalizers occur in with verb phrases resemble relative clauses, but there are some differences:

- The phrase to the left of the nominalizer is obligatory, and therefore an argument of the nominalizer, as can be seen in (129).
- The nominalizer does not fill an argument position in the subcat frame of the verb, as can be seen in (126).

Nominalizers are organized in a type hierarchy of nominalizers (see Figure 53). All nominalizers inherit from the type *nom-lex*. This is a subtype of nouns, with its HEAD being a subtype of *noun_head*, which encodes the similarity of nominalizers to common nouns. The type *nom-lex* determines that the nominalizer subcategorizes for a specifier. Nominalizers that take a VP as their argument determine that the specifier's head is a *verb_head* and that the argument is obligatory, using cross-classification with the subcategorization hierarchy to *nom_sc*.

The MRS of a nominalization of a verb phrase (*nom-pred-lex*) contains the relation for the nominalizer (e.g., _koto_n_nom), and an underspecified determiner (udef_q). The verb relation is linked to the nominal predicate through a qeq in order to allow for scope ambiguities. The MRS can be seen in (130).

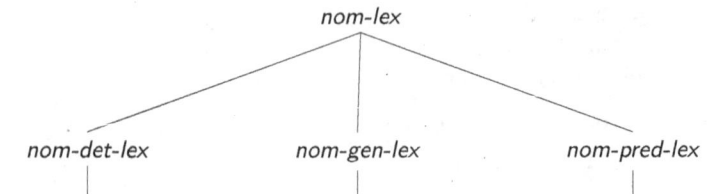

FIGURE 53 Type hierarchy of nominalizers

(130) a. 食べる こと
taberu NMLZ
eat   thing

"eating/to eat"

b. $\left\langle h_1, \left\{ \begin{array}{l} h_5\text{:\_taberu\_v\_1}(e_8, u_6, u_7), \\ h_9\text{:\_koto\_n\_nom}(x_4, h_{10}), \\ h_{11}\text{:udef\_q}(x_4, h_{13}, h_{12}) \end{array} \right\}, \right\rangle$
$\{h_{10} =_q h_5, h_{13} =_q h_9\}$

Nominalizers are typically used for some verbs that take verbal arguments, as in (131). In this case we do not directly link the verb *oyogu* "swim" to *suki* "like", the semantics are more like "I like the swimming thing".

(131) a. 泳ぐ の   が   好き だ
oyogu no   ga   suki da
swim NMLZ NOM like COP

"I like swimming."

b. $\left\langle h_1, \left\{ \begin{array}{l} h_3\text{:\_oyogu\_v}\left(e_5\left\{\text{TENSE } pres\right\}, i_4\right), \\ h_6\text{:\_no\_n\_nom}(x_7, h_8), \\ h_9\text{:udef\_q}(x_7, h_{10}, h_{11}) \\ h_{12}\text{:\_suki\_a\_1}\left(e_2\left\{\text{TENSE } pres\right\}, i_{13}, x_7\right) \end{array} \right\}, \right\rangle$
$\{h_{10} =_q h_6, h_8 =_q h_3\}$

6.5 Temporal Nouns

Temporal expressions are common in many genres. The Verbmobil domain of appointment scheduling requires precise analysis of various types of temporal expressions. (132) to (134) show some typical temporal expressions in Japanese, from the Verbmobil corpus.

Nouns used in temporal expressions can syntactically behave like ordinary nouns. An example is the word 日 *hi* "day" in (132).[7] We give specialized semantics to time expressions, due to their importance in the scheduling task in Verbmobil. For example, temporal nouns those that denote days of the week, such as 月曜日 *getsuyoubi* "Monday" and 火曜日 *kayoubi* "Tuesday" get a special semantic description dofw("_mon") and dofw("_tue"). In the lexical type hierarchy *day-lex*[8] has the subtypes *dofw-n-lex* (day of week), *dofm-n-lex* (day of month) and *mofy-n-lex* (month of year).

Another class contains the nouns that can modify a verb even without a dative particle such as 朝 *asa* "morning", 午後 *gogo* "afternoon", 一月 *ichigatsu* "January", or 三日 *mikka* "the third", and that belong to a type *temp_numeral-lex*, which is also a subtype of nouns.

(132) その 日 は いい です
 sono hi wa ii desu
 that day TOP good COP.AHON:+

 "That day is good."

(133) 六月 十 三 日 の 火曜日 から は いかが
 rokugatsu juu san nichi no kayoubi kara wa ikaga
 June ten three day ADN Tuesday from TOP how
 でしょう か
 deshou ka
 COP.AHON:+ Q

 "Would from Tuesday the 13th of June, in the afternoon, suit you?"

(134) 来週 の 水曜日 十 七 日 は どう
 raishuu no suiyoubi juu nana nichi wa dou
 next.week ADN Wednesday ten seven day TOP how
 です か
 desu ka
 COP.AHON:+ Q

 "How would next week Wednesday the 17th be?"

Temporal nouns that modify verbs directly are given an analysis that makes their semantics similar to that of nouns functioning as adverbial modifiers in combination with a post-position. This is achieved through a unary rule, licensed by this lexical type, which adds the semantics of an underspecified post-position: unspec_p. The MRSs given in (135) and

---

[7] Others are 週 *shuu* "week" and 時間 *jikan* "time/hour".
[8] This was a poor choice of name, as it is the supertype of both days and months.

(136) show how unspec_p parallels the predication of the post-position ni (_ni_p).

(135) a. 夜　に　行く
　　　　yoru ni iku
　　　　night LOC go

　　　　"I will go at night."

　　b. $\left\langle h_1, \left\{ \begin{array}{l} h_3\text{:\_yoru\_n\_5}(x_4), \\ h_5\text{:udef\_q}(x_4, h_6, h_7), \\ h_8\text{:\_ni\_p}(e_9 \{\text{TENSE } \textit{untensed}\}, e_2, x_4), \\ h_8\text{:\_iku\_v\_1}(e_2 \{\text{TENSE } \textit{pres}\}, u_{10}) \end{array} \right\}, \right.$
$\left. \{h_6 =_q h_3\} \right\rangle$

(136) a. 夜　行く
　　　　yoru iku
　　　　night go

　　　　"I will go at night."

　　b. $\left\langle h_1, \left\{ \begin{array}{l} h_3\text{:\_yoru\_n\_5}(x_4), \\ h_5\text{:udef\_q}(x_4, h_6, h_7), \\ h_8\text{:unspec\_p}(e_9 \{\text{TENSE } \textit{untensed}\}, e_2, x_4), \\ h_8\text{:\_iku\_v\_1}(e_2 \{\text{TENSE } \textit{pres}\}, u_{10}) \end{array} \right\}, \right.$
$\left. \{h_6 =_q h_3\} \right\rangle$

6.6 Noun Modification

6.6.1 Noun Modification by Post-Positional Phrases

Typically, Japanese nouns are modified by other noun phrases via the post-position の *no*, as in (137). This element inserts a relation to the MRS, which links the indices of the nouns via its argument structure: the external argument (the head) is ARG1 and the internal argument (the dependent) is ARG2. This behavior is the same for other post-positions (§ 7.5).

(137) a. 学生　の　本
　　　　gakusei no hon
　　　　student ADN book

　　　　"the student's book/the book of the student"

　　b. $\left\langle h_1, \left\{ \begin{array}{l} h_5\text{:\_gakusei\_n}(x_6 \{\text{PERS } 3\}), \\ h_7\text{:udef\_q}(x_6, h_9, h_8), \\ h_{10}\text{:\_no\_p}(e_{11} \{\text{TENSE } \textit{untensed}\}, x_4, x_6) \\ h_{10}\text{:\_hon\_n}(x_4), \\ h_{12}\text{:udef\_q}(x_4, h_{14}, h_{13}), \end{array} \right\}, \right.$
$\left. \{h_{14} =_q h_{10}, h_9 =_q h_5\} \right\rangle$

With direction nouns like 上 *ue* "above", 下 *shita* "under", 北 *kita* "north", and others there is the possibility of noun modification using から *kara* "from" or *yori* "than" より, as in (138).

(138) 大阪 は 東京 から 南 だ
 Osaka wa Tokyo kara minami da
 Osaka TOP Tokyo from South COP

 "Osaka is South of Tokyo (lit: South from Tokyo)"

The entry for this particle is of the same lexical type as the *no* entry, restricted to relational nouns (their head type being a subtype of *noun_head*).

6.6.2 Relative Clause Constructions

Noun phrases can be modified by predicates in the relative clause construction. Typically the verb will be in plain form (with no addressee honorification: § 9.1) as in (139).

(139) なかなか 空いて いる 時間 が ありません
 nakanaka ai-te iru jikan ga ari-mase-n
 more.and.more open-INF PROG time NOM exist-AHON:+-NEG
 ので
 node
 SFP

 "There is less and less free time." [Verbmobil Corpus]

The range of possible connections between head nouns and relative clauses in Japanese is similar to that found with topics (see § 7.5.3): The noun that is modified by the relative clause can fill a subject position in the argument structure of the verb (see (140)), a complement position (see (141)), or no position at all (see (142)). Sirai and Gunji (1998, 17) designate these as "internal relationship" and "external relationship".

(140) 本 を 読んだ 人
 hon wo yon-da hito
 book ACC read-PST person

 "the person that read the book"

(141) 人 が 読んだ 本
 hito ga yon-da hon
 person NOM read-PST book

 "the book that a person read"

(142) 魚　　を　焼く　匂い
　　　 sakana wo yaku ni'oi
　　　 fish   ACC grill smell

"the smell of grilling fish"

    This ambiguity is systematic and rarely if ever completely resolve by syntactic constraints. The decision can in many cases be made by selectional restrictions and world knowledge, which are currently not treated within **Jacy**. One solution is to not connect the head noun to the argument structure of any element within relative clause, thus leaving the decision to further NLP components that have access to world knowledge and selectional restrictions. Relative clauses are then seen as simple adjuncts to the head noun in all cases. This treatment is consistent with the tradition of underspecification, as for example scope representation in MRS. Another approach is to model the ambiguity, even though it can rarely be resolved. We can then select the best interpretation when treebanking and use the results for stochastic disambiguation.

    Sirai and Gunji (1998) give an approach for the relative clauses with internal relationship to the head noun which includes a lexical rule that builds up a SLASH list with subcategorized arguments of the head verb, such that elements on the SLASH list can be bound by the head noun. We opt for a more direct approach, circumventing the building of SLASH lists, as we did for the treatment of zero pronouns (see § 4.3.3). In order to allow for disambiguation by treebanking, we constructed four possibilities for relative sentence constructions. All relative clause rules are subtypes of head-final intersective modification rules.

    The *relative-clause-rule* views the relative clause as a simple modifier of the head noun and does not give the head noun any role in the verb's argument structure. Using C-CONT, it adds a distinctive predication (rel_p) to the MRS that takes the verbal event and the head noun as its arguments and thus links the structures of the relative clause and the head noun. The first daughter of the rule (the relative clause) is restricted to have the feature [POSTHEAD *rels*] in its HEAD. The POSTHEAD feature is determined by the verbal ending, such that plain endings like *ru* can undergo relative clause constructions, while the *te* ending, for example, is compatible instead with the coordinated sentence construction. (143) shows the MRS for (140) with the *relative-clause-rule* applied. It can be seen that the verbal relation _yomu_v_1 contains a zero pronoun i_{10} as its first semantic argument. *hito* is linked by the rel_p relation, giving analogous semantics to the topic reading of (144).

(143) $h_1, \left\{ \begin{array}{l} h_5\text{:udef\_q}(x_6 \{\text{PERS } 3\}, h_7, h_8), \\ h_9\text{:\_hon\_n}(x_6), \\ h_{10}\text{:\_yomu\_v\_1}(e_{12}\{\text{TENSE } past\}, i_{11}, x_6), \\ h_{13}\text{:udef\_q}(x_4, h_{14}, h_{15}), \\ h_{16}\text{:\_hito\_n}(x_4), \\ h_{10}\text{:rel\_p}(e_{17}\{\text{TENSE } untensed\}, e_{12}, x_4) \end{array} \right\},$
$\{h_7 =_q h_9, h_{14} =_q h_{16}\}$

(144) 人　　は　本　を　読んだ
hito　wa　hon　wo　yon-da
person TOP book ACC read-PST

"People read a book."

The *rel-cl-sbj-gap-rule* takes the index of the head noun and identifies it with the index of the subject of the highest verb in the relative clause. (145) shows the MRS for (140) with the subject gap reading. It can be seen that the verbal relation _yomu_v_1 contains the index of _hito_n_rel as its first argument. Because the subject reading is more common, (145) will be ranked higher than (143).[9]

(145) $h_1, \left\{ \begin{array}{l} h_5\text{:udef\_q}(x_6 \{\text{PERS } 3\}, h_7, h_8), \\ h_9\text{:\_hon\_n}(x_6), \\ h_{10}\text{:\_yomu\_v\_1}(e_{11}\{\text{TENSE } past\}, x_4, x_6), \\ h_{12}\text{:udef\_q}(x_4, h_{13}, h_{14}), \\ h_{10}\text{:\_hito\_n}(x_4), \end{array} \right\},$
$\{h_7 =_q h_9, h_{13} =_q h_{10}\}$

The *rel-cl-obj1-gap-rule* and the *rel-cl-obj2-gap-rule* do the same thing for the direct and indirect objects. As a result, **Jacy** can link head nouns to the subject, first or second complements of the highest verb in a relative clause, or note that the linking is an underspecified non-argument relation. This makes argument linking available through statistical parse selection, but avoids explicit enumeration of the lower-frequency, vaguer non-argument possibilities.[10]

One final detail of relative clause constructions in Japanese is that the nominative case inside of relative clauses can be changed to adnominal, as in (146). In this case, a lexical rule is applied to the verbal stem that changes the case of the subcategorized subject noun to *adn-case* and restricts the verb to only head relative clauses by setting the head

---

[9] Baldwin (2004) found that of 5,143 relative clause instances in the EDR corpus the subject gap interpretation is correct in 64.0% of cases.

[10] This is not a fully general account for argument linking as it does not accommodate long-distance dependency examples. These, however, are quite rare in corpus data.

feature MAIN-PRD to − on the verb. The distribution of these relative clause types is quite skewed: subject gap is the most common (941 instances), followed by non-gapped (576). Object relatives are rare — we find only 74 direct object relatives and no and indirect object relatives in our corpus.

(146) 田中 の 食べた ご飯
      Tanaka no tabe-ta gohan
      Tanaka ADN eat-PST rice

      "The rice that Tanaka *ate*."

6.6.3 Pre-Nominal Adjectives

As noted in § 5.2.7, there are two major types of inflecting adjectives in Japanese: *i*-adjectives and *na*-adjectives. When these appear as noun modifiers, we analyze them as heading relative clauses. In the case of *i*-adjectives, the adjective itself is the head of the relative clause. In the case of *na*-adjectives, the formative *na*, analyzed as a copula, is the head.[11] These two types of adjectives, in relative clauses and main clauses, are illustrated in (147)–(150). In either case, the copula (*na* or *da*) is treated as semantically empty, so that the semantic representations for the two adjective types are parallel.

(147) いい 時間 だ と 思います
      ii jikan da to omoi-masu
      good time COP COMP think-AHON:+

      "I think this is a good time. (lit: I think this is a time which is good.)" [Verbmobil]

(148) 時間 が いい
      jikan ga ii
      time NOM good

      "The time is good." [Verbmobil]

(149) きれい な ホテル に 泊まって みたい
      kirei na hoteru ni tomat-te mi-tai
      beautiful COP hotel LOC stay-INF try-want

      "I want to try to stay in a pretty hotel." [Verbmobil]

(150) ホテル が きれい *(だ)
      *hoteru ga kirei *(da)*
      hotel NOM pretty COP

      "The hotel is pretty."

---

[11]For the details of the analysis of *na*, see § 5.1.4.

The predicative adjective modification of nouns as in (147) and (148) is treated as a relative sentence construction, just as described in § 6.6.2. In both cases there is ambiguity between the adjunctive relative clause and the subject-gap relative clause constructions.

Just like any other relative clause in Japanese, those headed by adjectives are tensed, i.e., necessarily marked as past or non-past:

(151) きれい だった 人
 kirei dat-ta hito
 pretty COP-PST person

 "The person who was pretty."

(152) きれい な 人
 kirei na hito
 pretty COP.NONPST person

 "The person who is pretty."

This contrasts with noun-modifying adjectives in English, which are not marked for tense. Thus, there is no exact Japanese translation of the English phrases such as *the pretty person*, though normally the non-past tense relative clause is used to translate it.

6.7 Numeral Classifiers[12]

Much attention has been paid to the semantic aspects of Japanese numeral classifiers, and in particular, the semantic constraints which govern which classifiers cooccur with which nouns (Matsumoto, 1993; Bond and Paik, 2000). A more neglected aspect of this linguistic phenomenon is the syntax of numeral classifiers: How they combine with number names to create numeral classifier phrases, how they modify head nouns, and how they can occur as stand-alone NPs.

Paik and Bond (2002) divide Japanese numeral classifiers into five major classes: *sortal*, *event*, *mensural*, *group* and *taxonomic*, and several subclasses. The classes and subclasses can be differentiated according to the semantic relationship between the classifiers and the nouns they modify, on two levels: First, what properties of the modified noun motivate the choice of the classifier, and second what properties the classifiers predicate of the nouns. As we are concerned here with the syntax and compositional semantics of numeral classifiers, we will focus only on the latter. Sortal classifiers, (*kind*, *shape*, and *complement* classifiers) serve to individuate the nouns they modify. Event classifiers quantify events, characteristically modifying verbs rather than nouns.

---

[12]This section is an extended version of Bender and Siegel (2004).

Mensural classifiers measure some property of the entity denoted by the noun they modify (e.g., its length). NPs containing group classifiers denote a group or set of individuals belonging to the type denoted by the noun. Finally, taxonomic classifiers force a kind or species reading on an NP.

Internally, Japanese numeral classifier expressions consist of a number name followed by a numeral classifier (153), (154), and (155). In this, they resemble some date expressions (156):[13]

(153) 十 枚
juu mai
ten NUMCL
"ten sheets"

(154) 十 円
juu en
ten NUMCL:yen
"ten yen"

(155) 十 ヶ月
juu kagetsu
ten NUMCL:month
"ten months"

(156) 十 月
juu gatsu
ten month
"October"

In fact, both numeral classifiers and date expressions are tagged as numeral classifiers by the morphological analyzer **ChaSen** (Asahara and Matsumoto, 2000). However, date expressions do not have the same combinatoric potential (syntactic or semantic) as numeral classifiers. We thus give date expressions a distinct analysis.

Externally, numeral classifier phrases (NumClPs) appear in at least four different contexts: alone, as anaphoric NPs (157); preceding a head noun, linked by the particle の *no* (158); immediately following a head noun (159); and 'floated', right after the associated noun's case particle or right in front of the verb (160). These constructions are distinguished pragmatically (Downing, 1996).[14]

---

[13] Note that many of the time units are ambiguous with date expressions, although some, like the one for months shown in (155), are distinguished.

[14] Downing also notes NumClPs following the head noun with an intervening *no*. As this rare construction did not appear in our data, we have not incorporated it into our account.

(157) 二 匹   を 飼う
　　　 ni hiki wo kau
　　　 two NUMCL ACC raise

"I am raising two (small animals)."

(158) 二 匹   の 猫   を 飼う
　　　 ni hiki no neko wo kau
　　　 two NUMCL ADN cat ACC raise

"I am raising two cats."

(159) 猫   二 匹   を 飼う
　　　 neko ni hiki wo kau
　　　 cat two NUMCL ACC raise

"I am raising two cats."

(160) 猫   を (二 匹)   家   で (二 匹)   を 飼う
　　　 neko wo (ni hiki) ie de (ni hiki) wo kau
　　　 cat ACC (two NUMCL) house LOC (two NUMCL) ACC raise

"I am raising two cats in my house."

NumClPs can be modified by elements such as *yaku* 'approximately' (in front of the number name) or *mo* 'even' (after the floated numeral classifiers).

The above examples illustrate the possible uses of NumClPs with a sortal numeral classifier, but mensural numeral classifiers can also appear both as modifiers (161) and as NPs in their own right (162):

(161) 二 キロ の りんご を 買った
　　　 ni kiro no ringo wo kat-ta
　　　 two NUMCL:kg ADN apple ACC buy-PST

"I bought two kilograms of apples."

(162) 二 キロ を 買った
　　　 ni kiro wo kat-ta
　　　 two NUMCL:kg ACC buy-PST

"I bought two kilograms."

NumClPs serving as NPs can also appear as modifiers of other nouns:

(163) 三 人   の 出会い は 80 年 春
　　　 san nin no deai wa 80 nen haru
　　　 three NUMCL ADN meeting TOP 80 year spring

"The three's meeting was in the spring of 80."

(164) 一　キロ　　　の　値段　は　百　　　円
　　　 ichi kiro　　*no nedan wa hyaku en*
　　　 one NUMCL:kg ADN price TOP hundred NUMCL:yen
　　　 です
　　　 desu
　　　 COP.AHON:+

"The price of/for 1 kg is 100 yen."

As a result, tokens following the syntactic pattern of (158) and (161) are systematically ambiguous, although the non-anaphoric reading tends to be preferred.

Certain mensural classifiers can be followed by the word 半 *han* "half":

(165) 二　キロ　　　半
　　　 ni kiro　　*han*
　　　 two NUMCL:kg half

"two and a half kilograms"

In order to build their semantic representations compositionally, we make the numeral classifier (here, *kiro*) the head of the whole expression, and *ni* and *han* its dependents. *Kiro* can then orchestrate the semantic composition of the two dependents as well as the composition of the whole expression with the noun it modifies.

Although they aren't tagged as numeral classifiers by **ChaSen**, we extended our analysis of mensural classifiers to certain elements that appear in front of numbers, namely currency symbols (such as $), and prefixes like *No.* "number" in (166).

(166) 口座　　　　　No.　　 1 2 3 4　号
　　　 kouza　　*No.*　　*1234*　　*gou*
　　　 account number 1234　　NUMCL:number

"account number 1234"

We also found that number names can sometimes occur without numeral classifiers, either as modifiers of nouns or as anaphora:

(167) (口座)　　 1 2 3 4　を　閉じ　たい
　　　 (kouza)　　*1234*　　*wo toji-tai*
　　　 (account) 1234　　ACC close-want

"I want to close (account) 1234."

We used **ChaSen** to segment and tag 10,000 paragraphs of the Mainichi Shinbun 2002 corpus. Of the resulting 490,202 words, 11,515

(2.35%) were tagged as numeral classifiers. 4,543 of those were potentially time/date expressions, leaving 6,972 unambiguously numeral classifiers, or 1.42% of the words. 203 orthographically distinct numeral classifiers occur in the corpus. The most frequent is *nin* (the numeral classifier for people) which occurs 1,675 times. We sampled 100 sentences tagged as containing numeral classifiers to examine the distribution of the constructions outlined. These sentences contained a total of 159 numeral classifier phrases and the vast majority (128) were stand-alone NPs. This contrasts with a study of 500 examples from modern works of fiction and spoken texts, where most of the occurrences are not anaphoric (Downing, 1996). Furthermore, while our sample contains no examples of the floated variety, Downing's contains 96. The discrepancy probably arises because Downing only included sortal numeral classifiers, and not any other type. Another possible contributing factor is the effect of genre.

In the remainder of this section, we present our analysis of numeral classifiers. We begin with the semantic representations (described in § 6.7.1) we posit and then continue to a description of the grammar entities which interact in order to produce these representations (while ruling out ungrammatical combinations) in § 6.7.2.

6.7.1 Semantic Representations

One of our main goals in implementing an analysis of numeral classifiers is to compositionally construct semantic representations, and in particular, Minimal Recursion Semantics (MRS) representations. The representation we build for (158) and (159) is as in (168).

(168) $\left\langle h_1, \left\{ \begin{array}{l} h_3\text{:card}\left(e_5\left\{\text{TENSE }\textit{tense}\right\}, x_4\left\{\text{PERS }\textit{3}\right\}, 2\right), \\ h_6\text{:udef\_q}(x_4, h_7, h_8), \\ h_3\text{:\_neko\_n}(x_4), \\ h_9\text{:\_kau\_v\_2}\left(e_2\left\{\text{TENSE }\textit{pres}\right\}, i_{10}, x_4\right) \end{array} \right\} \right\rangle$
$\{h_7 =_q h_3\}$

This can be read as follows: A relation of raising holds between i_{10} (the unexpressed subject), and x_4. x_4 denotes a cat entity (neko_n), and is bound by an underspecified quantifier (as there is no explicit determiner). x_4 is also an argument of a card (short for cardinal relation), whose other argument is the constant value 2, meaning that there are in fact two cats being referred to. For anaphoric numeral classifiers, the representation contains an underspecified generic_entity, which can be resolved in further processing to a specific relation. Thus for (157) **Jacy** produces the representation in (169), which differs from (168) only in having generic_entity in place of neko_n.[15]

(169) $h_1, \left\langle \left\{ \begin{array}{l} h_3\text{:udef\_q}(x_4, h_5, h_6), \\ h_7\text{:generic\_entity}(x_4), \\ h_7\text{:card}\left(e_8\left\{\text{TENSE } tense\right\}, x_4\left\{\text{PERS } 3\right\}, 2\right), \\ h_9\text{:\_kau\_v\_2}\left(e_2\left\{\text{TENSE } pres\right\}, i_{10}, x_4\right) \end{array} \right\}, \right\rangle$
$\{h_5 =_q h_7\}$

Mensural classifiers have somewhat more elaborated semantic representations, which we treat as similar to English measure NPs (Flickinger and Bond, 2003). On this analysis, the NumClP denotes the extent of some dimension or property of the modified N. This dimension or property is represented with an underspecified relation (unspec_adj), and a degree relates the measured amount to the underspecified adjective relation. The underspecified adjective relation modifies the N in the usual way. This is illustrated in (170), which is the semantic representation assigned to (161).

(170) $h_1, \left\langle \left\{ \begin{array}{l} h_3\text{:card}\left(e_5\left\{\text{TENSE } tense\right\}, x_4, 2\right), \\ h_6\text{:udef\_q}(x_4, h_7, h_8), \\ h_3\text{:\_kiro\_n\_3}(x_4), \\ h_9\text{:degree}\begin{pmatrix} e_{11}\left\{\text{TENSE } tense\right\}, \\ e_{10}\left\{\text{TENSE } tense\right\}, \\ x_4 \end{pmatrix}, \\ h_9\text{:unspec\_adj}\left(e_{10}, x_{12}\left\{\text{PERS } 3\right\}\right), \\ h_{13}\text{:udef\_q}(x_{12}, h_{14}, h_{15}), \\ h_9\text{:\_ringo\_n\_1}(x_{12}), \\ h_{16}\text{:\_kau\_v\_1}\left(e_2\left\{\text{TENSE } past\right\}, i_{17}, x_{12}\right) \end{array} \right\}, \right\rangle$
$\{h_7 =_q h_3, h_{14} =_q h_9\}$

When mensural NumClPs are used anaphorically (162), the element modified by the unspec_adj is an underspecified noun relation (generic_entity), analogously to the case of sortal NumClPs used anaphorically, as in (171):

---

[15] It also differs in the order of the predications, but this is never interpreted as meaningful and is only an artifact of the composition process.

NOMINAL STRUCTURES / 149

(171) h_1, $\left\langle \left\{ \begin{array}{l} h_3\text{:udef\_q}(x_4, h_5, h_6), \\ h_7\text{:generic\_entity}(x_4), \\ h_8\text{:card}(e_{10}\{\text{TENSE } tense\}, x_9, 2), \\ h_{11}\text{:udef\_q}(x_9, h_{12}, h_{13}), \\ h_8\text{:\_kiro\_n\_3}(x_9), \\ h_7\text{:degree}\left(\begin{array}{l} e_{15}\{\text{TENSE } tense\}, \\ e_{14}\{\text{TENSE } tense\}, \\ x_9 \end{array} \right), \\ h_7\text{:unspec\_adj}(e_{14}, x_4), \\ h_{16}\text{:\_kau\_v\_1}(e_2\{\text{TENSE } past\}, i_{17}, x_4) \end{array} \right\} \right\rangle$,

$\{h_5 =_q h_7\}$

6.7.2 The Analysis

Having presented our target semantic representations, we now turn to a description of the analysis that produces them. It consists of:

- A lexical type hierarchy cross-classifying numeral classifiers along three dimensions (Figure 54).
- A pair of lexical rules for verb-adjacent floated numeral classifiers
- A special lexical entry for *no* for linking NumClPs with nouns.
- A unary-branching phrase structure rules for promoting NumClPs to nominal constituents.

6.7.2.1 Lexical Types

Figure 54 shows the lexical types for numeral classifiers, which are cross-classified along three dimensions:

1. Their semantic relationship to the modified noun (*individuating* or *mensural*)
2. Their modificational possibilities (NPs or PPs: *anymod*; NPs: *noun-mod*)
3. Their relationship to the number name (number name precedes: *spr-only*, number name precedes but may take some modifiers (such as 半 *han* "half", 強 *kyou* "a bit more" or 弱 *jaku* "a bit less"): *spr-obj* number name follows: *obj-only*).

Not all the possibilities in this space are instantiated in the grammar. For example, we don't yet provide for sortal classifiers which can take *han*. We leave such extensions to future work for now.

The constraint in Figure 55 ensures that all numeral classifiers have the head type *num-cl_head*, as required by the unary phrase structure rule discussed below. Furthermore, it identifies two key pieces of semantic information made available for further composition, the INDEX and

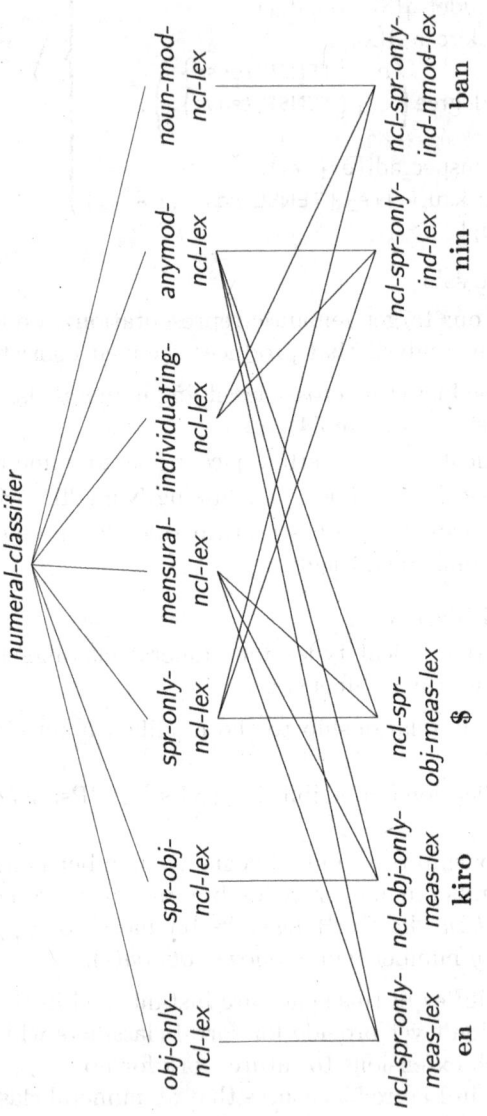

FIGURE 54 Type hierarchy under *numeral-classifier*

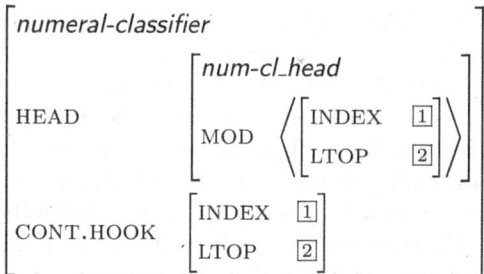

FIGURE 55 Constraints on *numeral-classifier*

LTOP (local top handle) of the modified element with the numeral classifier's own INDEX and LTOP, as these are intersective modifiers (Bender et al., 2002). The constraints on the type *num-cl_head* (not shown here) ensure that numeral classifiers can modify only saturated NPs or PPs (i.e., NPs marked with a case post-position *wo* or *ga*), and that they only combine via intersective head-modifier rules.

The constraints on the types *spr-only-num-cl-lex*, *obj-only-num-cl-lex* and *spr-obj-num-cl-lex* account for the position of the numeral classifier with respect to the number name and for the potential presence of *han*. Both the number name (a phrase of head type *int_head*) and *han* (given the distinguished head value *han_head*) are treated as dependents of the numeral classifier expression, but variously as specifiers or complements according to the type. In the **Jacy** grammar, specifiers immediately precede their heads, while complements are not required to do so and can even follow their heads (in rare cases; see § 3.3). Given all this, in the ordinary case (*spr-only-num-cl-lex*), we treat the number name as the specifier of the numeral classifier. The other two cases involve numeral classifiers taking complements: with no specifier, in the case of pre-number unit expressions like the symbol $ (*obj-only-num-cl-lex*) and both a number-name specifier and the complement *han* in the case of unit expressions appearing with *han* (*spr-obj-num-cl-lex*).[16] Finally, the type *spr-obj-num-cl-lex* does some semantic work as well, providing the plus_rel which relates the value of the number name to a cardinal relation with the value of 0.5 contributed by *han*, and identifying the ARG1 of the plus_rel with the XARG of the SPR and COMPS so that they will all share an index argument (eventually the index of the modified noun for sortal classifiers and of the measure noun relation for

---

[16]Because numeral classifiers are analyzed as taking posthead complements in these two cases, the head type *num-cl_head* is a subtype of *init_head*, which contrasts with *final_head*. These types are used by the head-complement rules to determine the order of the head and complements.

mensural classifiers). The constraints which implement these aspects of our analysis are sketched in Figure 56.

In the second dimension of the cross-classification, *anymod-num-cl-lex* and *noun-mod-num-cl-lex* constrain what the numeral classifier may modify, via the MOD value. When numeral classifiers appear in front of the head noun, they are linked to it with *no*, which mediates the modifier-modifiee relationship. However, numeral classifiers can appear after the noun (159), modifying it directly. Some numeral classifiers can also 'float' outside the NP, either immediately after the case postposition or to the position in front of the verb (160).[17]

We handle the former type by allowing most numeral classifiers to appear as post-head modifiers of PPs. Thus *noun-mod-num-cl-lex* further constrains the HEAD value of the element on the MOD list to be *noun_head*, but *anymod-num-cl-lex* leaves it as inherited (*noun-or-case-p_head*). This type does, however, constrain the modifier to show up after the head ([POSTHEAD *right*]), and further constrains the modified head to be [NUCL *nucl_plus*], in order to rule out vacuous attachment ambiguities between numeral classifiers attaching to the right and other modifiers appearing to the left of the NP. These constraints are illustrated in Figure 57.

The final dimension of the classification captures the semantic differences between sortal and mensural numeral classifiers. The sortal numeral classifiers contribute no semantic content of their own.[18] They are therefore constrained to have empty RELS and HCONS lists, as shown in Figure 58.

In contrast, mensural numeral classifiers contribute quite a bit of semantic information, and therefore have quite rich RELS and HCONS values. As shown in Figure 59, the *noun-relation* is identified with the lexical key relation value (LKEYS.KEYREL) so that specific lexical entries

---

[17]Those that can't include expressions like *gou* in (i), cf. (ii):

(i) 口座　　1 2 3 4 号　　を　閉じたい
　　kouza　　1234　　gou　　wo　toji-tai
　　account 1234　　　NUMCL ACC close-want

"I want to close account number 1234."

(ii) *口座　を　1 2 3 4 号　　閉じたい
　　kouza wo　1234　　gou　toji-tai
　　account ACC 1234　　NUMCL close-want

Intended: "I want to close account number 1234."

[18]The individuating function they serve we take to be implicit in the linkage they provide between the **card_rel** and the noun relation. Because they can specify the referent, some linguists prefer to give them some representation in the semantics, e.g., (Gunji, 2005).

$$\begin{bmatrix} \textit{spr-only-num-cl-lex} \\ \text{VAL} \begin{bmatrix} \text{SUBJ} & \textit{null} \\ \text{OBJ} & \textit{null} \\ \text{SPR} & \langle [\text{HEAD} \quad \textit{int\_head}] \rangle \end{bmatrix} \end{bmatrix}$$

$$\begin{bmatrix} \textit{obj-only-num-cl-lex} \\ \text{VAL} \begin{bmatrix} \text{SUBJ} & \textit{null} \\ \text{OBJ} & \langle [\text{HEAD} \quad \textit{int\_head}] \rangle \\ \text{SPR} & \textit{null} \end{bmatrix} \end{bmatrix}$$

$$\begin{bmatrix} \textit{spr-obj-num-cl-lex} \\ \text{VAL} \begin{bmatrix} \text{SUBJ} & \textit{null} \\ \text{OBJ} & \begin{bmatrix} \text{HEAD} & \textit{han\_head} \\ \text{HOOK} & \begin{bmatrix} \text{LTOP} & \boxed{1} \\ \text{XARG} & \boxed{2} \end{bmatrix} \end{bmatrix} \\ \text{SPR} & \begin{bmatrix} \text{HEAD} & \textit{int\_head} \\ \text{HOOK} & \begin{bmatrix} \text{LTOP} & \boxed{3} \\ \text{XARG} & \boxed{2} \end{bmatrix} \end{bmatrix} \end{bmatrix} \\ \text{CONT.RELS} \left\langle ! \begin{bmatrix} \text{PRED} & \textit{plus-relation} \\ \text{ARG1} & \boxed{2} \\ \text{ARG2} & \boxed{3} \\ \text{ARG3} & \boxed{1} \end{bmatrix} ! \right\rangle \end{bmatrix}$$

FIGURE 56 Constraints related to the order of numeral classifiers and number names

$$\begin{bmatrix} \textit{noun-mod-num-cl-lex} \\ \text{MOD} \quad \langle \begin{bmatrix} \text{HEAD} & \textit{noun\_head} \end{bmatrix} \rangle \end{bmatrix}$$

$$\begin{bmatrix} \textit{anymod-num-cl-lex} \\ \text{HEAD} \begin{bmatrix} \text{MOD} & \langle \begin{bmatrix} \text{LOCAL.NUCL} & \textit{nucl\_plus} \end{bmatrix} \rangle \\ \text{POSTHEAD} & \textit{right} \end{bmatrix} \end{bmatrix}$$

FIGURE 57 Constraints on MOD values for numeral classifiers

$$\begin{bmatrix} \textit{individuating-num-cl-lex} \\ \text{CONT} \begin{bmatrix} \text{RELS} & \langle ! \ ! \rangle \\ \text{HCONS} & \langle ! \ ! \rangle \end{bmatrix} \end{bmatrix}$$

FIGURE 58 Constraints restricting sortal classifiers to being semantically empty

of this type can easily further specify it (e.g., *kiro* constraints its PRED to be kiro_n).

The type also makes reference to the HOOK value so that the INDEX and LTOP (also the INDEX and LTOP of the modified noun, see (55)) can be identified with the appropriate values inside the RELS list. The length of the RELS list is left unbounded, because some mensural classifiers also inherit from *spr-obj-num-cl-lex*, and therefore must be able to add the plus_rel to the list.

The types in the bottom part of the hierarchy in Figure 54 join the dimensions of classification. They also do a little semantic work, making the INDEX and LTOP of the modified noun available to their number name argument, and, in the case of subtypes of *mensural-num-cl-lex*, they constrain the final length of the RELS list, as appropriate.

6.7.2.2 Lexical Rules

While numeral classifiers that have 'floated' directly to the right of a PP can be handled via the constraints on lexical types discussed above, those that appear instead adjacent to the verb require different treatment: Because the case-marking post-positions raise the INDEX value of their complement NP, in either case, the MOD's INDEX will be the same. NumClPs that appear just before the verb (and not adjacent to the PP they modify semantically) need to look elsewhere in their MOD's feature structure to find the relevant INDEX value.

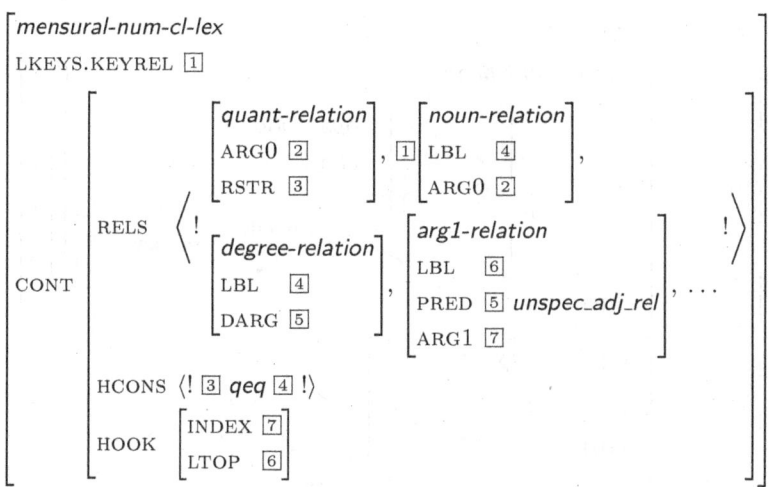

FIGURE 59 Constraints implementing the semantic contribution of mensural classifiers

Specifically, we model two different types of verb-adjacent floated NumClPs: One that provides information about the verb's subject, as in (172), and one that provides information about the verb's complement, as in (173).

(172) 友達 が 外 で 3 人 待って
 tomodachi ga soto de san nin mat-te
 friend NOM outside LOC three NUMCL wait-INF
 います
 i-masu
 PROG-AHON:+

 "Three friends are waiting for me outside."

(173) 友達 を 外 で 3 人 待って
 tomodachi wo soto de san nin mat-te
 friend ACC outside LOC three NUMCL wait-INF
 います
 i-masu
 PROG-AHON:+

 "I am waiting for three friends outside."

We handle these via two lexical rules which take a numeral classifier and turn it into a type that modifies the verb, but semantically combines with either the verbal external argument or the first complement:

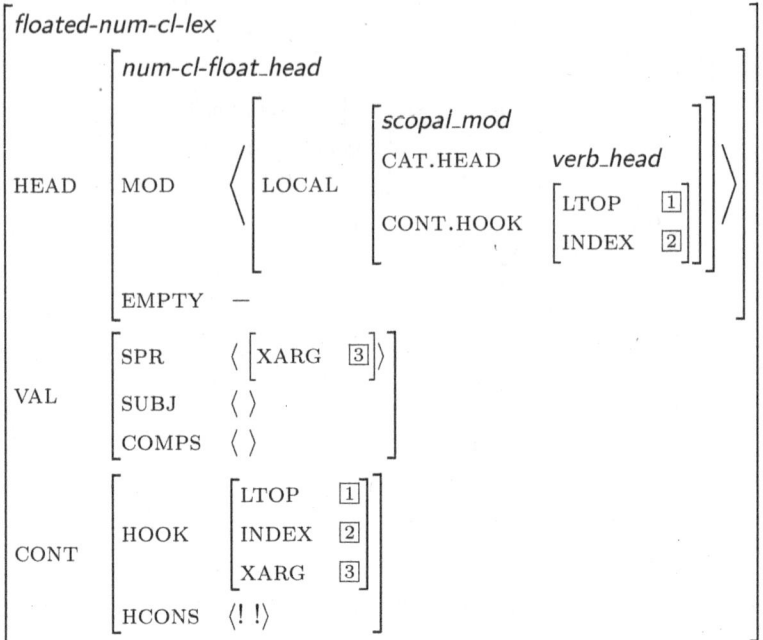

FIGURE 60 Constraints on floated numeral classifiers

numeral-classifier-sbj-float and *numeral-classifier-obj-float*. Because the floated NumClPs appear directly adjacent to the verb, the relevant arguments are still unsaturated (available on the SUBJ or COMPS lists). For subject-modifying floated numeral classifiers, this is not critical: The relevant information is available through the verb's XARG. For complement-modifying numeral classifiers, no such pointer is available. In this case, the relevant INDEX value is instead accessed through the verb's uncanceled COMPS list.[19]

The mother of these two lexical rules is of type *floated-num-cl-lex*, which is constrained as shown in Figure 60. This type identifies the XARG of its specifier (the number) with its own XARG. This type is supertype to subject- and object-modifying types.

The subtypes are shown in Figure 61. *floated-ind-sbj-num-cl-lex*, the type for subject-modifying floated numeral classifiers identifies the XARG of the modified verb with its specifier's XARG. *floated-ind-obj-num-cl-lex*, the type for complement-modifying floated numeral classifiers identifies the INDEX of the first argument of the modified verb with

---

[19] This is a case where the constraints in **Jacy** are not consistent with the MRS algebra proposed in Copestake et al. 2001.

$$\begin{bmatrix} \textit{floated-ind-sbj-num-cl-lex} \\ \text{MOD} \quad \langle [\text{XARG} \quad \boxed{1}\textit{full\_ref-ind}] \rangle \\ \text{VAL} \quad [\text{SPR} \quad \langle [\text{XARG} \quad \boxed{1}] \rangle] \end{bmatrix}$$

$$\begin{bmatrix} \textit{floated-ind-obj-num-cl-lex} \\ \text{MOD} \quad \langle [\text{VAL.COMPS} \quad \langle [\text{INDEX} \quad \boxed{1}\textit{full\_ref-ind}] \rangle] \rangle \\ \text{VAL} \quad [\text{SPR} \quad \langle [\text{XARG} \quad \boxed{x}] \rangle] \end{bmatrix}$$

FIGURE 61 Subtypes for subject and complement modifying floated quantifiers

its specifier's XARG. Both types constrain the relevant argument of the verb to be overtly expressed (via the type of its INDEX).

In order to prevent spurious ambiguity, we wish to keep the floated numeral classifiers from serving as the daughter of the *nominal-num-cl-rule* (discussed in § 6.7.2.5). We achieve this with the feature EMPTY: The *nominal-num-cl-rule* requires its argument to be [EMPTY +], while *num-cl-float_head* is [EMPTY −]. The type for the special *no* that is used in the case of numeral classifiers modifying the counted noun also requires its complement to be [EMPTY +].

The MRS for sentences with floated numeral classifiers reflect the fact that these modify verbs but count their arguments, as shown in (174), the MRS for (172).

(174) $\quad h_1, \left\langle \left\{ \begin{array}{l} h_3{:}\text{udef\_q}(x_4 \{\text{PERS } 3\}, h_5, h_6), \\ h_7{:}\_\text{tomodachi\_n}(x_4), \\ h_8{:}\text{def\_q}(x_9, h_{10}, h_{11}), \\ h_{12}{:}\_\text{soto\_n}(x_9), \\ h_{13}{:}\_\text{de\_p}\begin{pmatrix} e_{14} \{\text{TENSE } \textit{untensed}\}, \\ e_2 \{\text{TENSE } \textit{pres}\}, \\ x_9 \end{pmatrix}, \\ h_{13}{:}\text{card}(e_{15} \{\text{TENSE } \textit{tense}\}, x_4, 3), \\ h_{13}{:}\_\text{matsu\_v}(e_2, x_4, i_{16}) \end{array} \right\}, \right\rangle$
$\quad \{h_5 =_q h_7, h_{10} =_q h_{12}\}$

6.7.2.3 Special Types

Japanese has a special numeral classifier つ *tsu*, which can only be used with the native numerals from one to nine. **ChaSen** does not separate

$$\begin{bmatrix} \textit{nmod-numcl-p-lex} \\ \\ \text{VAL} \quad \begin{bmatrix} \text{COMPS} \quad \left\langle \begin{bmatrix} \text{HEAD} \quad \begin{bmatrix} \textit{num-cl-mod\_head} \\ \text{MOD} \quad \left\langle \begin{bmatrix} \text{INDEX} & \boxed{1} \\ \text{LTOP} & \boxed{2} \end{bmatrix} \right\rangle \end{bmatrix} \end{bmatrix} \right\rangle \end{bmatrix} \\ \\ \text{MOD} \quad \left\langle \begin{bmatrix} \text{INDEX} & \boxed{1} \\ \text{LTOP} & \boxed{2} \end{bmatrix} \right\rangle \\ \\ \text{CONT} \quad \begin{bmatrix} \text{RELS} & \langle ! \, ! \rangle \\ \text{HCONS} & \langle ! \, ! \rangle \end{bmatrix} \end{bmatrix}$$

FIGURE 62 Constraints on the linker *no* used with numeral classifiers

these into numeral and classifer, so we need a special type that combines the properties of both: *n_num+cl-spr-only-index*.[20]

6.7.2.4 The Linker *no*

We posit a special lexical entry for の *no* which mediates the relationship between NumClPs and the nouns they modify. In addition to the constraints that it shares with other entries for *no* and other modifier heading post-positions (see § 7.5.2.1), this special *no* is subject to the constraints shown in Figure 62. These specify that *no* makes no semantic contribution, that it takes a NumClP as a complement, and that the element on the MOD list of *no* shares its local top handle and index with the element on the MOD list of the NumClP (i.e., that *no* effectively inherits its complement's MOD possibility). Even though (most) numeral classifiers can either modify NPs or PPs, all entries for *no* are independently constrained to only modify NPs, and only as pre-head modifiers.

6.7.2.5 Unary-Branching Phrase Structure Rule

We treat NumClPs serving as nominal constituents by means of an exocentric unary-branching rule, shown in Figure 63.[21] This rule specifies that the mother is a noun subcategorized for a determiner specifier (these constraints are expressed on *noun_sc*), while the daughter is a numeral classifier phrase whose valence is saturated.

---

[20] Alternatively we could split, e.g., 一つ *hitotu* "one NumCl" into 一 *ichi* "one" and つ *tsu* "NumCl" in the pre-processor.

[21] In the analysis of number names used as NumClPs, we posit a second unary-branching rule. The mother of that rule (a NumClP) can then serve as the daughter of the rule discussed here.

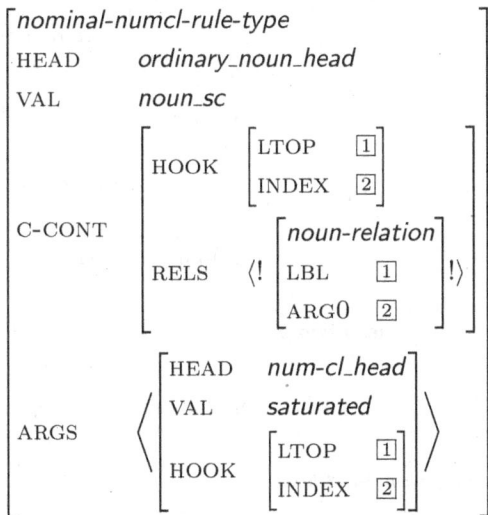

FIGURE 63   Unary rule for stand-alone NumClPs

Furthermore, it contributes (via its C-CONT, or constructional content feature) an underspecified noun-relation which serves as the thing (semantically) modified by the numeral classifier phrase. The reentrancies required to represent this modification are implemented via the LTOP and INDEX features. This rule works for both sortal and mensural NumClPs, as both are expecting to modify a noun.

6.7.2.6   Sample Derivations

We illustrate our analysis with sample derivations, displayed as trees with (abbreviated) rule names and lexical types on the nodes. Figures 64, 65 and 66 give the analyses for (158), (159), and an abbreviated version of (160) respectively. The analysis in Figure 67 illustrates the interaction of the unary-branching rule from § 6.7.2.5 with the rest of the grammar.

6.8   Summary and Further Reading

In this chapter, we gave an analysis of the syntax and semantics of Japanese noun phrases and also touched on their pragmatic constraints. We presented analyses of common nouns, names, pronouns, nominalizers, temporal nouns, and modifiers of nouns including numeral classifiers. In this final section we give some pointers to further reading related to the main themes of this chapter.

Our analysis of the basic structures of Japanese ordinary nouns illus-

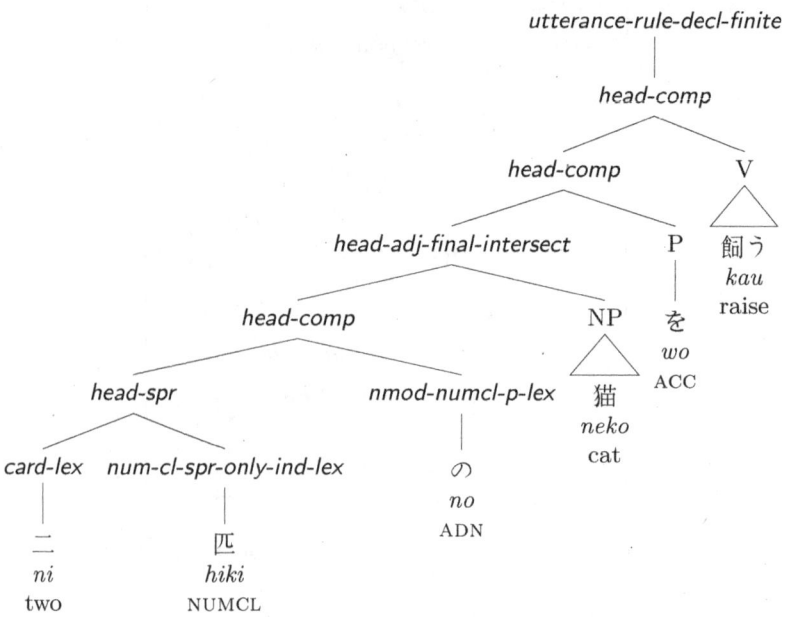

FIGURE 64 Analysis for (158)

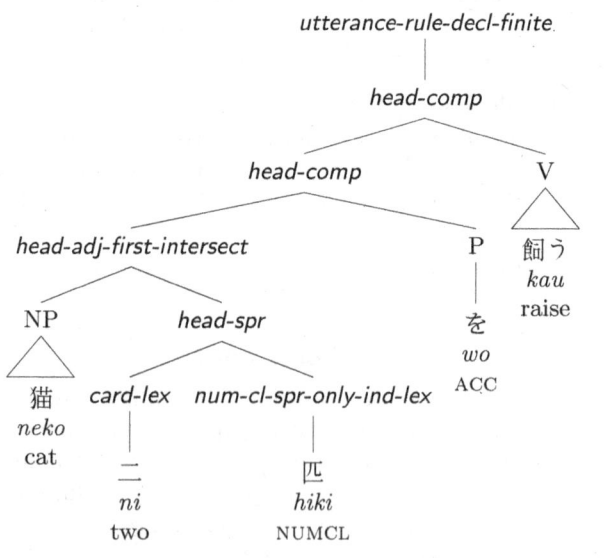

FIGURE 65 Analysis for (159)

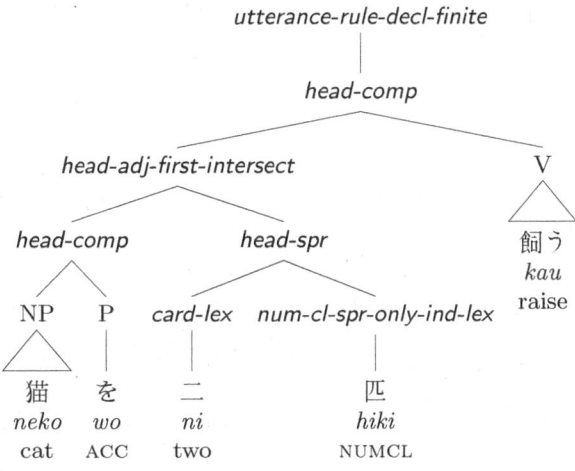

FIGURE 66 Analysis for (160)

trates the interaction of syntax, semantics, and pragmatics. For further reflection on the semantics and pragmatics of Japanese noun phrases and how they differ from English, see Bond (2005). Our analysis of named entities highlights how information from external resources is included into the grammar. The preprocessing method for POS detection is described in Matsumoto et al. (1999). Callmeier et al. (2004) illustrate how the information of the named-entity resolution module is integrated into the grammar analysis.

Pronouns are an area of perennial interest in linguistic theory. There is an interesting discussion of demonstratives in Backhouse (1993, 115–118). Although they are not commonly used, the characteristics of the Japanese reflexive express a system of interaction of linguistic levels. See also Katagiri (1991) and Tsujimura (1996, 215-227) for analyses of the Japanese reflexive.

Our analysis of temporal nouns is informed in part by the analysis of English temporal expressions in Flickinger 1996.

Relative sentence constructions in noun phrases show surprising similarities to pre-nominal adjectives and therefore get a similar analysis. See Baldwin (2004) and Tsujimura (1996, 263–269) for more detailed descriptions of Japanese relative clauses. Finally, numeral classifiers are a special class of noun modification, and show interesting behavior. See Bond and Paik (2000) for further material on these.

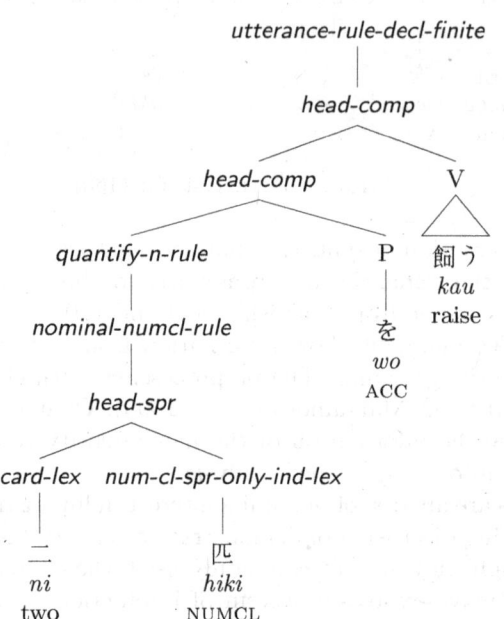

FIGURE 67 Sample derivation invovling stand-alone NumClP

7

Particles

The word 'particle' is used to describe a wide range of (usually very short) function words in Japanese, including case makers, semantically contentful post-positions, conjunctions, and sentence-final markers of sentential force/speaker attitude. These words are high frequency and bear central functions in Japanese syntax, and accordingly, their treatment is essential to Japanese language processing.

Table 18 contrasts the frequency of occurrence of a sample of particles with that of a highly topical noun in 800 Japanese dialogues on appointment scheduling from the Verbmobil corpus.

Word	Frequency
wa	5,765
ga	5,909
ni	4,358
kara	2,802
made	1,158
kaigi "meeting"	792

TABLE 18 Frequency of occurrence of particles and a representative noun in 800 Verbmobil dialogues

This high frequency can be explained by the grammatical functions borne by the particles, which include: the marking of case for subcategorized verbal arguments (case particles), heading adjuncts modifying both verbal and nominal heads (post-positions), marking topics (topic particles), and coordination (conjunctions). These functions make particles the 'work-horses' of Japanese syntax, in two senses: First, they have very high text frequency, as observed above, as these functions occur in most sentences. Second, the particles are closely involved in the analyses of a great many linguistic phenomena of Japanese, making the constraints on these elements both intricate and critical to the functioning of the grammar. Further complicating the analysis of Japanese particles are the following facts: Some particles may be omitted in spoken language; a given particle form can have more than function; and particles can cooccur, but there are constraints on their cooccurrence.

In order to create a broad-coverage grammar, we require a treatment of the full range of types of particles. Prior to the development of Jacy, there was no comprehensive investigation of Japanese particles at the level of detail necessary to implement the analysis.[1] As we developed our analysis of particles, we considered two kinds of solutions that have previously been proposed in the theoretical literature: Some analyses (e.g., Miyagawa 1988 and Tsujimura 1996) divide particles into two classes, 'post-positions', which are treated as heads and 'case particles', which are not. Others (e.g., Gunji 1987) treat particles as a single class which uniformly function as heads of phrases.

Looking at the full range of data handled in **Jacy**, we see that neither kind of analysis scales without problems. On the one hand, treating some as heads and others as non-heads leads to problems in cases where two or three particles appear in sequence, as we will show. On the other hand, without a means of drawing distinctions between subclasses of particles, we cannot capture their differing behavior in subcategorization and modification. We adopt a hybrid solution, in which all particles are treated as heads, but we take advantage of the type hierarchy to model the fine differences between different sub-classes.

This chapter begins with an empirical investigation of particle cooccurrence (§ 7.1), before turning to an overview of the type hierarchy under *p-lex* (§ 7.2) and discussions of the major classes of particles that we find: case particles (§ 7.3), other semantically empty particles (§ 7.4), semantically contentful particles (§ 7.5), including adnominal *no*, topic *wa*, and other noun and verb modifying post-positions, and sentence-final particles (§ 7.6). In § 7.7 we present our analysis of omitted particles before turning to an evaluation of our analysis of case markers and modifying particles (§ 7.8).

7.1 Cooccurrence of Particles

While in the simplest examples, particles occur once per constituent, there are also many examples where two or three particles occur in sequence. These data are important because they map out the territory

---

[1] Pollard and Sag (1994) mention a manuscript by Tomabechi (1989), but this does not appear to be available.

that our analyses must handle, but also because they reveal constraints on the possible combinations of particles. These constraints, in turn, allow us to classify particles based on their combinatoric potential, both in terms of the phrase types they subcategorize for and in terms of the phrase types they can modify. The analysis we report here is based on the 800 Japanese dialogues about appointment scheduling which were collected and transcribed as part of the Verbmobil project Wahlster (2000).

Table 19 shows the frequency of cooccurrence of two particles in the dialogue data.[2] In this table, the rows (labeled down the left hand side) show the first member of the combination and the columns (labeled across the top) the second. The last row shows the total occurrence of each particle as the second member of a particle sequence. The first thing to note here is that most combinations of particles are not found, and certain particles appear to be disallowed as either first (が *ga*, も *mo*) or second (へ *e*, から *kara*, まで *made*) members of such sequences.[3] なんか *nanka* should probably also be added to the second list, as the one example where it appears as the second in the sequence is a false positive: it is not a particle but an adverb *nanka*, because it does not relate to 来週 *raishuu* "next week", but to うまちゃってい る *uma-chatte iru* "be.filled-TERM PROG".

(175) 来週 は なんか うまっちゃって いる
       raishuu   *wa*   *nanka*   *umat-chat-te*   *iru*
       next.week TOP somehow be.filled-TERM-INF PROG
       んです けども
       ndesu   *kedomo*
       COP.AHON:+ SFP

"Next week is somehow occupied."

The core case-marking particles が *ga* and を *wo* appear relatively infrequently in particle sequences. In fact, we only have one instance of *wo* as the second member of a sequence (*made wo*) and three instances of it as the first member (all *wo to*). *ga*, for its part, never appears as the first member, but does appear after *de*, *kara*, *made*, and *nanka*.

The particle に *ni* occurs more frequently than *ga* as the second element in a two-particle sequence, but only after *kara* and *made*. It is noteworthy that these sequences include examples where *ni* appears

---

[2] We have not taken *no* into account here, because *no* is ambiguous between nominalizer (see § 6.4) and particle and occurs very often in both functions.

[3] として *toshite* and としまして *to-shimasite* also do not appear as the second member of any two-particle sequence in our data; for space we omit the columns for these particles.

	ga	wo	ni	de	e	kara	made	wa	mo	nanka	to
ga	–	–	–	–	–	–	–	–	–	–	–
wo	–	–	–	–	–	–	–	–	–	–	3
ni	–	–	–	19	–	–	–	137	49	–	15
de	2	–	–	–	–	–	–	158	241	–	30
e	–	–	–	1	–	–	–	1	–	–	–
kara	23	–	30	81	–	–	–	69	12	–	123
made	17	1	66	32	–	–	–	63	1	–	79
mo	–	–	–	–	–	–	–	–	–	–	–
nanka	3	–	–	1	–	–	–	30	–	–	–
to	–	–	–	1	–	–	–	17	58	–	–
toshite	–	–	–	–	–	–	–	36	15	–	–
toshimashite	–	–	–	–	–	–	–	15	–	–	–
wa	–	–	–	–	–	–	–	–	–	1	1
Total	45	1	96	135	–	–	–	526	376	1	251

TABLE 19 Cooccurrence of two particles in the 800 Verbmobil dialogues

in its case marking function (176) as well as examples where it is a post-position heading a modifier.

(176) 何時　　ぐらい から に　　します　　か
　　　nan-ji　gurai　kara　ni　shi-masu　ka
　　　what-hour about　from DAT do-AHON:+ Q

"At about what time shall we start?"

Like ni, で de occurs frequently after kara and made, but we also find it after ni, e, nanka and to. Here is an example of kara de where the whole constituent is a modifier, headed by de:

(177) 三時　　ぐらい から で よろしい でしょう　　か
　　　san-ji　gurai　kara　de　yoroshii　deshou　ka
　　　three-hour about　from INS good　COP.AHON:+ Q

"Would about 3 o'clock suit you?"

Note that ni and de can in fact appear in principle in sequence with themselves (as in ni ni or de de), provided that the first particle is a post-position and the second a case marker. The following invented example illustrates the point, as we did not find any examples like this in the data sample:

(178) 東京 で で いかが でしょう　　か
　　　Tokyo　de　de　ikaga　deshou　ka
　　　Tokyo LOC INS how　COP.AHON:+ Q

"Would it suit you (to meet in) Tokyo?"

	de mo	de wa	ni wa
ni	15	4	–
de	2	–	–
kara	12	5	–
made	2	1	16
wa	2	–	–
nanka	–	1	–

TABLE 20 Cooccurrence of 3 particles in the 800 Verbmobil dialogues

In some case three particles occur in a row, for example:

(179) 五 時   ごろ   まで に   は   お 電話
　　　go-ji   goro   made ni   wa   o-denwa
　　　five-hour about until LOC TOP   HON-telephone
　　　さしあげ ます   ので
　　　sashiage-masu   node
　　　do.SHON:−-AHON:+ SFP

"I will phone you before about 5 o'clock."

Note that the relative order of these three particles is fixed: *ni wa made*, *wa ni made* etc. are ungrammatical.

The three particle sequences we found in our data are summarized in Table 20. In this table, the rows (labeled down the left hand side) represent the first element of the sequence, and the columns (labeled across the top), the second and third. All three particle sequences we found involve *de* or *ni* as the second particle, and one of the topic particles (*mo* or *wa*) as the third. The particles *ga*, *wo*, *e*, *toshite*, and *toshimasite* don't appear in three-particle sequences at all, and *mo* can't be the first element. It would be surprising to observe a difference between *mo* and *wa* in this case, and in fact, the examples of *wa* followed by *de mo* in fact involve the adverb *demo* rather than the particles *de* and *mo*:

(180) 火曜日   は   でも   一日   空いて   います   ね
　　　kayoubi wa   demo   ichinichi   ai-te   i-masu   ne
　　　Tuesday TOP   also   whole.day   open-INF   PROG-AHON:+   TAG

"Also on Tuesday, the whole day is open."

A successful account of Japanese particles will need to allow for the observed particle sequences, while blocking the impossible ones. Of course, corpus data alone can't establish which sequences are impossible (as opposed to just rare), but the observations reported here do give a general impression of the range of sequences we are looking to account for.

7.2 The Type Hierarchy of Japanese Particles

The heart of our analysis of particles is the type hierarchy, the top of which is shown in Figure 68. The type hierarchy represents the similarities and differences among the various subtypes of particles. Looking to previous analyses, we see various ways to carve up this space. Kuno (1973) recognizes two classes of 'particles': those that are present in the deep structure (e.g., *kara*) and those that are introduced through transformations (*ga* (SBJ), *wo* (OBJ), *ga* (OBJ) and *ni* (OBJ2)). Our analysis doesn't make use of deep structure (nor transformations), but we do have an analog of this distinction in recognizing that some particles are semantically contentful (introducing their own elementary predication) while others are not.

Gunji (1987) assigns all particles the part of speech P, and treats them as heading their own phrases. In later work, however, he restricts the class P to *ga*, *wo* and *ni*, and classifies other particles as either adnominals (e.g., *no*) or adverbials (e.g, *de*) Gunji (2013, 110), essentially the same distinction as Kuno's (1973). Tsujimura (1996) draws a distinction between post-positions and case particles. The latter include *ga*, *wo*, *ni* (in its dative function) and the topic marker *wa*. The terminology here is confusing, because Tsujimura's 'post-position' class corresponds to Gunji's 'adnominals' and 'adverbials' and contrasts with his P ('post-positional') class. However, the distinction being drawn is largely the same. Nightingale (1996) focuses on a subset, arguing that some uses of *ni*, *de*, *na*, and *no* are actually forms of the copula (and thus to be distinguished from case markers and post-positions).

Our high-level classification of particles is shown in Figure 68. All particles inherit from *p-lex*. This type bears constraints that are in common to all particles, notably that they all take a single complement. Within *p-lex*, the first distinction is between case marking particles (*case-p-lex*) and all others (*cont-p-lex*). This distinction is consistent with those drawn by previous authors in the work discussed above. Like Kuno and others, we analyze the case markers as semantically null, and this constraint is represented on *case-p-lex*. Where our analysis differs significantly from previous work is in the fine-grained distinctions among the non-case markers (*cont-p-lex*).

Within the contentful class, we distinguish three major subclasses: conjunctions (*conj-lex*), an entry for *no* which heads specifiers of certain nominalizers (*nspec-p-lex*), and finally modifiers (*mod-p-lex*). As

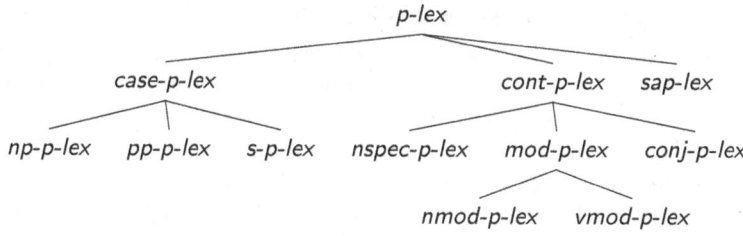

FIGURE 68 Type hierarchy of Japanese particles

case-p-lex-np	case-p-lex-postp
が ga	が ga
を wo	を wo
に ni	に ni
⋮	
と to	
は wa	
の no	

TABLE 21 Case particles

in Gunji 1991, modifiers are subdivided according to what they modify (adnominals inheriting from *nmod-p-lex* and adverbials from *vmod-p-lex-super*), and further subclassified. The following sections look in more detail at each type of particle, beginning with the case markers. It is important to note that a given form (e.g., *ni*) can be ambiguous: that is, there can be two (or more) lexical entries with the same orthography but belonging to different lexical types.

7.3 Case Particles **case-p-lex**

In this section we focus in on the analysis of case particles. The particles analyzed as case particles all inherit from *case-p-lex*. As shown in Figure 68, there are two subtypes of of *case-p-lex*, *case-p-lex-np* and *case-p-lex-postp*. As show in Table 21, *ga*, *wo* and *ni* have entries of both types, while the remaining case marking particles are treated as *case-p-lex-np* only. The distinction between these two types is the type of the complement: *case-p-lex-np* takes an NP complement while *case-p-lex-postp* takes a PP complement. This is an important piece of our analysis of two and three particle sequences.

7.3.1 General Properties of Case Particles

case-p-lex, shared by all case marking particles, has two key properties, shown in Figure 69: (i) it specifies a non-empty COMPS list and (ii) it is constrained to be semantically empty but identifies the INDEX value of the complement with its own INDEX. Thus on our analysis, case marking particles make no semantic contribution and are transparent to the semantics of their complements. This 'raising' of the INDEX value in particular makes it possible for verbs selecting the case-marked PP complements to access the semantic index of the NP inside the PP and link it to the appropriate role in the relation they introduce. The different particles then differ as to what values of case they supply and what other constraints they place on their complement.

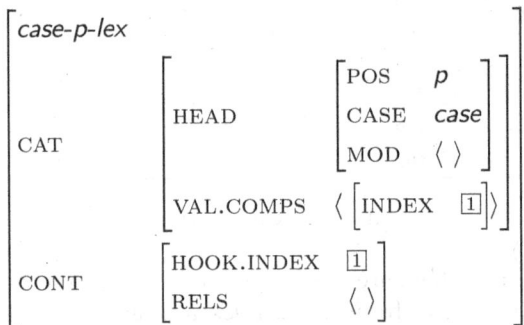

FIGURE 69 Constraints on *case-p-lex*

Given the word order flexibility of Japanese, case marking particles can be understood as serving to mark grammatical function, but they do not do so directly, on our analysis. Rather, they do so only in combination with the verbal valence patterns (described in § 5.1). That is, the case marking particles combine with their complement NP to build a PP with a particular value for CASE. Such PPs can only be used as arguments of verbs which place a compatible constraint on the arguments' CASE value.[4]

Treating case particles as elements which select NPs (or PPs) as complements entails treating them as heads of their phrases. This is contrary to the analyses presented by Pollard and Sag (1994, 45), Miyagawa (1988) and Yoshimoto (1998, 35), who all take the case particles in Japanese to be non-heads (markers, in Pollard and Sag's analysis). Miyagawa presents two arguments for this position, concerning the se-

---

[4]Ono (1996) investigates the particles *ni*, *ga* and *wo* and also states that grammatical functions must be clearly distinguished from surface cases.

mantic contrast between case markers and other particles on the one hand, and distributional facts regarding numeral classifiers on the other. Yoshimoto (1998) presents an argument from case ellipsis. We will address each of these points in turn, and then present evidence from multiple particle sequences which we argue supports an analysis of case particles as heads.

Miyagawa's (1988) first argument is that a distinction needs to be drawn between case particles and 'post-positions', because the latter but not the former, on his account, assign a theta-role to the NP they combine with. In essence, this is capturing the semantic contrast between the two, i.e., case particles are semantically empty, whereas other particles make a semantic contribution. We agree that this contrast needs to be captured, but in our framework, it needs not to correlate with whether or not the particles function as heads. Our type *case-p-lex* is constrained to be semantically empty.

The second argument that Miyagawa raises concerns the possible positions for numeral classifier phrases. He notes that they can appear after case marking particles but not after other particles:[5]

(181) a. 学生 三人 が 本 を 読んだ
gakusei san-nin ga hon wo yon-da
student 3-NUMCL NOM book ACC read-PST

"Three students read a book."

b. 先生 が 三人 来た
sensei ga san-nin ki-ta
teacher NOM 3-NUMCL come-PST

"Three teachers came."

c. 人 が 二つ の 小さい村 から来た
hito ga futa-tsu no chiisai mura kara ki-ta
person NOM 2-NUMCL ADN small village from come-PST

"People came from two small villages."

d. *人 が 小さい村 から二つ 来た
*hito ga chiisai mura kara futa-tsu ki-ta
person NOM small village from 2-NUMCL come-PST

Intended: "People came from two small villages."

Miyagawa (1988, 162) analyses this restriction in terms of *bijacency*, defined in (182):

---

[5](181b) is from Miyagawa 1988, 157 and (181c) and (181d) are from Miyagawa 1988, 162.

(182)   Definition: X is bijacent to NP, iff:
- X is a sister to NP, or
- X is immediately dominated by a sister of NP.

His restriction for numeral classifiers says that the classifier must be bijacent to the antecedent. Thus, every structure in which the antecedent of the numeral classifier is embedded in a PP is excluded.

However, there are counterexamples to a bijacency-based analysis. Gunji and Hasida (1998, 39) note the example in (183), where the numeral classifier refers to a subject but a complement intervenes:

(183)   去年   は   アメリカ人   が   日本   を   3000人
        kyonen   wa   Amerika-jin   ga   Nihon   wo   3,000-nin
        last.year TOP America-person NOM Japan ACC 3,000-NUMCL
        訪れた
        otozure-ta
        visit-PST
        "Last year, 30,000 Americans visited Japan."

Thus the bijacency-based analysis is not sufficient, and it seems that making a phrase-structural distinction between case-marked nominal phrases and NPs complements to P does not further help here. One might find traction for an analysis in the semantic distinction between *case-p-lex* and other particles: *case-p-lex* identifies its INDEX with that of the NP complement, so the INDEX value of the whole PP will be typical of nouns, i.e., of type *ref-ind*. Semantically-contentful post-positions, on the other hand, will have an INDEX value of type *event*, reentrant with the ARG0 of the predication they introduce.[6]

Yoshimoto (1998, 35) takes a different tack, arguing that Japanese case particles cannot function as heads, because they can be omitted in spoken language. Zwicky (1985, 13) includes obligatoriness as one of his criteria for headedness. However, Zwicky also notes that it is important to separate optionality from ellipsis, thus allowing for the possibility of heads being elided. Zwicky provides the example in (184), where the V in the second conjunct (independently argued to be the head) is elided:

(184)   I ate sushi, and Kiyoko a hamburger.

Zwicky also discusses the case of P+NP in English, coming down on the side of P being the head of that combination on the grounds that

---

[6] Gunji and Hasida (1998, 71) also argue that the distribution of numeral classifiers is best handled as a semantic phenomenon. They use the notions of measurability, coercion, contrastivity and incremental theme in order to explain the phenomena.

the NP is more optional than the P, if so-called particles in English are considered to be of the same category as prepositions, citing the VP *put the penguin on.* Japanese case particles cannot appear without their complement NPs, as shown in (185).

(185) リンゴを *(田中) に 手渡してください
      *ringo wo *(Tanaka) tewatashi-te kudasai*
      apple ACC Tanaka DAT hand-INF please

      "Please hand the apple to Tanaka."

On the other hand, treating the case particles as heads does not prevent us from analyzing examples where they are elided, as discussed in § 7.7 below. Thus treating case particles as heads is possible. We further find that it is helpful in the analysis of certain examples of multiple-particle strings, such as the following example from the Verbmobil corpus:

(186) 何時 から が よろしい です か
      nan-ji kara ga yoroshii desu ka
      what-hour from NOM good COP.AHON:+ Q

      "At what time would you like to start?"

All analyses agree that *kara*, a semantically contentful post-position, must be treated as a head. Thus *nanji kara* "from what time" is clearly a PP whose HEAD properties, including the ability to function a as modifier come from its head daughter *kara* (see § 3.2). If *ga* is treated as a non-head (e.g., as a marker) in this example, then *nanji kara ga* should have the same HEAD properties as *nanji kara*. But *nanji kara ga* cannot function as a modifier, as shown in (187):

(187)

(188) *セミナ- が 何時 から が 入って
      **seminaa ga nan-ji kara ga hait-te*
      seminar NOM what-hour from NOM enter-INF
      いらっしゃいます か
      irasshai-masu ka
      PROG.SHON:+-AHON:+ Q

      Intended: "From when is the seminar?"

Similar observations can be made about the following (Verbmobil) sentence:

(189)　一時　　から 三時　　ぐらい まで を　開けて
　　　　ichi-ji　kara san-ji　gurai　made wo　ake-te
　　　　one-hour from three-hour about　until ACC open-INF
　　　　いただけ ます　　　　か
　　　　itadake-masu　　　　ka
　　　　receive.SHON:−-AHON:+ Q

"Could you keep the time between one o'clock and three o'clock free?"

In the case of (189), *ichiji kara sanji gurai made* "from 1 o'clock until around 3 o'clock" is marked by *wo* and functioning as the object. If *wo* were not the head, we'd expect *sanji gurai made wo* to be acceptable as a modifier, just as *sanji gurai made* is, but in fact it is not:

(190)　一時　　から 三時　　ぐらい まで (*を)　寝て
　　　　*ichi-ji　kara san-ji　gurai　made (*wo)　ne-te*
　　　　one-hour from three-hour about　until (*ACC) sleep-INF
　　　　いた
　　　　i-ta
　　　　prog-PST

"They slept from one o'clock until around three."

Thus we conclude that not only is it possible to analyze all Japanese particles as heads, it is in fact desirable to do so. This means that Japanese is also head-final in this aspect, and all particles are analyzed uniformly as heads of PPs taking a complement. This complement is further more obligatory and always directly adjacent, as illustrated in the following examples:

(191)　a.　*が ある
　　　　　　ga aru
　　　　　　NOM exist

　　　　　　Intended: "It exists."

　　　　b.　家　が　ある
　　　　　　ie　ga　aru
　　　　　　house NOM exist

　　　　　　"A house exists."

　　　　c.　大きい 家　が　ある
　　　　　　ookii　ie　ga　aru
　　　　　　large　house NOM exist

　　　　　　"A large house exists."

d. その 大きい 家　が　ある
　　sono ookii　ie　ga　aru
　　that large　house NOM exist

"That large house exists."

e. *家　大きい が　ある
　　*ie　ookii　ga　aru
　　house large　NOM exist

Intended: "A large house exists."

f. *家　その 大きい が　ある
　　*ie　sono ookii　ga　aru
　　house that large　NOM exist

Intended: "That large house exists."

The remainder of this section looks at *ga*, *wo* and *ni* in more detail. In general, *ga* is associated with subjects, *wo* with direct objects and *ni* with indirect objects, but there are exceptions. As noted above, this means that we analyze the case markers as marking case, which verbs can select for, rather than marking grammatical function directly.

7.3.2 The Case Particle *ga*

In most cases a *ga*が-marked noun phrase is the subject of a sentence:

(192)　何　　日　　が　　よろしい でしょう　　　　か
　　　　nan　nichi ga　yoroshii deshou　　　　ka
　　　　which day　NOM good　　COP.AHON:+　Q

"Which day would suit you?"

However, this is not always the case. Notably stative verbs subcategorize for *ga*-marked objects. An example is the stative verb *dekimasu*:[7]

(193)　彼女　　が　泳ぎ　　　　が　でき ます
　　　　kanojo ga　oyogi　　　ga　deki-masu
　　　　3SG.F NOM swimming NOM do.POT-AHON:+

"She can swim."

These and other cases are sometimes called 'double-subject constructions' in the literature, but these *ga*-marked noun phrases do not behave like subjects in terms of subject honorification or reflexive binding by the subject. This can be shown by the following example:

---

[7] See Kuno (1973) for a semantic classification of verbs that take *ga*-objects.

(194) 午後   の   ほう が   ゆっくり 話   が
       gogo   no   hou ga   yukkuri hanashi ga
       afternoon ADN side NOM at.ease talk   NOM
       で き ま す   ね
       deki-masu   ne
       do.POT-AHON:+   TAG

"We can talk at ease in the afternoon."   [Verbmobil]

If *hanashi* were the subject of *dekimasu*, then it should be the target of any subject honorification marked on that verb.

(195) 私   が   ゆっくり   話   が   でき て
       watashi ga   yukkuri   hanashi   ga   deki-te
       I   NOM   at.ease   talk   NOM   do.POT-INF
       お り ま す
       ori-masu
       PROG.SHON:--AHON:+

"I can talk at ease."

We conclude that *ga*-marking, while typical of subjects, is not strictly correlated with subjecthood. Rather, it is typical of Japanese verbs to select for a *ga*-marked element as their subject, but it is also possible for Japanese verbs to select for *ga*-marked elements in other argument positions.

There are even *ga*-marked adjuncts, as in (194) and the following:

(196) いつ が   ご 都合   が   よろしい でしょう   か
       itsu ga   go-tsugou   ga   yoroshii deshou   ka
       when NOM   HON-convenience NOM   good   COP.AHON:+   Q

"When does it suit you?"

The first NP-*ga* in (194) and (196) is not only not a subject, it is not even subcategorized for by the verb. できます *dekimasu* in (194) subcategorizes for two *ga*-marked NPs, but *gogo no hou ga* can neither be the subject nor the object, as it does not fulfill the semantic restrictions for these. In (196), the NP marked by *ga* is the temporal interrogative *itsu* "when", which is similarly not subcategorized for by the intransitive *yoroshii* "good".

Kuroda (1992) assumes these 'double-subject constructions' to be derived from adnominal relations. This means that, on Kuroda's analysis, the following sentence from Farmer (1984) is derived from one with a *no*-marked NP:

(197) a. 山　　　が　木　が　きれい です
　　　　　yama　　ga　ki　ga　kirei　desu
　　　　　mountain NOM tree NOM pretty COP.AHON:+

　　　　"The mountains: Their trees are pretty."

　　b. 山　　　の　木　が　きれい です
　　　　　yama　　no　ki　ga　kirei　desu
　　　　　mountain ADN tree NOM pretty COP.AHON:+

　　　　"The mountain's trees are pretty."

But this analysis cannot be straightforwardly extended to (194), because the following sentence is not acceptable:

(198) *午後　　の　ほう の　ゆっくり 話　　　が
　　　　*gogo　　no　hou　no　yukkuri　hanashi　ga
　　　　afternoon ADN side ADN at.ease　talk　　NOM
　　　　でき ます　　　ね
　　　　deki-masu　　　ne
　　　　do.POT-AHON:+ TAG

　　　Intended: "We can talk at ease in the afternoon."

We conclude that *ga* marks a true verbal adjunct in this example.

To summarize, *ga* is a case particle that usually attaches to the subjects and adds case information to the entity it attaches to. However, sometimes non-subject arguments are marked by *ga*. This means that the grammatical function is not allocated by the case particle, but by the verbal valence. In some cases *ga* can even mark an adjunct. The case particle *ga* subcategorizes for noun phrases (as in most of the examples) and post-positions, as in (186). Therefore, we have two entries for the case particle *ga*: a *case-p-lex-np* and a *case-p-lex-postp*. In addition, we posit a topic entry (see § 7.5.3 below).

7.3.3　The Case Particle *wo*

The case particle を *wo* typically attaches to direct objects:

(199) 澤田　　　の　ほう が　雑誌　　の　インタビュー を
　　　Sawada　no　hou　ga　zasshi　no　intabyuu　　wo
　　　Sawada ADN side NOM journal ADN interview　　ACC
　　　受け ます
　　　uke-masu
　　　accept-AHON:+

　　　"Sawada is interviewed by a journal."

In contrast to *ga*, no two phrases in one clause may be marked by *wo*. This restriction is called 'double-*wo* constraint' in research literature (see, for example, Tsujimura 1996, 249ff). Consider the following examples from the Verbmobil corpus:

(200) 近藤 に も 再度 確認 を して みます
Kondou ni mo saido kakunin wo shi-te mi-masu
Kondou LOC also again confirmation ACC do-INF try-AHON:+
けれども
keredomo
SFP

"I will confirm it with Kondou again."

(201) 近藤 の スケジュール を 確認 いたし ます
Kondou no sukejuuru wo kakunin itashi-masu
Kondou ADN schedule ACC confirm do.SHON:−-AHON:+

"I will confirm Kondou's schedule."

The verb *suru* can occur with an *wo*-marked argument or in a light verb construction. The noun *kakunin* is an argument in (200) and the verbal noun in a light verb construction in (201). *kakunin* as an argument would not be possible in (201), according to the 'double-*wo* constraint', because there is already an *wo*-marked argument in the sentence:

(202) *近藤 の スケジュール を 確認 を
*Kondou no sukejuuru wo kakunin wo
Kondou ADN schedule ACC confirmation ACC
いたし ます
itashi-masu
do.SHON:−-AHON:+

Intended: "I will confirm Kondou's schedule."

As illustrated by the following examples, the domain of the double-*wo* constraint is the clause; a single sentence may have more than one *wo* provided they are not in the same clause:

(203) 近藤 の 研究室 の ほうで 実演 を
Kondou no kenkyuushitsu no hou de jitsuen wo
Kondou ADN institute ADN side LOC presentation ACC
する という 予定 を 立てて いる んです
suru toiu yotei wo tate-te iru ndesu
do COMP plan ACC build-INF PROG COP.AHON:+
けれども
keredomo
SFP

"There is a plan to do the presentation at Kondou's institute."

In fact, we find some violations of the double-*wo* constraint in the Verbmobil corpus. Examples are:

(204) 今日　お電話　　　　　した　　　　　の　は
kyou o-denwa　　　shi-ta　　　　 no　wa
today SHON:--telephone do.SHON:--PST ADN TOP
(P)(h)ええと本　を　　出版　　する　ため　　に　(P) その
(P)(h)/eeto/ hon　wo　shuppan suru　tame　 ni　(P) sono
(pause)　　　book ACC publish　do　purpose LOC (P) that
原稿　　　を　いつ (P) こう 一緒　　に　打ち合わせ
genkou　 wo　itsu (P) kou　issho　　ni　uchiawase
manuscript ACC when (P) so　　together LOC appointment
を　したら　よろしい か という　　で　　(P)
wo shi-tara　yoroshii ka toiu　 koto　de　(P)
ACC do-COND good　　 Q　COMP　NMLZ LOC (P)
お電話　　　　　さして　　　いただいた
o-denwa　　　 sashi-te　　itadai-ta
SHON:--telephone do.SHON:--INF receive.SHON:--PST
んです　　　けれとも
ndesu　　　 keredomo
COP.AHON:+ SFP

"This is the reason, why I am calling today: When would it suit you to have a joint discussion in order to publish that manuscript?"

(205) うちの　　佐藤　が　(P)あの　学会誌　　　　　の
uchi no　 Satou ga　(P)/ano/ gakkaishi　　　 no
we　 ADN Satou NOM (pause)　academic.journal ADN
特集　　　　の　出費　計画　　を　(P) (h) 近藤
tokushuu　　no　shuppi keikaku wo　(P) (h) Kondou
special.edition ADN expense plan　ACC (P) (h) Kondou
先生　と　打ち合わせ　を　したい　と　　申して
sensei to　uchiawase　 wo　shi-tai　 to　moushi-te
Prof　COM appointment ACC do-want COMP say.SHON:--INF
おりました　　　　けれとも
ori-mashi-ta　　　keredomo
PROG.SHON:--AHON:+-PST SFP

"Satou said that he would like to make an appointment with Prof Kondou to discuss the budget for the special edition of the academic journal."

However, native speakers we consulted find these examples to be ungrammatical. These examples are very complex utterances and in both cases there are pauses between the *wo*-marked entities. The *wo*-marked nominal phrases その原稿 *sono genkou* "that manuscript" in (204) and 学会誌の特集の出費計画 *gakkaishi no tokushuu no shuppitsu keikaku* "the budget for the special edition of the academic journal" in (205) are not subcategorized by 打ち合わせ *uchiawase* "appointment". The examples become acceptable if one replaces *wo* with について *nitsuite* "regarding" and thus mark the NPs as adjuncts. These exceptions of the 'double-*wo* constraint' are therefore effects of spoken language (possibly performance errors) and should not be licensed by the grammar.

Object positions with *wo*-marking as well as subject positions with *ga*-marking can be saturated only once. There are neither double subjects nor double objects. It will be shown that this restriction is also valid for indirect objects. Arguments found in the clause must be assigned a saturated status in the subcategorization frame, so that they cannot be saturated again (as it is in German and English). The verbs subcategorize for at most one subject, object and indirect object. Only one of these arguments may be marked by *wo*, while a subject and an object may both be marked by *ga*. These attributes are determined by the verbal valence. The effects of the so-called 'double-*wo* constraint' come from the fact that *wo* has only the function of marking direct objects, while *ga* and *ni* can have different functions.

Furthermore, though we find the verbal nouns both taking *wo*-marked objects (201) and appearing as the *wo*-marked object of the light verb (200), **Jacy** does not allow examples like (202) because the examples like (200) and (201) involve different lexical entries for the light verb. In examples like (200), the light verb combines with the verbal noun after the latter has been nominalized, and does not take over its argument structure. In examples like (201), on the other hand, the light verb combines directly with the verbal noun and the combination inherits the argument structure of the verbal noun. There is thus no entry for a light verb that could combine with a verbal noun marked with *wo* and then also combine with that verbal noun's complement again marked with *wo*.[8]

7.3.4 The Case Particle *ni*

The particle *ni* can have the function of a case particle as well as that of an adjunct particle modifying the predicate and is therefore the one that causes most problems in interpretation and processing. The task of distinguishing *ni*-marked adjuncts from *ni*-marked arguments is not

---

[8]For more on our analysis of verbal nouns, see § 3.2.6 and § 5.1.

a trivial one. Sadakane and Koizumi (1995) also analyze *ni* in terms of homophonous elements that mark adjuncts and complements. Ono (1996) suggests using the possibility of passivation as a diagnostic. This is helpful in many cases.

Some verbs subcategorize for a *ni*-marked object, as for example なる *naru*:[9]

(206) 来月 に なる んです が
raigetsu ni naru ndesu ga
next.month DAT become COP.AHON:+ SFP

"It will be next month."

ni-marked objects cannot occur twice in the same clause, just as *ga*-marked subjects and *wo*-marked objects. The 'double-*wo* constraint' is neither a specific Japanese restriction nor a specific peculiarity of the Japanese direct object. It is based on the mistaken assumption that grammatical functions are assigned by case particles.

There are a lot of examples with double NP-*ni*, but these all involve *ni*-marked adjuncts, as in (207):

(207) 十時 に 研究室 の ほう に お伺い
juu-ji ni kenkyuushitsu no hou ni o-ukagai
ten-hour LOC institute ADN side LOC SHON:−-visit
いたし ます
itashi-masu
do.SHON:−-AHON:+

"I'll visit your institute at 10 o'clock."

In order not to cause massive spurious ambiguity in the interpretation of *ni*-marked entities, we follow a conservative approach to subcategorization. In the decision on adding entities with *ni* case to the subcategorization frame of a verb, we perform the tests sketched in § 4.1, considering as arguments those *ni*-marked entities that are obligatory, can be passivated and/or get a semantic restriction from the head verb. All others *ni*-marked elements are treated as adjuncts.

7.3.5 Other Case Particles

We note three other minor case particles. The first is の *no*, which occurs a case marker for subjects or objects when the verb has undergone derivational lexical rules such as that associated with the ending *kata* (see § 5.2.6). We also find examples of verbs subcategorizing for a と *to*-marked argument, as in (208):

---

[9]See § 5.1.2.3.

(208) 花子 と 喧嘩 した
    Hanako to kenka shi-ta
    Hanako COM fight do-PST
    "(I) fought with Hanako."

Therefore we posit entries for *no* and *to* which inherit from (subtypes of) *case-p-lex*.

We also treat the colon as a case marker, to handle its appearance in sentences like (209).

(209) 写真 : 馬 だ
    shashin : uma da
    photo NOM horse COP
    "The photo is a horse"

7.4 Other Semantically Empty Particles

In addition to the case particles, **Jacy** recognizes two other categories of semantically empty particles (i.e., particles which contribute no predications to the semantics): complementizers (§ 7.4.1) and certain coordination markers (§ 7.4.2).

7.4.1 Complementizers

Complementizers combine with sentences to make constituents which can serve as arguments of verbs. The two subtypes of *comp-lex* correspond to those that combine with proposition-expressing complements (*comp-prpstn-lex*; と *to*, かも *kamo*) and those that combine with question-expressing complements (*comp-int-lex*; か *ka*, かどうか *kadouka*, のか *noka*). These are illustrated in (210) and (211).

(210) そちら に 伺い たい と 思い ます
    sochira ni ukagai-tai to omoi-masu
    2 DAT visit-want COMP think-AHON:+
    "I would like to visit you."

(211) 花子 が ご飯 を 食べた か 分から ない
    Hanako ga gohan wo tabe-ta ka wakara-nai
    Hanako NOM rice ACC eat-PST Q know-NEG
    "(I) don't know if Hanako ate the rice."

The *to* complementizer attaches to complement sentences that are subcategorized for by verbs like 思う *omou* "think", 言う *iu* "say" or 書く *kaku* "write". These complement sentences are obligatory and obligatorily adjacent to the particle (see § 4.3) and are complete sentences in the sense that they can include sentence-final particles:

$$\begin{bmatrix} \textit{comp-prpstn-lex} \\ \text{HEAD} & \begin{bmatrix} \textit{case-p\_head} \\ \text{CASE} & \textit{to} \end{bmatrix} \\ \text{VAL} & \begin{bmatrix} \text{COMPS} & \begin{bmatrix} \textit{obl-1-arg} \\ \text{FIRST.INDEX.SF} & \textit{prop} \end{bmatrix} \end{bmatrix} \end{bmatrix}$$

FIGURE 70 The complementizer *to*

(212) そろそろ 打ち合わせ を しよう か と 思う
sorosoro uchiawase wo shi-you ka to omou
soon meeting ACC do-HOR Q COMP think
のです が
nodesu ga
COP.AHON:+ SFP

"I think we should soon arrange a meeting."

The HEAD value of a complementizer is akin to that of case markers, inheriting from *case-particle-head*. This allows it to be subcategorized for by verbs such as *omou*. The complementizers in turn subcategorize for projections of verbal or sentence-final particle heads (*to, ka, kadouka, noka*), or of heads of the type *sentence-valid*, which includes verbal heads, quotations or idioms (*kamo*). These constraints are illustrated in Figure 70.

7.4.2 Coordination Particles

A final type of semantically empty particle is the coordination particles found on final conjuncts (*postp-lex-coord*). As described in more detail in § 3.2.4 and in § 7.5.4 below, **Jacy** implements an approach to coordination (similarly to the ERG Flickinger (2000)) which is binary-branching in both the syntax and the semantics. This means that we produce MRSs with one coordination predication for each non-final conjunct. Typically, these coordination predications are contributed by the coordination markers. In the case of examples like (213a), however, there is as many coordination markers as conjuncts, and so the final coordination particle is treated as semantically empty.

(213) a. 太郎 と 次郎 と が 着いた
Tarou to Jirou to ga tsui-ta
Tarou CONJ Jirou CONJ NOM come-PST

"Taroo and Jirou came."

b. $h_1, \left\{\begin{array}{l} h_3\text{:def\_q}(x_4, h_5, h_6), \\ h_7\text{:named}(x_4, \textit{tarou\_2}), \\ h_8\text{:\_to\_p\_and}(x_{10}, u_{11}, x_4, u_{12}, x_9), \\ h_{13}\text{:udef\_q}(x_{10}, h_{14}, h_{15}), \\ h_{16}\text{:def\_q}(x_9, h_{17}, h_{18}), \\ h_{19}\text{:named}(x_9, \textit{jirou\_2}), \\ h_{20}\text{:\_tsuku\_v\_7}\left(e_2 \left\{\text{TENSE } \textit{past}\right\}, x_{10}\right) \end{array}\right\},$

$\{h_5 =_q h_7, h_{14} =_q h_8, h_{17} =_q h_{19}\}$

Lexical entries in this class include だの *dano*, か *ka*, なり *nari*, と *to*, とか *toka*, や *ya*, and やら *yara*.

7.5 Particles with Semantic Content cont-p-lex

We turn now to the subhierarchy under *cont-p-lex*, which is supertype to all the particles not considered case-marking. The classification of a given particle as belonging to one type or the other is based on its potential to contribute semantic information. This leads us in some cases to make classifications which are not consistent with previous analyses in the literature. For example, Tsujimura (1996, 134) classifies the particle の *no* in its noun-modifying use as a case particle. However, on our analysis it must introduce an elementary predication linking its complement to the modified noun, and thus must belong to *cont-p-lex*.

Tsujimura (1996, 135) uses omissibility as a criterion to distinguish case particles from 'post-positions' (in her terminology), noting that case particles are frequently omitted while the semantically contentful post-positions may not be.

Finally Tsujimura gives the criterion that case particles can follow modifying particles while 'post-positions' cannot follow particles. This criterion in particular implies that a finer distinction is necessary, this finer distinction can be realized with HPSG types. Further, topic particles are not taken into account in Tsujimura's classification.

In this section, we will examine the various subtypes of *cont-p-lex*, including adnominal *no* (§ 7.5.1), modifying particles (§ 7.5.2), topic particles (§ 7.5.3) and NP conjunctions (§ 7.5.4).

7.5.1 Adnominal-Specifying *no*

As described in § 6.4, some nominalizers (such as 方 *hou* "side" in (214)) subcategorize for a complement sentence, a determiner or an adnominal. In order to provide the adnominal structure (214), we need an entry for の *no* that has an appropriately constrained SPEC value, can be subcategorized for by the nominalizer and contributes some semantic relation. This is accounted for by the particle type *nspec-p-lex*, an immediate subtype of *cont-p-lex*. Because there are many possible semantic relations between the nominalizer and the NP complement of *no* in this construction, we leave the semantic contribution of *no* as the underspecified predication unspec_compound_rel, which can be disambiguated in further processing.

(214) そちら の 方
sochira no hou
you ADN side
"your side"

7.5.2 Modifying Particles mod-p-lex

The type *mod-p-lex* subsumes both noun modifying particles and verb modifying particles. All of these share the properties shown in Figure 71: they have a non-empty MOD value (the external argument), they subcategorize for a single complement (the internal argument: inherited from *p-lex*), and they bear a CASE value (*mod*) which is incompatible with any case required by a selecting verb, barring the modifiers from filling argument requirements of verbs. These are generally analogous to prepositions in English, differing only in their order with respect to their complement.

Here we briefly describe two subtypes of *mod-p-lex*: *nmod-p-lex*, for particles that build noun-modifying phrases (§ 7.5.2.1), and *vmod-p-lex*, for particles that build adverbial phrases (§ 7.5.2.2).

$$\begin{bmatrix} \textit{mod-p-lex} \\ \text{HEAD.MOD} \left\langle \begin{bmatrix} \text{INDEX} & \boxed{1} \\ \text{LTOP} & \boxed{2} \end{bmatrix} \right\rangle \\ \text{VAL.COMPS} \left\langle \begin{bmatrix} \text{INDEX} & \boxed{3} \end{bmatrix} \right\rangle \\ \text{CONT.RELS} \left\langle !\begin{bmatrix} \textit{prep-mod-relation} \\ \text{PRED} & \textit{relation} \\ \text{LBL} & \boxed{2} \\ \text{ARG0} & \textit{event} \\ \text{ARG1} & \boxed{1} \\ \text{ARG2} & \boxed{3} \end{bmatrix}! \right\rangle \end{bmatrix}$$

FIGURE 71 Constraints on *mod-p-lex*

7.5.2.1 Noun-Modifying Particle *no* **nmod-p-lex**

The particle の *no* builds PPs that can function as modifiers of nominal projections. The relationship between the modifiee and the complement of *no* can take a wide range of meanings, as the following examples indicate:[10]

(215)   a. ほか の 日
        hoka no hi
        other ADN day

        "another day"

     b. 次 の 日
        tsugi no hi
        next ADN day

        "next day"

     c. 私 の 研究室
        watakushi no kenkyuushitsu
        1SG ADN institute

        "my institute"

     d. 二十九日 の 午前中
        ni-juu-ku-nichi no gozen-chuu
        two-ten-nine-day ADN afternoon-during

        "the afternoon of the 29th"

     e. 京都 大学 の 川村
        Kyouto Daigaku no Kawamura
        Kyoto University ADN Kawamura

        "Kawamura of Kyoto University"

Our analysis of noun-modifying *no* is sketched in Figure 72. The underspecified semantics of *no* is represented by _no_p_rel, which takes as its two arguments the modified noun and the complement of *no*.

$$\begin{bmatrix} \textit{nounmod-p-lex} \\ \text{HEAD.MOD} & \langle \begin{bmatrix} \text{HEAD} & \textit{noun\_head} \end{bmatrix} \rangle \\ \text{CONT.RELS} & \langle ! \begin{bmatrix} \text{PRED} & \textit{\_no\_p\_rel} \end{bmatrix} ! \rangle \end{bmatrix}$$

FIGURE 72 Additional constraints on noun-modifying *no*

---

[10] See also Tsuda and Harada 1996.

As noted above, Tsujimura (1996, 134ff) assigns *no* to the class of case particles, but on our analysis, it fits in as a semantically contentful (if very bland in its meaning) modifying particle, similar to *of* in English. NP-*no* is an adjunct to a nominal phrase. As a result, we license NPs with multiple *no*-marked dependents:

(216) 私　　の　生駒　の　家　　が　美しい
　　　watashi no　ikoma no　ie　　ga　utsukusii
　　　1SG　 ADN Ikoma ADN house NOM beautiful

"My house in Ikoma is beautiful."

The particle *no* modifies a noun phrase and occurs after a noun (as in (216)) or a verb modifying particle, as in:

(217) 四日　　から の　週　　です　　　　ね
　　　yok-ka　kara no　shuu desu　　　　ne
　　　four-day from ADN week COP.AHON:+ TAG

"It's the week beginning from the fourth, isn't it."

We handle this by introducing lexical entries with different COMPS requirements.

We note that these lexical entries for *no* are part of quite a large collection of entries for this highly ambiguous particle. In addition to the entries that fit under *nmod-p-lex*, there are also the case marker *no*, described in § 7.5.1 above, nominalizer *no*, discussed in § 6.4,[11] and an entry of type *nmod-numcl-p-lex* used in numeral classifier constructions (§ 6.7).

7.5.2.2 Verb-Modifying Particles vmod-p-lex

We now turn to the very large class of verb-modifying particles. These particles all constrain their MOD value to be a verbal projection, and function semantically as intersective modifiers. In MRS terms, that means that they take the INDEX of the verbal projection they modify as their ARG1 and identify their own LTOP value with that of the verbal projection. Within the class of verb-modifying particles, we distinguish between post-positions, adverbial particles and topic particles. In light of their key role in Japanese grammar, topic particles are discussed in their own section (§ 7.5.3), below.

The post-positions modify a verb as an adjunct and subcategorize for a nominal object (*postp-lex*) or a verb (*postp-lex-varg*). The former

---

[11] Nominalizer *no* builds an NP and thus can be followed by any NP-complement-taking particle.

class includes directional, locative[12] and temporal post-positions (e.g., へ *e* "to", から *kara* "from", まで *made* "to, until"; see (218)–(219)), as well as forms such as として *toshite* "as" (220), について *nitsuite* "regarding", and にもかかわらず *nimokakawarazu* "despite".

(218) 九時　　に　　そちら へ　　伺い ます
ku-ji　　*ni*　*sochira e*　　*ukagai-masu*
nine-hour LOC 2　　　DIR visit-AHON:+

"I'll visit you at 9 o'clock."

(219) 先生　　　の　　おうち　　から 遠いので　　お昼　　　から
sensei　*no*　*o-uchi*　　*kara tooi node*　　*o-hiru*　*kara*
Professor ADN HON-home from far　because HON-noon from
に　　しましょう　　　か
ni　*shi-mashou*　　　*ka*
DAT do-HOR.AHON:+ Q

"Shall we start from noon, because it's far from your home?"

(220) こちら としては　　都合　　　　が　　いい んです
kochira toshite wa　*tsugou*　　　*ga*　*ii*　*ndesu*
1　　　　　as　　TOP circumstance NOM good COP.AHON:+
けれども
keredomo
SFP

"This is good for us."

Verb-modifying post-positions that take verbal complements (*postp-lex-varg*) include forms such as ほど *hodo* "as", まで *made* "until", and より *yori* "than", as illustrated in (221)–(222).

(221) 早い ほど いい
hayai hodo ii
early as　good

"The sooner the better."

(222) 十時　　　まで 寝ました
juu-ji　*made ne-mashi-ta*
ten-hour until sleep-AHON:+-PST

"(I) slept until 10 o'clock"

---

[12] Japanese has two locative particles. で *de* is mainly used to show the place at which an action occurs, while に *ni* is used to mark the location of an entity or the goal of a motion verb (Makino and Tsutsui, 1986, 105–111).

(223) バラ より チューリップ が 好き
     bara yori chuurippu   ga suki
     rose than tulip   NOM like

"(I) like tulips better than roses."

The class of particles we call adverbial particles share the property of potentially occuring after post-positions. In this class, we find directional ni に (224), temporal, locative and instrumental で *de* (225), and certain uses of と *to*.

(224) 二十四日   から に   迫って   います
     ni-juu-yok-ka   kara ni semat-te   i-masu
     two-ten-four-day from LOC draw.near-INF PROG-AHON:+

"The 24th is already close."

(225) 一時   から で お昼ご飯   の ほう は
     ichi-ji kara de o-hiru-gohan no hou wa
     one-hour from LOC HON-noon-meal ADN side TOP

だいじょうぶ です   ね
daijoubu   *desu*   *ne*
okay   COP.AHON:+ TAG

"Lunch from one o'clock be okay, right?"

Note that the adverbial particle *ni* can also subcategorize for infinitival verbs:

(226) 花   を 見 に 行く
     hana *wo* *mi ni* *iku*
     flowers ACC see LOC go

"(Someone) goes to see flowers."

7.5.3 Topic Particles

The particle は *wa*, traditionally called the topic particle,[13] is a verb modifying particle that can mark arguments as well as adjuncts. In the case of argument marking it replaces the case particle (see (227), where it replaces *ga*). In the case of adjunct marking it can replace the verb modifying particle (see (228), where it replaces *ni*) or it can occur after it (see (229)):

(227) 午後   は 開いて   おります   ので
     gogo   *wa* *ai-te*   *ori-masu*   *node*
     afternoon TOP be.free-INF PROG.SHON:--AHON:+ SFP

"The afternoon is free."

---

[13]Song (2014) argues convincingly that so-called topic markers in Japanese and Korean actually have a more flexible information structural value. We will stick with the traditional terminology here while acknowledging that it is inaccurate.

(228) 二十八日　　の　月曜日　　は　会議　　が
　　　 ni-juu-hachi-nichi no getsuyoubi wa kaigi   ga
　　　 two-ten-eight-day ADN Monday   TOP meeting NOM
　　　 午後　　に　入って　　おります
　　　 gogo   ni   hait-te   ori-masu
　　　 afternoon LOC enter-INF PROG.SHON:−-AHON:+

"On Monday the 28th there is a meeting in the afternoon."

(229) 今月中　　　　　に　は　ぜひ　　　お会い
　　　 kongetsu-chuu   ni wa zehi   o-ai
　　　 this.month-during LOC TOP certainly SHON:−-meet
　　　 したい　　　　と　思うんです　　　　が
　　　 shi-tai   to   omou ndesu   ga
　　　 do.SHON:−-want COMP think COP.AHON:+ SFP

"I would certainly like to meet you within the month."

The particle *wa* introduces a great deal of ambiguity: semantically, it can be anaphoric, generic or contrastive (see Kuno 1973). Syntactically, it can mark both arguments and adjuncts. Since arguments can also be dropped, any use of *wa* that could be an argument could also be an adjunct, and the ambiguity can only be resolved with reference to lexical semantics. In (230), for example, the subject of 働きます *hatarakimasu* "work" is unexpressed, and yet the *wa*-marked element is best interpreted as an adjunct:

(230) 明日　　　は　働きます
　　　 ashita   wa hataraki-masu
　　　 tomorrow TOP work-AHON:+

"Tomorrow (I) will work."

Gunji (1991) analyzes Japanese topicalization with a phonologically null element (a 'trace') that introduces a value in SLASH and the 'Binding Feature Principle' that unifies the value of SLASH with a *wa*-marked element.[14] This treatment is similar to the one introduced by Pollard and Sag (1994) for the treatment of English topicalization.

---

[14] Harada et al. (1990, 10) give the following statement of the Binding Feature Principle, where M is the mother, H is the head daughter, and D is the non-head daughter:

> In the phrase structure rule in [...] the value of a binding feature at the M category unifies with the union of its value at the D category and its value at the H category minus the category bound at this local branching.

There as well a trace introduces a SLASH value which is bound by the topicalized element.

However, Japanese topicalization is fundamentally different from that found in English. First, it occurs more frequently. Up to 50% of the sentences are concerned Yoshimoto (1998). Second, there are examples where the topic occurs in the middle of the sentence, unlike the English topics that occur sentence-initially. Yoshimoto (1998, 33) gives the following example:

(231) ビル が 東京 へ は 行く
      Bill *ga* *Toukyou* *e* *wa* *iku*
      Bill NOM Tokyo DIR TOP go

"Bill goes to Tokyo."

There are also examples in the Verbmobil dialogue corpus:

(232) 来週 中 に 打ち合わせ は し たい んです
      raishuu-chuu *ni* *uchiawase* *wa* *shi-tai* *ndesu*
      next.week-during LOC meeting TOP do-want COP.AHON:+
けれども
keredomo
SFP

"I would like to hold a meeting in the next week."

Third, Japanese verbal arguments are optional. Suppressing of verbal arguments could be called more a rule than an exception in spoken language. The SLASH approach would introduce traces in almost every sentence. This, in connection with scrambling and suppressed particles, could not be restricted in a reasonable way. If one follows Gunji's interpretation of those cases where the topic-NP can be interpreted as a noun modifying phrase, an adnominal gap has to be assumed. But this leads to assuming an adnominal gap for every NP, whether or not it is otherwise modified.

Fourth, multiple occurrences of NP-*wa* are possible in one utterance, whereas English sentences contain only one topic at most:

(233) ご予定 の ほう は 来週 は 先生 は
      go-yotei *no* *hou* *wa* *raishuu* *wa* *sensei* *wa*
      HON-plan ADN side TOP next.week TOP Professor TOP
いかが でしょう か
ikaga *deshou* *ka*
how COP.AHON:+ Q

"Concerning your plans: Would next week suit you?"

Thus, we decided to assign topicalized sentences the same syntactic structure as non-topicalized sentences and to resolve the problem in post-processing. Still, there is a problem of massive ambiguity (where topics can be linked to arguments or not) that asks for a decision: We have the possibility to introduce ambiguous readings in many cases and leave the disambiguation to a disambiguation module, or analyze all topics as modifiers to the sentence and leave the linking to a zero pronoun resolution module. In both cases, there is the necessity to rely on a natural language processing module that has access to a different type of information than the HPSG grammar processing. The introduction of ambiguity is useful when parsing relatively short sentences and building up treebanks with human disambiguation, such as being done in the Hinoki project Bond et al. (2004a). The underspecification of information is useful when parsing large amounts of data containing long sentences and much topicalization, such as was done in the Verbmobil project Wahlster (2000). As there are different demands for different kinds of processing and applications, we decided to leave the possibility for ambiguous readings in the grammar. There is a switch on the root node of the grammar that allows the user to choose whether to allow the case particle replacing lexical entry for *wa* or not.

The topic particle gets three lexical entries. The first one is for the verb modifying topic variant, as in (228), (229) and (230). The second entry is for the case marking variant of *wa*, as in (227), where the CASE value assigned is *ga*. It gets the same HEAD value as the other case marking particles and adds a _wa_d_rel to the semantics. In the case of a topic particle *wa* replacing *wo*, there is furthermore CONTEXT information, with the empathy set to the entity denoted by the particle's complement NP, following Watanabe et al. 2000.

Though *wa* is the canonical topic marker in Japanese, there are also others. も *mo* "also/even" is similar to *wa* in some aspects. It can mark a predicative adjunct and can follow *ni* or *de*. It implies that there is more than one referent: that referred to and at least one other, similar to *too* or *also*. Unlike English, it can appear in positive and negative contexts.

(234) 私　に　も　出来る　！
 watashi ni　mo　dekiru　!
 I　　　DAT TOP can

"I can do it too!"

The particle *dake* "only" だけ can replace *ga* or *wo*, as in (235) and adds to the semantics. We have thus an entry for *dake* that is a topic particle.

complement type	type name	particles in this type
nominal	plain-topic-nobj-lex	wa, ga, demo, koso, mo, nanowa, nomi, notame, sura, tteiunowa, tte, ja, shika, nado
topic modifying particle	topic-pobj-lex	wa, ga, koso, mo, shika
topic complementizer phrase	topic-cobj-lex	wa
verbal	topic-vobj-lex	wa, mo, shika
adverbial	topic-advarg-lex	wa, mo, dewa, made
cardinal	topic-cardarg-lex	shika

TABLE 22 Types and instances of particles

(235) 学生　の　半分　だけ　参加　しました
gakusei no hanbun dake sanka shi-mashi-ta
student ADN half only participate do-AHON:+-PST

"Only half of the students have participated."

Other topic particles in the lexicon that attach to nouns, replace case particles or are adjuncts to the sentence and add to the semantic content are でも *demo* "but", こそ *koso* "especially", など *nado* "etc", のみ *nomi* "only", すら *sura* "even", っていうのは *tteiunowa* "called", って *tte* "such as", じゃ *ja* "contraction of で わ *de wa*" and しか *shika* "only (requires negative concord)". The topic particles can attach to (i.e., subcategorize for) nominal, verbal, particle, conjunctional, cardinal and adverbial heads. The subtypes of *topic-p-lex* reflect this variation (see Table 22).

Most occurrences are topic particles attaching to nominal heads, such as in (232). They insert a relation to the MRS and link this with the subcategorized entity and the modified event. (236) gives the MRS for a *wa*-marked noun (*hon* "book"):

(236) $\langle h_1, \{ \begin{matrix} h_4\text{:\_hon\_n}(x_5), \\ h_9\text{:\_wa\_d}(e_{10}, x_5, e_2) \end{matrix} \}; \rangle$
$\{\}$

As already discussed in § 7.1, topic particles can follow modifying particles and complementizers. This is accounted for in the types *topic-pobj-lex* and *topic-cobj-lex*. In this case as well, a topic relation is added, which links the nominal entity with the verbal event. (237b) gives the MRS for (237a):

(237) a. 本　から　は
hon　kara　wa
book from TOP

"from the book"

$\left\langle h_1, \left\{ \begin{array}{l} h_4{:}\_hon\_n(x_5), \\ h_9{:}\_kara\_p(e_{10},\ e_2,\ x_5), \\ h_9{:}\_wa\_d(e_{11},\ e_2,\ x_5) \end{array} \right\}, \right\rangle$
$\{\ \}$

Topic particles can attach to verbs in *te* form, as in (238).

(238) 寝て　は　なら　ない
ne-te　wa　nara-nai
sleep-INF TOP become-NEG

"It is not allowed to sleep."

The topic particle links the subcategorized event and the modified event with its arguments in the MRS. The same happens when attaching topic particles to adverbs like *hayaku* "fast".

The topic particle *shika* attaches to cardinals; this accounted for by the type *topic-cardarg-lex*.

(239) 百　しか　ない
hyaku　shika nai
hundred only NEG

"It is only 100."

The final particle that we consider under the heading of topic particles is the *ga* that is used to mark adjuncts. One can find several examples with *ga*-marked adjuncts in the Verbmobil data. On the level of information structure it is said that *ga* marks neutral descriptions or exhaustive descriptions Gunji (1987); Kuno (1973). Gunji analyzes these exhaustive descriptions syntactically in the same way as he analyzes his 'type-I topicalization'. They build adjuncts that control gaps or reflexives in the sentence. He analyzes *ga* marked adjuncts without control relations as relying on a very specialized context.

However, this treatment leads to the following problems:

1. In all cases where *ga* marks a constituent that is subcategorized as *ga*-marked by the verb, a second reading is analyzed that contains a *ga* marked adjunct controlling a gap. This is not reasonable. The treatment of the different meaning of *ga* marking arguments and *ga* marking adjuncts belongs to the semantics and not into the phrase structure.

2. This treatment assumes gaps, which as noted above, we are avoiding with the goal of minimizing ambiguity.
3. The Verbmobil dialogue data contains mostly examples with *ga*-marked adjuncts without syntactic control relation to the rest of the sentences.

On the level of syntax, we do not decide whether a *ga*-marked subject or object is a neutral description or an exhaustive listing. This decision must be based on context information, where it can be found out whether the noun phrase is generic, anaphoric or new. We distinguish occurrences of NP+*ga* that are verbal arguments from those that are adjuncts.

The examples for *ga*-marked adjuncts in the Verbmobil dialogues can be classified into two kinds: those describing temporal entities (240)–(241) and those describing personal entities (242).

(240) 私　　の　ほう　の　都合　　　は
watakushi no　hou　no　tsugou　　wa
1SG　　　ADN side ADN circumstance TOP
二十八日　　　　が　午後　　に　会議　　が　一件
ni-juu-hachi-nichi ga　gogo　ni　kaigi　ga　ikken
two-ten-eight-day NOM afternoon LOC meeting NOM one
入って　おります
hait-te　ori-masu
enter-INF PROG.SHON:−-AHON:+

"On our side, there is a meeting in the afternoon of the 28th."

(241) こちら　は　月曜日　　　が　ちょっと　スケジュール　が
kochira wa　getsuyoobi ga　chotto　sukejuuru　　ga
1　　　TOP Monday　NOM somewhat schedule　　NOM
いっぱい なんです　　けれども
ippai　　nandesu　　keredomo
full　　　COP.AHON:+ SFP

"On our side, the schedule is full on Monday."

(242) 私　　　　が　十二時　　　に　会議　　が　終わります
watakushi ga　juu-ni-ji　　ni　kaigi　ga　owari-masu
1SG　　　 NOM ten-two-hour LOC meeting NOM end-AHON:+

"As far as I am concerned, the meeting ends at 12 o'clock."

We restrict the adjunctive *ga* to those cases where the subject of the sentence is saturated and not a zero pronoun. This is achieved by having it require the XARG of the modified verbal projection to be of type *full_ref_ind*, as can be seen in Figure 73.

$$\begin{bmatrix} \textit{topic-nobj-lex} \\ \text{HEAD} \begin{bmatrix} \text{PTYPE} & \textit{topic} \\ \text{MOD} & \left\langle \begin{bmatrix} \text{HEAD.EMPTY} & - \\ \text{VAL.SUBJ} & \langle \, \rangle \\ \text{XARG} & \textit{full\_ref\_ind} \end{bmatrix} \right\rangle \end{bmatrix} \\ \text{CONT.RELS} \quad \langle ! \, [\text{PRED} \quad \_ga\_p\_rel] \, ! \rangle \end{bmatrix}$$

FIGURE 73 Constraints on adjunctive *ga*

One of the most interesting results from the analysis of particles in Jacy is the range and number of topic particles that are found. This is a prime example of the value of working with corpus data and grammar engineering methodology in the study of natural language syntax and semantics.

7.5.4 Noun Phrase Conjunctions conj-p-lex

Conjunctions are part of the particle type hierarchy, because they share several peculiarities with particles: They attach to nouns and postpositions, they are head-final, and they have the same distributional behavior as (other) particles. They also contribute semantic information, and so on our analysis, they fit in under *cont-p-lex*.

Japanese coordination (as in most languages) presents intriguing conundrums. First we note that the conjuncts can differ in their honorification information, but that the honorification properties of the conjoined NP must match those of the second daughter:[15]

(243) a. 花子　と　　田中　先生　が　本　を　お買い
　　　 Hanako to Tanaka sensei ga hon wo o-kai
　　　 Hanako CONJ Tanaka Prof NOM book ACC SHON:+-buy
　　　 に　なった
　　　 ni nat-ta
　　　 COP SHON:+-PST

　　　 "Hanako and Prof Tanaka bought the book."

　　 b. *田中　先生　と　花子　が　本　を
　　　 *Tanaka sensei to Hanako ga hon wo
　　　 Tanaka Prof CONJ Hanako NOM book ACC

---

[15]Thanks to Akira Kusamoto for verifying the examples.

お買い　　　に　なった
o-kai　　　*ni*　*nat-ta*
SHON:+-buy COP SHON:+-PST

Intended: "Prof Tanaka and Hanako bought the book."

This might suggest that there is not in fact coordination going on, but rather two PPs independently combining with the verb, one as a modifier. However, there are examples which argue for coordination, in at least some cases. One type of example involves floating numeral classifiers. The example in (244) can be interpreted in the two ways shown:[16]

(244)　犬 と　猫 が　三　匹　います
　　　　inu to　neko ga　san　biki　i-masu
　　　　dog CONJ cat　NOM three NUMCL exist-AHON:+

"There are cats and dogs, amounting to three animals." / "There are three cats with some dogs."

The floated numeral classifier scopes over the verbal subject in this example. Thus, in the first interpretation, the subject is the coordination of the animals, while in the second interpretation, only the cats — the second conjunct — are counted. See § 6.7 for more discussion.

Thus, we propose to analyze some NP *to* NP examples as involving true coordination. Where the constraints on the two conjuncts in the substructures that should be shared (e.g., HEAD) do not unify, as in the given examples on honorification, we provide an alternative analysis that does not involve coordination. Rather, the particle *to* is then interpreted as a modifying particle with the meaning of "with". The conjunct not marked by *to* is interpreted as the actual argument, and this is the one that verb must agree with in terms of honorification.

In order to work with the analysis of coordination presented in § 3.2.4, the lexical entry for the particle *to* (of type *n_conj-p-lex*) must add the coordination relation to the semantics and link the nominal indices that participate in the conjunction. This is mediated by the feature C-MOD. The non-coordination analyses of sentences with *to*, on the other hand, involve the post-position *to* of type *adv-p-lex-np*. In addition to coordinated NPs marked by *to* on all non-final conjuncts, Japanese allows the marker to appear on all conjuncts. We analyze this in terms of another subtype of *mod-p-lex*, *postp-lex-coord*, discussed in § 7.4.2 above.

---

[16] Thanks to Chikara Hashimoto for evaluating this example.

7.6 Sentence Particles and Sentence Force sa-p-lex

A high frequency feature of spoken Japanese is the use of sentence final particles. Sentence final particles can express the speaker's attitudes, such as emotions, doubt, emphasis, caution, hesitation, wonder, or admiration. Some are also stylistically marked, associated with either masculine or feminine speech. Sentence final particles can also assign the sentence mood (declarative, interrogative or negative imperative) or be conjunctive.

Three basic types of sentence-final particles are distinguished in the type hierarchy:

1. Sentence conjunctions (*s-conj-lex*), conjoining sentences in coordinative structures.
2. Sentence end particles (*s-end-lex*), ending sentences and expressing the speaker's attitude.
3. Elliptical sentence-final particles (*s-ell-end-lex*), ending sentences with a conjunction, leaving the inferring of the second conjunct to the addressee.

Sentence conjunctions, such as が *ga* "but, and", けれども *keredomo* "however", ので *node* "because", are quite similar to nominal conjunctions. The *conj-rule* that we described above applies to these as well. In the MRS, they add a new vague predicate (*conjunction-rel*) which is linked to the conjoined sentences with L-HNDL and R-HNDL. The type for these conjunctions in the type hierarchy is *s-conj-lex*.

Most of the sentence-final particles take the addressee honorification from their complement, i.e., the sentence. Some, though, mark the utterance as honorific with regard to the addressee. Examples for these are かな *kana*, かしら *kashira*, な *na*. They are of type *s-end2-lex* and add an [AHON +] restriction to the HEAD.

Sentence-final particles can add sentence mood information, such as declarative (*keredomo, kedo, yo* etc.), tag question mood (*ne, kane, yone* etc.) or interrogative (*no* and *ka*). For these, we have the types *s-end1-decl-lex*, *s-end1-declint-lex* and *s-end1-quest-lex*, respectively. There is also a sentence-final particle for negative commands: *iku na* "don't go" (*s-end1-neg-imp-lex*). This both changes the mood and adds a negative relation outscoping the main verb.

Those particles that are associated with masculine style and extremely informal situations get the HEAD information of [AHON −] and the empathy (in CONTEXT) set to the speaker INDEX. We found examples of declarative sentence-final particles such as *i* and interrogatives such as *nokai* or *kai*.

Elliptical sentence-final particles (*s-ell-end-lex*) leave some inference to the addressee, when ending the sentence. An example for these is given in (245). Therefore, we add a subordinate predication to the MRS which is an arg1-relation with the PRED value of *ellipsis*. The elliptical particle then functions like a conjunction, conjoining the expressed sentence and an elliptical predication.

(245) ヒロミ が　ご飯 を　食べた ので
Hiromi ga　gohan wo　tabe-ta node
Hiromi NOM rice　ACC eat-PST because

"Because Hiromi ate the rice..."

7.7 Omitted Particles

Some particles can be omitted in Japanese spoken language. Here are three examples from the Verbmobil corpus:

(246) 五月　十三日　　の　火曜日　φ 午後　　から は
gogatsu juu-san-nichi no　kayoubi　φ gogo　　kara wa
May　ten-three-day ADN Tuesday　afternoon from TOP
いかが でしょう　　か
ikaga deshou　　ka
how　COP.AHON:+ Q

"How about from Tuesday afternoon on the 13th of May?"

(247) 先生　　φ ご 都合　　　の　ほう は　いかが
sensei　φ go-tsugou　　no　hou wa　ikaga
Professor　HON-convenience ADN side TOP how
でしょう　　か
deshou　　ka
COP.AHON:+ Q

"Would that suit you?"

(248) 今　の　所　φ 午後　　は　なにも　予定 が
ima no tokoro φ gogo　　wa nanimo yotei ga
now ADN time　afternoon TOP anything plan NOM
入って　おり ません　　　ので
hait-te　ori-masen　　　node
enter-INF PROG.SHON:—-NEG.AHON:+ SFP

"Up to now I have no plans for the afternoon."

This phenomenon can be found frequently in connection with pronouns and temporal expressions in the domain of appointment scheduling. Hinds (1977) assumes that exclusively *wa* can be suppressed.

Yatabe (1993) however shows that there are contexts, where *ga*, *wo* or even *e* can be omitted. He assigns it as 'phonological deletion'. Kuroda (1992) analyzes omitted *wo* particles and explains these with linearization: A particle *wo* can only be omitted when it occurs directly before a verb. Yatabe (1993) however gives some counterexamples, one of which is shown in (249). He judges it to be 'slightly awkward but acceptable':

(249) どの 学生　φ おれ が　殴った か 覚え　てる
dono gakusei φ ore ga nagut-ta ka oboe teru
which student 1SG NOM hit-PST Q remember PROG

"Do you remember which student I have hit?"

The Verbmobil data available to us did not include information such as intonation contours, and so we are not at present able to elaborate a phonological analysis. However, it is noteworthy that pauses often occur in place of missing particles; this suggests that a phonological analysis might be appropriate.

Looking at the examples from a syntactic point of view, we find NPs without particles fulfilling the functions of verbal arguments (249) and verbal adjuncts (246)–(248). Therefore, we posit a unary rule *pp_np_rule_case* that builds a PP with the HEAD value *empty-case-p_head* out of an NP. That PP is compatible with nominative ([CASE *ga*]) or accusative ([CASE *wo*]) requiring environments.[17] NPs functioning as verbal adjuncts are discussed in § 6.5 and § 8.1.1.

7.8 Evaluation of Case and Modifying Particles

Here we present an analysis from an early version of the grammar. We randomly chose 100 sentences out of the Verbmobil spoken dialogue data on appointment scheduling to process for evaluation. Of these 100, 83 were parseable with the grammar.[18] We then observed the accuracy of the analysis of the particles in the examples. The results are shown in Table 23. The main problem was that adjuncts were bound to the wrong predicate where more than one predicate occurred in the data. There were seven combinations of particles that occurred in the test data: *kara ga, kara de mo, de wa, kara wa, ni wa, de wa* and *de mo*. All of them were correctly analyzed.

---

[17] In distributions of the grammar that are aimed to parse mainly written language, however, this rule is commented out. It is only useful in parsing spoken language and adds massive ambiguity.

[18] Failures came from transliteration problems (6 cases), mistakes in lexical entries (5 cases), very complex adnominal modification (1 case) and the occurrence of interrogatives without question markers (2 cases).

Type	Analysis	Frequency	Percentage
Single	correct	153	92%
	incorrect	14	8%
Multiple	incorrect	7	100%
Missing	correct	14	82%
	incorrect	3	18%

TABLE 23 Analysis of particles from 83 sentences of Verbmobil dialogues

In seventeen cases particles were missing. Three cases were wrongly analyzed. The problem was the same as with particle marked adjuncts: The adjuncts were bound to a wrong predicate in the case were more than one predicate occurred. One parse failed, because of an unexpected missing particle.

7.9 Summary and Further Reading

Particles are a core part of the Japanese grammar. They are the words that occur most frequently and fulfill central functions at the syntactic, semantic and pragmatic levels. The syntactic behavior of Japanese particles has been analyzed based on an empirical investigation concerning their cooccurrence. For an overview of the Verbmobil data that was used for this investigation, see Burger et al. (2000). We adopted the view that all Japanese particles build the head of their phrases, but extended this idea with a type hierarchy of particles. See Gunji (1987) and Gunji and Hasida (1997) for the all-head interpretation of Japanese particles. For an analysis as particles and post-position, see Yoshimoto (1998), Miyagawa (1988) and Tsujimura (1996). Pollard and Sag (1994) view case particles as markers.

Using a type hierarchy, we have adopted a lexical treatment of the differences between particles instead of a syntactic treatment based on phrase structure. The analysis is based on the different kinds of modification and subcategorization that occur with the particles. We analyzed the Japanese particles according to their cooccurrence potential, their modificational behavior and their occurrence in verbal arguments. We capture common characteristics and individual differences through inheritance in the hierarchy. A two way distinction into case particles and post-positions did not capture all the differences in usage, so we created a more elaborate type hierarchy.

On our analysis, the assignment of the grammatical function is done by the predicate valence and not directly by the case particles.

For another approach to the double-*wo* constraint, see Tsujimura (1996). The ambiguity of particle *ni* case marking and modifying uses is described by Ono (1996). We analyzed the topic particle as ambiguous between a case marker and a verbal adjunct, but argued against an analysis in terms of head-filler structures (as Pollard and Sag (1994) propose for English) on efficiency grounds. For a SLASH-based analysis of topics in Japanese, see Gunji (1991). Coordinate structures are analyzed as binary syntactic structures. See Kasai and Takahashi (2001) for the idea that NP coordination does not exist in Japanese. We gave an analysis for omitted particles that occur in spoken language. See also Yatabe (1993) and Kuroda (1992) for this phenomenon. sentence-final particles add propositional information and honorific information to the feature structures.

The approach presented here has been proved to be essential for the processing of a large amount of Japanese language data.

8
Other Word Classes

In this chapter we discuss other word classes, including adverbs, interrogatives and demonstratives.

8.1 Adverbs

Japanese adverbs modify verbs, adjectives and other adverbs, typically appearing before their modificant. Adverbs are typically one-place predicates, with their argument ARG1 being restricted to events. We take their characteristic variable (ARG0) to also be an event, both to serve as the variable to be modified by other adverbs and so that we can share predicate symbols between adjectives and adverbs.

From a lexical-semantic viewpoint, Japanese adverbs can be grouped into three categories:

1. Adverbs of manner, e.g., 速く *hayaku* "quickly"
2. Adverbs of time, e.g., 今 *ima* "now"
3. Adverbs of degree, e.g., 随分 *zuibun* "quite"

Other languages have additionally adverbs of place, which is expressed by nominal categories and particles in Japanese.

8.1.1 Adverb Morphology and Derived Adverbs

Japanese genuine adverbs are a non-inflecting class. An example (直接 *chokusetsu* "directly") is given in (250).

(250) 直接　　聞いて　みます
chokusetsu kii-te　mi-masu
directly　ask-INF　try-AHON:+

"I will ask directly."

However, other part-of-speech classes can inflect to behave like adverbs. Adjectives in the continuative form can modify verbs in the same way as adverbs:

$$\begin{bmatrix} \textit{isect-adv-lex} \\ \text{LKEYS.KEYREL.PRED} & \boxed{1} \\ \text{HEAD} & \textit{adv\_head} \\ \text{CONTEXT} & \boxed{2} \\ \text{HOOK} & \boxed{3} \\ \text{NON-LOCAL} & \boxed{4} \end{bmatrix} \rightarrow \begin{bmatrix} \textit{base-adj-stem-lex} \\ \text{LKEYS.KEYREL.PRED} & \boxed{1} \\ \text{CONTEXT} & \boxed{2} \\ \text{HOOK} & \boxed{3} \\ \text{NON-LOCAL} & \boxed{4} \\ \text{STEMTYPE} & \textit{adj-stem} \end{bmatrix}$$

FIGURE 74 *adj2adv-lexeme-infl-rule*

(251) 弱い → 弱く
       yowai *yowaku*
       weak   weakly

This is done by a fully productive derivational rule that changes the category of adjective to adverb: *adj2adv-lexeme-infl-rule*. It changes the adjective ending い *i* to く *ku*, makes the head type of the result to be an *adv_head* (therefore modifying predicates), copies PRED, CTXT, CONT.HOOK and NONLOCAL from the adjective stem entry and makes the result an intersective adverb (*isect-adv-lex*, see § 8.1.2 below). The semantics of the resulting adverb thus contains an ARG0 and an ARG1 (just as the adjective) (see Figure 74).

Some temporal nouns can also behave just like adverbs:

(252) 今日   東京   に   行き ます
       kyou *Toukyou* LOC *iki-masu*
       today Tokyo   to   go-AHON:+

"Today I go to Tokyo."

A unary rule (*adv_np_rule*) takes these temporal nouns and adds a new underspecified modification relation that looks like a post-position (*unspec_p*). This then can modify verbs. See § 6.5 for more discussion.

8.1.2 Types of Adverbial Modification

Adverbs can be modifiers or complements. As modifiers, they can be intersective or scopal. In order to account for this, we make use of the type hierarchy: the type *adv-lex* contains subtypes *scopal-adv-lex* and *isect-adv-lex*. They add the basic form of the semantic relation contributed by the adverb and a modification type which is used to ensure that the appropriate head-adjunct rule (scopal or intersective) is used (see § 3.2.3). The examples in (253) and (254) illustrate intersective and scopal adverbial modification, respectively.

(253) a. そろそろ 食べる
    sorosoro taberu
    soonish   eat

    "I'll eat soonish."

  b. $\left\langle \begin{array}{l} h_3, \\ \{\} \end{array} \left\{ \begin{array}{l} h_3\text{:\_sorosoro\_a}\left(\begin{array}{l} e_4\,\{\text{TENSE }untensed\}, \\ e_2\,\{\text{TENSE }pres\} \end{array} \right), \\ h_3\text{:\_taberu\_v\_1}(e_2, u_6, u_5) \end{array} \right\}, \right\rangle$

(254) a. たぶん 食べる
    tabun   taberu
    probably eat

    "I'll probably eat."

  b. $\left\langle \begin{array}{l} h_3, \\ \{h_5 =_q h_6\} \end{array} \left\{ \begin{array}{l} h_3\text{:\_tabun\_r}(e_4\,\{\text{TENSE }tense\}, h_5), \\ h_6\text{:\_taberu\_v\_1}(e_2\,\{\text{TENSE }pres\}, u_8, u_7) \end{array} \right\}, \right\rangle$

A further function of adverbs in Japanese is to express comparative and superlative forms of adjectives. That is, this is not done via adjectival morphology in the language but rather by modification by degree adverbs of the adjectives:

(255) もっと 安い
    motto yasui
    more   cheap

    "cheaper"

(256) 一番 安い
    ichiban yasui
    most   cheap

    "cheapest"

8.2 Interrogatives

The major interrogatives are listed along with a gloss and a simplified version of their semantics in Table 24. Interrogatives also set the sentential force to be a question (*ques*, see § 5.1.4.3 for more discussion).

Interrogative words, such as 何 *nani* "what" or どこ *doko* "where" are given a decomposed semantics. For example, *nani* "what" is treated as "what thing", and *doko* "where" as "what place". The decomposition is different from, for example English, where *when* "at what time" and *where* "in what place" also contain the equivalent of a preposition in their semantics, whereas in Japanese they must be followed by a

Word	Gloss	Variants	Lexical Type
何 *nani* "what"	what thing	なに	*wh-word-thing-lex*
誰 *dare* "who"	what person	だれ, 何方, となた, とち様	*wh-word-person-lex* *wh-word-person-hon-lex*
何時 *itsu* "when"	what time	いつ	*wh-word-temp-lex*
何処 *doko* "where"	what place	とこ	*wh-word-place-lex*
何故 *naze* "why"	for what reason	なぜ, どうして, 何で, なんで	*adv-wh-lex*
いくら *ikura* "how much"	how much	幾ら	*adv-wh-lex*
とう *dou* "how"	[in] what way	如何, いかが	*lex-mod-adv-wh-lex*

TABLE 24 Interrogative Semantics

post-position. In normal use, 何時 *itsu* "when" undergoes the same unary rule (*adv_np_rule*) as other temporal nouns and ends up with the prepositional semantics as well (**unspec_p**).

何 *nan-* "which" with a classifier afterwards, builds up an expression meaning "which number of X", where X is the thing classified. This is a common way of asking questions about "how many" or "how much" in Japanese. For example, to ask how heavy a bag is, you you would often say something like (257).

(257) カバン は 何 キロ です か
      kaban wa nan kiro desu ka
      bag TOP what kilogram COP.AHON:+ Q

"How heavy is the bag (lit: how many kilograms is the bag)?"

8.3 Demonstratives

The Japanese demonstratives differ from English in that there is a three-way split between proximal *ko-*, medial *so-* and distal *a-*. Along with an interrogative form *do-*, these appear in a wide range of words, as

Part of speech	Proximal ko-	Medial so-	Distal a-	Interrogative do-
Determiner	*kono*	*sono*	*ano*	*dono* "which"
Pronoun	*kore*	*sore*	*are*	*dore* "which"
Locative	*koko*	*soko*	*asoko*	*doko* "where"
Locative	*kochira*	*sochira*	*achira*	*dochira* "where"
Manner Adverb	*koo*	*soo*	*aa*	*doo* "how"

TABLE 25 Demonstrative words

show in Table 25. See Backhouse (1993, 115–118) for more discussion.

In order to capture the regularity, we give a decomposed analysis for the demonstrative pronouns and locatives, effectively treating *kore* "this" and *koko* "here" as "this thing" and "this place". This decomposition is also done by other DELPH-IN grammars such as the ERG and **GG**, and makes it easy to model similarities across languages (Seah and Bond, 2014). We therefore have two predicates for each kind: one that corresponds to the actual determiner (e.g., _kono_q, marked with an initial underscore) and one that corresponds to the demonstrative component of the demonstrative pronoun (kono_q), shown in Figure 75. We need to distinguish between actual words and subcomponents of pronouns in order to distinguish between *koko* "here" and *kono tokoro* "this place". On the other hand, we want to model the similarity in meaning, which we do by making both predicates subtypes of the common supertype proximal_q. Finally, note that the which_q relation is one of a set of proposed universals for the Grammar Matrix (Bender et al., 2002): we expect all languages to have a quantifier that behaves similarly to this. See Seah and Bond 2014 for a fuller discussion of the decomposition of pronouns.

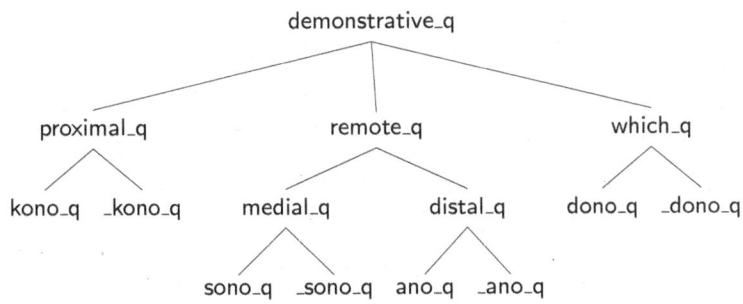

FIGURE 75 Type Hierarchy for Demonstratives

The presence of an interrogative like *dono* means that the entire utterance should be a question. Because this is a non-local effect, we model this by making the feature NON-LOCAL.QUE (question) a non-empty list. The rule for making declarative sentences is constrained to only fire when NON-LOCAL.QUE is empty, thus blocking the ungrammatical **doko-e ikimasu* "You go where".[1] In speech, this is acceptable with a rising inflection, we model this by having a rule for speech (and informal text) that allows sentences without an overt question particle to be interpreted as questions.

8.4 Summary and Further Reading

This chapter describes the basic analysis of Japanese adverbs and demonstratives. Japanese genuine adverbs are non-inflecting. On the other hand, adjectives in the continuative form are adverbs. We account for this with a derivational rule. Japanese adverbs can be modifiers or complements in syntax. Modification can be intersective or scopal. See Kasper (1995) for the differentiation. From the semantic point of view, Japanese adverbs can be adverbs of manner, time, or degree. Degree adverbs occur with adjectives and fulfill the task of comparison, as comparatives and superlatives are not marked by inflectional forms of adjectives in Japanese. We give a decomposed analysis for the demonstrative pronouns and locatives. Therefore, we treat *kore* "this" as "this thing" and *koko* "here" as "this place", as in other HPSG descriptions like the ERG (Flickinger, 2008).

For a general description of adverbs in Japanese, see Backhouse (1993, 73–74) and Tsujimura (1996, 131–132). Many Japanese adverbs are mimetic—their sound mimics the meaning in some way, because these are not syntactically or semantically irregular we do not discuss them here, see Hamano 1998 for a full description.

---

[1]This is a simplified version of the analysis for English wh-questions presented in Pollard and Sag (1994, 159).

9

Honorifics

An important feature of Japanese (particularly the spoken varieties) is its elaborate system of honorifics. Honorifics serve to encode the social distance between the speaker and the addressee or other third person referents.[1] Systems of honorifics are reasonably common in the world's languages, but can vary in their complexity. Examples (258)–(260) give near-translational equivalents of the same sentences in German, French and Japanese, respectively.

(258) *Wann haben   Sie   Zeit?*
      when have.2.AHON:+.PRES 2.AHON:+ time

  "When do you have the time?"

(259) *Quand est-ce que vous   avez   du*
      when Q   2.AHON:+ have.2.AHON:+.PRES of.the
      temps?
      time

  "When do you have the time?"

(260) いつ ご 都合   が   よろしい でしょう   か
      itsu go-tsugou   ga   yoroshii deshoo   ka
      when HON-convenience NOM good   COP.AHON:+ Q

  "When are the conditions (hon, i.e., your convenience) good?"

Each of these utterances has the semantic content indicated by the English translation, but there is also additional pragmatic content not captured by the gloss. The speaker is expressing social distance from the addressee. In German and French, this is expressed by the honorific second-person pronouns *Sie* and *vous* (together with the appropriate

---

[1]More generally, this system is used in the construction of social situations, speakers' stances, and personae; see Okushi (1997).

210 / JACY

form of the verb). In the Japanese example it is expressed by the following attributes:

- The honorific prefix *go* in front of *tsugou* "convenience"
- The honorific adjective *yoroshii* "good"
- The honorific copula *deshoo* "probably is"

A Japanese utterance with the same semantic content addressed to a more familiar (socially closer) addressee could be:

(261) いつ 時間 が ある の
     itsu jikan ga aru no
     when time NOM exist.AHON:− Q

"When do you have the time?"

We model honorifics in **Jacy** for several reasons: First, there are interactions between the honorific markers and syntactic phenomena (e.g., honorific agreement or the fact that addressee honorifics don't appear in certain subordinate clauses). Second, correct modeling of honorifics is critical to machine translation as well as other applications of generation. Finally, honorifics encode information that is key to reference resolution, particularly of zero pronouns: Siegel (1996a) calculated that 23.9% of the zero pronouns can be resolved using lexical pragmatic restrictions about honorification.

The rest of this chapter is structured as follows: § 9.1 gives an overview of the system of honorifics in Japanese and explores the interaction between the different types of honorifics. § 9.2 gives reviews a selection of previous analyses of Japanese honorifics, before § 9.3 explains the analysis developed and implemented in **Jacy**, which is briefly evaluated in § 9.4. Finally, § 9.5 and § 9.6 explore how the analysis can be useful in a machine translation scenario on the one hand and in the analysis of other languages on the other.

9.1 Honorific Forms in Japanese

9.1.1 Three Types of Honorifics

Compared to western European languages, Japanese has a relatively elaborate system of honorifics. In this section, we briefly review the contrasts encoded by these honorifics and the forms they take. Japanese honorifics can be understood as encoding social relationships between the speaker and addressee, the referent of subject of the sentence, and/or the third-person referent of a non-subject constituent.[2] While the addressee can also be the referent of the subject of the sentence

---

[2]See note 1.

and thus these categories can overlap, we nonetheless separate them as they relate differently to the morphosyntactic devices for marking honorification.

Addressee honorifics include variation in verbal endings, sentence final particles (especially those related to questions) and the choice of first-person pronouns.[3] The verbal endings are illustrated in (262) and (263), where the so-called plain form in (262) is appropriate for familiar addressees and the so-called *masu*-form in (263) is appropriate for socially distant (or superior) addressees.

(262) 田中　さん を　待つ
　　　Tanaka san wo matsu
　　　Tanaka HON ACC wait.AHON:−

　　　"I wait for Mr/Ms Tanaka."

(263) 田中　さん を　待ち ます
　　　Tanaka san wo machi-masu
　　　Tanaka HON ACC wait-AHON:+

　　　"I wait for Mr/Ms Tanaka."

The sentence final particles are illustrated in (260) and (261) above, where の *no* is used with familiar addressees and か *ka* with distant ones. The choice of first person pronouns is sensitive to both social distance and gender: The neutral pronoun in a feminine style is わたし *watashi* and the formal one (used with a socially distant addressee) is わたくし *watakushi*. For masculine styles, 僕 *boku* is neutral, while わたし *watashi* is formal. There are also pronouns which are used specifically in familiar (socially close) contexts.

Subject honorifics are expressed through changes in verbal stems and/or verbal inflection. Most verbs have a neutral form and a pair of derived forms one for a socially distant subject and one for the case where the subject is the speaker and the speaker is expressing social distance with respect to some other argument (the so-called 'humble' form). These map to the traditional categories of 尊敬語 *sonkeigo* and 謙譲語 *kenjougo*. Some verbs have suppletive stems for these two functions, rather than derived forms, such as 行く *iku* with the sonkeigo form いらっしゃる *irassharu* and the kenjougo form 参る *mairu*. Consider (264):

(264) 先生　　を　お待ち　　します
　　　Sensei wo o-machi shi-masu
　　　Professor ACC SHON:−-wait do.SHON:−-AHON:+

　　　"I wait for the professor."

---

[3]Addressee honorifics are traditionally called 丁寧語 *teineigo*.

In this example, the speaker chooses a (productively derived) humble form of the verb to indicate social distance between him/herself and the object of the sentence (先生 *sensei* "professor"). In addition, the ending on the verb (ます *mase*) expresses social distance to the addressee.

Finally, there are so-called entity honorifics, which are not restricted to subject position. These include contrasts in referring expressions for second and third person (e.g., the second person pronoun そちら *sochira* or the honorific name-suffix さん *san* as contrasted with another second-person pronoun 君 *kimi* or the familiar name-suffix 君 *kun*). Note that in second person uses, these are closely related to addressee-honorifics. In addition there are lexical contrasts for some nouns as well as semi-productive prefixes 御 *o* and 御 *go* (and very occasionally 御 *mi*) which attach to nouns.[4]

9.1.2 Interaction of Different Kinds of Honorification

The relationship between speaker, addressee and subject can be one of three possible constellations:

1. The addressee is the subject of the utterance.
2. The speaker is the subject of the utterance.
3. A third person is the subject of the utterance.

When the addressee is the referent of the subject of the sentence, then the subject honorifics and addressee honorifics must agree. For first-person subjects, the subject honorifics also tend to reflect addressee honorifics: If the speaker is using addressee honorifics, then s/he is (more) likely to use humble forms of verbs with first-person subjects.

In many cases utterances contain multiple honorifications as can be seen in the following example:

(265) 私　　が　　お 電話　　　　いたし ました
　　　 watashi ga   o-denwa   itashi-mashi-ta
　　　 I   NOM SHON:–-telephone do.SHON:–-AHON:+-PST

"I made a phone call."

The verbal stem いたし *itashi* "do" as well as the prefix *o-* on the verbal noun express subject honorification (with negative polarity, i.e., a humble form), the verbal ending まし *mashi* and the pronoun わたくし *watakushi* "1SG" express addressee honorification.

Japanese honorification undergoes different kinds of restrictions. The first kind to mention is called 'pragmatic agreement' by Pollard

---
[4]These are part of the traditional category *sonkeigo*.

and Sag (1994). There must be agreement between the honorification of the subject and the verb, as the following examples show:

(266) a. 私　　　が　先生　　に　お電話
   watakushi ga   sensei   ni   o-denwa
   1SG   NOM professor DAT SHON:−-telephone
   いたし まし た
   itashi-mashi-ta
   do.SHON:−-AHON:+-PST

   "I called the professor."

b. #先生　　が　私　　　に　お電話
   #sensei ga   watakushi ni   o-denwa
   professor NOM 1SG   DAT SHON:−-telephone
   いたし まし た
   itashi-mashi-ta
   do.SHON:−-AHON:+-PST

   Intended: "The professor called me."

c. 先生　　が　私　　　に　お電話
   sensei   ga   watakushi ni   o-denwa
   professor NOM 1SG   DAT SHON:+-telephone
   なさい まし た
   nasai-mashi-ta
   do.SHON:+-AHON:+-PST

   "The professor called me."

The pronoun 私 wata(ku)shi "I" can be used with a humble verb form, but not the noun 先生 sensei "professor", which refers to a honorable person. This must be used with an honorific (or at least neutral) verb form.

Another kind of restriction concerns certain embedded clauses, as illustrated in the following examples from Harada (1976):[5]

(267) a. 太郎 は　花子　　が　来 まし た　　　と　言った
   Taro wa Hanako ga   ki-mashi-ta   to   it-ta
   Taro TOP Hanako NOM come-AHON:+-PST COMP say-PST

   "Taro said that Hanako came."

b. 太郎 は　花子　　が　来 た　と　言った
   Taro wa Hanako ga   ki-ta   to   it-ta
   Taro TOP Hanako NOM come-PST COMP say-PST

   "Taro said that Hanako came."

---

[5]Note that こと koto is a bleached head noun that functions to nominalize the clause that attaches to it. See § 6.4 for an overview of our analysis of such nouns.

c. *太郎 は 花子 が 来ました こと を
   *Taro wa Hanako ga ki-mashi-ta koto wo
   Taro TOP Hanako NOM come-AHON:+-PST NMLZ ACC
   しら なかった
   shira-nakat-ta
   know-NEG-PST

   Intended: "Taro did not know that Hanako came."

d. 太郎 は 花子 が 来た こと を
   Taro wa Hanako ga ki-ta koto wo
   Taro TOP Hanako NOM come-PST NMLZ ACC
   しら なかった
   shira-nakat-ta
   know-NEG-PST

   "Taro did not know that Hanako came."

Clausal complements of verbs (such as 言う *iu* "say") allow the addressee-honorific verbal endings, while the clausal complement of nominalizers such as こと *koto* do not.

9.2 Previous Approaches

Investigations of Japanese honorifics have been made from the point of view of sociolinguistics, formal grammar and machine translation. For sociolinguistic studies, see for example McGloin 1976, Ide 1986, Hori 1986, Hill et al. 1986, Coulmas 1987, and Okushi 1997. These authors analyze honorification as an expression of the social distance or 'perceived distance' Hill et al. (1986) between speaker and addressee and/or an expression of belonging to a social group Coulmas (1987). They also investigate the relation between gender and the use of honorific expressions Hori (1986).

Grammatical investigations of Japanese honorification include Ikeya 1983; Kuno 1973 and Harada 1976. Hori (1986) suggests the use of honorification in the definition of 'subject' in Japanese. Kuno (1973) classifies honorification into that concerning style and that concerning respect. These classes map onto our addressee and subject honorifics, respectively. Kuno also shows that there are differences of grade in various expressions of honorification.

Harada (1976) gives a classification of honorific forms that is quite similar to ours. Harada's classification is shown in Figure 76, and ours in Figure 77. Harada's 'subject honorifics' and 'object honorifics' both correspond to our subject honorifics, with opposite polarities. In addition, we classify entity honorifics as a subtype of propositional honorifics, along side subject honorifics.

Ikeya (1983) gives a GPSG analysis of Japanese honorifics, with a Boolean head feature EHON (for subject honorifics, corresponding to our SHON, see below), where the Head Feature Principle accounts for the agreement restrictions on subject honorification. Gunji (1987) also analyzes syntactic restrictions on honorification in terms of a head feature HON.

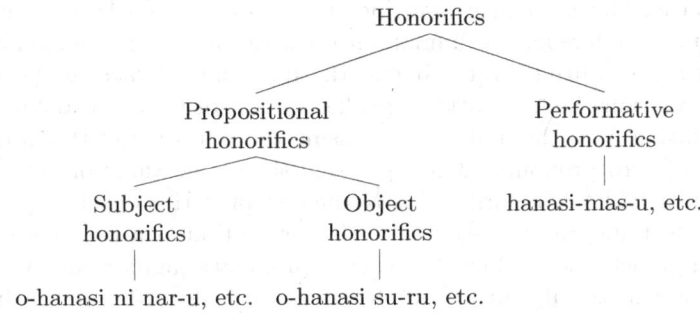

FIGURE 76 Classification of honorifics by Harada (1976)

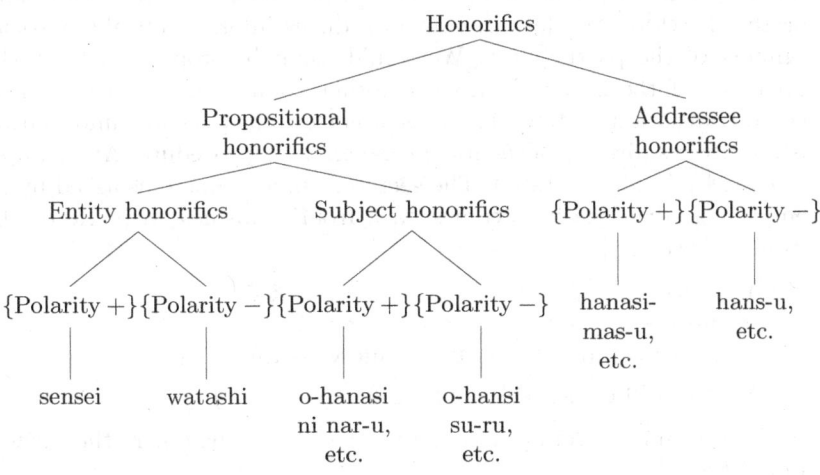

FIGURE 77 Classification of honorifics in **Jacy**

Dohsaka (1990) looks at Japanese honorifics from the point of view of machine translation. He describes how information about honori-

$$\left[\text{BACKGROUND} \left\{ \begin{bmatrix} \text{RELATION} & \textit{owe-honor} \\ \text{HONORER} & \boxed{1} \\ \text{HONORED} & \boxed{2} \\ \text{POLARITY} & 1/0 \end{bmatrix} \right\} \right]$$

FIGURE 78 owe-honor relation from Pollard and Sag 1994

fication can be used in a machine translation system to resolve zero pronominal references to human entities. He builds up a model of social relations during processing of the dialogue, extracting the pragmatic relations honorification, speaker's point of view and territory of information from the dialogue and using them to restrict the interpretation of zero pronouns. This approach shows the value of extracting information about honorification to the interpretation of zero pronouns.

Pollard and Sag (1994) analyze honorification as a pragmatic fact, and approach the problem they call 'pragmatic agreement' with information in the BACKGROUND feature. BACKGROUND takes a list of relations as its value, including owe-honor relations for honorification as shown in Figure 78.

This approach can handle subject honorification, but not the full range of kinds of honorification presented above. Green (1997) elaborates the CONTEXT feature and introduces information about social ranking of the participants. We would, though, propose to leave the inference of the social relations to other components of, e.g., a machine translation system. The reason is that all necessary information is not always directly accessible in the analysis procedure. An example is given by Coulmas (1987): The secretary in a company is asked by an employee, when the boss comes back from a business trip. He or she would answer:

(268) 来週　　 帰って　　 いらっしゃい ます
　　　 raishuu　 kaet-te　　 irasshai-masu
　　　 next.week return-INF PROG.SHON:+-AHON:+
　　　 "He will come back next week"

If the same secretary would be asked by a customer, the answer would be:

(269) 来週　　 帰って　　 まいり ます
　　　 raishuu　 kaet-te　　 mairi-masu
　　　 next.week return-INF PROG.SHON:−-AHON:+
　　　 "He will come back next week"

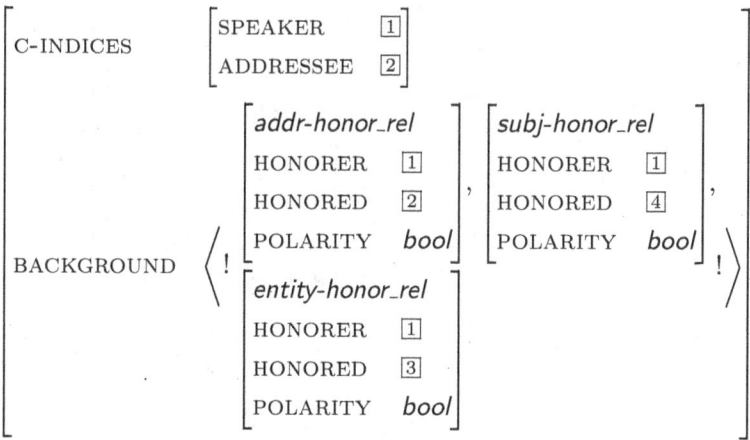

FIGURE 79 Structure inside CONTEXT

In both cases, the ます *masu* addressee honorific is used. The form of the verb changes, however, from a positive subject honorific (いらっしゃる *irrasharu*) in (268) to a negative subject honorific (まいる *mairu*) in (269). This is because the addressee is in-group in (268) and out-group in (269). The interpretation of the complex social relations must be left to a module that has access to the information about the actual social relations of the participants in the context. The grammar's job is to encode the pragmatic constraints associated with utterances.

9.3 Japanese Honorification in Jacy

Our analysis builds on that of Pollard and Sag (1994). To account for the fact that Japanese honorification has more dimensions, we propose the feature structure inside CTXT (CONTEXT) shown in Figure 79. The C-INDICES structure contains the indices for speaker and addressee, as proposed by Pollard and Sag (1994). The value of BACKGROUND contains all of the honorific relations expressed by the sign. Each relation gets classified into *addr-honor_rel*, *subj-honor_rel* and *entity-honor_rel*.[6] The HONORER is co-indexed with the speaker in all cases here, but in cases of indirect speech, other values for HONORER are possible. The HONORED value is co-indexed with the addressee in C-INDICES in the

---

[6]In Figure 79 we have shown one of each for purposes of illustration, but they aren't necessarily always all present and a given utterance can have more than one of a given type. As with the RELS and HCONS lists, we model this notional multiset with difference lists.

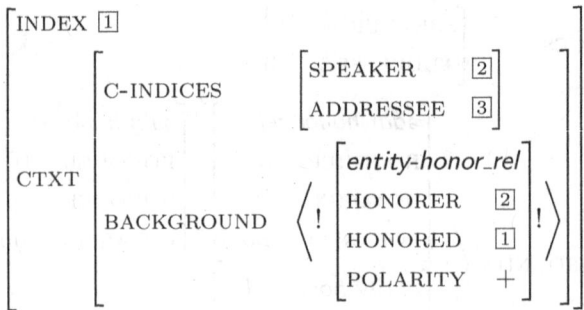

FIGURE 80 Honorification in the lexical type of *o-uchiawase* "meeting"

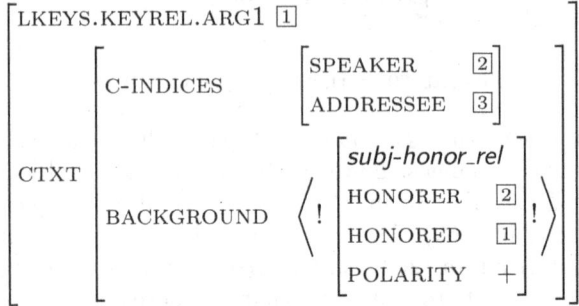

FIGURE 81 Constraint on a subject honorification verb

addr-honor_rel case, with the subject's CONTENT.INDEX value in the *subj-honor_rel* case and with the CONTENT.INDEX value of the noun that introduces the relation in the *entity-honor_rel* case. In addition, these relations all bear a feature POLARITY, to account for the fact that there can be forms that are honorific, humble or neutral. A [POLARITY −] *subj-honor_rel*, for example, reflects a situation where the speaker or a third person that socially belongs to the inner circle of the speaker is the subject of the utterance.

The next question is: how does the information enter into the BACKGROUND? Let us start with the *entity-honor_rel*. This relation is encoded in the nouns that express honorification. For example, the entry for お打ち合わせ *o-uchiawase* "meeting" is subject to the constraint in Figure 80.

A verb expressing (positive) subject honorification is subject to the constraint in Figure 81. Note that this constraint is in fact stated in terms of the semantic feature ARG1, such that, for example, passive

$$\left[\text{HEAD}\left[\text{FORMAL}\begin{bmatrix}\text{AHON} & \textit{bool}\\ \text{SHON} & \textit{bool}\end{bmatrix}\right]\right]$$

FIGURE 82 Syntactic features for honorification

subject honorification verbs in fact express honorification of the demoted subject. If it happens to be the case that an entity with an *entity-honor_rel* in its BACKGROUND becomes the subject of the sentence, the mother node must get the *subj-honor_rel* from the predicate, identified with the index of that entity. However, because examples with mismatches in honorifics between subjects and predicates are judged ungrammatical and because there are syntactic contexts in which certain honorific forms are disallowed, we decided to represent honorifics at the syntactic level, too.

In this we are following Gunji (1987), who also argues for a syntactic approach.[7] He describes in his JPSG-account of Japanese syntax honorification as a kind of agreement: "Since Japanese does not have syntactic agreement phenomena such as number, person, etc., the honorification system is more or less a counterpart." (p.25) Gunji introduces the boolean feature HON. HON is a head feature, and thus subject to the Head Feature Principle. Gunji's HON is, however, only a representation of subject honorification. Honorification concerning the addressee or other entities is not considered. Therefore, we expanded the syntactic part of the representation of honorification, using a head feature called FORMAL. FORMAL groups together two features, SHON and AHON, for subject and addresee honorofication respectively. This is shown in Figure 82.

Only by representing honorification on the syntactic **and** contextual levels can we account for all the phenomena presented here. A purely syntactic approach cannot capture the meaning of honorifics; in particular it cannot represent honorification relations between the speaker and addresee, entity honorifics, or multiple honorific relations within a sentence. On the other hand, a purely pragmatic approach cannot account for the syntactic restrictions on subjects and certain subordinate clauses. The CONTEXT structure gives information about the conditions for pragmatic felicity of an utterance, while the CAT structure gives information about syntactic correctness of an utterance. For honorification in Japanese, we need both. With the fundamental concept of HPSG, the sign, it is possible to incorporate **both** levels of linguistic analysis.

---

[7]See also Ikeya (1983).

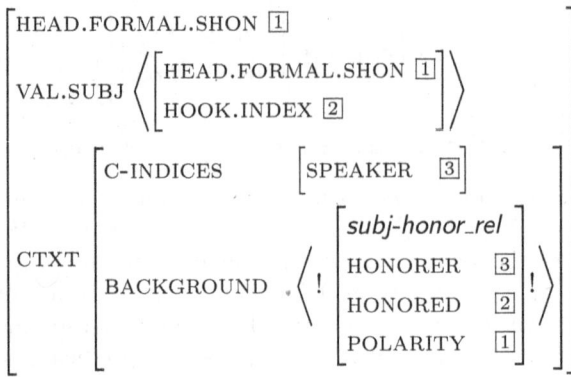

FIGURE 83 Principle of Subject Honorification

In order to model honorific agreement, i.e., the fact that certain nouns such as 先生 *sensei* "professor" cannot serve as the subject of so-called "humble" verbs and conversely others, such as *watashi* "1SG" cannot appear as the subject of "honorific" verbs, we constrain SHON on nouns as well as verbs. In addition, humble and honorific verbs are subject to the constraint in Figure 83, dubbed the Principle of Subject Honorification.[8]

According to this constraint, verbs which introduce a *subj-honor_rel* must agree in their SHON feature with their subjects. Furthermore, the POLARITY on the *subj-honor_rel* must also match the SHON value. This ensures that humble forms are never used with subject nouns that require honorific (or at least neutral) predicates and vice versa. More generally, this principle accounts for the compatibility of the information on the syntactic (CAT) and pragmatic (CTXT) levels.

In the case of addressee honorification, we do not find such examples of apparent syntactic agreement: non-addressee-honorific and addressee-honorific verbs may combine. However, we still need a syntactic reflex of addressee-honorific forms, in order to restrict them from appearing in certain subordinate clauses (see (267a)–(267d) above). The lexical entries for the various verbal endings set the value of AHON as appropriate, while the relative clause construction restricts it to [AHON −]. As for the *addr-honor_rel* in the BACKGROUND, we introduce it through the rules which license stand-alone utterances (instances of *utterance-type*), as shown in Figure 84.[9] This type adds the *addr-honor_rel* to the

---

[8]This principle should be implemented as a constraint on the type *v-lex*.

[9]The ⊕ in this figure indicates an append relation, actually implemented with difference lists.

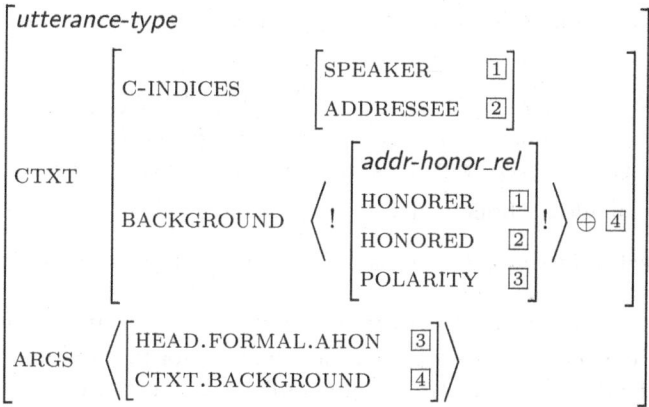

FIGURE 84 Partial constraints from *utterance-type*, introducing the *addr-honor_rel*

BACKGROUND list, while preserving the relations assembled from lower in the tree. Here, the polarity of the *addr-honor_rel* is determined by the (syntactic) AHON value of the head daughter; all utterances have some *add-honor_rel*, as there are no neutral forms in this regard. Once again, we see the coordination of syntactic and pragmatic information that is possible thanks to the sign-based approach of HPSG.

While the syntactic information goes up the tree thanks to the Head Feature Principle, the contextual information needs separate treatment. Pollard and Sag (1994, 333) propose the following "Principle of Contextual Consistency":

> The CONTEXT|BACKGROUND value of a given phrase is the union of the CONTEXT|BACKGROUND values of the daughters.

This approach assumes that all BACKGROUND information comes in with lexical items, and the role of phrase structure rules is only to gather it up. Our analysis almost conforms to this constraint: The one exception is the introduction of an *addr-honor_rel* by the utterance rules. Thus almost all phrase structure rules construct the BACKGROUND value of the mother on the basis of the BACKGROUND value of the daughters. The utterance rules simply add an addition relation, as shown in Figure 84 above. Finally, in order to make sure that the contextual indices (C-INDICES) are consistent across the sentence, they are shared between the mother and all daughters in each phrase structure rule.

To see how the various pieces of this analysis work together, let's take an example of multiple honorifications, (265), repeated here as (270):

(270) 私 が お電話 いたしました
   watakushi ga *o-denwa* *itashi-mashi-ta*
   1SG NOM SHON:−-telephone do.SHON:−-AHON:+-PST
   "I made a phone call."

The self-referring pronoun *watakushi* introduces an **entity-honor_rel** with POLARITY −, where the HONORER and HONORED are co-indexed with both the C-INDICES|SPEAKER and the CONTENT|INDEX. In other words, the speaker is using a self-deprecating form. This information is passed up the tree in the head-complement structure of *watakushi ga*. At the same time, the values of HEAD|FORMAL are introduced: [AHON +] and [SHON −]. As particles are assumed to be heads (see Siegel 1999 and Chapter 7), they must take their SHON value from their complements. (This constraint is included in the definition of the lexical type for particles). The honorific form *o-denwa itashi-mashi-ta* introduces a **subj-honor_rel** in the context with POLARITY −. The HONORED attribute is co-indexed with the subject's CONTENT|INDEX. The HEAD|FORMAL values are the same as those of *watakushi*. The Principle of Subject Honorification applied to a sentence with this pronoun then leads to the situation that the verb itself and its subject are constraint to be [SHON −], and the **subj-honor_rel** is introduced. The **utterance-rule** introduces an **addr-honor_rel** with POLARITY +, since the value of HEAD|FORMAL|AHON, contributed initially by the verbal ending まし *mashi* is +.

This was an example of the special case where the speaker is the subject. (271) provides an example where the addressee is the subject:

(271) あなたが お電話 を くださいました
   anata ga *o-denwa* *wo* *kudasai-mashi-ta*
   2SG NOM HON-telephone ACC give.SHON:+-AHON:+-PST
   "You made a phone call."

All three types of honorification relations are introduced here: subject honorification by the addressee-referring pronoun あなた *anata* and the verb くださる *kudasaru*, entity honorification by the honorific noun お電話 *o-denwa* and addressee honorification by the まし *mashi* ending of the verb. The polarity is + in all cases.

Finally, note that there can be multiple different **entity-honor_rel**s in a sentence, if multiple nouns have honorific markers. Furthermore, this analysis could be extended to handle honorification in embedded

	Addressee	Subject	Entity	Total
precision	1	1	1	1
recall	1	0.86	0.79	0.93

TABLE 26 Evaluation of analysis of honorifics

clauses which is distinct (or even contradictory to) that of the matrix clause, as in (272): The key point is to make sure that the embedding context blocks the propogation of the relevant CTXT features.

(272) 私　　が　　スケジュール　を　　立てたい　　　　と
watashi ga　　sukejuuru　　wo　tate-tai　　　　to
1SG　　NOM　schedule　　ACC set.up-want.AHON:−　COMP
おっしゃい まし た
osshai-mashi-ta
say.SHON:+-AHON:+-PST

"She said 'I want to set up a plan'."

9.4 Evaluation

In order to evaluate the coverage of our analysis against naturally occurring text, we randomly chose 100 utterances from the Verbmobil corpus. Then we tagged these with expected values for subject, entity and addresee honorifics. The utterances contained 170 occurrences of honorification, with 99 addressee honorifics, 32 entity honorifics and 39 subject honorifics. We parsed the utterances and compared the manual tagging with the parsing result. Then we calculated precision and recall as follows:

Precision = number of correctly assigned honorifics / number of assigned honorifics

Recall = number of correctly assigned honorifics / number of honorifics in the corpus

The results can be seen in Table 26. The very high precision results from the fact that honorofication is lexically triggered and rarely ambiguous.

9.5 Honorification and Machine Translation

The resolution of zero pronouns is a particularly difficult feature of Japanese-to-English machine translation. Modeling honorifics in the grammar can assist: lexical pragmatic restrictions for zero pronouns can be directly accounted for in the analysis, assisting in their resolution, as shown by Metzing and Siegel (1994). An example is given in (273).

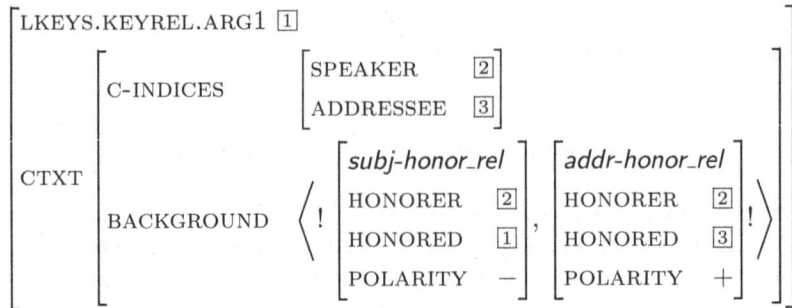

FIGURE 85 Honorific information in (273)

(273) お待ち　　して　　　おります
　　　 o-machi　 shi-te　　 ori-masu
　　　 SHON:--wait do.SHON:--INF PROG.SHON:--AHON:+

"I am waiting."

Our analysis of this sentence includes the information in Figure 85. This structure restricts the subject to one with a subject honorification with negative polarity. That is, only the speaker or a person of the speaker's social group can be the antecedent of the subject.

9.6 Honorification in Other Languages

Honorification in German concerns only the relation between speaker and addressee, as the following example shows:

(274)　*Sie sind nett*
　　　 you COP nice

　　　 "You (honorific or they) are nice."

The sentence is ambiguous, because it allows a first interpretation where *Sie* is a third person plural pronoun and therefore refers to a group of people and a second interpretation where it is a polite second person singular pronoun and refers to a single person. Honorification in German thus introduces entity honorification with honorific pronouns, but no special treatment of subjects and no addressee honorification relation separate from the use of second person pronouns. The agreement between subject and verb is a purely syntactic one. French differs somewhat from German (see Pollard and Sag 1994, 96f), but is similar in only using the entity honorific dimension. Honorification in Korean, as it is described by Lee (1996), is distinct from Japanese honorification in one point: There are no neutral forms of NPs and VPs in respect to subject honorification. Our approach thus seems to work for different kind of languages that express honorification.

9.7 Summary

This chapter has given an overview of the complex system of honorifics in Japanese, focusing primarily on syntactic constraints on the one hand, and the interface between syntax and pragmatics on the other. Honorification is mostly important when analyzing spoken language, especially dialogues, or interactive texts such as email, facebook, blogs or forum messages. It encodes the social distance between speaker, addressee and subject of the utterance. We briefly reviewed previous approaches and then presented the analysis of honorifics that is currently implemented in **Jacy**. It is based on the idea of honorific agreement, described in Gunji (1987) and the CONTEXT structure, introduced by Pollard and Sag (1994).

Our analysis allows for complex interaction between the three major types of honorifics as well as the parallel syntactic and pragmatic constraints they contribute. The general approach is applicable to other languages, such as German, French, and Korean. Nariyama et al. (2005) extend the approach with information on social ranking. Siegel (1996a) shows that honorific information is the basic source of information to resolve zero pronouns.

10
Grammar Engineering

The development of the grammar has been a combination of linguistic analysis and software development. In the previous chapters we have mainly talked about the linguistics. In this section, we talk more about the software engineering aspects. In our experience, grammarians are always the critical resource in grammar development: developing new analyses cannot be done automatically, and is a labor-intensive process. We therefore use (and have helped develop) a variety of tools and methods to aid the grammarian. We believe large grammars cannot be developed without these computational aids: the complexity of a realistic grammar is too great for a human to predict its behavior unaided.

In the following sections we describe the grammar development environment (§ 10.1) and the basic development process (§ 10.2). We then explore the broader grammar development process, including how to store information about the correct parse (§ 10.3) and embed documentation in the grammar (§ 10.4). Finally, we look at ways to automatically identify errors within the grammar itself not just identifying incorrect sentences, but trying to find where in the grammar is causing the problems (§ 10.5). Sections of this chapter have appeared in Oepen et al. 2002a; Hashimoto et al. 2007; Bond et al. 2008a and Goodman and Bond 2009a, although they have been unified and updated here.

10.1 The Development Environment

The core tool for grammar development is the LKB, a flexible grammar and lexicon development environment (Copestake, 2002b). It can be used to both parse and generate with the grammar, and has a wide variety of options for debugging, including tools for interactively unification, examination the type hierarchy, exploration of parse chart and so forth.

The results of processing an entire test suite can be stored, manipulated and compared to other runs using the [incr tsdb()] tool for grammar and system profiling (Oepen and Flickinger, 1998). This profiling environment allows us to take snapshots of the performance of the grammar, compare the same grammar being used with different settings of even different parsers and to compare different versions of the grammar on the same test suite. It can also be used to select trees and store them (§ 10.3). [incr tsdb()] can call multiple sub-processes, so that computation can be distributed over many processors.

For efficient parsing, using both less time and space than the LKB, we use CHEAP, from the PET system (Callmeier, 2002). It is typically an order of magnitude faster than the LKB. CHEAP pre-compiles the grammar for efficiency. It has several extensions to make it more useful in real world applications, including unknown word handling, parse ranking with a statistical model and partial parsing (returning hypothesis fragments even if there is no full parse).

The grammar also runs in ACE (Crysmann and Packard, 2012), another efficient processor for HPSG grammars, which can both parse and generate. The LKB, CHEAP and ACE all use the same grammar files, with some minor differences in the configuration files. This allows us to develop using an easy-to-use interactive grammar, but to test using a faster grammar.

The grammar sources are available at https://github.com/delph-in/jacy. It is released under an open license (the MIT license) which allows anyone the rights to use, extend and distribute the grammar, so long as they acknowledge the copyright holders.

It is (partially) documented in a wiki: http://moin.delph-in.net/JacyTop. The use of the wiki makes the documentation easily available to both developers and users. The various tools described above also have documentation pages at http://moin.delph-in.net. **Jacy** development is not done in a void: it is being developed in the DELPH-IN community and benefits from (and contributes to) the general discussions of both theory and implementation.

10.2 The Grammar Development Cycle

Grammar development is typically driven by the desire to parse some body of text. A representative sample of the text is chosen and formatted into one or more test suites.[1] The grammarian then parses the test-suite storing the results in a competence and performance profile using [incr tsdb()]. Typically, the grammar will not have perfect coverage of the test suite, and the grammarian will then examine sentences

---

[1]See § 11.2.1 for a discussion of the test suites used in developing **Jacy**.

which are problematic (e.g., those that cannot be parsed, or those that have higher than expected ambiguity). After identifying a problem, a solution is tested using the interactive environment of the LKB. When it appears correct, the new grammar is used to parse the test suite again, and a new profile created. The new profile can be compared against previous profiles, in various dimensions, including coverage and efficiency. The process is summarized in Figure 86.

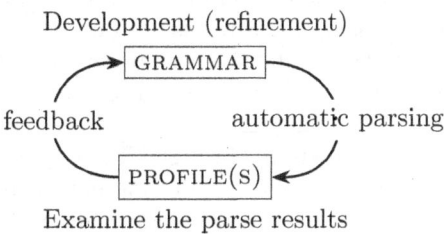

FIGURE 86 Grammar Development Cycle

Because of the complexity of the grammar, a change in one place can have hard-to-predict changes elsewhere. By regularly testing over a thousand or more sentences, it is possible to spot most changes early on. Periodically, the grammar should also be tested against other test suites, to check that it is not being over-fitted to any one particular test set.

Because the grammarian needs to keep many details of the system in their head, it is essential that the parsing does not take too long, so that it can be done frequently, even after small changes. With the current grammars typically we keep test suites to around a thousand sentences, and with several cpus these can be parsed in a couple of minutes or less.

This cyclical development strategy has proved extremely effective in developing new analyses without breaking the old ones. However, for the grammar to be truly correct, it is not enough to simply return some (or many) parses for a sentence; the parse forest must also contain the correct parse. As one sentence may have hundred or thousands (or many, many more) parses, it is not practical to search the results for the correct parse each time. We therefore began to incorporate information on the correctness of parses into the grammar develop cycle through the activity of treebanking (see next section).

10.3 Integrating Treebanking

Treebanks constructed with detailed linguistic information play an important role in various aspects of natural language processing; for example, grammatical knowledge acquisition or statistical language model induction. Such treebanks are typically constructed manually, but in the HPSG context they are constructed semi-automatically using a linguistically rich computational grammar.

A detailed grammar in turn is a fundamental component for **precise** natural language processing. It provides not only detailed syntactic and morphological information on linguistic expressions but also precise and usually language-independent semantic structures.

However, such a deep linguistic treebank and a grammar are often difficult to keep consistent through development cycles. This is both because multiple people, often in different locations, participate in a development activity, and because deep linguistic treebanks and grammars are complicated by nature. Thus, it is often the case that developers lose sight of the current state of the treebank and grammar, resulting in inconsistency. We therefore aim to integrate the treebanking into the grammar development process, as shown in Figure 87.

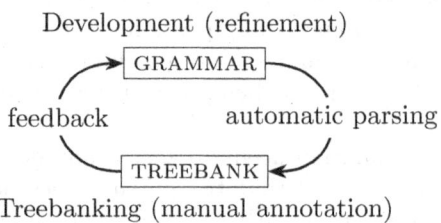

FIGURE 87 Treebanking Development Cycle

A new step is added into the grammar development cycle: periodically, as well as storing the results of the parse, the grammarian (or possibly a co-developer) chooses the intended interpretation from the possible interpretations generated by the grammar. In doing so, we find the grammar's flaws such as insufficient coverage and spurious ambiguities. The feedback allows us to refine the grammar so that it can have wider coverage and be more appropriately restricted. This integration is made possible by the fact that our treebanking is dynamic: information about which parse is correct is stored as discriminants which can be used to re-select the appropriate parse automatically (if there is no change) or semi-automatically if there are some changes. The tree-banker ideally only needs to look at places where the grammar has changed the range of interpretations: either the parse has become more ambiguous, so new decisions have to be made, or existing rules or lexical items have changed so much that the system cannot reconstruct the parse (Oepen et al., 2004a).

The basic approach to the syntactic annotation is grammar-based corpus annotation (Dipper, 2000). First, the corpus is parsed, and then the annotator selects the correct analysis (or, occasionally rejects all analyses). Selection is done through a choice of discriminants (following Oepen et al. (2004b), using a similar approach to Carter (1997)). The system computes features that distinguish between parses, and the annotator selects or rejects features until only one parse is left. The average number of decisions for each sentence is proportional to its length (around $\log_2$ of the number of parses). In general, even a sentence with 5,000 parses requires around 12 decisions (Tanaka et al., 2005). Experiments with sentences from the definition sentence corpus annotated by 3 speakers of Japanese with a high score in a Japanese proficiency test but no linguistic training gave an average annotation speed of 50 sentences an hour (Bond et al., 2008a).

The primary data stored in the treebank is the derivation trees: the series of rules and lexical items the parser used to construct each parse. This, along with the grammar, can be combined to rebuild the complete HPSG sign. The annotators task is to select the appropriate derivation tree or trees. The possible derivation trees for the definition of カーテン$_2$ *kaaten* "curtain" are shown in Figure 88. Nodes in the trees indicate applied rules, simplified lexical types or words. Each symbol below word is POS from a tagger output. We will use it as an example to explain the annotation process. The glossed definition is (275).

(275) ある 物事 を 隠す 物
aru monogoto o kakusu mono
certain something ACC hide thing

"a thing that hides something"

This example has two major sources of ambiguity. One is lexical: *aru* "a certain/have/be" is ambiguous between a reading as a determiner "a certain" (**det-lex**) and its use as a verb of possession "have" (**aru-verb-lex**). If it is a verb, this gives rise to further structural ambiguity. In addition to the different parses arising from the different parts of speech, there is further ambiguity in the relative clause (§ 6.6.2). In the gapped reading 物 *mono* "thing" is the subject of 隠す *kakusu* "hide". In the non-gapped reading there is some unspecified relation between

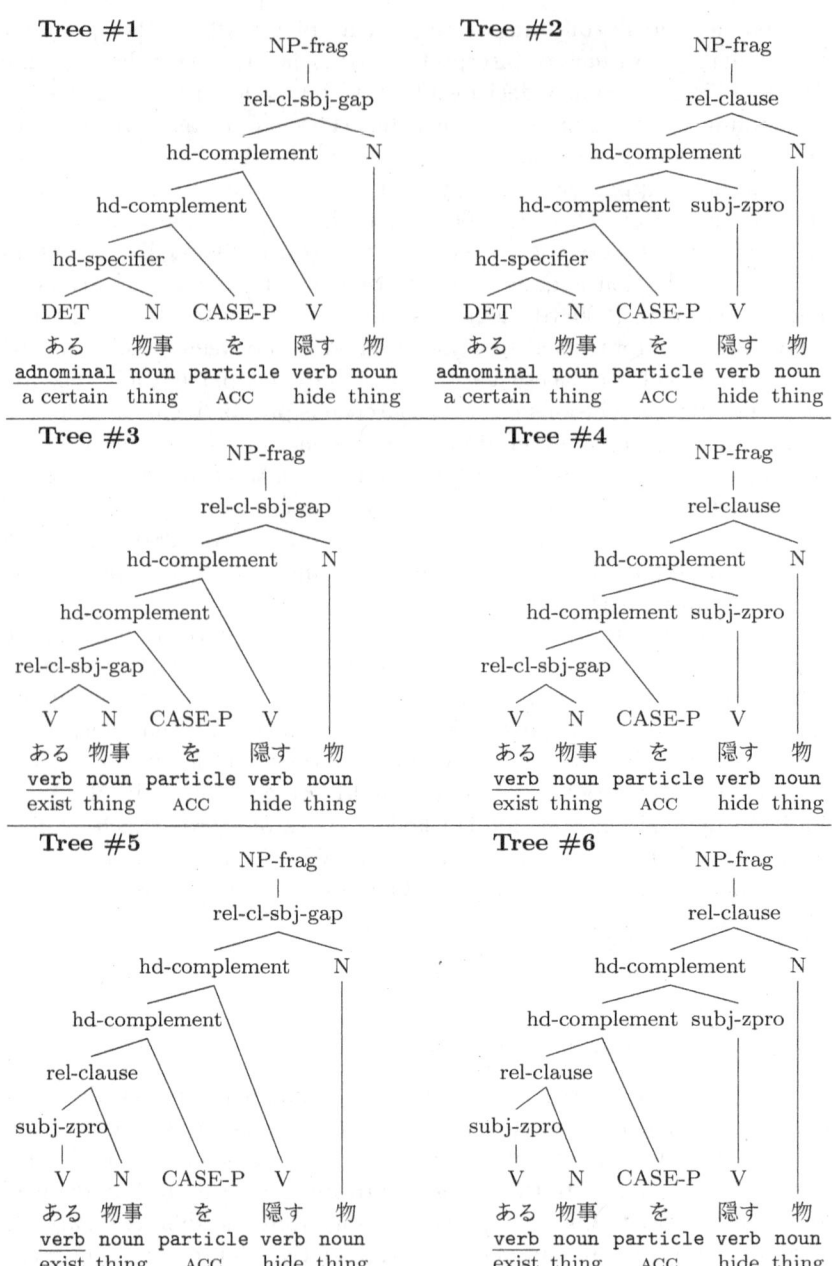

FIGURE 88 Derivation Trees of the Definition of カーテン₂ *kaaten* "curtain"

the thing and the verb phrase.[2] This is similar to the difference in the two readings of *the day he knew* in English. Such semantic ambiguity is resolved by selecting the correct derivation tree.

Overall, this five-word sentence has 6 parses. The annotator does not have to examine every tree but is instead presented with a range of 9 discriminants, as shown in Figure 89, each local to some segment of the utterance (word or phrase) and thus presenting a contrast that can be judged in isolation. Here the first column shows deduced status of discriminants (typically toggling one discriminant will rule out others), the second actual decisions, the third the discriminating rule or lexical type, the fourth the constituent spanned (with a marker showing segmentation of daughters, where it is unambiguous), and the fifth the parse trees having the rule or lexical type.

D A	rules / lexical types	subtrees / lexical items	parse trees
? ?	rel-cl-sbj-gap	ある物事 を 隠す ‖ 物	2,4,6
? ?	rel-clause	ある 物事 を 隠す ‖ 物	1,3,5
- ?	rel-cl-sbj-gap	ある ‖ 物事	3,4
- ?	rel-clause	ある ‖ 物事	5,6
+ ?	hd-specifier	ある ‖ 物事	1,2
? ?	subj-zpro	隠す	2,4,6
- ?	subj-zpro	ある	5,6
- ?	aru-verb-lex	ある	3–6
+ +	det-lex	ある	1,2

+ positive decision
- negative decision
? indeterminate / unknown
D deduced decisions, A actual decisions

FIGURE 89 Discriminants (marked after one is selected).

After selecting a discriminant, the system recalculates the discriminant set. Those discriminants which can be deduced to be incompatible with the decisions are marked with −, and this information is recorded. The tool then presents to the annotator only those discriminants which still select between the remaining parses, marked with ?.

In this case the desired parse can be selected with a minimum of two decisions. If the first decision is that ある *aru* is a determiner (det-lex), it eliminates four parses, leaving only three discriminants (corresponding to Tree #1 and #2 in Figure 88) to be decided on in the second round of decisions. Selecting 物 *mono* "thing" as the gapped subject

---
[2]See § 6.6.2.

of 隠す *kakusu* "hide" (rel-cl-sbj-gap) resolves the parse forest to the sinegle correct derivation tree #1 in Figure 88.

The annotator also has the option of leaving some ambiguity in the treebank. For example, the verbal noun オープン *oopun* "open" is defined with the single word 開く *aku/hiraku* "open". This word however, has two readings: *aku* which is intransitive and *hiraku* which is transitive. As *oopun* can be either transitive or intransitive, with no further context both parses could be correct. In such cases, we leave both parses.

Finally, the annotator has the option of rejecting all the parses presented, if none had the correct syntax and semantics. This decision has to be made even for sentences with a unique parse.

We measured inter-annotator agreement when we treebanked the Lexeed Corpus (§ 11.2.2.1). We used 5,000 sentences from the definition sentence corpus annotated by 3 speakers of Japanese with a high score in a Japanese proficiency test but no linguistic training (Tanaka et al., 2005). The average annotation speed was 50 sentences an hour.

The proportion of sentences for which two annotators selected the exact same parse was 65.4%. The proportion for which both chose parses, but there was no agreement, was 18.2%, the proportion for which both annotators found no suitable analysis was 12.4%. For 4.0% of sentences, one annotator found no suitable parses, but one selected one or more.

10.4 Embedded Documentation: The Lexical Type Database

Jacy has been built collaboratively, with multiple developers, separated both physically and temporally. This makes it easy to lose track of information and end up with inconsistent analyses. To counter this, we take a "snapshot" of one important aspect of the treebank and grammar for each development cycle. To be more precise, we extract information about lexical items that are being used in treebanking from the treebank and grammar and convert it into an electronically accessible structured database (the lexical type database). Such a snapshot helps treebank annotators and grammar developers to share precise and detailed knowledge of the treebank and grammar and thus to make them consistent throughout the development cycle.[3]

In particular, as we augment the grammar with finer distinctions, the grammar becomes more and more opaque and difficult to maintain, and so does the treebank. This is problematic in three ways. Firstly,

---

[3] We think we also need another snapshot, that of the grammar rules and principles being used. This has not yet been implemented.

when we annotate parser outputs of one sentence, we have to see which parse is correct for the sentence. Consequently, we have to distinguish which lexical type is correct for each word in the sentence. However, this task is not always trivial, since our grammar's lexical type distinctions are very fine-grained as shown above. Secondly, when we add a word to the grammar to get wider coverage, we have to see which lexical type the word belongs to. That is, we are required to be familiar with lexical types of the grammar. Thirdly, in collaborative grammar development, it sometimes happens that a developer accidentally introduces a new lexical type that represents overlapping functionality with an existing type. This causes spurious ambiguity. As a result, the grammar will be unnecessarily bloated, and the treebank will also be easily inconsistent. Again, we see that comprehensive knowledge of the grammar's lexical types is indispensable.

We include the following information for each type in the lexical type database.

1. Linguistic description of the types
    (a) Name (possibly in multiple languages)
    (b) A brief description
    (c) Criteria to judge a word as belonging to a given lexical type (positive and negative examples)
    (d) Reference to relevant literature
    (e) Comments related to the portion
    (f) ToDo items
2. Usage examples and distribution based on the grammar and treebanks
    (a) Lexeme and type frequencies
    (b) Examples of utterances that contain instances of the type
3. Typed feature structure definitions of the lexical type
    (a) The portion of grammar source file that corresponds to the usage

10.4.1 Linguistic Discussion

To understand lexical types precisely, linguistic observations and analyses are a basic source of information. Firstly, the requirements for naming lexical types in a computational system is that they be short (so that they can be displayed in large trees) and easily distinguishable. Type names are not necessarily understandable for anyone but the developers, so it is useful to link them to more conventional names. For example *naadj2adv-end-lex* is a *Nominal Adjective to Adverb Postposition*, in Japanese 形容動詞語幹助詞副詞化. Next, the description field contains a brief explanation of the lexical type. For example, *ga-wo-ni-p-lex* can be defined as "a particle that indicates that a noun it attaches to functions as an argument of a predicate." Grammar developers, treebankers, and other users can grasp the main characteristics from this.

Thirdly, the criteria field provides users with means of investigating whether a given word belongs to the class. That is, it provides positive `<ex>` and negative `<nex>` usage examples. Using these examples, developers can easily find differences among lexical types. For example, *adv-p-lex-1* subcategorizes for nouns, while *adv-p-lex-6* subcategorizes for adjectives. Ideally these sentences should be treebanked as part of the functional test suites (see § 11.2.1) so that they can be used to test that the grammar covers what it claims. This is especially important for regression testing after new development. The (optional) reference field points to representative papers or books dealing with the lexical type. This allows the grammar developers to quickly check against existing analyses, and allows users to find more information.

Finally, it is often the case that the grammar developer notices issues that they do not have time to solve. These should be noted in the ToDo field, both as a record of what needs to be done and to help users of the grammar to understand when it does not behave as expected.

10.4.2 Exemplification

Examples help users understand lexical types concretely. As we have constructed a treebank that is annotated with linguistic information, we can automatically extract relevant examples. We give the database two kinds of examples: words (instances of the lexical types) and sentences (treebanked examples that contain the words). This link to the linguistically annotated corpus examples helps annotators to check for consistency, and grammar developers to check that the lexical types are grounded in the corpus data.

10.4.3 Implementation

Grammar developers need to know exactly how the lexical types are implemented in the grammar. Figure 90 shows the implementation of *naadj2adv-end-lex*, along with the annotations for the various non-automatically generated fields of the lexical type database.

In addition to the actual implementation shown above, we automatically extract and hyperlink its parent type or types, the category of the head, i.e., the value at the end of the path SYNSEM.LOCAL.CAT.HEAD, its valence information (at the path SYNSEM.LOCAL.CAT.VAL, and its semantic type (at SYNSEM.LOCAL.CONT).

```
; <type val="naadj2adv-end-lex">
; <name-ja>承形容動詞語幹助詞副詞化
; <description>na-adj-lexの直後につく助詞の「に」。「na-adj-lex+に」の形で、
; 1つの副詞として働く。(since 2005)v-soc-adv-stem-lexやv2a-c-stem-lexの
; ように、adverbを格として取る動詞に対して使う。 ; <ex>部屋 を きれい に する
; <ex>桜 が 有名 に なる
; <nex>部屋 を きれい に 掃除 する
; <nex>確か に 鐘 が なった
; <todo>(TK 07-04-11)「そうに+V」(lkb::do-parse-tty "寒 そう に 振る舞う")
; や「na-adj-lex+に+助詞」
; (lkb::do-parse-tty "簡単 に は 譲ら ない")の場合にもこのtypeを選ぶかどうか
; の選択肢が出てしまう。(TK 07-04-11)また、「na-adj-lex+に+助詞」の場合、
; このtypeを選ぶことは可能だが、格にはなれない
; (lkb::do-parse-tty "きれい に は し ない")。
; </type>
naadj2adv-end-lex := lexical_sign-word &
  [SYNSEM j-synsem &
          [LOCAL[CAT[HEAD case-adv_head,
                     VAL obj-arg &
                         [COMPS #comps &
                                [FIRST[OPT -,
                                       LOCAL[CAT[HEAD na-adj_head,
                                                 VAL.UNSAT +],
                                             CONT[RELS <!#key & [ARG1 #xarg]!>,
                                                  HOOK[LTOP #tophand,
                                                       INDEX #ind]]]]]]],
                 ARG-S #comps,
                 CONT[HOOK[LTOP #tophand,
                           XARG #xarg,
                           INDEX #ind],
                      RELS <! !>,
                      HCONS <! !>]],
           LKEYS.KEYREL #key & [ LBL #tophand],
           NON-LOCAL[QUE <! !>,
                     AFFIX <! !>]],
   INFLECTED +].
```

FIGURE 90 Actual Implementation of *naadj2adv-p-end-lex*

10.4.4 Building the Lexical Type Database

In order to keep the documentation synchronized with the grammar, we embed it in the actual grammar description files, as shown in Figure 90. The description is written in XML, before the type it describes. It is extracted and stored in the database by a script. This approach was first suggested in Hypertextual Grammar development Dini and Mazzini (1997) but without our linking to examples in a treebank. The general idea of embedded documentation in code comes from literate programming (Knuth, 1992). This is extremely important for grammars that change constantly.[4]

We show examples of the lookup for the word に *ni* in Figure 91. It gives examples of all lexical types that have a lexeme with that orthography. For each lexical type, it shows the most common three instances; how many lexemes exist with that type in the lexicon, and how many appear with that type in the treebank.

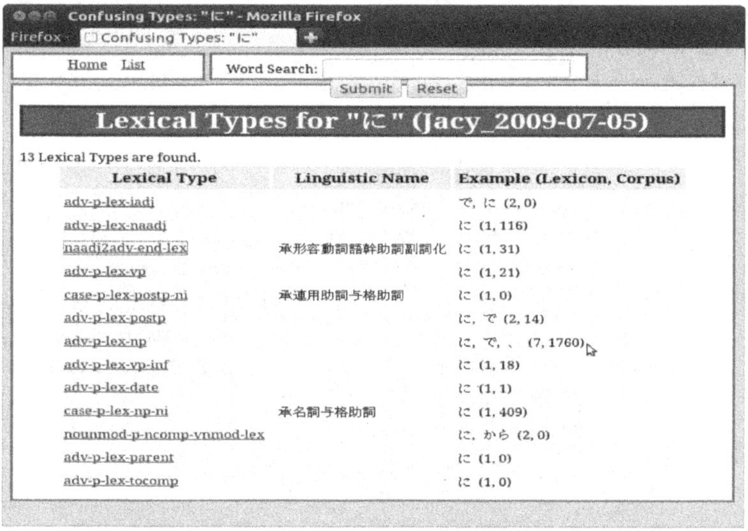

Lexical Type	Linguistic Name	Example (Lexicon, Corpus)
adv-p-lex-iadj		で, に (2, 0)
adv-p-lex-naadj		に (1, 116)
naadj2adv-end-lex	承形容動詞語幹助詞副詞化	に (1, 31)
adv-p-lex-vp		に (1, 21)
case-p-lex-postp-ni	承連用助詞与格助詞	に (1, 0)
adv-p-lex-postp		に, で (2, 14)
adv-p-lex-np		に, で, 、 (7, 1760)
adv-p-lex-vp-inf		に (1, 18)
adv-p-lex-date		に (1, 1)
case-p-lex-np-ni	承名詞与格助詞	に (1, 409)
nounmod-p-ncomp-vnmod-lex		に, から (2, 0)
adv-p-lex-parent		に (1, 0)
adv-p-lex-tocomp		に (1, 0)

FIGURE 91 Screenshot of the results of searching for に *ni*

We show examples of the lookup for the lexical type *naadj2adv-end-lex* in Figure 92. It gives the lexical description, the most common instances, three examples (and links to more) the full description from the implementation, and the links to other relevant types. As far as

[4]The lexical type database was originally developed for **Jacy**, but is also used for other DELPH-IN grammars.

possible, more information (such as the actual parse trees, super types and so on) is hyperlinked, so it is easy to access it.

10.5 Automatic Error Detection and Correction

To improve the efficiency of the grammarian even further, it is useful to identify (i) which problems are most common and (ii) which part of the grammar causes them. Work by van Noord (2004) identified problems in coverage by parsing a large corpus and identifying differences between sentences that parsed and those that didn't. A parsability score is calculated for all n-grams, depending on how often they occur in sentences that parse compared to the overall distribution. N-grams with low parsability identify input that is problematic for the grammar. This solves (i) but does not really solve (ii).

Jacy can both parse and generate, so in theory, for any sentence that it can parse, we should be able to generate the exact same sentence from the semantic representation. In practice, most effort has been put into parsing, so the generation coverage is not perfect. However, since both parsing and generation use the same grammar, their performance is closely related: in general improving the performance or cover of one direction will also improve the other (Flickinger, 2008). We produced a system (**Egad**: Goodman and Bond 2009b) that attempts to parse and generate all utterances in one or more test-suites and then uses machine learning to detect differences between those sentences that could successfully generate and those that couldn't. The differences are expressed as n-grams of rules from the parser. The system can output the most common problematic n-grams, with example sentences. By focusing on the rule combinations in the n-grams the developer could quickly identify and fix errors, starting with the most common.

Using **Egad** greatly reduced the amount of time the grammar developer spent finding bugs and helped to make informed decisions about which bugs are best to fix. Using the system, we were able to improve **Jacy**'s absolute generation coverage by 18% absolute (45% to 63%) with only four weeks of grammar development (Goodman and Bond, 2009b).

A similar process of error-mining can also be applied to other sentences which parse but are ill-formed in some way, for example if the MRS does not scope, or is not well formed (Flickinger et al., 2005).

10.6 Summary and Further Reading

To enable the construction of large grammars, we make a range of a variety of computational aids including: distributed processing; re-

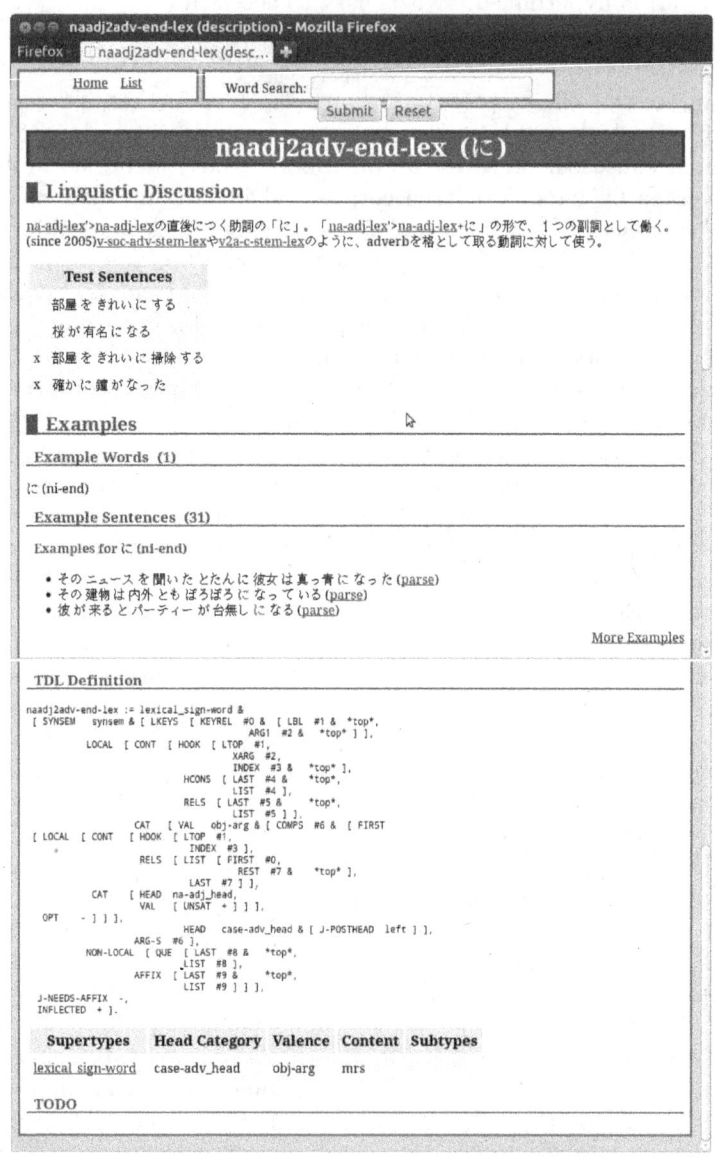

FIGURE 92 Screenshot of the entry for the type *naadj2adv-end-lex*

gression testing; dynamic treebanking; embedded documentation and automatic error detection. All of these serve to make the grammarian more productive.

For more information on collaborative language engineering in the DELPH-IN tradition, see Oepen et al. (2002b). For an example of grammar building in the lexical functional grammar community, see Butt et al. (1999). For more discussion of open source software development, see Raymond (1999). For more recent work on automatic error detection in precision grammar development, see Letcher et al. (2015).

11

The Current State of the Grammar

This chapter presents an overview of the different ways in which **Jacy** has been evaluated. The evaluation of deep grammars is complicated by several factors: the lack of any independent gold standard annotations which match the richness and detail of the output of the grammar, differences among target applications in requirements for robustness v. precision, and the range of genres that a linguistically motivated grammar aims to handle. We will thus approach the evaluation from multiple angles.

One axis along which to divide approaches to evaluation is intrinsic v. extrinsic evaluation, or developer-oriented v. operational. Intrinsic evaluation is part of grammar development at all stages, as we run regression tests to check that additions or refinements to the grammar haven't reduced coverage over previously handled phenomena or increased ambiguity in unmotivated ways. It is useful to supplement this regular regime of intrinsic evaluation with extrinsic evaluation, in order to see whether the analyzes are useful for NLP tasks (and for what kinds of tasks). Different tasks lay value on different aspects of the grammar. For example, argument structure is particularly important for the task of grammar checking. An information retrieval task would need a grammar which is good at getting the correct scope of negation. Generation, for text summarization or machine translation, needs highly precise and formally correct MRSs. Dialogue systems would need a grammar that can be parsed efficiently, as the application is time critical.

A second dimension of evaluation is internal (within-system) or external (between-system) evaluation. We do not have a comparable grammar of Japanese and therefore evaluate internally. Quantitative measures, such as coverage and size, shall be given as well as qualitative measures about the behavior of the grammar. The data the evaluation is based on can be constructed data to show the constructions the grammar can cover, as well as corpus-based data to show the usefulness in real-world applications.

Evaluation can be performed manually or automatically. Manual evaluation has an advantage in the level of detail it can provide and in the precision of its results, but is time consuming and cannot be performed on large amounts of data. Automatic evaluation can give information such as coverage on large amounts of data, but does not give precise information about output validation. We report results for both kinds of evaluation; manual evaluation by treebanking parsed sentences and inspection of MRS output, as well as automatic evaluation by coverage on constructed and natural data in different domains.

In grammar engineering as elsewhere in NLP, evaluation is a complex task, many difficult matters have to be considered and there is no one "magic number" (Sparck-Jones, 1994). For **Jacy** we try to to answer the following questions:

1. What is the size of the grammar? How many rules and lexical entries does it contain?
2. What is the general coverage on what kinds of data?
3. Can we select the best interpretation?
4. How domain-adaptable is the grammar?
5. To what extent can the grammar be used in multilingual applications?

We will try to answer these questions by considering the different applications and domains the grammar was part of.

11.1 What is the Size of the Grammar?

The number of grammar rules, lexical entries and types are shown in Table 27 for different versions of the grammar from 2000 to 2015.[1] The Japanese HPSG grammar in Verbmobil in October 2000 (Siegel, 2000) consisted of 27 rule schemata, 1,246 types and a lexicon of 3,399 entries. In the end of the follow-up project with the Californian company YY in September 2003 (Siegel and Bender, 2002), there were 5,147 words in the lexicon, 54 rule schemata and 1860 types.

When the Hinoki project started in 2005, there had been some pruning of rules and increase in the size of the lexicon, using semi-automatic techniques to add more words. We added the 30,000 most familiar words of Japanese from the Lexeed project (Fujita et al., 2006), which gave very good coverage of common words. By 2008, similar lexical entries

---

[1]In this table, 'rules' include inflectional and derivational rules from 2008.

Year	2000	2001	2002	2003	2005	2008	2009	2015
Rules	27	50	51	54	47	81	86	137
Lexemes	3,399	5,369	5,681	5,147	35,220	30,898	56,944	56,914
Types	1,246	1,709	1,736	1,889	2,204	2,185	2,324	2,473

TABLE 27 Change in grammar size over time

had been merged into under-specified types, reducing the size of the lexicon, without reducing the coverage of the grammar. In 2009, the grammar was tested on a new corpus (the Tanaka Corpus) and the lexicon expanded again, this time covering more informal and archaic terms.

The number of rules and types generally increased over time, as we add more complexity to the grammar to handle more phenomenon. Part of the jump between 2005 and 2008 was an expansion of rules to cover fragments: utterances that were not complete sentences. Between 2009 and 2015 there were many smaller phenomena added, attacking the long tail of rarer utterance types. Many of these were motivated by semantics: we had a parse before, but it did not get the correct meaning.

11.2 What is the General Coverage on Different Kinds of Data?

In this section we describe the coverage of the current version of the grammar (2015-12) using the open-source test suites distributed with the grammar. This methodology builds on that developed in the project Test Suites for Natural Language Processing (TSNLP: Lehmann et al., 1996) and the grammar profiling tool [incr tsdb()] (Oepen and Carroll, 2000) which we use for evaluation of our grammar origins from this project.

The test suites and corpora are parsed under two different configurations. In the first, the only pre-processing we use is segmentation, provided by **mecab** (Kudo et al., 2004) with the IPA Lexicons (Information-technology Promotion Agency, 1987). In this configuration, if there is any word not in **Jacy**'s lexicon, the parser will fail to parse the sentence. In the second, we also get part-of-speech information from **mecab**. Unknown open-class words are then assigned a generic lexical type based on their POS (currently, only for three types: proper nouns are mapped to named entities, common nouns are mapped to common nouns and verbal nouns to transitive verbal nouns).[2]

---

[2] Most new Japanese verbs are verbal nouns, Japanese does not appear to add new native-Japanese verbs or adjectives easily.

11.2.1 Test Suites and Coverage

We now describe the test suites we have used in grammar development. A test suite is a curated collection of test items (sometimes including both grammatical an ungrammatical examples) meant to test specific properties of a grammar.

The first three test suites are functional, designed specifically to cover different grammatical phenomena. The first is the MRS test-suite ('mrs'), a small set of sentences, originally in English, that are meant to cover some of the basic semantic phenomena (argument structure, quantification, negation, modification and so on). The second ('vanilla') contains a collection of phenomena that are specific to Japanese and was built during the development of the grammar to document phenomena analyzed as we added analyses.

The third is a 3,715 sentence Japanese machine translation test suite ('kinou': Ikehara and Shirai, 1990), which includes a variety of items from morphologically tricky input to extremely long sentences (200 words!). This test suite was later used as the basis for the Japan Electronic Industry Development Association MT test suite (Isahara, 1995) and is used to compare different MT systems. The system had also been tested on several smaller in-house test suites that we do not describe here, but are documented in Siegel (2006).

A method to evaluate the grammar coverage on grammatical phenomena we are interested in is to build up test sets, parse and evaluate the results manually (evaluation of constructed data). We therefore set up test sets containing of example sentences from a grammar book (Makino and Tsutsui, 1986), ordered by the grammar book chapters. We performed a coverage test on nominalizations (grammar book examples in the chapters of こと *koto*, もの *mono* and ため *tame*), the chapters of *ageru* "give", *dake* "only", *dake de wa naku* "not only", *darou* "it would be", *garu* "want", *goro* "about", the particles *ka* and *ni* and a manually constructed test suite of verbal endings. Figure 11.2.1 shows the results of coverage evaluation on these selected phenomena.

We also present results for two corpora of naturally occurring text. The first is the Tanaka Corpus ('tanaka': Tanaka, 2001), a freely available set of example sentences compiled by Tanaka Kouji and his students. The second is a translation of the Hiking corpus used in the LOGON machine translation project ('haikingu': Lønning et al., 2004). These give a better idea of its coverage on unrestricted text. The Tanaka Corpus was used to a certain extent as a development corpus (mainly inspiring the addition of lexical entries from this corpus). The hiking test-suite is completely unseen, and so provides a measure of the

Phenomenon	Coverage (%)
nominalizations	88.5
あげる *ageru* "give"	96.9
だけ *dake* "only"	71.0
だけではなく *dake de wa naku* "not only"	75.8
だろう *darou* "it would be"	66.7
-がる *-garu* "want"	72.7
ごろ *goro* "about"	100.0
か *ka*	57.5
に *ni*	83.1
verbal endings	89.4

TABLE 28 Coverage on selected phenomena

Type	Test Suite	Total # Sents	Parsed as is # Sents	Parsed as is Cover (%)	Handling unknowns # Sents	Handling unknowns Cover (%)
Functional	mrs	135	126	93	127	94
	vanilla	120	105	87	105	87
	kinou1	1500	1321	88	1328	88
	kinou2	1099	918	83	940	85
	kinou3	1116	866	77	883	79
Natural	tanaka/tc-003	1500	1145	76	1172	78
	tanaka/tc-004	1500	1136	75	1173	78
	tanaka/tc-005	1500	1114	74	1145	76
	haikingu	104	34	32	66	63

TABLE 29 Coverage on Test suites

grammar's ability to generalize: the system gets 63% coverage with the unknown word processing turned on.

Table 29 gives coverage results for the grammar over these test suites and test corpora, as of 2015-12. As noted above, we provide coverage data both with and without unknown word handling.

11.2.2 The Hinoki Treebank

The coverage numbers presented in Table 29 provide a first impression of the robustness of a grammar, but they do not in themselves provide a complete evaluation. In particular, they do not give us any information about precision: Just because we can get a parse for a sentence, does not guarantee that it is the right parse. In order to evaluate the correctness of the parses we use the methodology of treebanking.[3]

The treebank that accompanies **Jacy** is known as the Hinoki (檜)

---
[3] Portions of this section appeared in Bond et al. (2008a,b).

treebank. Hinoki (or Japanese Cyprus) is grown in Japan for its high quality timber. It is used as a material for building palaces, temples, shrines, traditional noh theatres, baths, table tennis blades and masu (the cups for drinking sake). The wood is lemon-scented, light pinkish-brown, with a rich, straight grain, and is highly rot-resistant. We chose the name as we wanted the treebank to serve as a strong building material for further research into the Japanese language.

The Hinoki treebank was produced at Nippon Telegraph and Telephone Corporation from 2004-2008, as part of their research into natural language understanding. We report results with two corpora: Lexeed (§ 11.2.2.1) and Tanaka (§ 11.2.2.2). The first was built using dictionary definition sentences from the machine-readable dictionary Lexeed (Kasahara et al., 2004). The second was built on dictionary example sentences from the Tanaka Corpus (Tanaka, 2001).

The structure of our treebank is inspired by the Redwoods treebank of English (Oepen et al., 2002c) in which utterances are parsed and the annotator selects the best parse from the full analyzes derived by the grammar. We had three main reasons for selecting this approach. The first was that we wanted to develop a precise broad-coverage grammar in tandem with the treebank. Treebanking the output of the parser allows us to immediately identify problems in the grammar, and improving the grammar directly improves the quality of the treebank in a mutually beneficial feedback loop, as we discussed in § 10.2.

The second reason is that we wanted to annotate to a high level of detail, marking not only dependency and constituent structure but also detailed semantic relations. **Jacy** simultaneously annotates syntactic and semantic structure without overburdening the annotator. The treebank records the complete syntactic-semantic analysis provided by the HPSG grammar, along with an annotator's choice of the most appropriate parse. From this record, all kinds of information can be extracted at various levels of granularity.

The third reason was that use of the grammar as a base enforces consistency — all sentences annotated are guaranteed to have well-formed parses. The drawback to using only the parser output is that any sentences which the parser cannot parse remain unannotated.

11.2.2.1 The Lexeed-Based Treebank

At NTT, we created a syntactically and semantically annotated corpus based on the machine-readable dictionary Lexeed (Kasahara et al., 2004). Lexeed is a manually built self-contained lexicon: it consists of headwords and their definitions for the most familiar 28,000 words of Japanese. These were selected by presenting all head words from two existing machine-readable dictionaries to 32 subjects, who were asked to rank them on a familiarity scale from one to seven, with seven being the most familiar Amano and Kondo (1999). Lexeed consists of all words with a familiarity greater than or equal to five. Their definitions and examples where then rewritten to use only these 28,000 words. Each rewritten definition and example sentence was parsed, and the most appropriate analysis selected using the process described in § 10.3.

Each content word in the sentences has been marked with the appropriate Lexeed sense. The syntactic model is embodied in a grammar, while the semantic model is linked by an ontology. This makes it possible to test the use of similarity and/or semantic class-based back-offs for parsing and generation with both symbolic grammars and statistical models.

One concern with Redwoods style treebanking is that it is only possible to annotate those trees that the grammar can parse. Sentences for which no analysis had been implemented in the grammar or which fail to parse due to processing constraints are left unannotated. This makes grammar coverage a significant issue. We extended **Jacy** during the treebanking by adding the 30,000 words of the defining vocabulary, and added some new rules and lexical types (more detail is given in Bond et al. 2004b). None of the rules were specific to the dictionary domain. The grammatical coverage over all sentences in Lexeed is 86%. The coverage is high because of the repetitive structure and short length of definition and example sentences. They represent a relatively easy genre to handle.

Around 12% of the parsed sentences were rejected by the treebankers due to an incomplete semantic representation. The total size of the treebank is 53,600 definition sentences and 36,000 example sentences: 89,600 sentences in total. Because the treebank was constructed as part of research within Nippon Telegraph and Telephone Corporation (NTT) using proprietary resources it was never released (and is thus not included in § 11.2.1).

The lexeed corpus is also annotated with sense tags from the lexeed dictionary itself, which is then linked to other resources, such as the Goi-Taikei Japanese Lexicon (Ikehara et al., 1997a) and WordNet (Fellbaum, 1998). Each content word of the definition and example sentences is annotated with sense tags from the same lexicon. The parsed dictionary definition sentences were used to extract ontological information, as described in § 2.4.

	Type	Number	%
Good	Single Good Tree	7,809	52.1
	Multiple Good Trees	679	4.5
Bad	No Good Trees	1,604	10.7
	No Parse Found	2,826	18.8
	Resource Limitation	2,082	14.0
	Total	15,000	100

TABLE 30 Tanaka Corpus Treebank

11.2.2.2 The Tanaka-Corpus-Based Treebank

We wanted to have a treebank that could be freely distributed with the grammar, and would be useful for a variety of tasks. We therefore chose an open corpus for our next treebank, using sentences from the Tanaka Corpus (Tanaka, 2001). This was a collection of 150,000 short, multilingual sentences, suitable for use as dictionary examples, that had been released into the public domain. The original corpus was compiled by students and very noisy, but had been extensively cleaned by the JDICT project (Breen, 2003).

At the Japanese National Institute of Information and Communications Technologies (NICT), we tree-banked a subset of 15,000 sentences of the Tanaka Corpus (Bond et al., 2008b). This treebank is released along with the grammar. The tree-banked coverage of the grammar over the corpus is shown Table 30.

For the 15,000 sentences, **Jacy** produced a good parse in 56.6% of the cases. Sometimes there was spurious ambiguity: multiple parses gave the same correct interpretation. In 14.0% of the sentences, the parser encountered resource limitations (e.g., time out). In 18.8% of sentences, the parser failed to find a valid parse. Some of these were due to ungrammatical input (misspellings and typos in the corpus) but most were due to lack of coverage of phenomena, such as rare honorific constructions. Finally, in 10.7% of the parses, we found an interpretation, but the treebanker considered it to not be the desired interpretation. These also suggest that the grammar needs to be extended further.

11.3 How Can We Select the Best Interpretation?

The grammar **Jacy** does two things: distinguish grammatical and ungrammatical utterances, and associate syntactic and semantic structure to grammatical utterances. For many applications, we would also like to assign a ranking to the interpretations: given what we know so far, of all the grammatical interpretations, which is the most likely? We do this by associating a statistical model with the grammar, trained on the treebank. This model ranks the outputs based on two assumptions: (i) the

	Definitions		Examples	
Method	Accuracy (%)	Features (×1000)	Accuracy (%)	Features (×1000)
Baseline	20.3	random	22.8	random
Syntactic	63.8	316	76.2	245
Semantic	63.3	2,546	69.2	2,679
Combined	**69.8**	2,861	**78.8**	2,923

TABLE 31 Parse Selection Results

interpretation of the utterance can be predicted by combining the interpretations of its sub-parts and (ii) the interpretations of the parts can be predicted by looking at the interpretations of previous utterances.

In this section we show the results of training parse-selection models on syntactic features, semantic features and combinations of both. There has been much previous work on parse ranking (Riezler et al., 2002; Oepen et al., 2004b; Malouf and van Noord, 2004; Miyao and Tsujii, 2008). We took as a starting point for our models the work in the DELPH-IN project (Toutanova et al., 2005).

The parses are ranked using a discriminative Maximum Entropy (ME) model, where the probability of each parse, given an input string, is estimated on the basis of selected properties (called features) of the parse (Abney, 1997; Johnson et al., 1999). We show the results for three models here, Fujita et al. (2010) give much more detail. Table 11.3 shows the results on the Lexeed corpus for the best preforming syntactic, semantic and combined models. Overall, the semantic models achieve almost the same accuracy as the syntactic ones, although with many more features. The combined model achieves the best result.

The accuracy is an exact match for the entire sentence: a model gets a point only if its top-ranked analysis for some item provides the same semantic structure as the analysis selected as correct in Hinoki. This is a stricter metric than component-based measures (e.g., labeled precision), which award partial credit for incorrect parses. Because we are scoring based on MRS matching, the baseline is also calculated accordingly: A given sentence might have multiple analyses with distinct parse trees but identical semantic structures. In this case all sentences with the correct semantics are scored as good. This gives baselines of 20.3% for the definitions and 22.8% for the example sentences. Definition sentences are more ambiguous and thus present a wider range of options to the parse ranker. This is mainly because the examples have fewer relative clauses and coordinate NPs, which are both large sources of ambiguity.

We illustrate the input of different parse selection features using the example in (276).

(276) 河童 は わさびを 抜いて ください
   kappa ha wasabi wo nui-te kudasai
   cucumber.roll TOP wasabi ACC leave.out-INF please

"Leave the wasabi out for the cucumber rolls, please."

In this example, the syntactic model preferred the parse where 河童 *kappa* "cucumber roll" is interpreted as the first argument (subject) of 抜く *nuku* "leave out", such that the gloss would be "Cucumber roll leave out the wasabi, please." But in the correct parse, it is the topic. The semantic features give the information that *kappa* is a kind of sushi and this can be combined with the Goi-Taikei ontology to show that ⟨848:rice/cooked rice/meal/diet⟩ (⊂ ⟨533:objects⟩). In general ⟨533:objects⟩ are not preferred as the subject, so this parse gets a low score from the semantic model. The semantic information is also effective in the problematic cases of post-position attachment ambiguity, coordinate structures and deciding whether something is an argument or adjunct.

Because the semantic model is much more complicated (it requires sense-disambiguation, more features and access to the semantics), we currently only use the syntactic model for selecting the best interpretation. **Jacy** comes with models trained for both parse selection and realization ranking (selecting the best string in generation), trained on the Tanaka Corpus.

11.4 How Domain-Adaptable is the Grammar?

The grammar is aimed at working with real-world data, rather than just experimenting with linguistically interesting examples. Therefore, robustness and performance issues play an important role. Grammar development is carried out in the LKB (Copestake, 2002b), but processing (both in the application domain and for the purposes of running test suites) is done with either the highly efficient PET parser (Callmeier, 2000) or the Answer Constraint Engine (ACE; Crysmann and Packard 2012). ACE and PET are both more efficient and more robust than the LKB, with greatly reduced memory usage and support for handling unknown words.

We first approached the task of adapting the grammar to a new domain first when going from Verbmobil (spoken dialogues) to YY Technologies (customer service email, including the banking domain). Continuous evaluation of coverage and performance gives a picture of the development. We had four different test suites in the new domain, constructed from data produced by actual customers:

- Banking data (864 items)
- Document request (317 items)
- Customer service (952 items)
- Support email (1982 items)
- Status of service (204 items)

A first test on a smaller test set in the domain in August 2001 showed that lexicon extension and linking to named-entity recognition is the main challenge in extending the coverage of the grammar in a new domain. Of 457 items tested, 213 parsed. Of those that didn't parse, 202 involved lexicon errors, including numbers, names placeholders (X), email addresses (total: 150 items) and ordinary words (52 items, 20 unique words). Additionally, 42 of the non-parsed items showed problems with grammatical phenomena, including evidential よう *you*, causative, the nominalizing suffix 方 *kata*, NP fragments, and interrogative complement sentences. In three months, with two developers, it was possible to bring the coverage of over these test suites up to over 90% on the 'banking' set and the other domains to between 50% and 70%.

Another experiment to adapt the grammar to a new domain was done at the Japanese company NTT Communication Science Laboratories (Nippon Telegraph and Telephone Corporation). We had a summer sprint, with the goal of extending the coverage on the Lexeed defining sentences to over 80% in four weeks. Six people were involved in this task, three of them had little experience in HPSG, none of them were previously involved in developing **Jacy**. First tests on the data gave a coverage of 39.3%. Adding some orthographemic variants to the lexicon extended the coverage to 46.2%.

The coverage increased to 82% in four weeks of work. First of all, the lexicon was expanded (up to 32,000 lexicon entries), using semi-automatic conversion from the Lexeed lexicon, with some guidance from the NTT machine translation lexicons (Ikehara et al., 1997b), which gave an increase of up to 55%. Further, some rules were added to account for compound verbs, increasing the coverage up to 70%. Domain-specific adaptation in the syntax added rules like one for a structure for dictionary definitions: "driver: In Golf, a long-distance club". This experiment showed that the grammar can be adapted to cover a high proportion of sentences from a new domain, and that most of the work is in the area of lexicon extension.

A later experiment on another data set showed a similar behavior. For the functional test suite of 3,715 test items that were originally set up for evaluation of machine translation by NTT, we had an initial coverage of 66%. After three months of mostly lexicon work, we reached 83%. However, it has to be mentioned that the ambiguity went up as well: from 18.6 analyses on average to 68.1. It is thus very important to work on parse selection when extending grammar coverage.

11.5 How Far Can the Grammar Be Used in Multilingual Applications?

The DeepThought project set a strong focus on multilinguality in grammar development and application. As we have shown in 10.2, we included the Grammar Matrix types in order to make the semantic output compatible and reliable. In this project we chose Robust MRS as a compatible semantic output format for languages and NLP modules. Chapter 2 shows the compatibility of analysis output of the six language's grammars.

Bond et al. (2004e) report on using the grammar for automatic ontology extraction by parsing dictionary definition sentences. The fact that it uses MRS as output is explicitly mentioned as a strength for the knowledge acquisition task and multilingual application. Nichols et al. (2005) show how **Jacy** is more precise for the task of ontology acquisition than robust semantic representations derived from ChaSen.

11.6 Summary and Further Reading

General evaluation of a large-coverage deep analysis grammar is difficult, because of the lack of gold-standard data to compare to and because of the range of applications and genres it can support. To address this, we split the evaluation into five areas: grammar size, coverage, application domains, multilinguality, and semantic precision. Concerning grammar size, Bond et al. (2008a) describe the Hinoki treebank that was built on the grammar. Hashimoto et al. (2005) give an introduction to the type hierarchy of the grammar. The coverage on different types of data was measured using the grammar profiling tool [incr tsdb()] (Oepen and Carroll, 2000). Robustness and performance in different application domains of the grammar was evaluated. Bond et al. (2004c) shows the possibility of adapting the lexicon to a new domain to increase coverage. We showed the usage of the grammar in multilingual applications. See Bond et al. (2004e) for using the grammar in an ontology extraction system. The semantic preciseness was evaluated using the treebanking mechanism. See Bond et al. (2004d) for results on the Hinoki treebank.

12

Conclusion

We described a broad-coverage Japanese grammar, using the framework of Head-driven Phrase Structure Grammar with Minimal Recursion Semantics. It encodes precise morphological, syntactic, semantic, and pragmatic information in feature structures. The grammar system is connected to a morphological analyzer and uses default entries for words unknown to the HPSG lexicon. The grammar has been developed within many different research projects and has been used to annotate naturally occurring Japanese language data from different domains. It covers core, well-studied phenomena of the Japanese language, as well as many common but lesser-studied ones, and gives morphological, syntactic, semantic and pragmatic analyses. The grammar is being developed in a multilingual context, where much value is placed on parallel and consistent semantic representations. The development of this grammar thus constitutes an important test of the cross-linguistic validity of the HPSG and MRS formalisms. **Jacy** also participated in the Heart of Gold project (Callmeier et al., 2004), where consideration of RMRS (Copestake, 2003) and hybrid deep/shallow processing informed the development the grammar's robustness and interoperability with external resources.

As the development of **Jacy** has been driven by and grounded in a series of applications, we began our description with an overview of those applications (§ 2). During the long history of the development of this grammar, it has been used in various applications, requiring the work on different types of data. This has led to a high demand for robustness and precision. The grammar must be compatible with grammars of other languages, able to work with large amounts of data, flexible enough to adapt to a new domain and must have a large and extensible lexicon. The embedding in a hybrid approach brought a breakthrough in coverage. The cooperation with external partners in lexicon development brought breakthroughs in the organization and documentation of lexical types.

The basic phrase structures of **Jacy** are built on the multilingual Grammar Matrix (Bender et al., 2002) phrase structure types (§ 3). In addition, rules for phenomena on the border between morphology and syntax are included in the formal class of phrase structure rules. Japanese has a strong tendency to be head-final, but the peripheral exceptions noted in the section about head-initial constructions show that this is not a categorical generalization. They illustrate once again the fact that languages seamlessly combine general tendencies with particular exceptions (Fillmore et al., 1988). In order to build consistent grammars that scale up to ever larger fragments of the languages we wish to model (such as is required for practical applications), we require a framework that allows the statement of generalizations at varying degrees of granularity. Furthermore, we believe that the construction of broad-coverage precision grammars such as **Jacy** in the context of applications which require robustness in the face of real-world language use provides a useful discovery procedure for many of the smaller generalizations and exceptional cases (Baldwin et al., 2004).

We went into considerable detail about our treatment of subcategorization in Japanese, both in terms of how we analyze scrambling and optional arguments and in terms of the range of subcategorization frames we have found (§ 4). The discussion of subcategorization leads into our presentation of our analysis of verbs and adjectives, which are not only central to the construction of semantic representations but are also the main locus of inflection in Japanese (§ 5). Our approach is to organize lexical types in a type hierarchy and thus the approach is highly modular. We have shown how inflectional and productive derivational morphology can be expressed in this approach of using a type hierarchy and rules operating on it. Our account includes analyses of valence changing constructions including passive, causative and additional auxiliary constructions. Our treatment of these is furthermore consistent with our approach to subcategorization in general.

The description of nominal constructions shows the various relations between syntax, semantics and pragmatics (§ 6). The HPSG feature structure is well suited for expressing these relations. The discussion of nominal constructions also presents the connection between named-entity recognition and part-of-speech tagging and the **Jacy** grammar. This analysis uses a combination of hand-coded lexical information with default lexicon entries. We also go into detail about one important class of noun modifiers, namely numeral classifiers. Our approach allows us to build semantic representations for strings that contain these prevalent elements—representations suitable for applications requiring natural language understanding, such as (semantic) machine translation and automated email response.

Particles play a central role in Japanese syntax and need a close investigation and a structured type hierarchy (§ 7). The syntactic behavior of Japanese particles was originally analyzed using dialogue data from the Verbmobil machine translation project. We observed 25 different particles in 800 dialogues on appointment scheduling. We set up a type hierarchy of Japanese particles which allowed us to adopt a lexical treatment of both the similarities and fine-grained differences between classes of particles, including the different kinds of modification and subcategorization they display. We analyzed the Japanese particles concerning to their possibilities of cooccurrence, their behavior of modification and their occurrence in verbal arguments. We clarified the question of which common characteristics and differences between the individual particles exist. The simple distinction into case particles and post-positions, as often proposed in theory-oriented research literature, was shown to be insufficient. Furthermore, we found that the assignment of grammatical function is best done by the verbal valence and not directly by the case particles. The evaluation of the particle treatment showed that 91.6% of particles in a 100 test sentences could be correctly analyzed. All combinations of particles and 82.35% of the elided particles were analyzed correctly.

Other word classes that we give an analysis for are adverbs and demonstratives (§ 8). Japanese adjectives can be inflected to be adverbs, but also genuine adverbs exist in Japanese. We handle these by derivational rules on the one hand and lexical types on the other. The different types of semantic modification are also handled, such that these analyses also give good examples for the necessity to describe the interaction between morphology, syntax and semantics.

The Japanese language has a complicated system of honorifics which are used to express the social relations between speaker, addressee and subject of an utterance (§ 9). Honorifics involve verbal stem alternations, verbal conjugations, nominal prefixes and pronouns and displays syntactic, semantic, pragmatic and domain-specific restrictions. We have shown that for Japanese it is necessary to distinguish subject honorification, entity honorification and addressee honorification and to introduce polarity for these. The number and kind of the dimensions is language-specific; German and French, for example, have only one dimension, while Korean and Japanese have three. In one sentence, different dimensions of honorification can be expressed. We have given a treatment of honorifics in the HPSG framework that covers all three dimensions of Japanese honorifics and makes it possible to account for honorific agreement as well as restrictions in complement sentences and restrictions for zero pronouns. The approach also allows a uniform treatment of honorific dimensions in different languages.

The chapter on grammar engineering describes tools and methods that we used to develop the **Jacy** grammar with high, robust coverage on large amounts of data in different application domains. It provides insights on best practices of grammar engineering (§ 10).

Finally, we gave numbers on the current state of the grammar (§ 11). The evaluation shows that the grammar is at a stage where domain adaptation is possible in a reasonable amount of time. We have given answers to the leading questions of grammar evaluation that apply to our approach of multi-level annotation. The **Jacy** grammar is of a reasonable size, has a good coverage on different types of data, is flexible and useful for applications, adaptable to new domains, useful in multilingual applications and gives precise and correct semantic output. Thus, it is a powerful resource for linguistic applications for Japanese.

The HPSG framework has proven to be well-suited for the task of describing Japanese: The type hierarchy facilitates a modular grammar design, the lexicon is easy to extend, once the lexical types are well organized and documented, and the sign-based approach to representing different levels of linguistic information (from morphology to pragmatics) has proven to be suitable for expressing the complex interactions between these levels evident in Japanese. The MRS framework has similarly proven to be expressive enough for the Japanese semantics, flexible enough for a wide-coverage grammar used in applications and well defined to generate compatible output in multilingual grammars.

The DELPH-IN open-source community working with HPSG provides a set of extremely useful tools to make the grammar developers life easy: LKB for grammar development (Copestake, 2002b), PET for efficient processing (Callmeier, 2000), Heart-of-Gold for hybrid processing (Callmeier et al., 2004) and [incr tsdb()] for grammar profiling and treebanking (Lehmann et al., 1996). In the combination of a rich formalism and efficient processing, we could implement a grammar that is theoretically complex and application-oriented at the same time. We have provided an NLP source for applications that need deep semantic information. **Jacy** is also the basis of the the Hinoki treebank (Bond et al., 2008a), a rich annotated treebank for Japanese, which is a useful resource for further research in machine learning of language-specific rules, as it contains — different to most treebanks up to date — semantic information.

In future work, this grammar should be further adapted to other domains, such as the newspapers (including the grammar of headline text) and general text such as Wikipedia. Further improving generation will be a certain topic in the near future, to open up the perspective for new applications and to give further means to evaluate the grammar and increase precision. In all of these endeavors, we expect the resource grammar approach, where each new domain and application inspires additions and refinements to one shared implementation of grammatical knowledge and each requires less adaptation effort than the previous ones, to continue to serve us well.

References

Abney, Steven P., 1997. Stochastic attribute-value grammars. *Computational Linguistics*, 23: 597–618.

Amano, Shigeaki and Tadahisa Kondo, 1999. *Nihongo-no Goi-Tokusei (Lexical properties of Japanese)*. Sanseido.

Asahara, Masayuki and Yuji Matsumoto, 2000. Extended models and tools for high-performance part-of-speech tagger. In *Proceedings of the 18th International Conference on Computational Linguistics, Coling 2000*, pp. 21–27. Saarbrücken, Germany.

Backhouse, A. E., 1993. *The Japanese Language: An Introduction*. Oxford: Oxford University Press.

Baldwin, Timothy, 2004. Making sense of Japanese relative clause constructions. In *Proceedings of the 2nd Workshop on Text Meaning and Interpretation*, pp. 49–56. Barcelona, Spain.

Baldwin, Timothy, Emily M. Bender, Dan Flickinger, Ara Kim, and Stephan Oepen, 2004. Road-testing the English resource grammar over the British national corpus. In *Proceedings of the Fourth International Conference on Language Resources and Evaluation (LREC 2004)*, pp. 2047–50. Lisbon.

Beavers, John and Ivan A. Sag, 2004. Coordinate ellipsis and apparent non-constituent coordination. In Stefan Müller (ed.), *Proceedings of the HPSG-2004 Conference, Center for Computational Linguistics, Katholieke Universiteit Leuven*, pp. 48–69. Stanford: CSLI Publications. URL http://cslipublications.stanford.edu/HPSG/5/.

Bender, Emily M., 2008. Radical non-configurationality without shuffle operators. In Stefan Müller (ed.), *Proceedings of HPSG 2008*. Stanford, CA: CSLI Publications ONLINE.

Bender, Emily M., Scott Drellishak, Antske Fokkens, Laurie Poulson, and Safiyyah Saleem, 2010. Grammar customization. *Research on Language & Computation*, 8(1): 23–72. URL http://dx.doi.org/10.1007/s11168-010-9070-1. 10.1007/s11168-010-9070-1.

Bender, Emily M., Dan Flickinger, Frederik Fouvry, and Melanie Siegel, 2005. Special issue on shared representations in multilingual grammar engineering: Introduction. *Journal of Research on Language and Computation*, 3(2): 131–138.

Bender, Emily M., Dan Flickinger, and Stephan Oepen, 2002. The grammar matrix: An open-source starter-kit for the rapid development of cross-linguistically consistent broad-coverage precision grammars. In *Proceedings of the Workshop on Grammar Engineering and Evaluation at the 19th International Conference on Computational Linguistics*, pp. 8–14. Taipei, Taiwan.

Bender, Emily M. and Melanie Siegel, 2004. Implementing the syntax of Japanese numeral classifiers. In *Proceedings of the IJC-NLP-2004*.

Bierwisch, Manfred, 1963. *Grammatik des deutschen Verbs*, volume II of *Studia Grammatica*. Akademie Verlag.

Blunsom, Phil and Timothy Baldwin, 2006. Multilingual deep lexical acquisition for HPSGs via supertagging. In *Proceedings of the 2006 Conference on Empirical Methods in Natural Language Processing*, pp. 164–171. Sydney, Australia: Association for Computational Linguistics. URL http://www.aclweb.org/anthology/W/W06/W06-1620.

Bond, Francis, 2005. *Translating the Untranslatable: A solution to the Problem of Generating English Determiners*. CSLI Studies in Computational Linguistics. CSLI Publications.

Bond, Francis, Timothy Baldwin, Kentaro Inui, Shun Ishizaki, Hiroshi Nakagawa, and Akira Shimazu (eds.), 2016. *Readings in Japanese Natural Language Processing*. CSLI Publications.

Bond, Francis, Sanae Fujita, Kaname Kasahara Chikara Hashimoto, Shigeko Nariyama, Akira Ohtani Eric Nichols, Takaaki Tanaka, and Shigeaki Amano, 2004a. The Hinoki treebank: A treebank for text understanding. *Lecture Notes in Computer Science*.

Bond, Francis, Sanae Fujita, Chikara Hashimoto, Kaname Kasahara, Shigeko Nariyama, Eric Nichols, Akira Ohtani, Takaaki Tanaka, and Shigeaki Amano, 2004b. The Hinoki treebank: A treebank for text understanding. In *Proceedings of the First International Joint Conference on Natural Language Processing (IJCNLP-04)*, pp. 158–167. Springer Verlag.

Bond, Francis, Sanae Fujita, Chikara Hashimoto, Kaname Kasahara, Shigeko Nariyama, Eric Nichols, Akira Ohtani, Takaaki Tanaka, and Shigeaki Amano, 2004c. The Hinoki treebank: Working toward text understanding. In *Proceedings of the 5th International Workshop on Linguistically Interpreted Corpora (LINC-04)*, pp. 7–10. Geneva.

Bond, Francis, Sanae Fujita, Chikara Hashimoto, Shigeko Nariyama, Eric Nichols, Akira Ohtani, and Takaaki Tanaka, 2004d. Development of the Hinoki treebank based on a precise grammar. In *2004-NLC-159*, pp. 91–98. (in Japanese).

Bond, Francis, Sanae Fujita, and Takaaki Tanaka, 2008a. The Hinoki syntactic and semantic treebank of Japanese. *Language Resources and Evaluation*, 42(2): 243–251. URL http://dx.doi.org/10.1007/

s10579-008-9062-z. (Re-issue of DOI 10.1007/s10579-007-9036-6 as Springer lost the Japanese text).

Bond, Francis, Takayuki Kuribayashi, and Chikara Hashimoto, 2008b. Construction of a free Japanese treebank based on HPSG. In *14th Annual Meeting of the Association for Natural Language Processing*, pp. 241–244. Tokyo. (in Japanese).

Bond, Francis, Eric Nichols, Sanae Fujita, and Takaaki Tanaka, 2004e. Acquiring an ontology for a fundamental vocabulary. In *20th International Conference on Computational Linguistics: COLING-2004*, pp. 1319–1325. Geneva.

Bond, Francis, Stephan Oepen, Eric Nichols, Dan Flickinger, Erik Velldal, and Petter Haugereid, 2011. Deep open source machine translation. *Machine Translation*, 25(2): 87–105. URL http://dx.doi.org/10.1007/s10590-011-9099-4. (Special Issue on Open source Machine Translation).

Bond, Francis, Stephan Oepen, Melanie Siegel, Ann Copestake, and Dan Flickinger, 2005. Open source machine translation with DELPH-IN. In *Open-Source Machine Translation: Workshop at MT Summit X*, pp. 15–22. Phuket.

Bond, Francis and Kyonghee Paik, 2000. Reusing an ontology to generate numeral classifiers. In *Proceedings of the 18th International Conference on Computational Linguistics, Coling 2000*, pp. 90–96. Saarbrücken, Germany.

Borsley, Robert D., 1993. Heads in HPSG. In Greville C. Corbett and McGlashan (1993), pp. 292–315.

Branco, António and Francisco Costa, 2010. A deep linguistic processing grammar for Portuguese. In *Computational Processing of the Portuguese Language*, volume LNAI6001 of *Lecture Notes in Artificial Intelligence*, pp. 86–89. Berlin: Springer.

Breen, James W., 2003. Word usage examples in an electronic dictionary. In *Papillon (Multi-lingual Dictionary) Project Workshop*. Sapporo. (http://www.csse.monash.edu.au/~jwb/papillon/dicexamples.html).

Bresnan, Joan and Ronald M. Kaplan, 1982. Lexical-Functional Grammar: A Formal System for Grammatical Representation. In J. Bresnan (ed.), *The Mental Representation of Grammatical Relations*, pp. 173–281. Cambridge, MA: MIT Press.

Bresnan, Joan and Annie Zaenen, 1990. Deep uunaccusativity in LFG. In K. Dziwirek, P. Farrell, and E. Mejías-Bikandi (eds.), *Grammatical Relations: A Cross-Theoretical Perspective*, pp. 45–57. Stanford: CSLI.

Burger, Susanne, Karl Weilhammer, Florian Schiel, and Hans G Tillmann, 2000. Verbmobil data collection and annotation. In *Verbmobil: Foundations of Speech-to-Speech Translation*, pp. 537–549. Springer.

Butt, Miriam, Mary Dalrymple, and Anette Frank, 1997. An architecture for linking theory in LFG. In *Proceedings of the LFG97 Conference*, pp. 1–16. Stanford: CSLI Publications.

Butt, Miriam, Helge Dyvik, Tracy Holloway King, Hiroshi Masuichi, and Christian Rohrer, 2002. The parallel grammar project. In *Proceedings of COLING 2002 Workshop on Grammar Engineering and Evaluation*, pp. 1–7.

Butt, Miriam, Tracy Holloway King, María-Eugenia Ni no, and Frédérique Segond, 1999. *A Grammar Writer's Cookbook*. CSLI publications.

Callmeier, Ulrich, 2000. PET - a platform for experimentation with efficient HPSG processing techniques. *Natural Language Engineering*, 6(1): 99–108.

Callmeier, Ulrich, 2002. Preprocessing and encoding techniques in PET. In Oepen et al. (2002b), chapter 6, pp. 127–143.

Callmeier, Ulrich, Andreas Eisele, Ulrich Schäfer, and Melanie Siegel, 2004. The DeepThought core architecture framework. In *Proceedings of LREC-2004*, volume IV. Lisbon.

Carter, David, 1997. The TreeBanker: a tool for supervised training of parsed corpora. In *ACL Workshop on Computational Environments for Grammar Development and Linguistic Engineering*. Madrid. (http://xxx.lanl.gov/abs/cmp-lg/9705008).

Chomsky, Noam, 1981. *Lectures on Government and Binding*. Dordrecht: Foris.

Copestake, Ann, 2002a. Definitions of typed feature structures. In Stephan Oepen, Dan Flickinger, Jun-ichi Tsujii, and Hans Uszkoreit (eds.), *Collaborative Language Engineering*, pp. 227–230. Stanford, CA: CSLI Publications.

Copestake, Ann, 2002b. *Implementing Typed Feature Structure Grammars*. CSLI Publications.

Copestake, Ann, 2003. Report on the design of RMRS. Technical Report D1.1a, University of Cambridge, UK.

Copestake, Ann, 2007. Semantic composition with (robust) minimal recursion semantics. In *ACL 2007 Workshop on Deep Linguistic Processing*, pp. 73–80. Prague, Czech Republic: Association for Computational Linguistics. URL http://www.aclweb.org/anthology/W/W07/W07-1210.

Copestake, Ann, 2009. Slacker semantics: Why superficiality, dependency and avoidance of commitment can be the right way to go. In *Proceedings of the 12th Conference of the European Chapter of the ACL (EACL 2009)*, pp. 1–9. Athens.

Copestake, Ann, Dan Flickinger, Ivan A. Sag, and Carl Pollard, 2005. Minimal Recursion Semantics. An introduction. *Research on Language and Computation*, 3(4): 281–332.

Copestake, Ann, Alex Lascarides, and Dan Flickinger, 2001. An algebra for semantic construction in constraint-based grammars. In *Proceedings of the 39th Annual Meeting of the Association for Computational Linguistics (ACL 2001)*. Toulouse, France.

Coulmas, Florian, 1987. Höflichkeit und soziale Bedeutung im Japanischen. *Linguistische Berichte*, 107: 44–62.

Crysmann, Berthold, 2005. Relative clause extraposition in German: An efficient and portable implementation. *Research on Language and Computation*, 3(1): 61–82.

Crysmann, Berthold, Anette Frank, Bernd Kiefer, Stefan Müller, Günter Neumann, Jakub Piskorski, Ulrich Schäfer, Melanie Siegel, Hans Uszkoreit, Feiyu Xu, Markus Becker, and Hans-Ulrich Krieger, 2002. An integrated architecture for shallow and deep processing. In *Proceedings of ACL-2002, Association for Computational Linguistics 40th Anniversary Meeting*.

Crysmann, Berthold and Woodley Packard, 2012. Towards efficient HPSG generation for German, a non-configurational language. In *COLING*, pp. 695–710.

Dini, Luca and Giampolo Mazzini, 1997. Hypertextual grammar development. In *Computational Environments for Grammar Development and Linguistic Engineering*, pp. 24–29. Madrid: ACL.

Dipper, Stefanie, 2000. Grammar-based corpus annotation. In Anne Abeillé, Thorsten Brants, and Hans Uszkoreit (eds.), *Proceedings of the COLING Workshop on Linguistically Interpreted Corpora LINC-2000*, pp. 56–64. Luxembourg. URL http://www.ling.uni-potsdam.de/~dipper/papers/linc00.pdf.

Dohsaka, Kohji, 1990. Identifying the referents of zero-pronouns in Japanese based on pragmatic constraint interpretation. In *Proceedings of ECAI 1990*, pp. 240–245.

Downing, Pamela, 1996. *Numeral Classifier Systems, the case of Japanese*. Amsterdam: John Benjamins.

Drellishak, Scott and Emily M. Bender, 2005. A coordination module for a crosslinguistic grammar resource. In Stefan Müller (ed.), *The Proceedings of the 12th International Conference on Head-Driven Phrase Structure Grammar, Department of Informatics, University of Lisbon*, pp. 108–128. Stanford: CSLI Publications. URL http://cslipublications.stanford.edu/HPSG/6/.

Dridan, Rebecca, 2013. Ubertagging. Joint segmentation and supertagging for English. In *EMNLP:13*, pp. 1–10.

Dridan, Rebecca and Timothy Baldwin, 2007. What to classify and how: Experiments in question classification for japanese. In *Proceedings of the 10th Conference of the Pacific Association for Computational Linguistics (PACLING)*, pp. 333–41. Melbourne, Australia.

Dridan, Rebecca and Timothy Baldwin, 2010. Unsupervised parse selection for HPSG. In *Proceedings of the 2010 Conference on Empirical Methods in Natural Language Processing (EMNLP 2010)*.

Dridan, Rebecca and Francis Bond, 2006. Sentence comparison using robust minimal recursion semantics and an ontology. In *Proceedings of the Workshop on Linguistic Distances*, pp. 35–42. Sydney. URL http://www.aclweb.org/anthology/W/W06/W06-1106.

Drozdzynski, Witold, Hans-Ulrich Krieger, Jakub Piskorski, Ulrich Schäfer, and Feiyu Xu, 2004. Shallow processing with unification and typed feature structures — foundations and applications. *Künstliche Intelligenz*, 1(1): 17–23.

Dubinsky, Stanley, 1997. Syntactic underspecification and light-verb phenomena in Japanese. *Linguistics*, 35(4): 627–672.

Eckert, Penelope and Sally McConnell-Ginet, 1992. THINK PRACTICALLY AND LOOK LOCALLY: Language and gender as community-based practice. *Annual Review of Anthropology*, pp. 461–490.

Farmer, Ann Kathleen, 1984. *Modularity in Syntax: A Study of Japanese and English*. Massachussetts: MIT Press.

Fellbaum, Christine (ed.), 1998. *WordNet: An Electronic Lexical Database*. MIT Press.

Fillmore, Charles J., Paul Kay, and Mary Catherine O'Connor, 1988. Regularity and idiomaticity in grammatical constructions: The case of let alone. *Language*, 64(3): 501–538.

Flickinger, Dan, 1996. English time expressions in an HPSG grammar. In Takao Gunji (ed.), *Studies on the Universality of Constraint-Based Phrase Structure Grammars*, 06044133, pp. 1–8. International Scientific Research Program, Osaka University, Japan.

Flickinger, Dan, 2000. On building a more efficient grammar by exploiting types. *Natural Language Engineering*, 6(1): 15–28. (Special Issue on Efficient Processing with HPSG).

Flickinger, Dan, 2008. The English resource grammar. Technical Report 2007-7, LOGON, http://www.emmtee.net/reports/7.pdf. (Draft of 2008-11-30).

Flickinger, Dan, 2011. Accuracy v. robustness in grammar engineering. In Emily M. Bender and Jennifer E. Arnold (eds.), *Language from a Cognitive Perspective: Grammar, Usage and Processing*, pp. 31–50. Stanford, CA: CSLI Publications.

Flickinger, Dan and Emily Bender, 2003. Compositional semantics in a multilingual grammar resource. In Bender et al (ed.), *A Workshop on Ideas and Strategies for Multilingual Grammar Engineering, ESSLLI*, pp. 17–24.

Flickinger, Dan and Francis Bond, 2003. A two-rule analysis of measure noun phrases. In *The 10th International Conference on Head-Driven Phrase Structure Grammar*, pp. 111–121. Michigan.

Flickinger, Dan, Alexander Koller, and Stafan Thater, 2005. A new well-formedness criterion for semantics debugging. In *Proceedings of the 12th International Conference on HPSG*, p. 129–142. URL http://cslipublications.stanford.edu/HPSG/6/abstr-hb.shtml.

Flickinger, Daniel, Ann Copestake, and Ivan A. Sag, 2000. HPSG analysis of english. In Wolfgang Wahlster (ed.), *Verbmobil. Foundations of Speech-to-Speech Translation*, pp. 254–263. Berlin, Germany: Springer, artificial intelligence edition.

Frellesvig, Bjarke, 2010. *A History of the Japanese Language*. Cambridge: Cambridge University Press.

Fujii, Atsushi and Tetsuya Ishikawa, 2004. Summarizing encyclopedic term descriptions on the web. In *20th International Conference on Computational Linguistics: COLING-2004*. Geneva.

Fujita, Sanae, Francis Bond, Takaaki Tanaka, and Stephan Oepen, 2010. Exploiting semantic information for HPSG parse selection. *Research on Language and Computation*, 8(1): 1–22. URL http://dx.doi.org/10.1007/s11168-010-9069-7.

Fujita, Sanae, Takaaki Tanaka, Francis Bond, and Hiromi Nakaiwa, 2006. An implimented description of Japanese: The Lexeed dictionary and the Hinoki treebank. In *Proceedings of the COLING/ACL 2006 Interactive Presentation Sessions*, pp. 65–68. Sydney. URL http://www.aclweb.org/anthology/P/P06/P06-4017.

Goodman, Michael Wayne and Francis Bond, 2009a. Automatic error detection for natural language generation. In *15th Annual Meeting of the Association for Natural Language Processing*, pp. A2–5. Tottori.

Goodman, Michael Wayne and Francis Bond, 2009b. Using generation for grammar analysis and error detection. In *Joint conference of the 47th Annual Meeting of the Association for Computational Linguistics and the 4th International Joint Conference on Natural Language Processing of the Asian Federation of Natural Language Processing*, pp. 109–112. Singapore.

Green, Georgia M., 1997. The structure of context: The representation of pragmatic restrictions in HPSG. In James Yoon (ed.), *Studies in the Linguistic Sciences. Proceedings of the 5th annual meeting of the Formal Linguistics Society of the Midwest*.

Greville C. Corbett, Norman M. Fraser and Scott McGlashan (eds.), 1993. *Heads in Grammatical Theory*. Cambridge University Press.

Grimshaw, Jane and Armin Mester, 1988. Light verbs and theta-marking. *Linguistic Inquiry*, 19(2): 205–232.

Gunji, Takao, 1983. Generalized phrase structure grammar and Japanese reflexivization. *Linguistics and Philosophy*, 6: 115–156.

Gunji, Takao, 1987. *Japanese Phrase Structure Grammar: A Unification-Based Approach*. Dordrecht: D. Reidel (Kluwer).

Gunji, Takao, 1991. An overview of JPSG: A constraint-based descriptive theory for Japanese. In *Proceedings of Japanese Syntactic Processing Workshop*. Duke University.

Gunji, Takao, 1996. On lexicalist treatments of Japanese causatives. In Takao Gunji (ed.), *Studies in the Universality of Constraint-Based Structure Grammars*, pp. 61–89. Osaka University.

Gunji, Takao, 2005. Measurement and quantification revisited. *Theoretical and Applied Linguistics at Kobe Shoin*, 8: 21–36.

Gunji, Takao, 2013. An overview of jpsg: A constraint-based grammar for japanese. In Reiko Mazuka and Noriko Nagai (eds.), *Japanese Sentence Processing*, pp. 105–134. Psychology Press.

Gunji, Takao and Kôiti Hasida, 1997. *Topics in constraint-based grammar of Japanese*. Springer.

Gunji, Takao and Koiti Hasida, 1998. Measurement and quantification. In Takao Gunji and Koiti Hasida (eds.), *Topics in Constrained-Based Grammar of Japanese*, pp. 39–79. Kluwer Academic Publishers.

Hamano, Shoko, 1998. *The sound-symbolic system of Japanese*. Tokyo: Kuroshio Shuppan.

Harada, Shinichi, 1976. Honorifics. In Shibatani (1976).

Harada, Yasunari, Koichi Hashida, Takao Gunji, Hideo Miyoshi, and Hidetoshi Shirai, 1990. JPSG - a phrase structure grammar for Japanese. In *Advances in Software Science and Technology 1*. Academic Press.

Hasegawa, Yoko, 2014. *Japanese: A Linguistic Introduction*. Cambridge University Press.

Hashimoto, Chikara and Francis Bond, 2005. A computational treatment of V-V compounds in Japanese. In *Proceedings of the 12th International Conference on HPSG*, pp. 143–156. URL http://cslipublications.stanford.edu/HPSG/6/abstr-hb.shtml.

Hashimoto, Chikara, Francis Bond, Takaaki Tanaka, and Melanie Siegel, 2005. Integration of a lexical type database with a linguistically interpreted corpus. In *6th International Workshop on Linguistically Integrated Corpora (LINC-2005)*, pp. 31–40. Cheju, Korea.

Hashimoto, Chikara, Francis Bond, Takaaki Tanaka, and Melanie Siegel, 2007. Semi-automatic documentation of an implemented linguistic grammar augmented with a treebank. *Language Resources and Evaluation*, 42(2): 117–126. URL http://dx.doi.org/10.1007/s10579-008-9065-9. (Special issue on Asian language technology).

Haugereid, Petter, 2009. *A constructionalist grammar design, exemplified with Norwegian and English*. Ph.D. thesis, NTNU, Norwegian University of Science and Technology. URL http://urn.kb.se/resolve?urn=urn:nbn:no:ntnu:diva-5755.

Haugereid, Petter and Francis Bond, 2011. Extracting transfer rules for multiword expressions from parallel corpora. In *Proceedings of the Workshop on Multiword Expressions: from Parsing and Generation to the Real World*, pp. 92–100. Portland, Oregon: ACL.

Heine, Julia, 1998. Definiteness predictions for Japanese noun phrases. In *36th Annual Meeting of the Association for Computational Linguistics and 17th International Conference on Computational Linguistics: COLING/ACL-98*, pp. 519–525. Montreal, Canada.

Hellan, Lars and Petter Haugereid, 2003. NorSource: An exercise in Matrix grammar-building design. In Emily M. Bender, Dan Flickinger, Frederik Fouvry, and Melanie Siegel (eds.), *Proceedings of the Workshop on Ideas and Strategies for Multilingual Grammar Development, ESSLLI 2003*, pp. 41–48.

Hill, Beverly, Sachiko Ide, Shoko Ikuta, Akiko Kawasaki, and Tsunao Ogino, 1986. Universals of linguistic politeness. quantitative evidence from Japanese and American english. *Journal of Pragmatics*, 10: 347–371.

Hinds, John, 1977. Particle deletion in Japanese and Korean. *Linguistic Inquiry*, 8(4): 602–604.

Hori, Motoko, 1986. A sociolinguistic analysis of the Japanese honorifics. *Journal of Pragmatics*, 10: 373–386.

Ide, Sachiko, 1986. The background of Japanese sociolinguistics. *Journal of Pragmatics*, 10: 281–286.

Ikehara, Satoru, Masahiro Miyazaki, Satoshi Shirai, Akio Yokoo, Hiromi Nakaiwa, Kentaro Ogura, Yoshifumi Ooyama, and Yoshihiko Hayashi, 1997a. *Goi-Taikei — A Japanese Lexicon*. Tokyo: Iwanami Shoten. 5 volumes/CDROM.

Ikehara, Satoru, Masahiro Miyazaki, Satoshi Shirai, Akio Yokoo, Hiromi Nakaiwa, Kentaro Ogura, Yoshifumi Ooyama, and Yoshihiko Hayashi, 1997b. *Goi-Taikei — A Japanese Lexicon*. Tokyo: Iwanami Shoten.

Ikehara, Satoru and Satoshi Shirai, 1990. A function test system for Japanese to English machine translation. In *IEICE Technical Report NLC90-43*, pp. 17–24. IEICE. (in Japanese).

Ikeya, Akira, 1983. Japanese honorific systems. In *Seoul Papers in Formal Grammar Theory. Proceedings of the 3rd Korean-Japanese Joint Workshop*. Seoul: Hanshin Publishing Company.

Information-technology Promotion Agency, 1987. *IPA Lexicon of the Japanese Language for Computers IPAL*. IPA. (in Japanese).

IPA, 1987. IPAL (basic verbs). Lexicon, Information-Technology Promotion Agency, Tokyo, Japan. (ftp://ftp.mgt.ipa.go.jp/pub/ipal).

Isahara, Hitoshi, 1995. JEIDA's test-sets for quality evaluation of MT systems — technical evaluation from the developer's point of view —. In *The Fifth Machine Translation Summit: MT Summit V*.

Ito, Chizuru and Rui P. Chaves, 2008. Apparent non-constituent coordination in japanese. In Stefan Müller (ed.), *The Proceedings of the 15th International Conference on Head-Driven Phrase Structure Grammar*, pp. 95–115. Stanford: CSLI Publications. URL http://cslipublications.stanford.edu/HPSG/9/.

Johnson, Mark, Stuart Geman, Stephan Canon, Zhiyi Chi, and Stefan Riezler, 1999. Estimators for stochastic "unification-based" grammars. In *37th Annual Meeting of the Association for Computational Linguistics: ACL-1999*, pp. 535–541. University of Maryland.

Kageyama, Taro (ed.), 2001. *Nichieitaisyou, Doushi no Imi to Koubun (Comparative Study of Japanese and English, Semantics and Construction of Verbs)*. Taishukan (Tokyo).

Kanasugi, Yuuko, Kaname Kasahara, Nozomi Inago, and Shigeaki Amano, 2002. Selection of a basic vocabulary based on word familiarity ratings. In *IEICE Technical Report NLC2002*, 27, pp. 21–26. IEICE. (in Japanese).

Kanayama, Hiroshi, Kentaro Torisawa, Yutaka Mitsuishi, and Jun ichi Tsujii, 2000. A hybrid japanese parser with hand-crafted grammar and statistics. In *Proceedings of the 18th International Conference on Computational Linguistics, Coling 2000*, pp. 404–410. Saarbrücken, Germany.

Kasahara, Kaname, Hiroshi Sato, Francis Bond, Takaaki Tanaka, Sanae Fujita, Tomoko Kanasugi, and Shigeaki Amano, 2004. Construction of a Japanese semantic lexicon: Lexeed. In *IPSG SIG: 2004-NLC-159*, pp. 75–82. Tokyo. (in Japanese).

Kasai, Hironobu and Shoichi Takahashi, 2001. Coordination in japanese. In *Proceedings of the Third Formal Approaches to Japanese Linguistics Conference FAJL3*.

Kasper, Robert, 1995. The semantics of recursive modification. http://www.essex.ac.uk/linguistics/external/clmt/papers/hpsg/modification.ps.

Katagiri, Yasuhiro, 1991. Perspectivity and the Japanese reflexive '*zibun*'. In Jon Barwise, Jean Mark Gawron, Gordon Plotkin, and Syun Tutiya (eds.), *Situation Theory and its Applications*, volume 2, chapter 18, pp. 425–447. CSLI.

Kiefer, Bernd, Hans-Ulrich Krieger, and Melanie Siegel, 2000. An HPSG-to-CFG approximation of Japanese. In *Proceedings of Coling 2000*.

Knuth, Donald E., 1992. *Literate Programming*. CSLI Publications.

Koehn, Philipp, Wade Shen, Marcello Federico, Nicola Bertoldi, Chris Callison-Burch, Brooke Cowan, Chris Dyer, Hieu Hoang, Ondrej Bojar, Richard Zens, Alexandra Constantin, Evan Herbst, Christine Moran, and Alexandra Birch, 2007. Moses: Open source toolkit for statistical machine translation. In *Proceedings of the ACL 2007 Interactive Presentation Sessions*. Prague. URL http://www.statmt.org/moses/.

Koenig, Jean-Pierre and Anthony R. Davis, 2006. The KEY to lexical semantic representations. *Journal of Linguistics*, 42: 71–108. doi: 10.1017/S0022226705003695.

Kordoni, Valia and Julia Neu, 2005. Deep analysis of Modern Greek. In Keh-Yih Su, Jun'ichi Tsujii, and Jong-Hyeok Lee (eds.), *Lecture Notes in Computer Science*, volume 3248, pp. 674–683. Springer-Verlag.

Kudo, Taku, Kaoru Yamamoto, and Yuji Matsumoto, 2004. Applying Conditional Random Fields to Japanese Morphological Analysis. In Dekang Lin and Dekai Wu (eds.), *Proceedings of EMNLP 2004*, pp. 230–237. Barcelona, Spain: Association for Computational Linguistics.

Kuno, Susumu, 1973. *The Structure of the Japanese Language*. Cambridge, MA: MIT Press.

Kuroda, Kow, Takayuki Kuribayashi, Francis Bond, Kyoko Kanzaki, and Hitoshi Isahara, 2011. Orthographic variants and multilingual sense tagging with the Japanese WordNet. In *17th Annual Meeting of the Association for Natural Language Processing*, pp. A4–1. Toyohashi.

Kuroda, Shigeyuki, 1992. *Japanese Syntax and Semantics. Collected Papers*, volume 22 of *Studies in Natural Language and Linguistic Theory*. Dordrecht: Kluwer Academic Publishers.

Kurohashi, Sadao and Makoto Nagao, 1994. A syntactic analysis method of long Japanese sentences based on the detection of conjunctive structures. *Computational Linguistics*, 20(4).

Lavie, Anton and Abhaya Agarwa, 2007. METEOR: An automatic metric for MT evaluation with high levels of correlation with human judgments. In *Proceedings of Workshop on Statistical Machine Translation at ACL-2007*. Prague.

Lee, Dong-Young, 1996. An HPSG account of the Korean honorification system. In Claire Grover and Enric Vallduvo (eds.), *Studies in HPSG*, volume 12, pp. 165–190. Centre for Cognitive Science, Univ.of Edinburgh.

Lehmann, Sabine, Stephan Oepen, Sylvie Regnier-Prost, Klaus Netter, Veronika Lux, Judith Klein, Kirsten Falkedal, Frederik Fouvry, Dominique Estival, Eva Dauphin, Hervé Compagnion, Judith Baur, Lorna Balkan, and Doug Arnold, 1996. Tsnlp - test suites for natural language processing. In *Proceedings of the 16th International Conference on Computational Linguistics*, pp. 711–716.

Letcher, Ned, Timothy Baldwin, and Rebecca Dridan, 2015. gDelta: A missing link in the grammar engineering toolchain. *Language Resources and Evaluation*, 49(1): 51–75. URL http://dx.doi.org/10.1007/s10579-014-9293-0.

Lønning, Jan Tore, Stephan Oepen, Dorothee Beermann, Lars Hellan, John Carroll, Helge Dyvik, Dan Flickinger, Janne Bondi Johannessen, Paul Meurer, Torbjørn Nordgård, Victoria Rosén, and Erik Velldal, 2004. LOGON. A Norwegian MT effort. In *Proceedings of the Workshop in Recent Advances in Scandinavian Machine Translation*. Uppsala, Sweden.

Lunde, Ken, 1999. *CJKV Information Processing*. Sebastopol, CA: O'Reilly.

Makino, Seiichi and Michio Tsutsui, 1986. *A Dictionary of Basic Japanese Grammar*. The Japan Times.

Malouf, Robert and Gertjan van Noord, 2004. Wide coverage parsing with stochastic attribute value grammars. In *IJCNLP-04 Workshop: Beyond shallow analyses - Formalisms and statistical modeling for deep analyses*. JST CREST. URL http://www-tsujii.is.s.u-tokyo.ac.jp/bsa/papers/malouf.pdf.

Manning, Christopher D. and Ivan A. Sag, 1998. Dissociatons between argument structure and grammatical relations. In A. Kathol, J.-P. Koenig, and G. Webelhuth (eds.), *Lexical and Constructional Aspects of Linguistic Explanation*. Stanford: CSLI Publications.

Manning, Christopher D., Ivan A. Sag, and Masayo Iida, 1998. The lexical integrity of japanese causatives. In Robert Levine and Georgia Green (eds.), *Readings in Modern Phrase Structure Grammar*. Cambridge University Press.

Marimon, Montserrat, 2010. The Spanish resource grammar. In Nicoletta Calzolari, Khalid Choukri, Bente Maegaard, Joseph Mariani, Jan Odijk, Stelios Piperidis, Mike Rosner, and Daniel Tapias (eds.), *Proceedings of the Seventh conference on International Language Resources and Evaluation (LREC'10)*. Valletta, Malta: European Language Resources Association (ELRA).

Martin, Samuel E., 1988. *A Reference Grammar of Japanese*. Tokyo: Tuttle, first tuttle edition edition.

Masuichi, Hiroshi and Tomoko Ohkuma, 2003. Constructing a practical Japanese parser based on Lexical-Functional Grammar. *Journal of Natural Language Processing*, 10(2): 79–109. (in Japanese).

Masuoka, Takashi and Yukinori Takubo, 1992. *Kiso Nihongo Bunpoo (Basic Japanese Grammar)*. Kuroshio (Tokyo).

Matsumoto, Yō, 1993. Japanese numeral classifiers: a study of semantic categories and lexical organization. *Linguistics*, 31: 667–713.

Matsumoto, Yō, 1996a. *Complex Predicates in Japanese*. Tokyo & Stanford: Kuroshio Shuppan & CSLI.

Matsumoto, Yo, 1996b. *Complex Predicates in Japanese: A Syntactic and Semantic Study of the Notion 'Word'*. CSLI Publications and Kurosio.

Matsumoto, Yuji, Kitauchi, Yamashita, Hirano, Matsuda, and Asahara, 2000. *Nihongo Keitaiso Kaiseki System: Chasen*. http://chasen.naist.jp/hiki/ChaSen/.

Matsumoto, Yuuji, Akira Kitauchi, Tatsu Yamashita, and Yoshitake Hirano, 1999. *Japanese Morphological Analysis System ChaSen Version 2.0 Manual*. Technical Report NAIST-IS-TR99009, NAIST.

McCawley, James D, 1976. Relativization. In Shibatani (1976).

McGloin, Naomi Hanaoka, 1976. Negation. In Shibatani (1976).

Metzing, Dieter and Melanie Siegel, 1994. Zero pronoun processing: Some requirements for a Verbmobil system. Verbmobil-Memo 46, Universität Bielefeld.

Mima, Hideki, Osamu Furuse, and Hitoshi Iida, 1997. A situation-based approach to spoken dialog translation between different social roles. In *Seventh International Conference on Theoretical and Methodological Issues in Machine Translation: TMI-97*, pp. 176–183. Santa-Fe.

Miyagawa, Shigeru, 1988. Predication and numeral quantifiers. In William J Poser (ed.), *Papers from the Second International Workshop on Japanese Syntax*, pp. 157–191. CSLI Publications.

Miyagawa, Shigeru, 1989. *Structure and Case Marking in Japanese*, volume 22 of *Syntax and Semantics*. Amsterdam: Academic Press.

Miyao, Yussuke and Jun'ichi Tsujii, 2008. Feature forest models for probabilistic HPSG parsing. *Computational Linguistics*, 34(1): 35–80.

Miyata, Takashi, Akira Ohtani, and Yuji Matsumoto, 2001. An HPSG account of the hierarchical clause formation in Japanese — HPSG-based Japanese grammar for practical parsing. In *Proceedings of the 15th Pacific Asia Conference (PACLIC,15)*, pp. 305–316.

Motomura, Mitsue, 2001. Zibun as a residue of overt a-movement. In *Proceedings of the Third Formal Approaches to Japanese Linguistics Conference FAJL3*.

Mouret, François, 2006. A phrase structure approach to argument cluster coordination. In Stefan Müller (ed.), *The Proceedings of the 13th International Conference on Head-Driven Phrase Structure Grammar*, pp. 247–267. Stanford: CSLI Publications. URL http://cslipublications.stanford.edu/HPSG/7/.

Müller, Stefan, 1999. *Deutsche Syntax deklarativ. Head-Driven Phrase Structure Grammar für das Deutsche*. Tübingen, Germany: Max Niemeyer Verlag.

Müller, Stefan and Walter Kasper, 2000. HPSG analysis of german. In Wahlster (2000), pp. 238–253.

Nariyama, Shigeko, Hiromi Nakaiwa, and Melanie Siegel, 2005. Annotating honorifics denoting social ranking of the referents. In *6th International Workshop on Linguistically Integrated Corpora (LINC-2005)*, pp. 91–100. Cheju, Korea.

Nichols, Eric, Francis Bond, Darren Scott Appling, and Yuji Matsumoto, 2007. Combining resources for open source machine translation. In *The 11th International Conference on Theoretical and Methodological Issues in Machine Translation (TMI-07)*, pp. 134–142. Skövde.

Nichols, Eric, Francis Bond, Darren Scott Appling, and Yuji Matsumoto, 2010. Paraphrasing training data for statistical machine translation. *Journal of Natural Language Processing*, 17(3): 101–122. Special Issue on Empirical Methods for Asian Language Processing.

Nichols, Eric, Francis Bond, and Daniel Flickinger, 2005. Robust ontology acquisition from machine-readable dictionaries. In *Proceedings of the International Joint Conference on Artificial Intelligence IJCAI-2005*, pp. 1111–1116. Edinburgh.

Nichols, Eric, Francis Bond, Takaaki Tanaka, Sanae Fujita, and Daniel Flickinger, 2006. Robust ontology acquisition from multiple sources. In *Proceedings of the 2nd Workshop on Ontology Learning and Population: Bridging the Gap between Text and Knowledge*, pp. 10–17. Sydney. URL http://www.aclweb.org/anthology/W/W06/W06-0502.

Nightingale, Stephen, 1996. *An HPSG Account of the Japanese Copula and Related Phenomena*. Master's thesis, University of Edinburgh.

van Noord, Gertjan, 2004. Error mining for wide-coverage grammar engineering. In *42nd Annual Meeting of the Association for Computational Linguistics: ACL-2004*. Barcelona.

Oepen, Stephan, Emily M. Bender, Ulrich Callmeier, Dan Flickinger, and Melanie Siegel, 2002a. Parallel distributed grammar engineering for practical applications. In *Proceedings of the Workshop on Grammar Engineering and Evaluation, COLING 2002*. Taipei, Taiwan.

Oepen, Stephan and John Carroll, 2000. Performance profiling for grammar engineering. *Natural Language Engineering*, 6(1): 81–97.

Oepen, Stephan and Dan Flickinger, 1998. Towards systematic grammar profiling: Test suite technolgy ten years after. *Journal of Computer Speech and Language. Special Issue on Evaluation*, 12(4).

Oepen, Stephan, Dan Flickinger, and Francis Bond, 2004a. Towards holistic grammar engineering and testing — grafting treebank maintenance into the grammar revision cycle. In *Beyond Shallow Analyses — Formalisms and Statistical Modelling for Deep Analysis (Workshop at IJCNLP-2004)*. Hainan Island. URL http://www-tsujii.is.s.u-tokyo.ac.jp/bsa/.

Oepen, Stephan, Dan Flickinger, Kristina Toutanova, and Christoper D. Manning, 2004b. LinGO redwoods: A rich and dynamic treebank for HPSG. *Research on Language and Computation*, 2(4): 575–596.

Oepen, Stephan, Dan Flickinger, Jun-ichi Tsujii, and Hans Uszkoreit (eds.), 2002b. *Collaborative Language Engineering*. Stanford: CSLI Publications.

Oepen, Stephan, Kristina Toutanova, Stuart Shieber, Christopher D. Manning, Dan Flickinger, and Thorsten Brant, 2002c. The LinGO redwoods treebank: Motivation and preliminary applications. In *19th International Conference on Computational Linguistics: COLING-2002*, pp. 1253–7. Taipei, Taiwan.

Oepen, Stephan, Erik Velldal, Jan Tore Lønning, Paul Meurer, and Victoria Rosen, 2007. Towards hybrid quality-oriented machine translation. on linguistics and probabilities in MT. In *11th International Conference on Theoretical and Methodological Issues in Machine Translation: TMI-2007*, pp. 144–153.

Ohtani, Akira, Takashi Miyata, and Yuji Matsumoto, 2000. On HPSG-based Japanese grammar — refinement and extension for implementation —. *Journal of Natural Language Processing*, 7(5): 19–49. (In Japanese).

Okushi, Yoshiko, 1997. *Patterns of Honorific Use in the Everyday Speech of Four Japanese Women*. Ph.D. thesis, University of Pennsylvania.

Ono, Kiyoharu, 1996. Syntactic behaviour of case and adverbial particles in Japanese. *Australian Journal of Linguistics*, 16(1): 81–129.

Oshima, David Yoshikazu, 2003. Out of control: A unified analysis of japanese passive. In *Proceedings of HPSG*.

Paik, Kyonghee and Francis Bond, 2002. Spatial representation and shape classifiers in Japanese and Korean. In David Beaver, Stefan Kaufmann, Brady Clark, and Luis Casillas (eds.), *The Construction of Meaning*, pp. 163–180. Stanford: CSLI Publications.

Papineni, K., S. Roukos, T. Ward, and W. J. Zhu, 2002. BLEU: a method for automatic evaluation of machine translation. In *40th Annual Meeting of the Association for Computational Linguistics: ACL-2002*, pp. 311–318.

Pollard, Carl and Ivan A Sag, 1994. *Head-Driven Phrase Structure Grammar*. Chicago: University of Chicago Press.

Raymond, Eric S., 1999. *The Cathedral & the Bazaar*. O'Reilly.

Reape, Mike, 1993. *A Formal Theory of Word Order: A Case Study in West Germanic*. Ph.D. thesis, University of Edinburgh.

Riezler, Stefan, Tracy H. King, Ronald M. Kaplan, Richard Crouch, John T. Maxwell III, and Mark Johnson, 2002. Parsing the Wall Street Journal using a Lexical-Functional Grammar and discriminative estimation techniques. In *41st Annual Meeting of the Association for Computational Linguistics: ACL-2003*, pp. 271–278.

Sadakane, Kumi and Masatoshi Koizumi, 1995. On the nature of the "dative" particle *ni* in Japanese. *Linguistics*, 33: 5–33.

Sag, Ivan A. and Tom Wasow, 1999. *Syntactic Theory: A Formal Introduction*. Stanford: CSLI Publications.

Sag, Ivan A., Tom Wasow, and Emily Bender, 2003. *Syntactic Theory: A Formal Introduction*. Stanford: CSLI Publications, 2 edition.

Saussure, Ferdinand de, 1949. Cours de linguistique générale (1916). *Paris: Payot*.

Schlangen, David and Gabriel Skantze, 2009. A general, abstract model of incremental dialogue processing. In *Proceedings of the 12th Conference of the European Chapter of the ACL*, pp. 710–718. URL http://www.ling.uni-potsdam.de/~das/papers/schlangenetal_agmo_eacl2009.pdf.

Seah, Yu Jie and Francis Bond, 2014. Annotation of pronouns in a multilingual corpus of Mandarin Chinese, English and Japanese. In *10th Joint ACL - ISO Workshop on Interoperable Semantic Annotation*. Reykjavik.

Shibatani, Masayoshi, 1976. *Japanese Generative Grammar*, volume 5 of *Syntax and Semantics*. Academic Press.

Shibatani, Masayoshi and Taro Kageyama, 1988. Word formation in a modular theory of grammar: Postsyntactic compounds in japanese. *Language*, 64: 451–484.

Siegel, Melanie, 1996a. Definiteness and number in Japanese to German machine translation. In D. Gibbon (ed.), *Natural Language Processing and Speech Technology*, pp. 137–142. Berlin: Mouton de Gruyter.

Siegel, Melanie, 1996b. Preferences and defaults for definiteness and number in Japanese to German machine translation. In Byung-Soo Park and Jong-Bok Kim (eds.), *Selected Papers from the 11th Pacific Asia Conference on Language, Information and Computation*, pp. 43–52. Language Education and Research Institute, Kyung Hee University, Seoul.

Siegel, Melanie, 1999. The syntactic processing of particles in Japanese spoken language. In Jhing-Fa Wang and Chung-Hsien Wu (eds.), *Proceedings of the 13th Pacific Asia Conference on Language, Information and Computation (PACLIC-99)*, pp. 43–52. Taipei, Taiwan.

Siegel, Melanie, 2000. HPSG analysis of Japanese. In Wahlster (2000), pp. 265–280.

Siegel, Melanie, 2006. *JACY - A Grammar for Annotating Syntax, Semantics and Pragmatics of Written and Spoken Japanese for NLP Application Purposes*. habilitation, Bielefeld University.

Siegel, Melanie and Emily Bender, 2004. Head-initial constructions in Japanese. In Stefan Müller (ed.), *Proceedings of the 11th International Conference on Head-Driven Phrase Structure Grammar*, pp. 244–260. Center for Computational Linguistics, Katholieke Universiteit Leuven.

Siegel, Melanie and Emily M. Bender, 2002. Efficient deep processing of Japanese. In *Proceedings of the 3rd Workshop on Asian Language Resources and International Standardization at the 19th International Conference on Computational Linguistics*, pp. 1–8. Taipei.

Sirai, Hidetoshi, 1996. Constraints based grammar formalism for Japanese. In Takao Gunji (ed.), *Studies in the Universality of Constraint-Based Structure Grammars*. Osaka.

Sirai, Hidetoshi and Takao Gunji, 1998. Relative clauses and adnominal clauses. In Takao Gunji and Koiti Hasida (eds.), *Topics in Constrained-Based Grammar of Japanese*, pp. 17–38. Kluwer Academic Publishers.

Smith, Jeffery D., 1999. English number names in HPSG. In Gert Webelhuth, Jean-Pierre Koenig, and Andreas Kathol (eds.), *Lexical and Constructional Aspects of Linguistic Explanation*, pp. 145–160. Stanford: CSLI.

Song, Sanghoun, 2014. *A Grammar Library for Information Structure*. Ph.D. thesis, University of Washington.

Song, Sanghoun, Jong-Bok Kim, Francis Bond, and Jaehyung Yang, 2010. Development of the korean resource grammar: Towards grammar customization. In *Proceedings of the Eighth Workshop on Asian Language Resouces*, pp. 144–152. Beijing, China: Coling 2010 Organizing Committee. URL http://www.aclweb.org/anthology/W10-3219.

Sparck-Jones, Karen, 1994. Towards better nlp system evaluation. In *Proceedings of the Second ARPA Workshop on Human Language Technology*. San Mateo,CA: Morgan Kaufmann.

Tan, Liling and Francis Bond, 2012. Building and annotating the linguistically diverse NTU-MC (NTU-multilingual corpus). *International Journal of Asian Language Processing*, 22(4): 161–174.

Tanaka, Takaaki, Francis Bond, Stephan Oepen, and Sanae Fujita, 2005. High precision treebanking – blazing useful trees using POS information. In *ACL-2005*, pp. 330–337.

Tanaka, Yasuhito, 2001. Compilation of a multilingual parallel corpus. In *Proceedings of PACLING 2001*, pp. 265–268. Kyushu. (http://www.colips.org/afnlp/archives/pacling2001/pdf/tanaka.pdf).

Teramura, Hideo, 1984a. *Nihongo no Shintakkusu to Imi, Dai-ik-kan (The Syntax and Semantics of Japanese 1)*. Taishukan (Tokyo).

Teramura, Hideo, 1984b. *Nihongo no Shintakkusu to Imi, Dai-ni-kan (The Syntax and Semantics of Japanese 2)*. Taishukan (Tokyo).

Tomabechi, Hideto, 1989. Zero-pronominals, point-of-view, empathy perspective, and context parameters. Ms.

Toutanova, Kristina, Christopher D. Manning, Dan Flickinger, and Stephan Oepen, 2005. Stochastic HPSG parse disambiguation using the redwoods corpus. *Research on Language and Computation*, 3(1): 83–105.

Tsuchiya, Masatoshi, Sadao Kurohashi, and Satoshi Sato, 2001. Discovery of definition patterns by compressing dictionary sentences. In *Proceedings of the 6th Natural Language Processing Pacific Rim Symposium, NL-PRS2001*, pp. 411–418. Tokyo.

Tsuda, Hiroshi and Yasunari Harada, 1996. Semantics and pragmatics of adnominal particle NO in Quixote. In Takao Gunji (ed.), *Studies in the Universality of Constraint-Based Structure Grammars*. Osaka.

Tsujimura, N., 2006. *An Introduction to Japanese Linguistics*. Blackwell Textbooks in Linguistics. Wiley. URL http://books.google.de/books?id=LKoo7Zi63PkC.

Tsujimura, Natsuko, 1996. *An Introduction to Japanese Linguistics*. Cambridge, MA: Blackwell.

Tsujimura, Natsuko (ed.), 1999. *The Handbook of Japanese Linguistics*. Blackwell.

Uda, Chiharu, 1994. *Complex Predicates in Japanese*. Garland Publishing.

Uda, Chiharu, 1996. ARG-S feature and valence features: More evidence from Japanese passives. In Takao Gunji (ed.), *Studies in the Universality of Constraint-Based Structure Grammars*, pp. 203–215. Osaka University.

Uszkoreit, Hans, Ulrich Callmeier, Andreas Eisele, Ulrich Schäfer, Melanie Siegel, and Jakob Uszkoreit, 2004. Hybrid robust deep and shallow semantic processing for creativity support in document production. In *Proceedings of KONVENS 2004*, pp. 209–216. Vienna, Austria.

Vermeulen, Reiko, 2012. The information structure of Japanese. *The Expression of Information Structure*, 5: 186–215.

Wahlster, Wolfgang (ed.), 2000. *Verbmobil: Foundations of Speech-to-Speech Translation*. Berlin, Germany: Springer.

Waibel, Alex, Hagen Soltau, Tanja Schultz, Thomas Schaaf, and Florian Metze, 2000. Multilingual speech recognition. In *Verbmobil: Foundations of Speech-to-Speech Translation*, pp. 33–45. Springer.

Watanabe, Hideo, Sadao Kurohashi, and Eiji Aramaki, 2000. Finding structural correspondences from bilingual parsed corpus for corpus-based translation. In *Proceedings of the 18th International Conference on Computational Linguistics, Coling 2000*, pp. 906–912. Saarbrücken, Germany.

Wetzel, Dominikus and Francis Bond, 2012. Enriching parallel corpora for statistical machine translation with semantic negation rephrasing. In *Sixth Workshop on Syntax, Semantics and Structure in Statistical Translation (SSST-6)*. Jeju, Korea.

Yatabe, Shoichi, 1993. *Scrambling and Japanese Phrase Structure*. Ph.D. thesis, Stanford University.

Yatabe, Shuichi, 1996. Long-distance scrambling via partial compaction. In Masatoshi Koizumi, Masayuki Oishi, and Uli Sauerland (eds.), *Formal Approaches to Japanese Linguistics*, volume 2 of *MIT Working Papers in Linguistics*, pp. 303–317. MITWPL.

Yatabe, Shûichi, 2007. Evidence for the linearization-based theory of semantic composition. In Stefan Müller (ed.), *The Proceedings of the 14th International Conference on Head-Driven Phrase Structure Grammar*, pp. 323–343. Stanford: CSLI Publications. URL http://cslipublications.stanford.edu/HPSG/8/.

Yoshimoto, Kei, 1998. *Tense and Aspect in Japanese and English*. Frankfurt am Main: Peter Lang.

Zhang, Yi, Timothy Baldwin, and Valia Kordoni, 2007a. The corpus and the lexicon: Standardising deep lexical acquisition evaluation. In *ACL 2007 Workshop on Deep Linguistic Processing*, pp. 152–159. Prague, Czech Republic.

Zhang, Yi, Stephan Oepen, and John Carroll, 2007b. Efficiency in unification-based n-best parsing. In *IWPT:07*, pp. 48–59. Prague, Czech Republic.

Zhang, Yi, Rui Wang, and Stephan Oepen, 2009. Hybrid multilingual parsing with HPSG for SRL. In *Proceedings of the 13th Conference on Computational Natural Language Learning*.

Zwicky, Arnold M., 1985. Heads. *Journal of Linguistics*, 21: 1–29.

Zwicky, Arnold M., 1993. Heads, bases, and functors. In Greville C. Corbett and McGlashan (1993), pp. 292–315.

Index

—, 43, 71, 73, 75, 142

accusative, 69, 81, 202
ACE, 27, 230, 254
add-honor_rel, 223
addr-honor_rel, 219, 220, 222–224, 226
addressee, 10, 14, 89, 127, 128, 134, 139, 200, 201, 211–214, 216, 219–227
adj-stem, 93
adj2adv-lexeme-infl-rule, 206
adjacency, 18, 70
adjunct, 49, 129, 179, 182, 189, 191, 192, 194, 196, 204
adn-case, 141
adnominal, 56, 120, 134, 141, 166, 178, 186, 193, 202
adv-lex, 55, 206
adv-p-lex-1, 238
adv-p-lex-6, 238
adv-p-lex-np, 17, 199
adv-wh-lex, 208
adv_head, 206
adv_np_rule, 206, 208
adverb, 82, 167, 169, 206, 239
adverbial particle, 191
adversative, 106, 107, 109–112, 116, 131, 133
adversative-intrans-pass-end-lt, 110
adversative-pass-end-lt, 110

adversative-trans-pass-end-lt, 111
ambiguity, 6, 14, 16, 17, 111, 112, 140, 143, 157, 183, 192, 194, 197, 202, 204, 231, 233, 235–237, 254, 256, *see also* spurious ambiguity 263
anaphora, 14, 67, 146
antecedent, 69, 130–134, 174, 226, 288
anymod, 149
anymod-, 150
anymod-num-cl-lex, 152
appointment scheduling, 136, 165, 202
argument, 12, 16, 18, 33, 48, 49, 56, 62, 63, 68–71, 73–75, 78, 81, 82, 84, 85, 100, 103, 105, 107, 109–111, 123, 129, 132, 134, 135, 138–141, 147, 151, 154–157, 173, 178, 180, 182, 183, 187, 191, 192, 199, 205, 213, 238
argument optionality, 33, 70, 71
aspect, 62, 77, 78, 100, 101, 104, 106, 116, 117, 143, 176, 236
aspect-stem-lex, 102
automatic error detection, 243
aux-obj-id-stem-lex, 103, 105
auxiliary, 14, 16, 52, 77, 100, 106, 116, 134

banking domain, 9, 16, 255

base-adj-stem-lex, 206
basic-head-comp-type, 34
basic-head-complement-type, 33
bijacency-based analysis, 174
binary rule, 60
binary-modification-type, 38
binary-type-conj, 38
BLEU, 25, 26
broad-coverage grammar, 258
broad-coverage grammar, 5, 6, 60, 166, 250, 257

c-stem, 91–93, 112
c2-stem, 91, 93
card-lex, 160–162
cardinal relation, 147, 151
case, 4, 14, 25, 32, 41, 47–51, 54, 56, 57, 59–62, 64, 71, 72, 75, 78–80, 82–84, 86, 89, 95, 98, 99, 107, 110–112, 114–116, 128–130, 136, 141, 142, 144, 148, 151, 152, 154, 156, 157, 165, 166, 168–177, 179, 182–187, 189, 191, 194, 195, 202–204, 213, 220–222, 224, 232, 235, 238
case particle, 54, 86, 129, 144, 179, 182, 186, 191, 194
case-p-lex, 170–174, 184
case-p-lex-np, 17, 171
case-p-lex-postp, 171
case-p_head, 185
case-particle-head, 185
caus-trans-obj-end-lt, 115
causative, 77, 112–114, 116, 117, 255
ChaSen, 43, 49, 90, 256
collectivizing suffix, 119
colon, 16, 184
comp-int-lex, 184
comp-lex, 184
comp-prpstn-lex, 184, 185
compatibility, 18, 121, 222, 256
complement, 31, 33–35, 59, 68, 73, 80–88, 106, 110, 139, 151, 154, 155, 157, 158, 170–172, 174–176, 182, 184, 186–188, 194, 195, 200, 216, 255
complementizer, 184, 185, 195
complex-aspect-stem-lex, 102, 103
compositional semantics, 143
compound, 37
compound noun, 123
compound-name-rule, 124
compounds-rule, 124
cond-spoken-lexeme, 95
conj-lex, 170
conj-p-lex, 171, 198
conj-rule, 38–41, 200
conj-rule-type, 38
conjunct, 37, 39, 41, 174, 185, 199, 200
conjunction-rel, 200
conjunction-relation, 39, 40
cons, 72, 74
const-stem, 95
cont-p-lex, 170, 171, 186, 187, 198
cooccurrence, 166, 167, 203
coord, 36, 37
coordination, 37–39, 41, 65, 165, 184, 185, 198, 199, 204, 223
cop-arg, 79
cop-id-neg-stem-lt, 87
cop-light-lt, 79, 86, 87
cop-neg-lt, 87
cop-neg-stem-lt, 87
cop-stem, 93
copula, 11, 14, 23, 35, 68, 79, 82, 85–89, 99, 116, 142, 170, 212

da-stem, 93
day-lex, 137
decomposition, 83, 207, 209
DeepThought, 17, 28, 256
def_q, 123
default entry, *see also* generic entry 263
DELPH-IN, 29, 71
demonstrative, 125, 126, 209, 210
dependency, 250
derivation, 75, 116, 129, 162, 233, 235, 236

INDEX / 281

derivation tree, 75, 233, 235, 236
desu-stem, 93
det-lex, 121
determiner, 18, 42, 119–121, 123, 129, 134, 135, 147, 158, 186, 209, 233, 235
dialogue data, 128, 167, 197, 202
disambiguation, 140, 194
discriminants, 232, 233, 235
dofm-n-lex, 137
dofw-n-lex, 137
dropped argument, 74, *see also* zero pronoun 263

EDR corpus, 6, 141
elementary predication, 61, 80, 102, 170, 186
ellipsis, 38, 173, 174, *see also* zero pronoun 263
empathy, 10, 14, 101, 104, 105, 116, 125, 127, 128, 133, 134, 194, 200
empty-case-p_head, 202
English Resource Grammar, 6, 31
entity-honor, 127
entity-honor_rel, 127, 128, 219–221, 224
eru-lexeme-infl-rule, 98, 99
eval-rashii, 90
eval-te+ii, 90
evaluation
　extrinsic, 245
　intrinsic, 245
event, 174
event variable, 81, 107

final_head, 59, 151
final_head., 59, 60
floated-ind-obj-num-cl-lex, 156, 157
floated-ind-sbj-num-cl-lex, 156, 157
floated-num-cl-lex, 156
frag-pp-np-rule, 45, 47
fragment, 11, 44, 46, 47, 247
full_ref-ind, 157

ga, 78
ga+, 90
ga-ga, 90
ga-wo, 90
ga-wo-ni-p-lex, 238
ga-wo_transitive, 89
gaj, 202
generic entity, *see also* default entry 263
genre, 10, 147
grammar profiling, 247
grammar development cycle, 232
Grammar Matrix, 6, 7, 17, 28, 31, 70, 71, 209
grammar profiling, 256
grammar size, 246, 256
grammar-based corpus annotation, 233
grammatical coverage, 17, 251, 255
grammatical function, 78, 172, 177, 179, 203
grammaticality, 26, 27, 50, 89, 147, 169, 182, 210, 221

han, 59
han_head, 151
handle constraint, 62–64
head, 59
Head Feature Principle, 31
head daughter, 32, 35, 41, 43, 73, 192, 223
head feature, 31, 55, 142, 217, 221
Head Feature Principle, 31
Head Feature Principle, 47, 217
head noun, 36, 139–141, 143, 144, 152, 215
head type, 60, 121, 139, 149, 151, 206
head value, 151
head-adj-final-intersect, 160
head-adj-first-intersect, 161
head-adjunct, 73
head-adjunct rule, 36, 206
Head-Adjunct Schema, 30

head-adjunct-rule-final, 36, 37
head-adjunct-rule-first, 37
head-adjunct-rule-type, 35
head-comp, 160–162
head-comp-hf-type, 34
head-comp-hi-type, 34
head-comp-phrase, 32
head-comp-type, 34
head-comp2-types, 34
head-complement, 71
head-complement rule, 34
Head-Complement Schema, 30
head-complement-hf-rule, 33, 39
head-complement-hf-type, 33
head-complement-hi-rule, 33
head-complement-hi-type, 33
head-complement-rule-type, 34
head-complement-type, 33, 35
head-complement2, 71, 73
head-complement2-rule, 33, 34
head-complement2-type, 33, 34
Head-Filler Schema, 30, 31
head-final, 29, 34, 35, 37, 45, 49, 55, 57, 60, 65, 73, 124, 140, 176, 198
head-initial complementation, 56, 58, 59
head-initial modification, 49, 53, 55
Head-Marker Schema, 30, 31
head-marker-rule-type, 43
head-mod-phrase, 32
head-nexus-phrase, 31, 32
head-spec-phrase, 32
Head-Specifier Schema, 31
head-specifier-rule, 41, 42, 100, 110, 113, 116
head-specifier-rule-type, 95
head-spr, 160–162
head-subj-phrase, 32
head-subject, 73
Head-Subject Schema, 30, 33
Head-Subject-Complement Schema, 30, 31
head-valence-phrase, 32

headed-phrase, 31, 32
Heart-of-Gold, 17, 20, 123
Hinoki treebank, 2, 4, 246, 250, 256
honorific agreement, 212, 222, 227
honorific information, 204, 227
honorification, 7, 10, 13, 14, 67, 87, 89, 100, 104–106, 111, 116, 124, 125, 127, 128, 130, 134, 139, 177, 178, 198–200, 212–222, 224–227
HOOK, 239
hybrid architecture, 17
hypernym, 21, 24

i-lexeme-c-stem, 99
i-lexeme-c-stem-infl-rule, 95
i-lexeme-c2-stem, 99
i-lexeme-v-stem, 99
i-morph, 95
ind-lex, 150
ind-nmod-lex, 150
indicative, 95
individuating, 149
individuating-, 150
inflection, 10, 14, 15, 41, 48, 52, 77, 91, 93, 99, 116, 117, 210, 213
inflectional morphology, 42, 77
information extraction, 2, 9, 28
information structure, 14, 76, 196
init_head, 59, 60, 151
int_head, 59, 151
interrogative, 88, 178, 200, 207–209, 255
intersective, 35, 36, 55, 140, 151, 189, 206, 210
intersective_mod, 36
intransitive verb, 78, 109
ippan-name, 124
isect-adv-lex, 206
Italic sans serif, xv

JPSG, 8, 70, 221

kenjougo, 213
kuru, 91
kurusuru-stem, 93

lack-control-rel, 106
language generation, 3
language understanding, 2
left, 37, 55
lex-left, 55
lex-mod-adv-wh-lex, 208
lex-right, 55
Lexeed, 4, 21, 24, 246, 250, 251, 253, 255
lexeme, 70, 71, 240
lexical entry, 32, 39, 73, 91, 95, 116, 149, 158, 194, 199
lexical rule, 71, 87, 95, 141
lexical type database, 236
lexical type hierarchy, 55, 149
Lexical-Functional Grammar, 28
lexical-sign-word, 55
lexicon, 3, 15, 16, 27, 56, 65, 71, 78, 91, 123, 195, 229, 240, 246, 250, 255, 256
light verb construction, 180
linearization, 71, 76, 202, *see also* word order 263
linguistic competence, 2
list, 72, 74
LKB, 5, 7, 27, 230, 254
local, 36
locative, 125, 126, 190, 191

machine translation, 2, 4, 5, 9, 10, 20, 23, 25, 28, 122, 124, 212, 216–218, 225, 245, 248, 256, 259
Matrix, 6, 7, 17, 28, 31, 70, 71, 209, 256
meas-lex, 150
mensural, 149
mensural-, 150
mensural-num-cl-lex, 154
mod, 187
mod-p-lex, 170, 171, 187, 199

modality, 117, *see also* auxiliary 263
modifier, 23, 37, 45, 49, 50, 52–56, 88, 140, 152, 158, 168, 175, 176, 199
mofy-n-lex, 137
morphbindtype, 93, 94
morpheme, 87
morphology, 3, 4, 42, 43, 49, 57, 77, 91, 98, 113, 207
MRS, 3, 5, 8, 16–18, 20–23, 25, 61–63, 65, 78, 81, 83, 84, 86, 102, 106, 107, 109, 111, 114, 116, 120, 121, 123–125, 127, 133, 135, 138, 140, 141, 147, 156, 157, 189, 195, 196, 200, 201, 246, 253, 256
MRS algebra, *see also* semantic algebra 263
multilingual grammar development, 3, 4, 9, 17

n-lex, 125
n_conj-p-lex, 199
n_num+cl-spr-only-index, 158
naadj2adv-end-lex, 237, 238, 240, 242
naadj2adv-p-end-lex, 239
named-entity recognition, 3, 4, 20, 123, 124, 255
ncl-lex, 150
ncl-obj-only-, 150
ncl-spr-, 150
ncl-spr-only-, 150
negation, 26, 62, 63, 87, 90, 245
ni-ga, 90
nmod-numcl-p-lex, 160, 189
nmod-p-lex, 171, 187–189
nom-det-lex, 136
nom-exceptional-det-lex, 136
nom-exceptional-gen-lex, 136
nom-exceptional-pred-lex, 136
nom-gen-lex, 136
nom-lex, 135, 136
nom-pred-lex, 135, 136
nom_sc, 135

nominal phrase, 189
nominal-num-cl-rule, 157
nominal-numcl-rule, 162
nominalization, 135
nominalizer, 134
nomorphbind, 93
non-constituent coordination, *see also* coordination 263
non-final conjuncts, 41, *see also* coordination 263
non-head, 32, 41, 48, 51, 175, 192, *see also* head 263
non-subject argument, *see also* complement 263
nonlocal, *see also* local 263
nonrels, 37
noun modification, 120, 163
noun-mod, 55, 149
noun-mod-, 150
noun-mod-lex, 55
noun-mod-num-cl-lex, 152
noun-or-case-p_head, 59, 152
noun-relation, 152
noun_head, 42, 124, 135, 139, 152
noun_sc, 158
nounmod-p-lex, 188
NP complement, 86, 171, 174, 187
NP fragment, 22
np-p-lex, 171
nspec-p-lex, 170, 171, 186
nucl_plus, 152
null, 72, 74
num-cl-float_head, 156, 157
num-cl-spr-only-ind-lex, 160–162
num-cl_head, 59, 149, 151
number name, 58, 59, 144, 145, 149, 151, 154
numeral classifier, 42, 54, 56, 58, 59, 143–147, 151, 152, 155, 157–159, 173, 174, 189, 199
numeral-classifier, 150, 151
numeral-classifier-obj-float, 156
numeral-classifier-sbj-float, 156

obj-meas-lex, 150

obj-only, 149
obj-only-, 150
obj-only-num-cl-lex, 151
obl-1-arg, 185
obligatoriness, 70, 83, 174
ocons, 72, 74
olist, 33, 35, 72–74
omitted particle, *see also* particle ellipsis 263
ontology, 4, 28, 251, 256
onull, 72, 74
optionality, 7, 14, 18, 33, 50, 67, 69–71, 89, 174
ordinary-noun-lex, 120
organization, 124
orthography, 15, 49, 171, 240

p-lex, 166, 170, 171, 187
p_head, 59
parse chart, 229, *see also* parse tree 263
parse ranking, 27, 28, 230
parse selection, 20, 141, 254
parsing, 3, 9, 16, 20, 31, 194, 202, 225, 230, 231, 241, 251, 256
part-of-speech tagging, 2, 15, 23, 258
partial information, 130
pass-c-stem-lt, 112
pass-lteme-stem, 95
pass-v-stem-lt, 112
past, 43
performance profiling, 16
pers-pron-lex, 125
person name, 123, *see also* named entity 263
perspective auxiliary, 134
PET, 5, 27, 230, 254
phrase structure, 29–32, 57, 65, 70, 73, 90, 95, 116, 132, 149, 192, 203, 223
phrase type, 16
plain-topic-nobj-lex, 195
polarity, 104, 105, 125, 127, 128, 214, 218–220, 222–224, 226
positive polarity, 104

post-head modifier, 52
post-position, 49, 65, 77, 126, 137, 138, 151, 152, 168, 170, 175, 199, 203, 206, 208, *see also* particle 263
post-processing, 12, 23, 63, 124, 194
posthead, 37, 56, 151, 154
posthead, 37
postp-lex, 189
postp-lex-coord, 185, 199
postp-lex-varg, 189, 190
PP, 10, 22, 23, 31, 50–52, 80, 82, 84, 154, 171, 172, 174, 175, 202
PP complement, 84, 171
pp-mod, 55
pp-mod-lex, 55
pp-mod-lex-left, 55
pp-mod-lex-right, 55
pp-p-lex, 171
pp_np_rule_case, 202
pragmatic agreement, 120, 214, 218
pragmatic information, 42, 89, 223
pragmatic perspective, 128
preciseness, 17, 256
precision, 256
pred-adj-lex, 99
predicate, 41, 42, 61–64, 68, 69, 82, 84–86, 103, 112, 123, 135, 143, 182, 200, 202, 203, 205, 221, 238
predication, 61–63, 80–82, 85–87, 102, 103, 116, 138, 140, 170, 174, 185–187, 201
prefix, 212, *see also* suffix 263
prep-mod-relation, 187
preposition, 47, 207
preprocessing system, 3, 15, 162
progressive aspect, 100
pron-demon-lex, 125
pronoun, 14, 17, 74, 120, 125–130, 133, 140, 194, 197, 209, 213–215, 224, 226, 290

quantify-n-rule, 121, 122, 162
ques, 44
question answering, 28
question particle, 44, 210

rare_v_can, 112
Redwoods treebank, 2, 250, *see also* Hinoki treebank 263
ref-ind, 120, 174
reflexive, 69, 120, 126, 128–130, 133, 134, 162, 177, *see also* jibun 263
reflexive pronoun, *see also* jibun 263
reg-cop-stem-lt, 87
regression testing, 238, 243
regular-lex, 55
rel-cl-obj1-gap-rule, 141
rel-cl-obj2-gap-rule, 141
rel-cl-sbj-gap-rule, 141
relative-clause-rule, 140
rels, 37
right, 37, 55, 152
right2left-lex, 55
RMRS, 17, 28, 123, 256, *see also* Minimal Recursion Semantics 263
robustness, 3, 4, 7, 17, 27, 254

s-conj-lex, 200
s-ell-end-lex, 200, 201
s-end-lex, 200
s-end1-decl-lex, 200
s-end1-declint-lex, 200
s-end1-neg-imp-lex, 200
s-end1-quest-lex, 200
s-end2-lex, 200
s-p-lex, 171
sa-p-lex, 200
sap-lex, 171
saturated, 44, 74, 75
saturation, 18, 44
scopal modification, 36
scopal-adv, 55

scopal-adv-lex, 206
scopal_mod, 36, 156
scrambling, 7, 18, 31, 33, 67–71, 75, 258
selectional restriction, 69
semantic representation, 251
semantic composition, 98, 146
semantic preciseness, 256
semantic precision, 256
semantic predication, 82, 85
semantic representation, 39, 123, 127, 241
semantic transfer, 23, *see also* machine translation 263
sentence conjunction, *see also* coordination 263
sentence-final particle, 10, 11, 185, 200
sentence-te-coord-rule, 41
sentence-te-coordination-rule, 41
sentence-valid, 185
sentential coordination, 41
sentential force, 44, 62, 88, 165, 207
shallow processing, 17
sign, 29
simple-pass-end-lex, 107
simple-verb-sem-type, 97
sonkeigo, 213, 214
sortal numeral classifier, 145
specifier, 31, 41, 58, 120, 125, 135, 151, 156–158
speech recognition, 10, 12
spoken language, 4, 9, 11, 13–15, 95, 128, 174, 182, 193, 201, 202, 204, 227
spr-obj, 149
spr-obj-, 150
spr-obj-num-cl-lex, 151, 154
spr-only, 149
spr-only-, 150
spr-only-num-cl-lex, 151
spurious ambiguity, 17, 157, 183, 237, *see also* ambiguity 263
stative verb, 177

stochastic model, 27
subcategorization, 7, 14, 18, 33, 43, 48, 67, 69–71, 75, 77, 78, 86, 88, 89, 91, 116, 120, 135, 166, 182, 183, 203
subj-honor_rel, 111, 219–222, 224, 226
subject antecedent condition, 130, 132
subject honorification, 104, 125, 177, 178, 217, 218, 220, 221, 224, 226, 227
suffix, *see also* prefix 263
supertagging, 28
surface subject, 109, 132
surname, 124, *see also* named entity recognition 263
suru, 91
suru_noun_ditransitive, 71, 72
synonym, 24
synsem, 41, 71, 72
syntactic argument, 78, 82
syntactic category, 98, 99
syntactic head, 45, 49
syntactic information, 29, 121, 223

tam, 97
Tanaka Corpus, 26, 61, 122, 252
Tanaka corpus, 247, 248, 250
te-form, 100, 106
temp_numeral-lex, 137
temporal noun, 53
title-inst-lex, 125
title-lex, 125
title-pers-honsubj-lex, 125
title-pers-lex, 125
title-pers-minus-honsubj-lex, 125
tmorph, 93
top handle, 151, 158
topic particle, 79, 191, 194, 196, 204
topic-advarg-lex, 195
topic-cardarg-lex, 195
topic-cobj-lex, 195
topic-nobj-lex, 198

topic-p-lex, 195
topic-pobj-lex, 195
topic-vobj-lex, 195
topicalization, 13, 15, 192–194, 196
transfer grammar, 25, 27, see also machine translation 263
transfer rule, 25
transfer rule , see also machine translation 263
transitive verb, 31, 80, 81, 86
treebank, 2, 4, 60, 232, 233, 236–238, 240, 249–252, 256
tsdb++, 5, 16, 230, 247, 256, 260
type constraint, 72, 74
type hierarchy, 13, 30, 55, 59, 120, 125, 127, 135, 149, 166, 170, 198, 200, 203, 206, 229, 256
typed feature structure, see also TDL 263

udef_q, 123
unary rule, 60, 121, 123, 137, 202, 206, 208, see also binary rule 263
underspecification, 6, 12, 16, 62, 95, 121, 123, 130, 140, 141, 147, 148, 159, 187, 194, 206
unification, 30, 73, 229
unknown word handling, 4, 9, 27, 230, 257
utterance rule, 44, 75
utterance-rule, 224
utterance-rule-decl-finite, 160–162
utterance-rule_wh_without_ka, 44
utterance-type, 222, 223

v-cause-op-end-lt, 114
v-lex, 222
v-stem, 91–93, 95, 112
v2n-kata-rule, 99
v2vn-infl-rule, 99
v_-_lt, 78–80
v_adv*_lt, 79, 82
v_cp*_to_lt, 81

v_np*_coparg-subj_lt, 79
v_np*_ga+coparg-subj_lt, 86
v_np*_lt, 79
v_pp*_ni+to_lt, 79, 82, 83
v_pp-pp_wo-ni_lt, 79, 83
v_pp_ni+to_lt, 79, 80, 83
v_pp_ni_lt, 79, 80
v_pp_wo_lt, 79–81
v_to*cp_lt, 79
v_to_lt, 79
valence, 15, 18, 31, 33, 39, 42, 43, 47, 71, 73, 95, 100, 101, 107, 110, 114, 121, 132, 158, 172, 179, 182, 203, 238
valence, 44
vend-vend-rule, 44
verb_head, 59, 135
verbal adjunct, 49, 179, 204
verbal argument, 70, 129
verbal construction, 112
verbal ending, 41, 87, 111, 112, 114, 140, 214, 224
verbal inflection, 14, 15, 117, 213
verbal noun, 42, 43, 78, 99, 180, 182, 236
verbal stem, 75, 106, 107, 110, 112–114, 141, 214
Verbmobil, 10, 11, 13, 14, 28, 68, 71, 128, 136, 137, 165, 167–169, 175, 180, 181, 193, 194, 196, 197, 201–203, 225, 246, 254
vmod-p-lex, 171, 187, 189
vmod-p-lex-super, 171
vn-ditrans-lt, 79
vn-ditrans-toni-lt, 79
vn-intrans-lt, 79
vn-light-rule, 43
vn-trans1-lt, 79
vn-trans2-lt, 79
vn-trans3-lt, 79
vn-trans8-lt, 79
vn_head, 43
vp_pp*_ni+to_lt, 82
vstem-morph, 95

vstem-vend, 42, 75, 95
vstem-vend-rule, 107, 110, 113, 114, 116

wh-word-person-hon-lex, 208
wh-word-person-lex, 208
wh-word-place-lex, 208
wh-word-temp-lex, 208
wh-word-thing-lex, 208
wo, 202
word lattice, 12
word order, 67, 76, 172, *see also* linearization 263
world knowledge, 140

zcons, 74, 75
zero pronoun processing, 17
zlist, 44, 74, 75
znull, 74
zpro_ref-ind, 74, 75